Personal
Risk Management
and
Insurance

Volume II

Personal
Risk Management
and
Insurance
Volume II

CLAUDE C. LILLY, Ph.D., CPCU, CLU

*Director, Risk Management and Insurance Research
Center for the Study of Financial Institutions
University of Southern California*

GLENN L. WOOD, Ph.D., CPCU, CLU

*Professor of Finance
California State College*

JERRY S. ROSENBLOOM, Ph.D., CPCU, CLU

*Executive Director
The S.S. Huebner Foundation for Insurance Education
The Wharton School
University of Pennsylvania*

First Edition • 1978

AMERICAN INSTITUTE FOR
PROPERTY AND LIABILITY UNDERWRITERS
Providence and Sugartown Roads, Malvern, Pennsylvania 19355

Table of Contents

Health Maintenance Organizations

Blanket Accident and Sickness Insurance

Franchise Accident and Sickness Insurance

National Health Insurance ～ *The Issues; Types of Insurance Plans*

Introduction

Exposure Analysis ～ *Chances of Survival; Estimating Financial Needs During Retirement; Major Problems in Retirement Planning*

Techniques for Meeting the Exposure ～ *Social Insurance; Individual Annuities; Pension Plans*

Introduction

Profit Sharing Plans ～ *Eligibility Provisions; Employer Contributions; Allocation Formulas; Benefits; Comparison of Pension and Profit Sharing Plans*

Savings Plans ～ *Eligibility Provisions; Contributions; Investment of Funds; Benefits; Comparison of Savings Plans and Profit Sharing Plans*

Pension and Profit Sharing Plans for the Self-Employed ～ *Eligibility and Coverage Requirements; Contributions; Funding Instruments; Benefits; Arranging an HR-10 Plan*

Individual Retirement Savings Programs ～ *Eligibility Requirements; Contributions and Deductions; Funding; Distributions; Comparison of IRAs and Other Plans*

Tax Deferred Annuities ～ *Eligibility Requirements; Contributions; Funding Instruments; Distributions*

Nonqualified Deferred Compensation ～ *Types of Deferred Compensation Plans; Arranging a Deferred Compensation Plan; Funding Deferred Compensation Plans*

Employee Stock Ownership Plans ~ *ESOP as a Financing Technique; ESOP as an Employee Benefit*

Introduction

Factors Involved in the Selection of Savings and Investment Vehicles ~ *Investment Returns; Investment Risks; Marketability; Divisible Amounts; Tax Considerations; Financial Leverage*

Types of Savings and Investment Vehicles ~ *Savings Accounts; U.S. Government Securities; Corporate Bonds; Municipal Bonds; Annuities; Common Stocks; Preferred Stocks; Investment Companies; Speculative Stock Market Investments; Real Estate; Art and Antiques; Precious Metals; Coin Collecting; Stamp Collecting*

Combining Various Investment Vehicles

Introduction

Key Employee Insurance ~ *Identifying Key Employees; Estimating Key Employee Losses; Key Employee Life Insurance Arrangements; Tax Aspects of Key Employee Life Insurance; Key Employee Health Insurance*

Split Dollar Life Insurance ~ *Variations of the Basic Split Dollar Plan; Implementation*

Business Continuation Sole Proprietorship Insurance ~ *Types of Losses; Plans to Avoid or Minimize Losses; Arranging Proprietorship Insurance; Disposition of Policies; Tax Aspects*

Partnership Insurance ~ *Types of Losses; Problems in Reorganizing a Partnership; Arranging Partnership Insurance*

Corporation Insurance ~ *Types of Losses; Problems in Reorganizing a Closely Held Corporation; Arranging Closely Held Corporation Insurance*

CHAPTER 9

Health Insurance
Planning and Individual Coverage

FINANCIAL IMPACT OF A SICKNESS
OR AN INJURY

Need for Sickness and Injury Protection

Adequate financial preparation for loss caused by sickness or accident is important in the risk management planning of an individual or a family. Extended periods of disability can result in a large loss of income. Huge medical costs can arise from the use of hospital services, drugs, Xrays, prosthetic devices, doctors, and therapy. Miscellaneous additional expenses, such as travel for an individual to and from a hospital or the cost of replacing the services of a family member, also can deplete a family's budget. Table 9-1, for example, lists the medical care expenses incurred by two individuals during stays in a hospital. These figures exclude any loss of income.

The cost of health services has risen rapidly in recent years relative to the cost of other services. Figure 9-1 illustrates the rapid increase in the past of health care between 1967 and 1976. During that period, health care prices rose 85 percent while the consumer price index for all items rose only 70 percent. In aggregate dollar terms, national health care expenditures were $139.3 billion in 1976, nearly three times the 1967 spending level of $47.9 billion. One result of the steady growth in health care prices and expenditures is that national health care expenditures now consume a larger proportion of the gross national product (GNP) than in the past. For example, national health care

Table 9-1

Hospital Costs of Two Patients

	Patient with Heart Attack	Patient with Acute Pancreatitis
Emergency room	$ 606.25	$ 24.00
Drugs	1,924.75	1,916.75
Laboratory fees	1,272.50	2,826.74
X-rays	276.00	140.00
Medical/surgical supplies	2,200.55	1,635.00
EKG/EEG	105.00	0
Physical therapy	40.00	0
Inhalation therapy	1,789.00	0
Miscellaneous	1.50	22.00
Intensive care unit	4,800.00	2,875.00
Private room	456.00	0
Semi-private room	477.00	0
Total medical care costs	$13,948.55	$9,439.49

expenditures were slightly more than $12 billion in 1950 representing 4.6 percent of the GNP. The corresponding figures in 1976 were $139.3 billion and 8.6 percent of GNP, respectively. On an individual level, consider the hospital bill of the heart patient given in Table 9-1. The total bill was $13,948.55. Assuming this bill had been incurred in 1967, the same services in 1977 probably could have cost over $23,000.

Handling Sickness and Injury Exposures

The risk management techniques discussed in CPCU 1 can be applied to the reduction of health losses. For example, individuals may "prevent" poor health by taking better care of themselves; and, by receiving physical checkups periodically, they may be able to "reduce" the financial impact of a health problem. Frequent dental checkups are an example. Some insurance companies which underwrite dental expense coverage provide benefits for routine checkups in the hope that in the long run, losses will be reduced because of preventative care.

"Retention" also can be utilized in health coverage. Some individuals buy major medical coverage with a large deductible so that they pay first dollar losses. This action avoids dollar swapping and can result in substantial premium savings.

Figure 9-1
Medical Care Prices and Consumer Price Index (1967 = 100)*

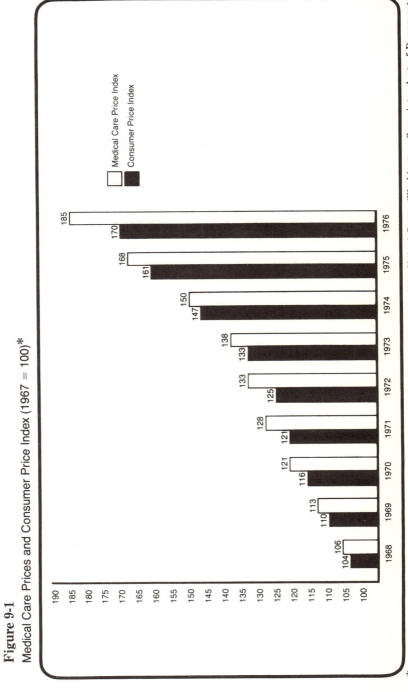

*Reprinted from United States Department of Commerce, *Statistical Abstract of the United States* (Washington: Superintendent of Documents, 1976), p. 439.

Table 9-2

Number of Persons Covered by Group and Individual Health Insurance Policies Issued by Private Insurance Companies—by Type of Coverage for Selected Years*

Type of Coverage	Year			
	1950	1960	1970	1975
Hospital Expense				
Individual Policies	17,296,000	22,181,000	26,658,000	30,115,000
Group Policies	22,305,000	54,416,000	80,505,000	87,185,000
Total †	36,955,000	69,226,000	89,688,000	99,547,000
Surgical Expense				
Individual Policies	13,718,000	16,025,000	17,961,000	18,468,000
Group Policies	21,219,000	55,464,000	81,549,000	87,958,000
Total †	33,428,000	65,093,000	85,661,000	92,089,000
Regular Medical Expenses				
Individual Policies	2,714,000	5,487,000	10,283,000	11,775,000
Group Policies	5,587,000	35,522,000	74,899,000	87,027,000
Total †	8,001,000	37,442,000	74,888,000	86,567,000

† These numbers represent the net number of people protected; that is, duplication among those with more than one policy has been eliminated.

*Adapted from *Source Book of Health Insurance Data 1976–77* (New York: Health Insurance Institute, 1977), pp. 23, 25, and 26.

Most health insurance is underwritten on a group basis. This can be attributed to the extensive use of health insurance as an employee benefit. Group health coverage tends to be cheaper and more comprehensive than coverage written on an individual basis since the threat of adverse selection can be minimized.

Approximately three-fourths of all health insurance coverage is made available on a group basis. Of course, the exact percentages differ by type of coverage (whether it is for hospital, surgical, regular medical, major medical or some combination of these) as well as the kind of insuring organization (private insurance companies, Blue Cross-Blue Shield plans, or independent health plans). Table 9-2 shows the substantial difference between the number of persons covered under group and individual policies issued by insurance companies, by type of coverage. The table also reveals how rapidly the health insurance field has grown over the years and the fact that most of the growth has taken place in the group health market.

Changing Health Insurance Environment

In 1965, Congress passed Amendments XVIII and XIX to the Social Security Act which established the Medicare and Medicaid Programs. The former shifted from individuals to the federal government much of the responsibility for providing health care for the elderly (over age sixty-five). Medicaid enables medically indigent individuals, regardless of age, to receive joint federal-state governmental help. In 1973, Congress passed the Health Maintenance Organization (HMO) Act to encourage the development of HMOs.

Numerous national health insurance (NHI) plans have been proposed in Congress that would broaden the federal government's role in the health field. These programs range from relatively limited plans that protect against catastrophic losses to plans that would allow the government to control most aspects of the health delivery system. Who would operate a national health insurance program is an unanswered question. Some persons would like to see the federal government operate any national health insurance program that is developed. Others feel a partnership between government and the private insurance sector would be the best solution to the problem. The following sections explain what types of health coverages are available to individuals and how these coverages can be obtained. Chapter 10 examines group insurance, governmental programs, and health maintenance organizations.

INDIVIDUAL HEALTH INSURANCE POLICIES

Individual health insurance contracts fall into two categories, medical expense and disability income. The next section discusses medical expense coverages while a later section of this chapter deals with disability income coverages.

Medical Expense Insurance

Most health insurance companies issue basic medical expense contracts and major medical contracts. Basic medical expense contracts contain one or more of the following coverages: (1) hospital, (2) surgical, or (3) physician's services. Major medical contracts usually contain all three coverages.

The health insurance industry provides numerous types of accident and sickness protection defined as "any policy or contract providing insurance against loss resulting from sickness or from bodily injury or death by accident or both."[1] While the definition appears clear, the meaning of some of the words in the definition can vary significantly between health insurance policies. "Sickness" is considered an illness or disease of the body. However, insurers often restrict the term sickness by means of exclusions or limitations. Until recently, alcoholism was not considered a sickness. Health insurance benefits for individuals suffering from this disease were almost nonexistent. Similarly, the acceptance of mental disturbance as a form of sickness under health insurance policies has become widespread only in the last ten years.

The American Psychiatric Association has taken this stand:

> Psychiatric services should be considered an integral part of total health services. Accordingly, it is recommended that prepayment and other health insurance plans should include coverage of all significant health or medical conditions, including mental disorders.[2]

In keeping with this philosophy, many Blue Cross and private plans include coverage for psychiatric treatment and in some instances the services of a psychologist. Some organizations, e.g., General Motors and the United Mine Workers, have added psychiatric benefits to their employee benefit programs.

Medical expenses arising from bodily injury may or may not be covered by a particular contract. Some contracts cover only bodily injury that is caused by "accident," which is not easily defined. One court has stated:

> The word "accident" is derived from the Latin word meaning to happen and the literal meaning of the word is "befalling," though in common parlance it has (a) much more restricted meaning which is difficult to define. [3]

In the past, most contracts covered bodily injury losses caused either by accidental injury or accidental means. Although these phrases sound similar, they have different meanings. Accidental injury is "an unintended and undesigned result arising from acts done."[4] Injuries caused by accidental means arise "from acts unintentionally done and where the cause of injury . . . is an act of the insured."[5]

The difference between these two terms can be better understood by means of an example. Assume that Charles Pennell climbed up on a box to wash the windows of his home. After washing one window, Charles jumped from the box and sprained his ankle. This injury would be covered in a policy which covered accidental injury. Although Charles jumped, he did not mean to sprain his ankle. A policy which covered injuries caused by accidental means would not have insured the loss since the action causing the injury was not accidental.

Types of Coverage

Hospital Coverage. Hospital coverage provides benefits for room and board charges and also for miscellaneous services and supplies which an insured may utilize while staying in the hospital.

The definition of what constitutes a miscellaneous service or supply varies. One health insurance publication lists forty-five miscellaneous types of benefits. Some of the miscellaneous benefits categories found in health policies are:[6]

- General nursing care
- Registered graduate nurse for private duty nursing care
- Up to one-half of hospital benefit for convalescent or nursing home confinement
- Drugs, medicines requiring written prescription of physician
- Microscopic or laboratory tests
- Electrocardiogram
- Diagnostic x-ray and laboratory examinations
- Treatment by x-ray
- Treatment by radium
- Radioactive therapy
- Physiotherapy
- Anesthetics and administration
- Blood, blood plasma
- Blood or blood derivatives
- Rental of equipment for administration of oxygen
- Oxygen and administration
- Casts, splints, trusses, braces, crutches
- Initial emergency transportation by aircraft or railroad from place where sickness was contracted or injury occurred to nearest hospital

Most contracts limit the maximum amount that the insurer will pay for hospital room and board per day as well as the maximum number of days for which benefits are available. In addition, there will be an aggregate limit for all benefits, and there may also be internal limits for specific benefits. For example, a $50 per day limitation on the amount payable for hospital room and board would be an internal limit. To illustrate how an internal limit operates, consider the following example.

Recently, Edward Tiernan underwent major surgery. Tiernan was confined to a hospital for twelve days and incurred the expenses shown in Table 9-3. Tiernan's policy had a $50 per day benefit for hospital room and board expense for a maximum period of ten days. His policy also listed the miscellaneous benefits shown in Table 9-4. Consequently,

Table 9-3

Hospital Expenses

Intensive care unit	$ 300 (3 days x $100 per day)
Semi-private room	540 (9 days x $60 per day)
Drugs	212
X-ray	200
EEG	55
Total hospital bill	$ 1,307

Table 9-4

Miscellaneous Benefits

Drugs	$200
X-rays	150
EEG/EKG	100
Maximum amount payable for the combined total of all such expenses incurred in a single hospital stay	$300

Tiernan was paid a total of $800—$500 for room and board ($50 × 10 days) and $300 for the miscellaneous charges. Sometimes contracts provide additional room benefits when an insured is in an intensive care unit. This type of coverage would have increased Tiernan's reimbursement.

In lieu of the indemnity approach in which the policy stipulates dollar benefits, some health insurance contracts stipulate that particular services will be provided. For example, an insurer might pay for a semiprivate room regardless of cost.

Maternity benefits can be included as a hospital expense benefit, but on an individual basis, the purchase of maternity benefits may be too expensive relative to the benefits received. Those individuals who anticipate utilizing this benefit will elect to add it to their contracts. As a result, an insured introduces adverse selection into the insuring process, i.e., the probability of a loss is not fortuitous. The insurance company passes the cost of this adverse selection on to an insured. Therefore, the purchase of hospital maternity benefits might become a dollar swapping process for an insured. Usually, this is not the case in group insurance contracts because an insurer is able to obtain a spread of risk. The maternity benefit premium is paid by everyone, even those who have no need for maternity coverage.

Maternity benefits can be a stated amount, such as $350 or the regular policy coverage for room and board and miscellaneous expenses. Regardless of the method of providing coverage, pregnancy benefits are not available unless conception occurred during the policy period. This reduces adverse selection against the insurer. This provision may be stated in terms of a waiting period, such as nine months, before the coverage becomes effective.

Surgical Coverage. Surgery may result not only in the direct expenses related to an operation but also in some miscellaneous expenses. Surgical coverages are designed to pay for both types of expenses. To illustrate, a surgical expense contract might pay for an appendectomy as well as preoperative and postoperative care.

Normally, surgical expense benefit coverage is defined by means of a schedule which contains a list of operations and the amount that the insurer will pay for each. A sample schedule of operations can be found in Table 9-5.

Instead of using stated dollar amounts in a schedule of operations, an insurer may place various unit values on each operation; i.e., the insurer uses a relative value schedule. The value of a unit is indicated in the policy declarations. Therefore, to ascertain the amount of coverage available for a specific type of surgery, one multiplies the number of units for that surgery times the value of a unit. The relative values, i.e., the number of units, reflect the time and difficulty of the surgical procedure while the value of each unit is a function of area price levels and changes from year to year or in some cases even more frequently. As an example, a contract might specify fifteen units of coverage for an operation to fuse an ankle. If the policy stated that each unit of coverage was worth $10, then the total amount of insurance protection would be $150. Because of price level changes, the value of each unit might be changed to $15 by endorsement in which case the insurer would pay $225 (15 × $15), for the ankle fusion surgical procedure. Table 9-6 gives a surgical schedule with unit values.

For operations not listed on a schedule of operations, an insurance company will pay an amount based on the severity of the operation and the relation of this severity to the maximum amount paid in the schedule of operations.

An individual can have multiple surgical procedures performed at the same time. If only one incision is necessary for several surgical procedures, most insurers will pay up to the policy limits for the most expensive procedure. When more than one incision is required, the coverage for the most expensive incision is paid. Additionally, 50 percent of the amount of coverage for every other incision may be paid.

Physician's Coverage. This coverage is designed to provide insurance for both in-hospital and home visits by a physician as well as

Table 9-5
Schedule of Surgical Procedures

Procedure	Dollar Value	Procedure	Dollar Value
Abdomen		Arthrotomy with Exploration, Drainage, or	
Appendectomy	$200	Removal of Loose Body	
Colon resection, partial	400	Ankle	$250
Gall bladder, removal of	300	Elbow	250
Gastrotomy	250	Finger	75
Laparatomy, exploratory	200	Hip	350
Stomach, total resection of	500	Knee or shoulder	250
		Wrist	200
Amputations			
Arm, through humerus or radius and ulna	200	Arthrodesis—Fusion of a Joint	
Finger, one	75	Ankle	350
Foot, through ankle	250	Elbow	350
Hand, through wrist or metacarpal bones	200	Finger, one joint	100
Hip	400	Hip	500
Leg, through tibia and fibula	250	Knee	400
Thigh	300	Shoulder	450
Toe	50	Wrist	300

Table 9-6
Schedule of Surgical Procedures with Unit Values

Procedure	Units[†]
Incision and drainage of infected or non-infected sebaceous cyst	2.0
Incision and drainage of furuncle	2.0
Acne surgery, marsupialization, opening or removal of multiple milia, comedones, cysts, pustules, etc.	1.5
Incision and drainage of carbuncle, supperative hidradenitis, and other cutaneous or subcutaneous abscesses, simple	2.0
Drainage of pilonidal cyst	2.0
Drainage of onychia or paronychia	2.0
Incision and removal of foreign body, subcutaneous tissues, simple	2.0
Puncture aspiration of abscess or hematoma	1.0

[†]Each unit is worth $25.00.

visits by a patient to a physician's office. Most policies that provide this benefit contain limitations on the amount payable per visit or per day. Generally, there is a limitation on the number of visits per period of illness. Any excess charges are absorbed by the insured, as illustrated in the following example.

Sarah Rouse underwent surgery. Following the operation, Sarah's doctor visited her twice a day for two weeks. Each visit cost $15. Sarah had a medical expense policy which provided $10 for each in-hospital visit subject to a maximum of twenty visits. The amount of coverage provided by Sarah's policy was as shown in Table 9-7.

Types of Policies[7] In most cases, individual health insurance protection is afforded under either a basic medical expense policy or a major medical expense policy. Both types of policies contain one or more of the types of coverages that have been discussed.

A basic medical expense policy must be examined carefully to ascertain what coverage is provided. Frequently, contracts will indicate that they have coverage for hospital, surgical, and physician's expense benefits. However, the amount of protection provided for each category of expense benefit may vary significantly among contracts. One contract

Table 9-7

Physician's Coverage Provided by Medical Expense Policy

Visits	Doctor's Charge	Insurer Paid	Sarah Paid
1–20	$300	$200	$100
21–28	120	0	120
Total	$420	$200	$220

may contain physician's expense benefits for in-hospital visits only, while another contract also may provide coverage for physician's visits in an extended care facility where limited medical services are available during convalescence. The surgical schedules used by different insurers vary significantly. While policies may have the same surgical limit for some operations, the benefits for all operations may not be identical.

In lieu of, or in addition to, buying a basic medical expense policy, an individual or family may purchase a major expense insurance policy which contains coverage for hospital, surgical, and physician's care.

A major medical contract usually is written with a $100 to $150 deductible but it can range as high as $1,500. This deductible generally is applied once if one or more of the insureds are injured in the same accident.

Major medical policies normally contain an aggregate ceiling which can range from $5,000 to $250,000 or more. These policies may have internal limits, e.g., a maximum rate per day for hospital room and board to minimize possible abuses and to keep premiums within acceptable limits.

Most major medical policies stipulate that the insurer will only pay 80 percent of the eligible (covered) expenses in excess of the deductible. For example, assume that a policy covering a $10,000 loss was written with a $1,000 deductible. The insurer would pay only $7,200 of the claim (10,000 – 1,000) × 0.8. However, many insurers today provide that after a fixed dollar amount of medical expenses are incurred, such as four or five thousand dollars, the coinsurance clause does not apply and the insurer will pay 100 percent of the remaining expenses. The purpose of the "coinsurance" clause is to encourage insureds to keep costs to a minimum.

The coinsurance clause found in the major medical policy is not like the coinsurance clause used in property insurance which is designed to encourage property owners to carry a minimum amount of insurance protection. The 80 percent coinsurance clause in the major medical policy limits the amount of the total loss paid by an insurer. The insured is never reimbursed for 100 percent of his or her loss. In property insurance, an insured is reimbursed fully for a loss only if the insurance-to-value ratio is 80 percent or greater, and if the loss is less than the policy limits.

The distinction between major medical expense policies and basic medical expense policies has blurred in recent years. Many insurers are offering comprehensive policies which have some of the characteristics of both types of policies.

Some insurers offer a package of health insurance protection composed of a basic medical expense and a major medical expense policy. When this is done, there usually is a deductible between the hospital expense policy and the major medical policy which an insured has to absorb. This deductible, which is called a *corridor* deductible, is not as large as the flat deductible normally contained in a major medical policy when it is written separately.

Standard Health Insurance Policy Provisions   In the early 1950s, the National Association of Insurance Commissioners formulated a model Uniform Individual Accident and Sickness Policy Provision Law which listed a number of provisions the commissioners felt should be included in each accident and sickness policy. The model legislation also contained a list of optional policy provisions which could be utilized in an accident and sickness policy. All states have promulgated laws which incorporate at least some of the recommendations of the National Association of Insurance Commissioners. The following provisions are now required by statute in most states.

Entire Contract.   All health insurance policies contain an "entire contract" provision which stipulates that the policy along with attached endorsements and the application constitute the entire contract between the insurer and the insured. The insurer is not allowed to use provisions not found in these forms as a means for voiding coverage.

The policy cannot be changed unless the change is approved by an executive officer of the insurance company. Even then, the change is not effective until the policy itself has been endorsed to reflect the modification.

Time Limit on Certain Defenses.   Health insurance contracts have a type of incontestable clause known as a "time limit on certain defenses" provision. The provision is divided into two parts and reads as follows:

(a) after three years from the date of issue of this policy no misstatements, except fraudulent misstatements, made by the applicant in the application for such policy shall be used to void the policy or to deny claim for loss incurred or disability (as defined in the policy) commencing after expiration of such three year period.

(b) No claim for loss incurred or disability (as defined in the policy) commencing after three years from date of issue of this policy shall be reduced or denied on the ground that disease or physical condition not excluded from any coverage by named or specific description effective on the date of loss had existed prior to the effective date of coverage of this policy.

Most states have changed their laws to allow insurers only two years to contest coverage.

In lieu of part (a) of the provision, insurers that issue policies to individuals until the individuals are at least age fifty, or if older than age forty-four for at least five years, may substitute the following:

After this policy has been in force for a period of three years during the lifetime of the insured (excluding any period during which the insured is disabled), it shall become incontestable as to the statements contained in the application.

While the time limit protects the insured, it does not guarantee that an insurer will not attempt to void an insured's policy. An insurer may contend that the policy was void from its inception; i.e., that a contract never existed. As an example, if an individual sent someone else to take the examination in his or her place, the insurance company could contend that it issued a policy based on medical information on someone other than the insured. Consequently, the insurer could claim that it never entered into a contract with the policyholder.

Occasionally, an insurer will attempt to void a contract on the grounds that the statements in the application were fraudulent even when the policy is beyond the two or three year incontestable period. In the case of Massachusetts Casualty Insurance Company v. Forman, the insurer attempted to rescind a disability policy after the policy's two year contestable period had expired.[8] The insurer contended that the insured, in his application, had indicated that he was in good health. The insurer later learned that the insured had diabetes for a year before he applied for coverage. Therefore, the insurer felt the policy should be declared null and void.

The court ruled that the insurer could not rescind the contract because of the time limit on certain defenses provision, but that the insurer did not have to provide coverage for disability caused by diabetes. The court said that since sickness was covered only if it first manifested itself during the time of the policy, losses arising from the diabetes were not covered. The diabetes had manifested itself one year prior to the date of the policy.

Grace Period. Health insurance contracts contain a grace period which is applicable to all premiums except the first one. If premiums are paid weekly, then the grace period is seven days. If the premiums are paid monthly, the grace period is ten days; and when the premium payment is made on any other basis, the grace period is thirty-one days.

Policies renewable at the option of the company contain a provision that requires the insurer to give the insured five days written notice prior to cancellation by mailing to the insured's last known address a notice of the company's intention.

Reinstatement. Lapsed property and liability policies can be reinstated only at the underwriter's discretion. Life and health insurance contracts, on the other hand, contain a provision which allows the insured to reinstate the policy under some circumstances.

Most health insurance reinstatement provisions stipulate that if an insured pays the premium and no application is required, the policy is automatically reinstated. When an application is required and a conditional receipt is issued, the policy is reinstated when the application is approved by the insurer. If the insurer does not notify the insured of disapproval within forty-five days of the date of the conditional receipt, the policy is automatically reinstated. Coverage for losses from accidental injury commences upon reinstatement while coverage for losses resulting from sickness does not start for ten days.

The amount paid to reinstate a policy can be applied to previous unpaid premiums that span a period no more than sixty days prior to reinstatement. The sixty-day provision may be eliminated from contracts in which the insured has the right to continue the policy until age fifty or if issued after age forty-four for at least five years from the date of issue.

Notice of Claim, Claim Forms, and Proof of Loss. The insured in a health insurance policy must notify the insurer within twenty days after a claim arises barring unusual circumstances which preclude this from occurring. After notification, the insurer must furnish the insured with proof of loss forms within fifteen days. Otherwise, the insured's obligation with respect to the time requirements of providing proof of loss will be waived.

Most policies state:

> Written proof of loss must be furnished to the insurer at its said office in case of claim for loss for which this policy provides any periodic payment contingent upon continuing loss within ninety days after the termination of the period for which the insurer is liable and in the case of claim for any other loss within ninety days after the date of such loss.

If an insured does not furnish written proof of loss within the time required, coverage is voided unless circumstances prohibit notification within the allotted time. There is an overall limitation of one year to file written proof of loss unless an insured lacks the legal capacity to do so.

For example, Marian Lucas incurred numerous medical bills during a recent stay of one week in the hospital. Marian's hospital expense policy gave her twenty days from the time that she entered the hospital to notify her insurer about her loss unless she had a valid reason why she could not.

Instead of waiting twenty days, Marian notified her insurer about the claim three days after she left the hospital, but the notification took six days to reach the insurer. From the point that the insurer received notice of the claim, the insurer had fifteen days to get the claim forms to Marian. The insurer only took five days. Marian then had sixty-nine days (90 – 7 – 3 – 6 – 5) to file a written proof of loss.

Time of Payment of Claims and Payment of Claims. If a claim does not require periodic payments, such as those payable under a disability contract, then the claim is paid when the written proof of loss is received by the insurer. Where benefits are payable on a periodic basis, then the payments are made on whatever basis is stipulated in the contract. For example, benefits could be paid monthly under a disability contract. If an insured is deceased, unpaid benefits are paid either to the insured's designated beneficiary or the estate.

Legal Actions. The policy's legal actions provision prohibits any action against the insurer for sixty days after written proof of loss has been furnished. This is designed to allow the insurer adequate time to pay the policy proceeds.

This provision also contains a statute of limitations that prevents the insured from bringing action against the insurer more than three years after written proof should have been furnished. Consider the following example.

Jack Fontaine recently was injured in an automobile accident and spent a week in the hospital. The $1,000 of medical expenses were covered under Jack's hospital expense insurance policy. Jack notified his insurer which forwarded claim forms to Jack. Jack promptly filled out the forms and returned them to the insurer.

If the insurer does not pay Jack within sixty days, Jack can bring legal action against the insurer. However, he cannot wait more than three years after the date that written proof of loss was required, i.e., ninety days after the date of loss. Assuming the date of loss was the first day of hospitalization, he has three years from then to file a suit.

Physical Examinations and Autopsy. The insurer may examine an insured "as often as it may reasonably require during the pendency of a claim" to protect it against fraudulent claims. However, the insurer may not utilize this provision to harass an insured. An insurer could not require the insured to have a physical examination weekly or even monthly without a valid reason.

When death benefits are payable under a health insurance policy, the insurer has a right to have an autopsy performed, barring a state statute to the contrary. This proviso avoids any conflict between state statutes and the insurance policy.

Change of Beneficiary. An insured may change a beneficiary designation and may surrender or assign the policy if no irrevocable beneficiary exists.

The preceding provisions are required by state statute while use of the following provisions is optional with insurers. If an insurer elects not to utilize these provisions, the substitute wording utilized must be at least as favorable as that which is found in these provisions. This determination is made by the insurance commissioner in each state. Most insurance contracts contain one or more of these optional provisions.

Misstatement of Age. If an insured has misstated his or her age, the policy is adjusted to reflect the correct age which can benefit either the insurance company or the insured. If an insured overstates his or her age, then the insurer is charging too much, and vice versa. Upon the discovery of a discrepancy between the insured's stated and actual age, the insurer pays benefits equal to what would have been purchased with the premium had the insured's correct age been known.

Change of Occupation. When an insurer issues a policy, one of the primary underwriting factors is the insured's occupation. Individuals working in highly hazardous occupations represent a higher morbidity risk. For example, the injury and sickness exposure faced by a construction worker is greater than the same exposure encountered by an accountant or a lawyer; therefore, any change in an insured's occupation will have a direct bearing on the exposure faced by the insurance company.

To avoid this problem, an insurance company may include a change of occupation provision that stipulates that if the insured changes:

> ... his occupation to one classified by the insurer as more hazardous than that stated in this policy or while doing for compensation anything pertaining to an occupation so classified, the insurer will pay only such portions of the indemnities provided in this policy as the premium paid would have purchased at the rates and within the limits fixed by the insurer for such more hazardous occupation.

Thus, an insured will receive reduced benefits if he or she is injured while working in an occupation which is more hazardous than the one the insured had at the time the insurance coverage was purchased.

An insured who changes to a less hazardous occupation will have his or her premium rate reduced accordingly, and in addition, will receive a pro rata refund of premium for the time during which the insured had paid a premium based on the more hazardous occupation.

In order to use the occupational classifications and the rates for the classifications, an insurer must have the rates and classifications on file with the state insurance department.

Other Insurance in the Same Insurer. An insurer may include an "other insurance in the same insurer" provision in its policy which limits the maximum amount of coverage that the insured can obtain from the company.

Two methods are used to limit the benefits that the insured may collect. Under the first method, the insured (or the insured's beneficiary) may select the policy that provides the highest benefits. The insurer is then required to return the premium for the policy(ies) which is/are not utilized.

Second, an insurer can stipulate the maximum benefit for each category that an insured can collect regardless of the number of policies purchased. The premium for excess coverage is returned to an insured. The difference between these approaches is illustrated by the following example.

Recently, William Dixon had a heart attack and spent twenty-two days in the hospital. The cost per day in the hospital for room and board was $83. William had two insurance policies with the same insurance company. One policy provided a room benefit of $70 per day, and the other policy provided a room benefit of $50 per day.

If each of the two insurance policies had another insurance clause which gave William the option to select the insurance policy under which he wished to collect, William would select the policy with the $70 per day benefit. The premium for the other policy would be returned.

If the other insurance in the same insurer provision had set a maximum indemnity (e.g., $80), the insurer would have paid William $80 of his $83 bill for each day of confinement. Since this benefit is less than the total room benefit for which William had paid a premium, the insurer would have returned the premium for the excess coverage.

Insurance with Other Insurers. Conceivably, an insured can profit from a health loss not only by buying several policies from the same company but also from different companies. To keep an insured from profiting in the latter case, an insurance company can include an "insurance with other insurers" provision in its health insurance contract such as:

> If there be other valid coverage, not with this insurer, providing benefits for the same loss on a provision of service basis or an expense incurred basis and of which this insurer has not been given written notice prior to the occurrence or commencement of loss, the only liability under any expense incurred coverage of this policy shall be for

such proportion of the loss as the amount which would otherwise have been payable hereinunder plus the total of the like amounts under all other such valid coverages for the same loss of which this insurer had notice bears to the total like amounts under all other valid coverages for such loss, and for the return of such portion of the premiums paid as exceed the pro rata portion of the amount so determined.

This provision applies to expense-incurred benefits, such as room and board and miscellaneous hospital costs, and also to benefits other than those on an expense-incurred basis, such as daily or weekly income while in a hospital. The "insurance with other insurers" provision is not affected by the time limit on certain defenses, and the insurer has up until the time of payment of the loss to discover other valid coverage. The following example shows how this provision would have an impact on an insured's coverage.

Mary Levy entered the hospital on March 1 for the removal of cataracts. She was confined in a semiprivate room for twenty-two days following her operation.

Mary owned four insurance policies which contained an "insurance with other insurers" provision. Each policy was written by a different company. None of the insurers knew about the other contracts. Insurer A's policy provided a $50 per day room benefit while those issued by Insurers B and C provided a $100 per day room benefit. The contract issued by Insurer D was a service-provided contract that provided a benefit equal to the cost of a semi-private room. All of the policies provided hospital room and board benefits for a period of fifty days. The hospital in which Mary was confined charged $60 per day for a semiprivate room. Each insurer would pay the benefits as shown in Table 9-8.

If a policy does not define other valid coverage, it will not include:

... group insurance, automobile medical payments insurance, or coverage provided by hospital or medical service organizations or by union welfare plans or employer or employee benefit organizations.

Third-party liability coverage is not considered other valid coverage, but benefits provided by statute, such as workers' compensation benefits, are assumed to be other valid coverages. The assumption is made that the insurer has notice of these latter types of benefits.

Unpaid Premium. Conceivably, an insured could be eligible for insurance benefits without paying a premium because of the grace period. To protect itself, an insurance company can include a provision that permits it to reduce any benefit payment by any amount due and unpaid at the time of the loss.

Cancellation. An insurer may reserve the right to cancel its policy. Specifically, the insurer may:

Table 9-8

Benefits Paid by Each Insurer

$$\text{Insurer A} \quad \frac{50}{(50 + 100 + 100 + 60)} \times 1{,}320 = \$\ 212.90$$

$$\text{Insurer B} \quad \frac{100}{(50 + 100 + 100 + 60)} \times 1{,}320 = \quad 425.81$$

$$\text{Insurer C} \quad \frac{100}{(50 + 100 + 100 + 60)} \times 1{,}320 = \quad 425.81$$

$$\text{Insurer D} \quad \frac{60}{(50 + 100 + 100 + 60)} \times 1{,}320 = \quad \underline{255.48}$$

Total $1,320.00

The service basis contract is evaluated on the cost of the service it provides. In this case, a semi-private room costs $60; therefore, the basis of evaluation is $60.

... cancel this policy at any time by written notice delivered to the insured, or mailed to his last address as shown by the records of the insurer, stating when, not less than five days thereafter, such cancellation shall be effective; and after the policy has been continued beyond its original term, the insured may cancel this policy at any time by written notice delivered or mailed to the insurer, effective upon receipt or on such later date as may be specified in such notice. In the event of cancellation, the insurer will return promptly the unearned portion of any premium paid. If the insured cancels, the earned premium shall be computed by the use of the short-rate table last filed with the state official having supervision of insurance in the state where the insured resided when the policy was issued. If the insurer cancels, the earned premium shall be computed pro rata.

Cancellation of a policy does not prejudice any outstanding claims.

A cancellation provision obviously may not be placed in a noncancelable or guaranteed renewable policy. Even when it is used, certain insured rights are guaranteed. For example, the insured must be given notice of cancellation (e.g., five days), and a return of the unused premium on a pro rata basis must be afforded. To illustrate, the cancellation provision found in the New York Statutes reads:

Cancellation: Within the first ninety days after the date of issue, the insurer may cancel this policy by written notice delivered to the insured, or mailed to his last address as shown by the records of the insurer, stating when, not less than ten days thereafter, such cancellation shall be effective.[9]

Conformity with State Statutes. Most insurers stipulate that where there is a conflict between the statutes of the state in which a contract is issued and the policy, the policy is automatically amended "to conform to the minimum requirements of such statutes." Thus, insureds are protected against noncompliance.

Illegal Occupation. To protect themselves against losses incurred by insureds engaged in illegal occupations, insurers may include a provision that eliminates coverage when individuals are so engaged.

Intoxicants and Narcotics. An insurer may avoid losses which result from an insured's being intoxicated or under the influence of narcotics unless the intoxicant or narcotic is administered on the advice of a physician.

Policy Inspection. Health insurance contracts contain a provision known alternatively as the "policy examination" provision, the "refund upon examination" provision, or the "free policy examination" provision. Its purpose is to give the insured an opportunity to examine a policy for ten days without being obligated to keep it and with full premium refund available. This provision is not found in property and liability contracts. However, some life insurers are now including a ten-day free examination period provision in their life insurance policies.

Amount of Coverage Under a Medical Expense Insurance Policy The coverage provided under a medical expense contract is limited by policy exclusions (e.g., drug addiction or alcoholism), a schedule of surgical procedures (if there is one), the daily room and board rate, as well as any internal limits for the various miscellaneous benefits. In addition, any preexisting conditions clause may limit coverage. It can stipulate that no preexisting conditions are covered. For example, preexisting conditions may not be covered until after a specific period of time (e.g., twelve months) has elapsed. An alternative sometimes used is to limit coverage on all preexisting conditions until after the policy has been in effect for a specified period (e.g., twelve months) provided that there has been no recurrence of the condition. In lieu of a specific preexisting condition provision, many contracts limit coverage for any injury or sickness which manifests itself prior to the effective date of the policy. As an example, one policy defines sickness or disease as:

> Sickness or disease which first manifests itself while the Coverage Provision under which claim is made is in force for the Insured Person whose sickness is the basis of claim and which results in loss to which such Coverage Provision applies.

In some instances, insurers may insure preexisting conditions on a limited basis or may provide the coverage for an additional charge.

Some states specify how a preexisting condition can be used. In Texas:

> . . . if an insurer elects to use a simplified application form, with or without a question as to the applicant's health at the time of application, but without any questions concerning the insured's health history or medical treatment history, the policy must cover any loss occurring after 12 months from any pre-existing condition not specifically excluded from coverage by terms of the policy.[10]

Under this provision, the insured is covered for a preexisting condition after twelve months even if the preexisting condition occurred during the twelve months, provided that it is not excluded by the terms of the policy. This protects the insured against an insurer's attempting to underwrite business at the time of a loss rather than at the time of issue.

Other policy provisions also can limit the coverage provided. For example, the deductible is subtracted from the eligible expenses covered by the policy. However, the frequency with which a deductible is applied varies. For example, some policies provide that if two or more family members are involved in the same accident or are injured in the same event, then only one deductible amount applies for that occurrence. Moreover, many policies stipulate that the deductible need only be paid for each period of hospital confinement defined as:

> . . . successive periods of hospital confinement due to the same or related cause or causes unless between such confinement such insured person has resumed his *full and normal activities* for at least six consecutive months in which event such subsequent confinement shall be deemed a new confinement. *(emphasis added)*

Some insurers utilize a three-month period rather than a six-month period, and some insurers do not make the various periods dependent upon an individual returning to full and normal activity.

In lieu of a deductible per period of confinement, some contracts have an annual deductible based on either a calendar year or a policy year. In the former, a deductible has to be satisfied only once during any calendar year. Under the latter, a deductible has to be satisfied during every twelve month period following the anniversary of the policy.

An insurer's obligation is limited to the actual expenses incurred even if the insured's policy contains a higher limit for that type of coverage. For example, if the cost of a room in a hospital is $50 per day, and a policy's benefit limit is $60 per day, the insurer will pay $50 per day for room and board.

Insurers also do not provide coverage for losses excluded under a contract. Some of the exclusions that an insured might find in his or her health insurance contract are:[11]

- Self-inflicted injury
- Intentionally self-inflicted injury
- War or any act of war

- Suicide or attempt thereat
- Suicide while sane or insane
- Pregnancy, childbirth, miscarriage, abortion
- Infection, other than pus-forming or pyogenic infection through accidental wound or cut, is deemed sickness.
- While on active duty in military, naval, or air forces of any country or international authority (pro rata unearned premium is refunded)
- While participating in riot, insurrection, rebellion
- While outside of U.S. or Canada
- Loss covered under workers' compensation, or employer's liability act
- Medical care, services, or supplies paid for by national, state, or local government or agency thereof
- Alcoholism, drug addiction
- Cosmetic surgery except necessitated by injuries
- Eye glasses
- Eye refractions
- Rest cures
- Hearing aids or fitting thereof
- Transportation except local ambulance service to or from hospital

A brief examination of this list shows that some things which are covered in life insurance are not covered in health insurance. For example, life policies cover suicide after two years while many health contracts never cover suicide-related injuries.

Terms of Renewability and Rating All states have laws that specify that health insurance policies (i.e., medical expense and disability policies) must indicate on what basis the insured can continue the contract. The provisions relating to renewability can be divided into three categories. The first category includes those contracts which are renewable at the option of the insurer. The second category includes those policies which can be renewed for a specific time period, but the insurer is granted the right to increase premiums (i.e., guaranteed renewable). The final category is composed of those contracts which not only guarantee the insured the right to continue the policy for a specific time period but also guarantee the premium rate during the period (noncancelable).

The first category, i.e., policies that are renewable at the option of the company, is the least desirable from the insured's perspective. Cancellation can be restricted to the renewal date of the policy, or an insurer can be given the right to cancel at any time. Most state laws restrict cancellation to the renewal date as exemplified by the Georgia statute which reads:

> . . . right to refuse renewal shall not be exercised before the renewal date occurring on, or after and nearest, each anniversary, or in the case of lapse and reinstatement at the renewal date occurring on, or after and nearest, each anniversary of the last reinstatement, and that any refusal of renewal shall be without prejudice to any claim originating while the policy is in force.[12]

Generally, insurers have the right to change the premium rate of policies that are renewable at the company's option so long as the rate is changed for all policies in the same classification.

While an insurer has the right to change the premium rate of guaranteed renewable contracts, an insured is assured that his or her coverage cannot be canceled during the guaranteed period. Up until the middle 1960s, most health insurance contracts were issued on a guaranteed renewable basis until age seventy. An individual purchasing one of these contracts could continue coverage as long as the premium was paid. Following the passage of Medicare, nearly all insurance companies reduced the period during which their policies were guaranteed renewable to age sixty-five. Some insurers issue policies that are renewable until the first renewal date following the insured's eligibility for Medicare. A few companies also offer guaranteed renewable policies beyond age sixty-five which supplement Medicare benefits.

Noncancelable policies give insureds the greatest amount of protection since an insurer not only cannot cancel the policy until a stipulated time, but also cannot change the premium rates. The term "noncancelable" may be used in conjunction with the phrase "guaranteed renewable," such as "noncancelable and guaranteed renewable to age sixty-five." The addition of the term "guaranteed renewable" is redundant in a contract which is noncancelable.

Even a noncancelable policy has drawbacks. First, since the insurance company may not increase the premium rates, the charge for this coverage is higher than for a policy which is renewable at the option of the company.

Secondly, this type of policy tends to give an insured the feeling that he or she always will have adequate coverage, which is not the case. A noncancelable policy purchased thirty years ago with a $10 per day hospital room and board benefit provides protection, but this amount of coverage is not sufficient to cover current hospital room and board costs. The same situation arises in the case of guaranteed renewable policies.

Some contracts are written for one time period and consequently are not renewable. Trip insurance policies are an example.

Eligibility   Most medical expense contracts are written to cover not only the named insured but also eligible family members. The original National Association of Insurance Commissioners (NAIC) model bill specified that a contract could cover a single individual or two or more eligible family members which include a husband, wife, dependent children under the age of nineteen, and any other individuals dependent upon the policyholder. Some states have increased the age limit on children to twenty-four or up to age twenty-three if the children are attending school on a full-time basis.

Individuals can be added to a health insurance policy after it has been issued. As one policy states:

> Any person who is or becomes eligible for inclusion as an Insured Person after the Policy Effective Date, shall be added by amendment and become an Insured Person upon proper written application by the Insured, the furnishing of evidence of such person's eligibility and the payment of the additional premium, if any.

Newborn children are covered under many contracts without an immediate additional premium charge. Some insurers stipulate that no premium charges will accrue until the next premium due date following the birth of a child. Therefore, if a child is born on December 15 and the policy premium is paid annually on October 15, health insurance protection would be provided free for ten months.

If a premium charge is already being made for children, many contracts do not require the payment of any additional premium since normally one charge is made for coverage of all children.

Obviously, an individual is no longer eligible for coverage when a policy terminates. In addition, there may be other times when coverage terminates for a specific insured. For example, coverage automatically may terminate when an individual becomes eligible for Medicare. The spouse of an insured may lose all coverage upon completion of a divorce. Coverage on children may terminate at age nineteen or age twenty-three if the children are attending school on a full-time basis. Finally, some contracts stipulate that coverage on a child terminates if the child marries.

Normally, the coverage for dependent children who are mentally retarded or physically disabled can extend beyond age twenty-three. A typical provision relating to mentally or physically handicapped children states:

> In the event that a dependent child is mentally or physically incapable of earning his own living on such termination date, coverage shall continue for such child while the Policy is in force subject to the timely payment of premium in accordance with the Company's premium rate in force for such persons provided due proof of such incapacity is received by the Company within thirty-one days of such termination

date, such incapacity continues and, such dependent child remains unmarried.

Conceivably, an insurer could provide coverage for the entire life of a child.

Occasionally, medical expense policies include a conversion privilege. This privilege permits an individual who is terminated under the policy to purchase other health insurance coverage without proving insurability.

Disability Income Protection

Disability income policies are designed to replace a portion of the income which the insured loses when he or she is unable to work. Many individuals do not purchase disability income coverage because they think the cost is too high, because they think they will never be disabled, or because they are not aware of the importance of the coverage. This is despite the fact that over 286 million workdays are lost each year because of disabilities.[13]

At age twenty-two, the probability of being disabled for ninety days or longer is seven and a half times greater than the probability of dying. At age forty-two, the probability of being disabled is four times greater than the probability of dying, and at age sixty-two, the chance of being disabled is twice as great as the chance of dying.[14] While the probability of being disabled is an important statistic, severity (the duration of a disability) is equally important. Table 9-9 lists the probabilities of individuals at various ages being disabled for periods of six months, one year, two years, and five years. At age twenty-five there is a 15 percent probability that an individual will be disabled for at least five years. At age thirty-five this probability has not changed.

Types of Policy Benefits A disability income policy may include coverage for loss of income only or may include several other types of benefits as well.

Disability Income[15] Normally, a disability income policy stipulates that the periodic benefit is a function of an insured's income prior to disablement. Benefits always are less than 100 percent of income in order to prevent malingering.

The benefits are paid normally only when an insured is totally disabled. However, the term "total disability" has been defined in at least three ways. The most restrictive definition specifies that an individual is not totally disabled unless he or she cannot engage in any gainful occupation or employment. If this definition is strictly applied,

Table 9-9

Probability of Being Disabled During Remainder of Life*

Age	For 6 Months	For 1 Year	For 2 Years	For 5 Years
25	34%	27%	22%	15%
30	33	26	22	15
35	33	26	21	15
40	32	25	21	15
45	30	24	20	14
50	28	23	19	14

*Reprinted with permission from "*Why Disability Protection Is Vital for You*" (Cincinnati: National Underwriter Company, 1976), p. 3.

an individual almost would have to be confined to his or her home to qualify for benefits.

A less restrictive definition is "the inability of the Insured to engage in any gainful occupation or employment for which he is qualified or becomes qualified by reason of his education, training, or experience. . . ." Under this definition, an individual receives disability payments even though he or she was not confined to a bed or home.

A third definition stipulates that an insured is disabled if he or she cannot perform the duties of his or her own occupation. Thus, an individual unable to return to a job similar to the one previously held would qualify for benefits. Two court cases illustrate how this last provision is applied. In one case, an individual was deemed totally disabled because he developed calluses which prevented him from performing any and every duty of his own occupation as a spot welder. In another case, an insured was declared totally disabled after losing the ability to speak normally since the insured was unable to perform each and every duty of his own occupation.

Generally, insurance companies combine two of the definitions. For example, one approach is to apply the very liberal definition relating to own occupation for the first few years of disability and then to apply the less liberal definition relating to education, training, and experience for the remainder of the disability period.

Frequently, disability benefits are greater and are paid for a longer period of time when the disability results from an accident rather than from sickness. The benefit differential exists because a disability resulting from an accident is less likely to occur than disability resulting from sickness. Also, there is less chance of abuse (malingering) in cases involving accidents.

Controversy has arisen over whether pregnancy constitutes a disability. The argument has been made that failure to define pregnancy as disability violates the sex discrimination laws. As of September 1977, no federal statute requires employers to pay disability income benefits for maternity leaves. However, several bills pending before Congress would change this situation.

Contract provisions other than the definition of total disability can have a bearing on whether an insured is eligible for disability benefits. In Crowell v. Federal Life & Casualty Company, the insured had a policy which stated that total disability meant:

> . . . that as a result of Injury or Sickness, the Insured is under the regular care and attendance of a duly licensed doctor of medicine or osteopath, other than himself, is completely unable to perform each and every duty pertaining to his occupation and is not gainfully employed in any other occupation, except that if a monthly indemnity has been paid for twelve months during any period of continuous total disability, then for the balance of the period of such continuous total disability, the term total disability condition shall mean the complete inability of the Insured to engage in any gainful occupation for which he is reasonably qualified by education, training or experience.[16]

The policy also contained a provision relating to confining sickness which stipulated that confining sickness meant "that as a result of Sickness the Insured is confined to his residential premises or yard, except for necessary visits to hospitals or a doctor's office for treatment."[17]

The insured, Gerald Crowell, had a heart attack. The insurance company paid benefits for twenty-four months. Following the twenty-four month period, the insurance company denied the claim, contending that Mr. Crowell was not confined to his home or yard because daily he took two and one-half mile walks as recommended by his doctor.

The court stated that the provisions of the contract should be interpreted liberally and went on to point out:

> The courts recognize that it is just such provisions as these (referring to the confinement provision) which have brought health policies in disrepute, to the point where the public believes that the 'big print gives it to you, and the little print takes it away.' Since the buying public is not aware of the meaning of the average limited risk contract, the courts will hold them to be as little restrictive as possible.[18]

The court decided that the plaintiff was entitled to continue to receive benefits.

Partial Disability. In addition to benefits for total disability, some contracts provide benefits for partial disability. The amount of the partial disability payment is a percentage of the total disability benefit. Generally, the partial disability benefits are paid for a shorter period

Table 9-10
Accidental Death, Dismemberment, and Loss of Sight Schedules

For loss of:	
Life	The principal sum
Both hands or both feet or sight of both eyes	The principal sum
One hand and one foot	The principal sum
One hand or foot and sight of one eye	The principal sum
One arm or leg	Two-thirds the principal sum
One hand or foot	One-half the principal sum
Sight of one eye	One-third the principal sum

than total disability benefits. Partial disability is the inability to perform some but not all activity. The definition of disability is generally a function of the definition of total disability.

Accidental Death, Dismemberment, and Loss of Sight. Many disability policies also provide coverage for accidental death, dismemberment, and loss of sight that occurs within a certain time after an accident. Generally, the highest benefit is paid for loss of life or loss of two or more limbs. This maximum amount, known as a "principal sum," is set out in a schedule. Normally, the coverage for lesser injuries is a percentage of the principal sum. Table 9-10 illustrates a possible schedule of benefits for accidental death, dismemberment, or loss of sight.

Accidental Medical Expense. Some disability income policies contain a limited medical expense benefit which applies only to losses resulting from an accident. A time limit, such as one year, is placed on the period for which medical expense benefit costs are covered.

Waiver. Many policies contain a provision that waives the payment of premiums while the insured is disabled. The insured has no obligation to pay back the waived premiums but must resume the normal payment of premiums upon recovery. The waiver of premium benefit may also be added to many life insurance policies along with a limited disability income benefit.

Rehabilitation. Many insurance companies allow an insured to participate in a rehabilitation program without jeopardizing his or her disability payments. That is, the insured does not lose any benefits while undergoing treatment and usually does not lose any benefits following the completion of a rehabilitation program unless the individual is fully and totally rehabilitated. In addition, many programs provide additional funds for part or all of the costs of rehabilitation services.

Additional Policy Provisions The required and optional provisions found in medical expense policies also may be used in disability income contracts. Several of the additional and modified provisions found in disability contracts which are not found in a medical expense policy or are found in a different form require special attention.

Waiting or Elimination Periods. In lieu of a deductible, most disability income policies contain a waiting period which delays the time when an individual becomes eligible to receive disability benefits. For example, a contract may contain a seven-day waiting period for disability caused by injury and a fourteen-day waiting period for disability caused by sickness. Benefits would not begin until a waiting period had expired. Therefore, if an insured were disabled for thirty days, as a result of an accident, the insurance company would pay 76.6 percent (23/30) of the monthly benefit.

Insureds may eliminate any waiting period by paying a higher premium, but this results in dollar swapping with the insurance company. An insured normally maximizes coverage per premium dollar by utilizing as long a waiting period as possible.

Tables 9-11 and 9-12 indicate the difference in the incidence of disablement per thousand lives between a six-month waiting period and a twelve-month waiting period. The rate of disablement per thousand lives for the six-month period is 0.89 for all individuals under age forty and 0.78 and 1.02, respectively, for males and females under age forty. These rates of disablement compare with 0.47, 0.18, and 0.86 for a twelve-month waiting period. Thus, the longer the waiting period the lower the cost of disability coverage.

Some employers continue to pay an individual's salary even though the individual is disabled. In this situation, the insured employee should purchase coverage which has a waiting period equal to the duration of the salary continuation arrangement.

An insured can purchase a contract with a retroactive waiting period in which case benefits are earned unless disability lasts longer than the waiting period. Then benefits are paid from the first day of disability. The following illustrates the difference between a straight and a retroactive waiting period.

Carl Read was disabled for a month and Endora Jackson was

Table 9-11

Group Long-term Disability Insurance Rates of Disablement
Per 1,000 Lives Exposed (Six-Month Waiting Period;
Calendar Year of Issue Excluded)*

Attained Age	Life Years Exposed	Number of Claims	Rate of Disablement Per 1,000 Lives
All Experience: Males, Females and Sex Unknown			
Under 40	1,430,962	1,272	0.89
40–44	410,599	926	2.26
45–49	389,383	1,363	3.50
50–54	317,558	1,972	6.21
55–59	242,731	2,677	11.03
60–64	152,152	2,494	16.39
All ages	2,943,384	10,704	3.64
Male Experience Only			
Under 40	674,934	528	0.78
40–44	198,668	428	2.15
45–49	184,587	614	3.33
50–54	150,927	959	6.35
55–59	118,241	1,288	10.89
60–64	74,768	1,239	16.57
All ages	1,402,125	5,056	3.61
Female Experience Only			
Under 40	250,254	256	1.02
40–44	56,220	207	3.68
45–49	59,932	274	4.57
50–54	50,587	328	6.48
55–59	38,466	325	8.45
60–65	23,466	289	12.32
All ages	478,925	1,679	3.51

*Reprinted with permission from Committee on Group Life and Health Insurance, "Group Long-Term Disability Insurance," *Transactions: Society of Actuaries, Reports Volume* (Chicago: Society of Actuaries, 1974), p. 155.

Table 9-12

Group Long-term Disability Insurance Rates of Disablement Per 1,000 Lives Exposed (Twelve-month Waiting Period; Calendar Year of Issue Excluded)*

Attained Age	Life Years Exposed	Number of Claims	Rate of Disablement Per 1,000 Lives
All Experience: Males, Females, and Sex Unknown			
Under 40	104,587	49	0.47
40–44	31,686	42	1.33
45–49	30,767	84	2.73
50–54	25,832	116	4.49
55–59	20,284	173	8.53
60–64	12.060	128	10.61
All ages	225,216	592	2.63
Male Experience Only			
Under 40	59,880	11	0.18
40–44	14,839	11	0.74
45–49	14,283	33	2.31
50–54	11,251	36	3.20
55–59	9,186	69	7.51
60–64	5,806	71	12.23
All ages	115,245	231	2.00
Female Experience Only			
Under 40	12,859	11	0.86
40–44	2,985	6	2.01
45–49	4,012	13	3.24
50–54	4,252	21	4.94
55–59	3,878	29	7.48
60–64	2,183	17	7.79
All ages	30,169	97	3.22

*Reprinted with permission from Committee on Group Life and Health Insurance, "Group Long-Term Disability Insurance," *Transactions: Society of Actuaries, Reports Volume* (Chicago: Society of Actuaries, 1974), p. 161.

disabled for two months as the result of a skiing accident. Carl's disability income policy paid $500 per month for accident-related disabilities subject to a fourteen-day waiting period. Consequently, he received $266.67; that is, $500 × (16/30). Most insurers assume a thirty-day month when calculating benefits for fractions of a month.

Endora's disability income policy also had a $500 per month benefit but her policy had a fourteen-day retroactive waiting period. Therefore, she received $1,000 ($500 × 2 months). Even though the contract had a fourteen-day waiting period, it provided coverage retroactive to the first day of disability.

Notice of Claim. In addition to the requirement that an insured must notify the insurer within twenty days of the commencement of a loss, disability income policies generally contain a provision which requires an insured to periodically (e.g., every six months) prove that he or she is still disabled.

Recurrent Disability. Several periods of disability may be considered the same disability if they occur in rapid succession. A typical clause reads as follows:

> If, within 6 months a period of total disability due to injury or sickness for which monthly indemnity has been payable under Part I or Part II, the Insured sustains a subsequent period of disability from the same or related cause or causes, such subsequent period shall be considered a continuation of the prior period of total disability and indemnified as such.
>
> If, however, following a period of total disability, the Insured is engaged in his occupation, or any gainful occupation or employment for which he is qualified by reason of his education, training or experience, and has performed all the the important duties for 6 months or more, such subsequent period of disability resulting from the same or related cause or causes shall be considered as new disability resulting from sickness . . . .

An individual could be disabled because of a back injury for six months. If that individual returned to work for one month and then was disabled again because of the same back injury, an insurer whose policy had a recurrent disability provision like the one above would treat the two occurrences as the same disability.

Relation of Earnings to Insurance. To discourage abuse, disability income policies that are renewable until age fifty-five or that are issued after age forty-four and can be renewed for at least five years, frequently include a provision known as the "relation of earnings to insurance" clause which bars an insured from collecting benefits in excess of his or her salary despite the number of contracts owned. Specifically, the provision states:

If the total monthly amount of loss of time benefits promised for the same loss under all valid loss of time coverages upon the insured, whether payable on a weekly or monthly basis, shall exceed the monthly earnings of the insured at the time disability commenced or his average monthly earnings for the period of two years immediately preceding the disability for which claim is made, whichever is the greater, the insurer will be liable only for such proportionate amount of such benefits under this policy as the amount of such earnings or such average monthly earnings of the insured bears to the total amount of monthly benefits for the same loss under all such coverage upon the insured at the time such disability commences . . . .

Generally, this provision cannot act to reduce coverage below $200 per month or the sum of the coverages in all policies, whichever is less. A pro rata return of premium is made for the portion of the coverage not collected. The following example demonstrates how this relation of earnings to insurance provision reduces the coverage.

Becky Welch has two disability income policies issued by different insurers. One policy has a $600 per month benefit while the other contract has a $300 per month benefit. Becky's current monthly salary is $700, but her average monthly salary for the past two years has been $750. If Becky were disabled, each insurer would pay the amount shown as follows:

$$\text{Insurer } A: \frac{\$600}{\$900} \times \$750 = \$500$$

$$\text{Insurer } B: \frac{\$300}{\$900} \times \$750 = \$250$$

To prevent malingering, most insurers will not issue coverage for more than 66⅔ percent of an individual's monthly wage in recognition of the fact that disability benefits are received income tax free and the insured does not incur the normal costs associated with working. One insurer uses a formula which is more stringent than the 66⅔ percent rule. The formula is as shown in Table 9-13.

Health Insurance Underwriting

To properly rate an individual for any type of medical expense or disability income insurance contract, an underwriter must have the following information.

Age Age is a very important criterion not only in setting rates but also in determining if coverage will be issued with age.

Most insurers have a different rate for every age for medical

Table 9-13

Formula for Monthly Benefits*

$100 Minimum	
Maximum subject to:	
Earned Monthly Income	Maximum Monthly Benefit
Less than $1,000	None
$1,000—$2,499	55% of monthly income less $300
$2,500—$3,499	45% of monthly income less $50
$3,500 and up	35% of monthly income less $300

*Reprinted with permission from Price Gaines, Jr., *1976 Time Saver for Health Insurance* (Cincinnati: National Underwriter Company, 1976), p. 25.

expense and disability income coverage instead of a rate for age brackets. Therefore, there is a rate for ages thirty-five, thirty-six, thirty-seven, thirty-eight, and thirty-nine instead of a rate for ages thirty-five to forty.

Beyond age sixty-five, morbidity increases rapidly and many insurers limit their policies so that they cannot be renewed beyond that age. This has been true especially since the advent of Medicare.

Sex   Sex is another underwriting criterion since women are sick more often than men, and when disabled, are disabled for longer periods as can be seen by examining Table 9-14. As a result, women are charged higher rates than men. However, because of social pressure, this underwriting criterion probably will be eliminated.

Location   Individuals living or traveling outside of the United States may be subject to illnesses or injuries which would not be encountered in the United States. For example, the incidence of diseases is much higher in some South American countries than it is in the United States.

Physical Condition   The current health of an applicant as well as his or her past health record is pertinent to the underwriting decision. If a person has or has had a history of bad health, the underwriter, to compensate for the additional possibility of loss, will charge a higher premium, delete the coverage, or not issue coverage.

In evaluating a person's health, the underwriter will look for physical characteristics that indicate that the individual may be a bad risk. For example, an obese person, even in good health, is more susceptible to a heart attack, high blood pressure, and diabetes than a person with a normal build.

Alcoholism, drug addiction, and mental illness are three other

Table 9-14
Days of Disability—by Type and by Sex of Patient—1960 to 1974*

Item	Total Days of Disability (millions)						Days Per Person					
	1960	1965	1970	1972	1973	1974	1960	1965	1970	1972	1973	1974
Restricted-activity days[1]	2,830	3,086	2,913	3,402	3,392	3,566	16.2	16.4	14.6	16.7	16.5	17.2
Male	1,215	1,339	1,273	1,458	1,458	1,564	14.3	14.7	13.2	14.8	14.7	15.6
Female	1,615	1,747	1,640	1,943	1,934	2,001	18.0	18.0	15.8	18.4	18.1	18.7
Bed-disability days[2]	1,055	1,160	1,222	1,320	1,311	1,392	6.0	6.2	6.1	6.5	6.4	6.7
Male	454	484	503	539	528	584	5.3	5.3	5.3	5.5	5.3	5.8
Female	601	677	720	780	783	807	6.7	7.0	6.9	7.4	7.3	7.5
Work-loss days[3]	370	400	417	428	451	414	5.6	5.7	5.4	5.3	5.4	4.9
Male	244	261	243	258	264	245	5.5	5.7	5.0	5.2	5.2	4.8
Female	126	139	175	170	187	169	5.6	5.6	5.9	5.6	5.8	5.1
School-loss days[4]	196	214	222	235	222	242	5.3	5.2	4.9	5.3	5.1	5.6
Male	93	103	108	111	103	126	4.9	4.9	4.7	4.9	4.7	5.7
Female	102	111	114	125	118	116	5.6	5.4	5.1	5.8	5.5	5.5

1. A day when a person cut down on his usual activities for the whole day because of illness or injury. Includes bed-disability, work-loss, and school-loss days.
2. A day when a person was kept in bed either all or most of the day because of illness or injury. Includes those work-loss and school-loss days actually spent in bed.
3. A day when a person lost the entire work day because of illness or injury. Computed for persons 17 years of age and over in the currently employed population, defined as those who were working or had a job or business from which they were not on layoff during the 2-week period preceding the week of interview.
4. Child's loss of entire school day because of illness or injury. Computed for children 6–16 years of age.

*Reprinted from United States Department of Commerce, *Statistical Abstract of the United States* (Washington: Superintendent of Documents, 1976), p. 88.

factors which an underwriter will consider in evaluating a person's physical condition. Generally, if a person is an alcoholic or a drug addict, the underwriter will not issue a contract. People with minor mental problems are usually issued health disability income coverage since most contracts do not restrict benefits for mental illness. Minor mental problems would be those problems which do not increase a person's morbidity. Other policies contain limits such as two years for the payment of disability income benefits for mental illness.

Moral Hazard A person's moral habits may affect his or her health. Therefore, underwriters attempt to avoid providing coverage for individuals with undesirable character traits since they are more susceptible to conflict, mental problems, and undesirable health characteristics and may be more inclined to file fraudulent claims than other individuals.

Moral risk is not synonymous with a lack of ethics. To illustrate, a person may not take proper care of himself or herself, i.e., he or she may not get proper rest, eat properly, or obtain preventive medical care. While the person may be a respected individual in the community, he or she can be a moral hazard.

Occupation An individual's occupation can have an impact on his or her rate of sickness and injury. Most insurers grade the exposures presented by different occupational categories. As the exposure increases, the rates are increased. A construction worker, for example, is more likely to be disabled than an accountant. Therefore, the under-writer will charge a higher rate for a disability contract issued on the construction worker. Some occupations are so hazardous that insurers are unwilling to issue health or disability insurance at all.

Sources of Information An underwriter has several sources from which he or she can gather data for evaluating an applicant. The primary source of information is the application. It contains information about the applicant's current health, health history, family health history, and habits.

The producer is a source of information. He or she performs the first level of underwriting, and most applications provide space for the producer's evaluation of the applicant. This information is very important to the underwriter who probably will never see the applicant.

The underwriter also can get information from doctors who have treated the applicant and from hospitals in which the applicant has been a patient. The underwriter's primary source for the names of doctors and hospitals is the application provided by the prospective insured. If the applicant is dishonest, the underwriter may never have an accurate idea of the applicant's health history.

Other sources of information include credit reports and Medical

Information Bureau reports. These reports may provide information which the applicant is unwilling or unable to reveal.

Analysis of an Exposure After an underwriter has gathered the information, it must be evaluated. Normally, credits and debits are awarded for good and bad characteristics, respectively. Being overweight is a debit, while a good medical history is a credit. The debits and credits are totaled and the credits are used to offset the debits. If the net number of debits exceeds an acceptable level, an individual will be rated up or not insured.

In lieu of rating an individual, an insurance company may exclude coverage for some types of health conditions. As an example, a policy that excludes benefits for health care expenses resulting from a heart condition can be issued to an individual with a heart ailment. The exclusion may be permanent or may apply only to a period of time, e.g., five years. The latter approach is used when the underwriter feels that the increased exposure will be eliminated within the designated time period. For example, the heart condition exclusion may be added because the applicant has just had open heart surgery. However, if a complete recovery occurs, the exposure is no greater for the applicant than for any other person.

Miscellaneous Health Insurance Coverages

Some insurance contracts cover only a portion of the expenses that have been discussed or are designed to meet a specialized need. Several of the more common of these contracts are discussed in this section.

Dread Disease Some insurers specialize in policies that only cover specific illnesses such as cancer, meningitis, rabies, smallpox, and multiple sclerosis.

Cancer policies constitute a large segment of the dread disease policy market. These policies provide benefits for room and board in a hospital and for other miscellaneous expenses such as drugs, X-ray therapy, physician's visits, surgery, anesthesia, ambulance, blood, nursing, and transportation. Cancer policies have internal limits per benefit period in addition to an aggregate benefit limit, such as $10,000. Benefits normally are paid in addition to any other coverage that an insured may have.

Dread disease policies occasionally fill a definite need. However, an insured has to be careful not to concentrate on purchasing coverage for the catastrophic types of illnesses without having adequate health insurance protection for the less dramatic but equally expensive exposures.

Hospital Indemnity A hospital indemnity policy is similar to a disability income policy, the primary distinction being that the hospital indemnity contract only pays an individual while he or she is hospitalized. The benefit under the hospital benefit policy normally is stated in terms of a flat amount per day, week, or month. If benefits are stated on a weekly or monthly basis, an individual receives a portion of that benefit for every day that he or she is confined in a hospital. For example, a hospital indemnity policy that provides $1,000 per month pays $33.33 for each day of hospitalization.

The benefits under a hospital indemnity policy can be used to supplement gaps in a medical expense contract, to cover loss of income during a period of hospitalization, or to handle miscellaneous expenses such as child care. However, a hospital indemnity contract does not always replace a disability income or hospital expense policy. The hospital indemnity contract pays only while an insured is in the hospital. A disability income policy pays benefits if an insured is disabled regardless of hospitalization, and a hospital expense policy pays for specific charges. Consequently, these coverages may offer an insured better insurance protection than he or she would have under a hospital indemnity policy alone.

Credit Health Insurance Credit health insurance can be written on either an individual or a group basis. The coverage provides debtors with the funds necessary to meet loan obligations. The coverage is frequently sold in conjunction with mortgages, installment loans, and charge accounts.

In the past, rates for this coverage have been excessive relative to the exposure. However, many insurance departments have taken action to eliminate this problem. As a result, the coverage afforded under credit health insurance generally is a better buy now than previously.

Usually, individuals who have a disability income policy do not need to purchase credit or accident health insurance since it provides the funds necessary to meet installment loan commitments. This is not true, however, if an individual has a balloon or a large single installment note.

Business Overhead Expense Disabled individuals not only suffer loss of income but also may incur a loss because of continuing business expenses. This situation frequently arises among self-employed persons, such as doctors, lawyers, accountants, and other independent business personnel.

To meet the needs of these individuals, insurance companies have developed a business overhead expense policy which pays for continuing business expenses such as rent, electricity, taxes, fees, dues, cost of goods, equipment, fixtures, products of the business, depreciation, salaries, water, telephone, laundry, and postage. These policies pay only

Table 9-15

Expenses Incurred by the Law Firm

Rent	$500.00
Electricity	50.00
Heat	27.00
Water	8.00
Telephone	50.00
Postage/stationery	62.00
Office equipment and supplies	120.00
Taxes	100.00
Total	$917.00

for those expenses that are actually incurred by an individual. Thus, if an insured is an equal partner in a company, only that individual's proportionate share of expenses can be insured subject to the maximum benefit stated in the policy. An insurance company also will not be responsible for expenses which were not incurred regularly before the disability commenced. The following example illustrates how this type of policy works.

Pamela Crowell owns a law firm and pays all expenses and operating costs. The list of expenses incurred on a monthly basis is given in Table 9-15.

Pamela has a $900 business overhead expense policy which covers all the categories of expense listed. Therefore, the insurer will pay 100 percent of all expenses up to $900 if Pamela is disabled and Pamela must pay $17 of the monthly exposure.

The definition of disability used in most business overhead expense policies is "regular and own occupation." Premiums are tax deductible, and the insured must treat any payments under the contract as income. Most policies are written with a short maximum benefit period. Normally, if a person remains disabled for a long period of time the business will be sold or dissolved.

Buy-Sell Agreement. Covering overhead expenses is not the only way that disability insurance can be utilized in a business relationship. It may also be used to fund a buy-sell agreement between partners in the event that one partner is disabled.

Under a disability buy-sell agreement, the partners agree that if one partner is disabled, he or she will be paid a disability benefit. If it appears that the disabled partner will not return to work, the agreement compels the other partner(s) to purchase the disabled partner's share of the business by means of disability payments, normally for life. While a buy-sell disability agreement could be funded by the partnership's profits, the use of insurance guarantees that the dollars necessary for the disability payments will be available.

Insurance would be used in conjunction with a buy-sell agreement similar to the one shown below:

> In the event of the disability of one of the Partners the nondisabled Partner will, after . . . . . . days (months, years), purchase the partnership interest of the disabled partner. It is agreed: a. in the event that a Partner shall become totally disabled, the disabled Partner shall during the period of such disability, but for not more than . . . . . . months from the date on which such disability commenced, receive each week (monthly, semi-monthly) from the Partnership the sum of . . . . . . dollars in lieu of any share of the profits of the Partnership. b. If the period of disability should extend for a period of more than . . . . . . months, then the disabled Partner shall during the period of such continued disability, but for not more than for . . . . . . additional months, receive each week (monthly, semi-monthly) from the Partnership the sum of . . . . . . dollars in lieu of any share of the profits of the Partnership. c. Purchase of Partnership interest by nondisabled Partner. (1) in the event the disabled partner remains totally disabled for a continuous period of . . . . . . years, then and in that event the nondisabled Partner shall purchase and the disabled Partner shall sell all title and interest to the disabled Partner in and to the Partnership and all of its assets for the purchase price specified in Section 2 [Purchase Price Upon Death of Partner] of this agreement. (2) The purchase price shall be paid to such disabled Partner in equal monthly installments over a period of . . . . . . months . . . .[19]

This agreement makes the sale and purchase of the business mandatory in the event that a partner is disabled for an extended period. The mandatory nature of this agreement makes disability insurance desirable from the perspectives of both the disabled and the nondisabled partners.

Two methods of buying out a disabled partner are available under disability contracts. In the example presented above, the disabled partner is paid a periodic benefit over an extended period of time. Most disability policies can be used with this type of arrangement. Also available are disability policies that pay a lump sum to the disabled partner. This approach prevents the disabled partner from having to wait to obtain his or her money, and also relieves the other partner(s) of further obligation.

Key Employee Coverage   One other business use of disability income insurance involves the purchase (by the company) of a disability income policy on a key employee. If the employee becomes disabled, benefits are paid to the company which can be used to hire someone to continue the key employee's activities.

Travel Accident   A traveler can purchase accidental death and dismemberment insurance to pay for losses incurred while on a trip. Normally, this coverage insures a person against injury incurred on a plane, train, or other common carrier, but protection can be purchased to cover any type of transportation.

What Health Insurance Protection to Purchase

Criteria   The purchase of health insurance coverage is difficult since many factors must be considered when deciding which coverage is right for a particular individual or family. There are three primary areas that an individual should examine before purchasing health insurance protection. First, an individual must determine which is the right type of coverage for his or her needs. Second, a prospective insured must decide from which insurer he or she wants to purchase the coverage to meet the determined needs. Finally, the prospective insured must consider all the sources of insurance available to avoid underinsurance or overinsurance.

Selecting the Right Coverage   In determining what coverage to buy, an individual should consider his or her financial capability and should try to reduce dollar swapping by purchasing policies with a waiting period and with a deductible.

Table 9-16 contains the list of rates per $10 of monthly income for a disability income policy. Table 9-16 shows that the longer the waiting period, the lower the cost. For example, at age thirty-four, $100 of monthly income with a 30-day waiting period would be $42.70. The same contract with a 180-day waiting period would be $29.60. By selecting a policy with a waiting and/or a deductible period, an insured is combining the risk management principles of retention and transfer.

Another consideration in the selection of coverage is the cost of health benefits in the insured's geographical area. An individual who lives in New York City should purchase a higher room and board benefit than one who lives in Des Moines.

Policy provisions should be compared carefully in order that the insured might have a contract which meets his or her needs. Definitions, exclusions, renewability, and waiting periods are just a few of the factors that an insured should consider and evaluate.

Selection of the Insurer   Health insurers can be organized on a stock or mutual basis. Stock companies are owned by the stockholders, and generally issue policies that do not pay dividends. Mutual companies are owned by the policyholders who receive dividends based on experience. A third organizational structure is that of Blue Cross and Blue Shield. Blue Cross plans provide hospital expense benefits and Blue

Table 9-16

Disability Income Rates Per Ten Dollars of Monthly Income*

Age	Elimination Period		
	30 Days	90 Days	180 Days
18–25	3.14	2.43	2.15
26	3.37	2.64	2.32
28	3.53	2.78	2.44
30	3.70	2.93	2.57
32	3.96	3.13	2.75
34	4.27	3.39	2.96
36	4.63	3.68	3.21
38	5.04	3.99	3.49
40	5.50	4.37	3.81
42	6.11	4.92	4.30
44	6.80	5.52	4.86
46	7.55	6.19	5.45
48	8.32	6.89	6.05
50	9.15	7.60	6.67
52	9.68	8.00	6.98
54	10.07	8.38	7.26
56	10.21	8.57	7.40

*Reprinted with permission from Price Gaines, Jr., *1976 Time Saver For Health Insurance* (Cincinnati: National Underwriter Company, 1976), p. 135.

Shield pays surgical and physician's costs. In recent years, Blue Cross and Blue Shield have begun to move away from providing service benefits and now provide some coverage on an indemnity basis.

Each Blue Cross and Blue Shield organization is operated independently. A particular Blue Cross or Blue Shield plan may cover an entire state or a smaller area, such as a major metropolitan area. The Blue Cross/Blue Shield organizations are combined into a national network. As a result, while the individual units are autonomous, an individual covered by one plan will receive credit for that coverage from an association in another state.

Initially, Blue Cross plans issued only group coverage, but as members left the groups and converted to individual coverage, the number of individual policyholders grew. Today, Blue Cross sells not only group coverage but also individual contracts and is a strong competitor in all markets.

The "Blues" have two fundamental competitive advantages over other private health insurance carriers. Because of their nonprofit status, they receive preferential tax treatment. Secondly, the Blues deal directly with the providers of health services and receive a discount on services provided to their subscribers. As a result, both Blue Cross and Blue Shield have some control on the costs of the services provided their subscribers.

Another important factor in selecting an insurer is the type of marketing approach it uses. Some insurance companies utilize insurance agents or brokers to handle their business. Frequently, the agent will handle both life and health insurance. The agent or broker is responsible for services such as an explanation of the coverage, a discussion of what coverage is best suited to an individual's needs, and a determination of which insurer the prospective insured should use.

In lieu of using agents, some insurance companies use mass merchandising methods, such as advertisements in Sunday newspapers, magazines, and other publications. While the coverage offered through newspaper advertisements may include hospital expense benefits protection, more often they are hospital indemnity policies.

Another mass merchandising approach is direct mail solicitation in which an individual is mailed an application and an outline of coverage. The prospective insured completes and returns the application and is issued an insurance contract if he or she is in good health.

Other Sources of Health Insurance Insureds should be aware of all sources of available health insurance to avoid overinsurance and the wasting of premium dollars. To illustrate, an individual eligible for disability income benefits under Social Security should consider these benefits when deciding how much protection is needed on an individual basis. If Social Security provides $200 a month and an individual feels that $600 is needed, then a $400 policy should be purchased. The five-month Social Security waiting period should be considered. High disability benefits may have to be provided in the first portion of the disability until Social Security benefits are activated. Group health insurance benefits also should be considered before individual coverage is purchased. If the group coverage is adequate protection, individual coverage may be unnecessary.

Health Insurance Advertising

In most states, health insurers must provide applicants with an outline of coverage which describes the coverage being offered, the exclusions, terms of renewability, and other pertinent information.

Changing marketing methods have forced insurance regulators to closely examine the material contained in the outline of coverage. The use of direct mail and advertisements in newspapers and magazines has forced insurance regulators to require that brochures and outlines of coverage be very specific and clear.

In 1974, the National Association of Insurance Commissioners adopted model rules governing the advertisement of accident and sickness insurance contracts. These rules are designed to "assure truthful and adequate disclosure of all material and relevant information in the advertising of accident and sickness insurance."[20] The determination as to what constitutes truthful and adequate disclosure of policy material is left to the insurance commissioner in each state. A particular commissioner has to ascertain if "an advertisement has the capacity or tendency to mislead or deceive . . . a person of average education and intelligence, within the segment of the public to which it is directed."[21] The NAIC did not list all of the acceptable advertising practices in its rules and interpretive guidelines, but rather gave some examples of unacceptable advertising wording. Several of the (un)acceptable practices developed by the NAIC follow:

An advertisement which uses a phrase such as "no age limit," if benefits or premiums vary by age or if age is an underwriting factor, must disclose that fact.

Advertisements, applications, requests for additional information and similar materials are unacceptable if they state or imply that the recipient has been individually selected to be offered insurance or has had his eligibility for such insurance individually determined in advance when the advertisement is directed to all persons in a group or to all persons whose names appear on a mailing list.

Advertisements which indicate that a particular coverage or policy is exclusively for "preferred risks" or a particular segment of the population or that a particular segment of the population are acceptable risks, when such distinctions are not maintained in the issuance of policies, are not acceptable.

Any advertisement which uses any *phrase or* term such as *"here is all* you do to apply," "simply" or "merely" to refer to the act of applying for a policy which is not a guaranteed issue policy is unacceptable *unless it refers to the fact that the application is subject to acceptance or approval by the insurer.*

No advertisement shall employ devices which are designed to create *undue* fear or anxiety in the minds of those to whom they are directed. Unacceptable examples of such devices are: the use of phrases such as "cancer kills somebody every two minutes" and "total number of accidents" without reference to the total population from which such statistics are drawn. (As an example of a permissible device, data prepared by the American Cancer Society are acceptable provided their source is noted and they are not overemphasized.)

An advertisement which refers to "whenever you are hospitalized" or "while you are confined in the hospital" omitting the phrase "for covered injury or sickness," if the policy excludes certain injuries or sickness, is unacceptable. *Continued reference to "covered injury or sickness" is not necessary where this fact has been prominently disclosed in the advertisement and where the description of sicknesses or injuries not covered are prominently set forth.*

An advertisement which fails to disclose any waiting or elimination periods for specific benefits is unacceptable.

The term "confining sickness" is an abbreviated expression and must be explained in an advertisement containing the term. Such an explanation might be as follows: "Benefits are payable for total disability due to confining sickness only so long as the insured is necessarily confined indoors." Captions such as "Lifetime Sickness Benefits" or "Five-Year Sickness Benefits" are incomplete if such benefits are subject to confinement requirements. When sickness benefits are subject to confinement requirements, captions such as "Lifetime House Confining Sickness Benefits" or "Five-Year Confining Sickness Benefits" would be permissible.

A television, radio, mail, or newspaper advertisement *which is designed to produce leads either by use of a coupon or a request to write to the company* or a subsequent advertisement prior to contact must include information disclosing that an agent may contact the applicant if such is the fact.

An advertisement for a policy designed to supplement benefits under Medicare is unacceptable if the advertisement: fails to disclose in clear language which of the Medicare benefits the policy is designed to supplement and which of the Medicare benefits the policy is not designed to supplement or if it otherwise implies that Medicare provides only those benefits which the policy is designed to supplement.[22]

In addition to changing the requirements on the display of information, renewability, and other policy provisions, the 1974 NAIC advertising rules place constraints on the use of testimonials or endorsements by third parties. Testimonials or endorsements cannot be utilized unless they accurately represent the opinions of the individuals involved concerning the product being advertised.

When an individual receives remuneration for making an endorsement or giving a testimonial, this fact must be indicated in the advertising. The advertising also must indicate if the individual giving the testimonial or endorsement is somehow related to or has a financial interest in the insurer, such as stockholders, directors, officers, and employees.

Chapter Notes

1. Civil Statutes of Texas Annotated, Ch. 3, Art. 3.70-1, Sec. B.
2. American Psychiatric Association, *APA Guidelines* (Washington: American Psychiatric Association, 1969), p. 12.
3. Adams v. Metropolitan Life Insurance Company, 7 A. 2d 545 (1939).
4. Ibid., pp. 544-545.
5. Ibid., p. 545.
6. Price Gaines, Jr. *1976 Time Saver for Health Insurance* (Cincinnati: National Underwriter Company, 1976), p. vi.
7. Copies of a hospital expense policy and a major medical policy can be found in the policy kit.
8. Massachusetts Casualty Insurance Company v. Forman, 516 F. 2d 425 (1975).
9. Consolidated Laws of New York Annotated, Ch. 27, Art. 7, Sec. 164.
10. Civil Statutes of Texas Annotated, Ch. 3, Art. 3.70-1, Sec. H.
11. Gaines, Jr., pp. v, vi.
12. Code of Georgia Annotated, Ch. 56-30, Sec. 3006.
13. National Underwriter Company, "Why Disability Protection Is Vital For You," (Cincinnati: National Underwriter Company, 1976), pp. 4, 5.
14. Ibid., p. 4.
15. A copy of a disability income policy can be found in the policy kit.
16. Crowell v. Federal Life and Casualty, 232 N.E. 2d 711 (1975).
17. Ibid.
18. Ibid., p. 712.
19. R. R. Morse, J. C. Hartwig, F. W. Sager, and J. S. Couzens, *Business Agreements for Use with Life Insurance* (Milwaukee: Northwestern Mutual Life Insurance Company, 1970), p. 28.
20. *2 Proceedings of the National Association of Insurance Commissioners*, 421 (1974).
21. Ibid., 424.
22. *2 Proceedings of the National Association of Health Commissioners*, 425-428 (1974).

CHAPTER 10

Health Insurance Planning and Group Coverages

WORKERS' COMPENSATION

Early History

Most employees do not consider workers' compensation an employee benefit, but it is a part of the total package of coverage provided by an employer. Today, workers' compensation provides a broad range of benefits for disabled workers and their families or for the survivors of deceased workers.

The workers' compensation movement had its beginning in Europe in the nineteenth century. The first workers' compensation law enacted by a state legislature in the United States was passed in Maryland in 1902. The law had limited impact because it applied only to coal and clay mines, quarries, steam or street railroads, and municipal operations relating to the construction of sewers, excavations, or other physical structures. In 1904, the Maryland law was voided on the grounds that it violated the right of an injured party to a jury trial.[1]

President Theodore Roosevelt requested that Congress enact a workers' compensation law for federal employees. As a result, in 1908 a federal workers' compensation law was established.

Massachusetts adopted a state workers' compensation law in 1908. The plan was not effective because the program was optional. In 1909, Montana passed a compulsory workers' compensation law under which funds were collected and paid into the Employers' and Employees' Co-operative Insurance and Total Permanent Disability Fund. This law, like the Maryland law, was declared unconstitutional. The Montana law was overturned on the grounds that employers were required to contribute to the fund, but employees had the option of accepting benefits under the plan or suing the employer.[2]

The first state workers' compensation law which was effective and which survived legal challenges was passed in 1911, in Wisconsin. Although the law was voluntary, it was successful. State workers' compensation laws have subsequently been passed in all fifty states.

Benefits Available Under Workers' Compensation

Workers' compensation laws provide broad coverage for workers incurring job-related injuries or diseases. Benefits are available not only for a disabled employee but also for survivors of an employee who is killed because of a job-related activity.

Medical Coverage In nearly all states, the amount of medical expense coverage is unlimited.[3] A few states have established a maximum amount that can be paid for medical costs, but the state workers' compensation board can and does provide additional coverage, if necessary. Two states do not currently provide unlimited benefits and do not allow benefits to be extended. The amount of payment for medical expenses has no impact on the other benefits available to an employee.

Disability Four types of disability are covered under state workers' compensation laws: temporary total disability, permanent total disability, temporary partial disability, and permanent partial disability.

The amount paid during a period of disability varies with the severity and duration of the disability. For example, for permanent total disability, a state may provide an employee a disability benefit equal to 66 2/3 percent of his or her salary prior to disability.

States have established minimum payments that an employee can receive. A minimum amount will be stated as a dollar figure or as a percentage of the state average weekly wage. The state average weekly wage is the average weekly wage of employees in the state in which the workers' compensation claim is filed. A maximum amount also is stipulated and is stated either as a specific dollar amount or as a percentage of the state average weekly wage.

Benefits are payable either for the term of the disability or for a maximum number of weeks. For example, in Louisiana, permanent total disability payments are limited to 500 weeks, while Maryland's law requires benefits to be paid for the duration of the disability.

Most disability benefits under workers' compensation are subject to waiting periods. The maximum waiting period used by any state is twenty-eight days. However, a much shorter waiting period (e.g., seven days) is more common. Normally, compensation is paid retroactive to the beginning of the disability period after the waiting period requirement has been satisfied.

Scheduled Injuries In some cases an employee loses, or loses the use of, an eye, an arm, a hand, an ear, or some other body part. When one of these losses occurs, an employee is paid benefits for a specified number of weeks. For example, the loss of a hand may result in benefits being paid for 170 weeks. The amount paid is calculated in the same way that disability benefits are calculated.

Death Benefits Death benefits are available under all workers' compensation programs. These benefits include a burial allowance and payments to survivors. The amount of the burial allowance will vary, but generally it will not exceed $2,000.

The survivors' benefits are a function of a deceased worker's wages. For example, a widow's benefit might be equal to 50 percent of the worker's wage. If the widow has children, the benefit might be 66 2/3 percent of the worker's weekly wage. Like disability payments, the maximum and minimum survivors' benefits are stated as a percentage of the state average weekly wage or as a fixed dollar amount.

There is also a maximum benefit period, often stated in weeks. A state workers' compensation law may provide, however, that a widow receives benefits during her entire widowhood. Coverage for children continues until the children are over age eighteen or, if students, age twenty-five.

Rehabilitation State workers' compensation laws provide benefits for the rehabilitation of injured workers. The type of benefit varies significantly from state to state. For example, Connecticut has a maximum rehabilitation benefit of $40 a week, while North Carolina's law stipulates that all required rehabilitation services be provided. The following examples illustrate how some workers' compensation benefits are paid.

Tom Mason is the warehouse foreman for Ajax Electric Company. Recently, Tom was severely injured when a box was dropped on his leg. The leg was broken in several places, and Tom was disabled for three months. All of Tom's medical bills were paid by Ajax's workers' compensation carrier.

Tom also received disability payments equal to 66 2/3 percent of the state average weekly wage in his state: the maximum amount payable in his state. He received the maximum benefit because his salary exceeded the state average weekly wage.

This example illustrates workers' compensation death benefits.

Edgar Madison was killed by an explosion while examining a pipeline for his company. Edgar had one child, a son age seventeen.

Edgar's widow will receive an amount equal to 66 2/3 percent of his salary. (The assumption is made that 66 2/3 percent of Edgar's salary is less than the state maximum and more than the state minimum benefits.) However, the widow's benefit will drop to 50 percent of Edgar's salary when the son becomes eighteen, if he has completed his education. If the widow remarries after the son has left home, all benefits will cease.

Insuring Workers' Compensation

Employers can satisfy workers' compensation requirements in several ways. One method available to large employers is retention. Normally, a firm will have to post a bond with the state workers' compensation board if it decides to retain its workers' compensation exposures.

Retention programs may be operated by the firm or by independent administrative firms. A firm operating on a retention basis pays no premium. Instead, it provides whatever funding is necessary to pay benefits and administrative costs.

Even when a firm retains, it seeks to control exposures. To protect itself against unusual losses that might affect a large number of employees, a company can purchase a catastrophic workers' compensation policy. Under this policy, the firm retains only the normal flow of losses but not unusual fluctuations resulting from catastrophic losses.

In lieu of retention, an employer can purchase workers' compensation insurance coverage from an insurance company. An insurance company providing workers' compensation coverage promises to pay the benefits required by a state's workers' compensation law. In addition to covering workers' compensation claims, most workers' compensation insurance policies also provide employers' liability protection. This protection may seem unnecessary since a workers' compensation law restricts the right of an employee to sue. Conceivably, however, individuals working for an employer may have an action in law against the employer in spite of any workers' compensation law.

In some states, employers are required to participate in a state fund which handles workers' compensation claims. Other states have a competitive workers' compensation fund, allowing employers to retain, purchase insurance coverages, or participate in the state fund.

Covered Workers

Not all workers are covered under state workers' compensation laws. Most states allow employers who hire less than a stated number of employees not to provide workers' compensation protection. Some states do not require coverage on either farm or domestic employees or on employees of nonprofit organizations. Finally, employees of common carriers operating in interstate commerce do not have to be covered. Nearly all other classes of employees must be included under workers' compensation coverage.

Second Injury Fund

An employee only partially disabled may still be able to work on a full-time basis. However, most employers are not anxious to hire an individual who is partially disabled because another injury or the aggravation of an existing condition might result in permanent disability. To overcome this bias, states have established second injury funds. If another injury or the aggravation of preexisting disease results in permanent and total disability, the employer is not required to pay benefits for the total disability. Instead, a second injury fund pays the difference between the benefits that would be payable because of the second illness or injury and permanent total disability. The money for the operation of the second injury fund is provided through assessments of employers.

GROUP HEALTH INSURANCE

Disability Income Plans

When deciding what group disability benefits to provide an employee, an employer should examine all the sources of income that should be available to a disabled employee upon disability. Disability coverage, if not designed properly, frequently could give an employee the opportunity to make a profit. A prudent employer should integrate group disability benefits with other programs to prevent malingering.

Short-Term Disability Income Group disability protection may be either short-term or long-term. Many of the concepts relating to individual disability coverages are applicable to group coverage. A brief examination of the group coverages will illustrate the similarities and differences between individual and group disability protection.

Group short-term disability income contracts are designed to replace loss of income resulting from injury or sickness. Generally, the contracts do not cover disabilities caused by occupational injury or sickness. Thus, the coverage is used as a supplement to workers' compensation.

Benefits are paid for 90 or 180 days once the waiting period has been satisfied. Longer periods of coverage can be provided, but benefit periods longer than one year are unusual. The waiting period usually is seven days; however, some contracts contain fourteen- or thirty-day waiting periods.

Like individual coverage, the waiting periods may be retroactive. Once an insured is disabled for a period of time equal to the waiting period, benefits are paid from the first day of disability. Since most disabilities last only for short periods of time, a longer waiting period lowers the cost of group coverage.

Some states have mandatory disability programs for nonoccupational injuries. In these states, employers usually set benefit levels and group short-term disability income policies equal to or greater than the requirements of the state programs.

Benefits are paid either on the basis of a fixed schedule or as a percentage of salary. In the latter case a percentage of between 50 and 66 2/3 percent is common.

A few employers provide coverage under a group short-term disability income policy for all types of disability, not just nonoccupational disabilities. The expansion of the definition of disability is due in part to the impact of unions and the low level of workers' compensation benefits.

Short-term coverage normally is used as the first level of disability income protection. Many employers provide long-term disability income group coverage to supplement the short-term protection.

Long-Term Disability Income   The long-term policy is designed to provide benefits for an extended period of time. Many of the policies provide disability income benefits for an insured until age sixty-five.

Usually, benefits are provided for all types of disabilities (occupational and nonoccupational) subject to a waiting period. If there is an underlying short-term disability income policy, the waiting period in the long-term policy is equal to the period of coverage under the short-term policy. Waiting periods may or may not be retroactive.

The benefit levels under a group long-term disability income contract are determined by schedule or by taking a fixed percentage of the insured's salary. As a rule, benefits under long-term contracts will be significantly higher than those provided under short-term policies. The long-term contract also may include rehabilitation benefits, in an effort to return a disabled insured to the job market. If the rehabilitation effort fails, the benefits for the disabled insured are not reduced. If the insured is rehabilitated, disability payments are eliminated. The rehabilitation benefit has two advantages. First, it provides funds to help the disabled insured become employable. Second, if the total cost of rehabilitation efforts is less than the cost of the disability payments that are saved, the premium for group coverage may be lower.

The definition of disability in short-term contracts usually is restricted to disabilities which prevent the insured from being gainfully employed. Generally, the definition of disability under a group long-term disability income policy for the first one-to-five years covers an insured if he or she cannot perform the regular duties of his or her job. After the one-to-five year period, the definition reverts to the short-term definition (i.e., the insured must be unable to perform any job for which the insured is reasonably suited by education, training, or experience).

Integration Insurance is not the only means of replacing income. The first portion of a disability benefit package may consist of a salary continuation plan. Under this plan, an employee is paid all or a portion of his or her salary when he or she becomes disabled. A benefit formula may or may not be utilized. When a benefit formula is applied, an employee, while disabled, receives an amount equal to a percentage of his or her salary prior to the time of the disability. The amount of disability payment may vary directly with the employee's length of service.

Generally, salary continuation plans are not designed for extensive periods of disability. They should compensate the employee for loss of income because of short-term disability (i.e., less than a year, and are designed to be used instead of group short-term disability income policies). In addition to integrating salary continuation plans with group coverage, an employer also should subtract any benefits which are provided under pension plans or under social security from the total disability income benefit package available to an employee. Many insured trust fund and pension plans contain disability payments. The inclusion of disability payments in pension plans has resulted mainly from the demands of unions. There is no established pattern for disability provisions under private pension plans; however, the following outlines some of the prevalent pension disability benefits:

1. Provide regular early retirement to disabled employee meeting age and service requirement, but waive any requirement for company consent or advance notice

2. Pay a benefit equal to the full accrued pension, computed on the basis of service and earnings to disability, as though the disabled employee had reached normal retirement age
3. Pay the full accrued pension but with a special minimum dollar benefit such as $100 monthly, or a minimum benefit percentage such as 25 percent, in order to produce more realistic benefits for those who barely meet the service requirements for disability pension
4. Pay the full accrued pension plus a special supplement such as $100 monthly until social security benefits are payable
5. Use an alternate benefit formula for disability pensions such as 50 percent of final five-year average pay less 64 percent of the social security primary benefit
6. Pay the regular age retirement benefit computed on the basis of earnings to disability but extending service to age 65
7. Pay the regular age-retirement benefit starting at age 65 but add the period of disability to credited service. Usually this is combined with long-term disability benefits or an alternate formula disability pension payable up to age 65

Social security provides disability payments for eligible employees. The extent of these benefits are discussed in another chapter. Any disability income benefit program should be designed so that benefits received under social security are considered in the total benefits payable. Like the integration of other disability benefits, this action reduces the possibility that an individual will profit from being disabled. It also reduces the cost of the group coverage.

Medical Expense Insurance

Introduction Employee benefits have grown rapidly in recent years. A survey conducted by the United States Chamber of Commerce indicated that in 1975 the average amount paid for employee benefits by a firm in the private sector was $4,000. This represents a 23 percent increase in two years.[4]

The increase in employee benefits can be attributed to several factors. First, many group coverages have been developed as society's demand for broader protection has expanded. As an example, group prepaid legal plans have begun to gain national prominence even though the group prepaid legal concept has existed for years. Second, unions have sought increasingly larger employee benefit packages.

While the amount varies among companies, most employers make substantial expenditures on employee benefits. Workers' compensation,

Table 10-1

Health Insurance Benefit Payments of Insurance Companies in the United States*

Year	Group Medical Expense	Loss of Income	Individual and Family Policies Medical Expense	Loss of Income
1967	$ 3,953,000,000	$ 796,000,000	$ 824,000,000	$415,000,000
1968	4,360,000,000	948,000,000	894,000,000	461,000,000
1969	5,027,000,000	1,096,000,000	897,000,000	476,000,000
1970	6,043,000,000	1,293,000,000	1,090,000,000	523,000,000
1971	6,541,000,000	1,301,000,000	1,006,000,000	474,000,000
1972	7,315,000,000	1,427,000,000	1,148,000,000	531,000,000
1973	7,924,000,000	1,578,000,000	1,462,000,000	637,000,000
1974	9,260,000,000	1,847,000,000	1,517,000,000	680,000,000
1975	10,448,000,000	1,896,000,000	1,557,000,000	722,000,000

*Reprinted with permission from Health Insurance Institute, *Source Book of Health Insurance Data 1976–1977* (New York: Health Insurance Institute, 1977), p. 45.

unemployment, and social security benefits constitute a sizable expenditure for employee benefits, but a large portion of the employee benefit dollar is utilized to purchase or provide coverages which are not required or regulated by the government. One of the coverages frequently obtained by employers is health expense protection. The same health expense coverages found in individual contracts are available for groups. Basic health and major medical protection as well as disability income coverages can be purchased for groups. In the following sections, the characteristics of group protection are emphasized.

Health Care Financing Systems   A large portion of health insurance benefit payments are made under group insurance policies. Table 10-1 lists the medical expense and disability income benefits provided by private insurance companies under group coverage and under individual and family policies.

Employers can provide group health insurance by means of several health insurance financing systems. Included among the organizations which provide health coverage or services are Blue Cross-Blue Shield, private insurance companies, and health maintenance organizations. In addition, employers can use trust funds as conduits for paying employee health care expenses.

Blue Cross.   Of the group hospital insurance programs, probably none are better known than the Blue Cross plans. The Blue Cross idea started in the late 1920s in Texas when a group of school teachers agreed to pay Baylor University Hospital in advance for up to twenty-one days of semiprivate hospital care each year. The idea of prepaying health insurance benefits spread rapidly. Instead of limiting coverage to one hospital, however, some plans developed in the early 1930s offered subscribers a choice of hospitals on a communitywide basis. The communities which first established community plans include Sacramento, Newark, and New York City. In 1939 the Blue Cross symbol was adopted by the prepayment plans that had been developed, and these plans became known as Blue Cross plans.[5]

There are presently sixty-nine Blue Cross plans in the United States.[6] The area covered by a particular plan ranges from a state down to a city. All Blue Cross plans are operated on a nonprofit basis and are regulated by state insurance departments. The regulations applied to Blue Cross are not applicable to other private health insurance carriers.

The Blue Cross plans have a central clearinghouse in Chicago. The central clearinghouse founded in 1948, known as the Blue Cross Association, serves as a communications center for the individual plans and acts as a spokesman for the individual plans on matters which are important to the entire association.

Currently, 84 percent of all Blue Cross subscribers are members of a group plan.[7] Most of the Blue Cross subscribers who have individual coverages obtained the individual status by converting their group coverage or by purchasing Medicare supplementary protection. However, Blue Cross now has open enrollment periods during which persons can purchase individual coverage.

Blue Cross plans provide service benefits for their subscribers (i.e., Blue Cross contracts guarantee a subscriber certain services but not dollar amounts for these services). As an example, a Blue Cross contract would guarantee an individual a specific number of days of coverage in a semiprivate room rather than a specific amount per day of confinement. Blue Cross pays benefits directly to the hospital providing benefits to the subscriber. The amount paid for the services rendered by a hospital is developed by Blue Cross and the hospitals. Some hospitals are paid on a cost-based formula with the cost of each service subject to certain limits.

Other hospitals are reimbursed for their usual charges. However, these charges are established by contract, and a contract cannot be changed by the hospital without notifying Blue Cross.

Blue Cross has been attempting to develop new payment plans which encourage cost efficiency. Among the methods being tried are incentive payments or bonuses for hospitals that perform efficiently, and penalties for those which do not; target rates negotiated a year in advance; and payments based on a hospital's performance compared with the performance of other hospitals in the same area.[8] These efforts may result in lower costs for consumers who purchase hospital insurance protection from Blue Cross plans.

Blue Shield. Blue Cross plans have a counterpart in the physician expense area. The counterpart is Blue Shield. Blue Shield plans, like Blue Cross plans, permit consumers to prepay the costs of certain health expenses. If a physician provides service to an insured, then Blue Shield is responsible for paying for that service. Blue Shield plans are operated on a nonprofit basis.

Although Blue Cross and Blue Shield are very similar, each is a separate organization and each has a national association which coordinates activities for the members of the plans. However, in many areas, "Blue Cross and Blue Shield Plans cooperate closely and many, in fact, share office space, conduct joint enrollment and use joint billing. They may be under a single management. Often they are joint corporations. In other areas, they are separate organizations."[9] Together, the two organizations can offer almost any medical expense coverage that can be provided by a private health insurance company.

Insurance Companies. Those insurance companies which provide group health insurance cover approximately the same number of individuals as do Blue Cross and other medical society plans. Table 10-2 lists the number of individuals covered under group hospital expense policies compared with those under Blue Cross plans, Blue Shield plans, and other medical society plans.

Private health insurers agree to pay or provide (1) a flat dollar amount, (2) expenses up to a maximum benefit, or (3) a service benefit for services incurred by an insured. Insurance companies which provide service benefits do not negotiate with a hospital to establish the cost of a service and therefore do not have the competitive advantage enjoyed by Blue Cross. A typical group hospital expense policy might provide up to $50 per day of hospital confinement for room and board. If the insured must stay in a semiprivate room at a daily cost of $100, then he or she must absorb one-half of the cost of the room. If the insured had had a room benefit of $80 per day and the actual charge was $70, the private insurer would have paid the $70 charge not the $80. If a service benefit were provided, the cost of the room would be irrelevant since the insurer would have paid for the room regardless of the cost.

Most insurers use the reimbursement basis (i.e., they impose a maximum dollar benefit). The example that follows illustrates the difference between payment under a group Blue Cross plan and a private group health insurance plan with specific dollar benefits.

Clyde Duncan is confined to the hospital for seven days because of an automobile accident. Clyde's hospital expenses are as follows: semiprivate room—$80 per day, drugs—$190, x-rays—$150, and brac-

Table 10-2

Number of Persons in the United States with Hospital Expense Protection by Type of Insurer*

End of Year	Private Insurance Companies— Group Policies	Blue Cross, Blue Shield, and Medical Society Plans
1965	65,415,000	63,347,000
1966	67,799,000	65,310,000
1967	71,454,000	67,214,000
1968	74,073,000	70,019,000
1969	77,973,000	72,692,000
1970	80,505,000	75,055,000
1971	80,641,000	76,539,000
1972	81,526,000	78,206,000
1973	83,626,000	79,969,000
1974	85,385,000	83,845,000
1975	87,185,000	86,436,000

*Reprinted with permission from Health Insurance Institute, *Source Book of Health Insurance 1976–77* (New York: Health Insurance Institute, 1977), p. 23.

es—$100. If Clyde has a group Blue Cross plan which provides semi-private room coverage, then the entire hospital charge for the room will be paid. If the Blue Cross plan also covers drugs, x-rays, and braces, he would not have to pay for any of his medical treatment.

If Clyde is covered under a private group health insurance hospital policy which provides $80 or more of coverage per day, he will pay nothing toward the semiprivate room. In addition, if Clyde's plan also covers more than $190 for drugs, $150 for x-rays, and $100 for braces, he will incur no expense. However, if Clyde's contract pays less than the $80 per day of confinement for a semiprivate room, $190 for drugs, $150 for x-rays, or $100 for braces, Clyde would be required to absorb the differences between what the policy paid and the hospital bill. Deductibles have been ignored in this example.

There are several differences between Blue Cross and Blue Shield plans and private health insurance carriers other than the method used to provide benefits. First, Blue Cross plans receive special tax treatment since they are nonprofit corporations. They pay no premium tax and no income tax. These tax advantages give Blue Cross and Blue Shield a competitive edge.

Another distinction between Blue Cross and Blue Shield and private health insurance companies is centered on the nonprofit status of the

Blue Cross plans. Since Blue Cross plans are nonprofit, they need not provide sufficient income to pay stockholders a return on their investments. Thus, Blue Cross and Blue Shield plans may be very competitive with stock health insurance carriers. This same competitive edge does not accrue to Blue Cross plans compared with mutual health insurance carriers.

The cost savings which Blue Cross and Blue Shield have been able to implement because of their direct contractual relationship with hospitals are extremely beneficial from a competitive standpoint. Blue Cross can pressure hospitals and doctors to limit charges. Insurance companies cannot apply direct pressure.

Because of the preferential tax treatment and this monopolistic position, many individuals feel that a comparison of Blue Cross and Blue Shield with the private industry is unfair. Blue Cross and Blue Shield could be less efficient than private carriers and still *appear* to be more efficient. But private health insurance carriers do have some advantages. They have more flexibility in designing a benefit package than Blue Cross and Blue Shield have. Most Blue Cross and Blue Shield coverages are not subject to negotiation. In addition, private health carriers do not need to coordinate their activities on large groups with other carriers. Blue Cross and Blue Shield plans must be coordinated with other Blue Cross and Blue Shield plans to provide coverage for a group which is spread over a wide geographical area.

Trust Fund Plans. Several types of trust fund plans can be established. Some trust plans are based on retention. The employer makes contributions to the trustee, who is responsible for seeing that all eligible health insurance expenses of employees are paid. Frequently, the trustee uses a service company or an insurer to handle claims payments.

Trusts also may be used as a conduit between an employer and an insurance company. The trustee collects the premiums from the employer and pays them to the insurer. Multiple employer trusts (METs) are an example of this type of operation. Under a METs, two or more employers in the same industry form a trust. The trustee collects the premiums for each employer and pays the premium to an insurer. This type of trust may be beneficial to small firms who could not purchase group coverage or who could not obtain a competitive premium rate.

Taft-Hartley trusts are used where the covered employees are engaged in interstate or foreign commerce. Funds are placed by the employer(s) in a trust which is controlled jointly by labor and the employer(s). The program is used primarily where there is high mobility in the work force; that is, employees are frequently changing jobs within the same industry. Benefit levels are determined by the union through negotiations with an employer(s).

Benefits As mentioned earlier, most of the insurance coverages available on an individual basis are also available on a group basis. Hospital, surgical, and physicians' expense coverage can be purchased by an employer for his employees. The employee may pay none, some, or all of the cost for the group coverage.

Many employers provide either basic or major medical insurance protection, or both, for their employees. However, a growing number of firms are selecting a single comprehensive program of coverage which incorporates the features of both major medical and basic insurance protection plans.

Under a comprehensive contract, the deductible, if any, is generally small, but there is a coinsurance provision. Hospital, surgical, and physicians' expense benefits are afforded under a comprehensive policy. The comprehensive policy may take one of several forms. One of these provides for a deductible provision, followed by a coinsurance clause applicable to all covered medical expenses up to a stated maximum. Above the maximum, the insurer pays all of the eligible medical expenses. Another type pays 100 percent of the eligible medical expenses up to a maximum benefit level. Then a coinsurance clause becomes applicable.

Normally, group health insurance policies allow for the protection not only of an employee but also his or her dependents. Generally, the same coverage afforded to the employee is provided for all family members. Where a husband and wife both have group coverage that insures them and their dependents, a profit could be made because of duplicate coverage. The effects of this problem are reduced by the use of a coordination of benefits clause, which will be discussed later.

Some employers pay the premium for coverage for an employee and his or her family. Other employers pay the cost of the employee's coverage and require the employee to pay for optional dependents' coverage. Some few employers still do not pay any portion of the cost of group insurance plans that they make available to their employees.

Dental Care Expense Insurance

Prior to 1960, few employees had group dental insurance coverage, but since then, the number of individuals covered under group dental expense insurance plans has risen rapidly. In a survey of employer groups conducted by the Health Insurance Institute, 18 percent of the employees in the group surveyed had group dental coverage.[10]

Dental insurance coverage can be provided either under a group's existing coverage or under a separate comprehensive dental policy. Most dental expense coverages, whether provided on a major medical or basic group contract basis, have an aggregate limit per year. In addition, a contract may contain deductibles and individual limits on certain dental procedures.

Some plans have encountered extensive utilization in the early years of this coverage. Probably, the implementation of the dental plan has encouraged people to have all of their dental problems corrected— problems which had not been treated due to high dental costs. Once this adverse selection has been absorbed, a group's utilization rate stabilizes.

The benefits under group dental insurance vary significantly. One policy may cover only the cleaning of teeth and the filling of cavities. Another contract may also cover bridges, capping, and oral surgery.

Marketing of Group Health Insurance

Types of Groups There are many types of groups or organizations which may purchase or sponsor group insurance protection. The major groups include employer associations, labor unions, creditors, trust associations, in addition to individual employers.

Occasionally, employers will form an association in order to purchase group coverage for the employees of all of the employers. Frequently, the associations are comprised of smaller firms that want to obtain a better negotiating position when seeking insurance protection. The major problem from an employer's perspective is that he or she loses flexibility in selecting coverage since the same protection generally is provided for the entire employer's association group. The group plan may or may not be contributory.

Organizations, such as the American Bar Association and the American Medical Association, sponsor group coverage for their members. In this case, the sponsoring organization supports the group coverage. The participation of members of the organization under the group coverage is solicited by means of some mass merchandising approach—normally, a mail solicitation. Sometimes, the insurance is cited as one of the benefits of belonging to the group and, therefore, serves as a marketing tool for the organization in its efforts to obtain new members. Generally, these plans are 100 percent contributory.

Labor unions can purchase coverage for their members. A trust fund is established and premiums are paid into the trust. The trustee has responsibility for purchasing the insurance protection.

Creditors may purchase group insurance protection on debtors. The laws of most states stipulate that if the coverage is noncontributory, the coverage must be provided for all debtors. If the coverage must be purchased by the debtor, it is provided only on those individuals who elect to take it.

Selection and Sales Process Regardless of the type of group coverage provided, someone has the responsibility for selecting the benefits to be provided. Many factors affect the decision on what benefits will be made available. A few of these factors are discussed below.

Cost. The cost of the benefits will have a significant impact on the selection of benefits. For example, if an employer pays the entire cost, the benefit is constrained by the funds available for employee benefits. However, if employees contribute to the cost of a group policy, the combined employer-employee contribution will provide a better health insurance package.

Unions. When the benefits for employees are established through labor negotiations, the benefits will have to meet any limits established under the union contract. Cost is not a major consideration once the benefit levels have been established.

Income. The financial position of the group members sometimes will dictate the types of benefits made available under group coverage. If the members have low incomes, they may be more interested in first dollar coverage than in catastrophic health insurance protection. In addition, low income individuals might prefer lower benefits under a noncontributory plan than higher benefits under a contributory plan.

Specific Need. In some cases a specific type of benefit is needed, and the process of selecting coverage is simple. For example, group disability income coverage on debtors with monthly debt payments should provide benefits equal to the amount of the monthly payment.

When the benefit selection process is difficult, the individual or organization selecting benefit levels may obtain aid from several sources. The agent or broker selling the coverage should help select the appropriate coverages and place the business with an insurer. Some insurance companies have group representatives who work with agents and brokers in designing the appropriate coverage. Some brokerage firms are large enough to have employees who work full-time to assist in the development and design of group benefit packages.

The role of the agent or broker encompasses more than selling the coverage and aiding in the selection of benefits. He or she also gathers data on the group, recommends whether the plan should be contributory or noncontributory, and searches to find the best protection at the lowest cost.

Underwriting Group Health Insurance

Many factors must be considered by an underwriter deciding whether or not to cover a group. The basic concepts of individual underwriting can be applied to group underwriting. However, in group underwriting the underwriter looks at the characteristics of the group rather than those of an individual within the group.

Underwriting criteria vary from company to company. However, there are some criteria which are considered by nearly every insurance underwriter. A discussion of some of these criteria follows.

Group Size Underwriters always are concerned about the number of individuals participating in a particular group plan. Generally, a large group results in a diversity of exposure units and therefore a stable loss pattern. If a group is sufficiently large, it may be individually rated—that is, the group's rates are based upon its own experience. If a group is not large enough to be rated on an individual basis, the insurance carrier may want to apply its standard group rates or pool the small group with other small groups in order to obtain a distribution of exposure units. In the latter case, each group pays rates based on the overall experience of the combined groups.

Group Characteristics An underwriter is interested in the characteristics of the group. For example, the age of the group has a direct bearing on its overall utilization of health insurance coverages as well as utilization of specific health insurance benefits. An older group might not utilize pregnancy benefits but would use other services not needed by a younger group.

The underwriter will want to know the ratio of males to females. The cost of disability coverage will be higher if the percentage of women is high, especially if pregnancy is covered. For other types of health insurance services, utilization by men may be much higher than utilization by women.

Groups containing many seasonal workers pose special problems, particularly in the area of short-term disability. Employees who are going to work for only a portion of the year have a higher rate of fraudulent disability claims. This adverse selection can increase costs significantly.

Experience Underwriters are always interested in the reason a particular group is purchasing insurance. If a group is seeking insurance protection for the first time, the underwriter will want to know if the need for group insurance protection has resulted from dramatic changes in the health of individuals within the group.

If the group is changing carriers, the underwriter also may be concerned. Often, a group changes carriers because its experience is bad and, therefore, its rates have increased. A company writing a new policy may be able to eliminate the effects of the bad experience of a group by eliminating coverage for preexisting conditions or by imposing a waiting period. While this will handle the problem of increasing claims costs in the short run, the underwriter has not solved the basic problem of deteriorating health within the group.

Policyholder Any underwriter is concerned about who will be the group policyholder for several reasons. First, in employee groups, the type of policyholder dictates the type of employment. For employer-employee groups in industries with a high incidence of industrial accidents, the underwriter may not be anxious to provide insurance protection. Or, the underwriter may want to eliminate occupational injuries.

The policyholder is important from another perspective. If the policyholder is in an industry or area which will continue to grow, then the underwriter can anticipate a flow of new members into the group. However, if the industry or area is diminishing, the underwriter can anticipate increasing losses because the average age of the group will increase.

Plan Design An important health insurance underwriting goal is that benefits for injury or sickness do not result in financial gain to any covered person. Methods of achieving this goal include deductibles, waiting periods, selection of coverages and units, coinsurance, and coordination of benefits. When a plan offers benefits that exceed needs, higher than average losses can be expected.

Adverse Selection To avoid adverse selection, an underwriter requires that a substantial portion of a group participate in any group insurance plan. In addition, the underwriter should know if any employee classes are excluded from the contract. The group contract owner could attempt to put members who should have a low incidence of claims under one contract and all others under a second contract. By obtaining a representative proportion of the entire group, an under-writer can avoid this type of adverse selection.

Premium Payment The group plan may be contributory or noncontributory. Generally, underwriters prefer group contracts in which the contract owner absorbs some or all of the cost of the plan. This will increase participation in the group contract; whereas, if no contribution is made, participation may not be sufficient to overcome the impact of adverse selection.

Administration Implementing a group insurance contract is very difficult. The underwriter is interested in knowing how much expense will have to be incurred in order to put a group insurance policy on the insurance company's books. If above average administrative costs will be necessary, the contract may not be desirable from a profit perspective.

Persistency of the Group Coverage   Sometimes, the group policy owner may obtain a new group contract on a regular basis (i.e., the coverage will be put out for bid every one or two years). This situation is highly undesirable from an underwriting perspective. The underwriter does not have an opportunity to recoup administrative costs involved in writing group coverage if a contract is terminated. These expenses would include the development of booklets or certificates for employees, the establishment of a group insurance administration to deal with a specific group, and the issuance of the group insurance policy.

A process of continual bidding does not give the underwriter time to recover from an unprofitable year under the group policy. Thus, a year in which the insurance company faces higher than average claims cannot be counteracted by future profitable years.

Statutory Constraints   Underwriters must consider statutory constraints upon the issuance of group insurance coverages. Most state statutes stipulate what constitutes an eligible group, what minimum number of employees can be covered under a group plan, what organizations can be issued group insurance protection, what class of individuals can be covered, and what types of coverage can be provided.

A typical state statute is presented below. It illustrates some constraints an underwriter might face in issuing group insurance coverage.

Group accident and sickness insurance is that form of accident and sickness insurance covering groups of persons as defined below, with or without one or more members of their families or one or more of their dependents, or covering one or more members of the families or one or more dependents of persons in such groups, and issued upon the following basis:

(1) Under a policy issued to an employer or trustees of a fund established by an employer, who shall be deemed the policyholder, insuring at least five employees of such employer, for the benefit of persons other than the employer. The term "employees" as used herein shall be deemed to include the officers, managers, and employees of the employer, the individual proprietor or partners if the employer is an individual proprietor or partnership, the officers, managers, and employees of subsidiary or affiliated corporations, the individual proprietors, partners and employees of individuals and firms, if the business of the employer and such individual or firm is under common control through stock ownership, contract or otherwise. The term "employees" as used herein may include retired employees. A policy issued to insure employees of a public

body may provide that the term "employees" shall include elected or appointed officials;

(2) Under a policy issued to an association, including a labor union, which shall have a constitution and by laws and which has been organized and is maintained in good faith for purposes other than that of obtaining insurance, insuring at least 25 members, employees, or employees of members of the association for the benefit of persons other than the association or its officers or trustees. The term "employees" as used herein may include retired employees;

(3) Under a policy issued to the trustees of a fund established by two or more employers in the same industry or by one or more labor unions or by one or more employers and one or more labor unions, or by an association as defined in subsection (2) above, which trustees shall be deemed the policyholder, to insure not less than 25 employees of the employers or members of the union or of such association or of members of such association for the benefit of persons other than the employers or other unions, or such associations. The term "employees" as used herein shall be deemed to include the officers, managers and employees of the employer, and the individual proprietor or partners if the employer is an individual proprietor or partnership. The term "employees" as used herein may include retired employees. The policy may provide that the term "employees" shall include the trustees or their employees, or both, if their duties are principally connected with such trusteeship;

(4) Under a policy issued to any person or organization to which a policy of group life insurance may be delivered in this State, to insure any class or classes of individuals that could be insured under such group life policy....[11]

Important Group Policy Provisions

A group health insurance policy, unlike an individual life or health insurance policy, is not required by state law to contain a large number of standard policy provisions. For example, one state requires only three policy provisions in a group accident and sickness policy. These provisions are:

(1) A provision that, in the absence of fraud, all statements made by the policyholder or by any insured person shall be deemed representations and not guarantees ... (2) A provision that the insurer will furnish to the policyholder, for delivery to each employee or member of the insured group, an individual certificate setting forth in summary form a statement of the essential features of the insurance coverage of such employee or member and to whom benefits are payable ... (3) A provision that to the group originally insured may be added from time to time eligible new employees or members or dependents as the case may be, in accordance with the terms of the policy.[12]

Some states only require that there be a provision stating that a certificate be issued to an employee.

All states have the right to reject a group policy if the regulatory agency feels that the policy can be misrepresented easily. Policies also can be turned down if they are unfair, unjust, inequitable, misleading, deceptive, or contrary to public policy.

The contrast between the regulation of group policies and individual contracts is interesting. Individual health insurance contracts contain numerous required policy provisions while group policies which may run from several pages to several hundred pages have to contain only a few required policy provisions. The legislatures may have felt that a business firm is in a better position to negotiate for and evaluate insurance coverage than an individual. For example, an employer can call on his or her legal staff, employee benefits director, and other company personnel to examine an insurance contract to ascertain the types of benefits that should be purchased. Most individuals do not have these resources available.

Although only a few policy provisions are required in group health insurance policies in most states, there are still important policy provisions of which an insured should be aware. The discussion of policy provisions that follows concentrates on those provisions which are important both to the employer and to the employee. The form of these provisions will vary significantly. Therefore, it becomes the responsibility of the employer to ascertain whether or not a group health insurance contract provides the protection that is most beneficial to his or her employees.

Payment of Premiums A group health insurance policy will specify dates on which premium payments are due. The employer is responsible for forwarding the premium to an insurance company. In plans where the employer pays the entire cost of the program, premium payment is a simple process. Under a contributory plan, the employer is still responsible for making the entire premium payment to the insurer. However, he recovers part or all of his cost from the employees through payroll deductions. The employee has no direct contact with the insurance company providing the group insurance coverage other than filing a claim.

Eligible Employees A group health insurance policy contains provisions stating eligibility requirements for employees. Normally, an eligible employee is one who works more than a specified number of hours in a week or month. For example, a group insurance policy may stipulate that all employees who work thirty hours or more in a workweek are eligible. The eligibility requirements are usually determined by the employer. The employer will not want to cover employees who only work a small fraction of a week. By excluding these part-time employees, an employer is able to reduce costs and at the same time reward the full-time employees.

Dependent Coverage Group health insurance policies always cover the employees of an employer, but coverage does not have to be made available for dependents. The practice of most employers is to permit dependent coverage; but the final determination of whether or not dependents are covered is left to the employee. Where employers contribute the entire premium, the employee's decision is easy. If a plan is contributory, an employee will have to pay for some or all of the cost of the coverage for dependents. In this case, the employee may not want to insure family members who are eligible for coverage under other plans.

The definition of an eligible dependent varies from contract to contract. However, a typical provision might read:

> Dependent shall mean the spouse of an employee or retired employee and an unmarried child who is a registered full time student under 25 years of age including: (A) an adopted child and (B) a stepchild, foster child, or other child who is in regular parent-child relationship and (C) any such child, regardless of age, who lives with or whose care is provided by an employee or annuitant on a regular basis if such child is mentally retarded or physically incapacitated to such an extent as to be dependent upon the employee or retired employee for care or support.

Conversion A group hospital and major medical insurance policy will contain a provision explaining how an employee can convert the group coverage to individual coverage if he or she should leave the group. A conversion privilege is important to an employee who quits and goes to work for another employer who does not have group coverage or to an employee who is unemployed for an extended period of time. The provision also is important to an employee who is not in good health at the time of the conversion. The conversion privilege permits the employee to obtain insurance protection when it might not be available in the regular health insurance market.

An employee can convert an amount of insurance protection which will be equal to or less than the insurance protection provided in the group policy. For this coverage, the employee may have to pay a premium greater than that paid by the employee and/or the employer under the group policy. The increased cost results because the insurer is no longer able to insure a large number of people under one policy and thereby obtain administrative cost savings.

Extensions of Benefits The employer may find it desirable to change insurers, or a health insurer may decide that it does not want to renew a policy. When a contract is terminated, there may be some employees who are collecting benefits under the health insurance contract. To protect these employees, most group health insurance contracts have an extension of benefits provision. The NAIC Model Rules and Regulations for Group Continuance of Coverage and Replacement contains a provision on the extension of benefits. The model provision reads:

> c) In the case of a group plan providing benefits for loss of time from work or specific indemnity during hospital confinement, discontinuance of the policy during a disability shall have no effect on benefits payable for that disability or confinement.
>
> d) In the case of hospital or medical expense coverages other than dental or maternity expenses, reasonable extension of benefits or accrued liability provision is required. Such a provision would be considered "reasonable" if it provides an extension of at least 12 months under "major medical" and "comprehensive medical" type coverages, and under other types of hospital or medical expense coverages provides either an extension of at least 90 days or an accrued liability for expenses incurred during a period of disability or during a period of at least 90 days starting with a specific event which occurred while coverage was in force (e.g., an accident).

The model NAIC regulation or similar provision guarantees an employee receiving benefits that the benefits will not be truncated because of a change in carriers.

Coordination of Benefits In group disability contracts, employers may reduce disability payments by the amount received from other group plans. This reduction in coverage is designed to prevent an insured from profiting from a period of disability.

In group medical expense contracts, another option is available to employers and insurers for reducing any overlap in insurance benefits. The device is known as a coordination of benefits provision. The coordination of benefits provision stipulates that when two group policies cover the same individual, one of the policies will pay first and the other policy will serve as excess coverage. The order of benefit determination system used in the coordination of benefits provision might read:

> (1) A plan with no provision for coordination of other benefits will be considered to have paid its regular benefits before a plan which contains such provisions.
>
> (2) When two or more plans contain a nonduplication provision, the following sequence of payment is established:
>
> (a) The plan covering the patient as an employee pays before the plan covering the patient as a dependent;
>
> (b) The plan covering the patient as a dependent of a male person pays before the plan covering the patient as a dependent of a female person;

    (c) Where the order of payment cannot be determined by rules
        (a) and (b), the first plan to make payment will be the one
        that has covered the insured for the longer period of time.

Since the coordination of benefits provision establishes an order for determining which group policy provides primary coverage, theoretically an insured is unable to profit from his or her illness. The following example demonstrates how a typical coordination of benefits provision might operate.

    Julie Kruger and her six-year-old son are involved in an automobile accident. Both individuals are hospitalized for over two weeks. Julie works full time and is covered under a group policy at her place of employment. Julie's son and her husband are included as dependents under Julie's policy. Julie's husband has group insurance coverage where he works, and his wife and son are covered as dependents under that policy.

    Under a coordination of benefits provision, the coverage provided under Julie's policy would be primary coverage for her health expenses, and her husband's policy would provide protection for eligible health expenses not covered in Julie's policy. However, the expenses incurred by the son would be covered first under the policy of the father, and eligible excess expenses would be covered under Julie's policy.

    While coordination of benefits provisions bar the Kruger family from profiting from payment under two group policies, there is still a chance that the Krugers may collect more in benefits than they are required to pay in health expenses. For example, automobile medical payments coverage is not considered under the coordination of benefits provision. Therefore, if the Krugers have medical expense coverage under their family automobile policy, they will be able to collect additional benefits. Generally, individual policies are not affected by the coordination of benefits clause.

    Most states restrict use of the coordination of benefits provision. Generally, it cannot be utilized in the case of individual or blanket coverages. One provision which bars the application of coordination of benefits to individual coverages reads:

    ... no group policy of accident and sickness insurance offered for sale in this State shall be issued or renewed after the effective date of this section by any insurer or hospital service nonprofit corporation ... or medical service nonprofit corporation ... transacting business in this state which by the terms of such group policy excludes or reduces the benefits payable or services to be rendered to or on behalf of any insured by reason of the fact that benefits have been paid or are also payable under any blanket school accident policy regardless of who makes the premium contribution, or any individually underwritten and individually issued contract or plan of insurance which provides exclusively for accident sickness benefits and for which 100 per cent of the premiums have been paid by the insured or a member of the insured's family, irrespective of the mode or channel of premium payment to the insurer or any discount received on such premiums by virtue of the insured's membership in any organization or status as an employee.[13]

Entire Contract Most group policies contain an entire contract provision stipulating which documents constitute the entire contract. Generally, the group policy and the application constitute the entire contract. The enrollment cards or applications completed by the employees also may be part of the contract, but this is uncommon.

Grace Period Group insurance policies, like individual health insurance contracts, normally contain a grace period. The person responsible for forwarding the premium to the insurer may delay the premium payment until the end of the grace period. In some cases, an insurer may continue coverage even though the premium is not paid during the grace period; the insurer is then liable for any benefits that accrue before it notifies the policyholder of termination of coverage.

Certificates Insurance companies issuing group policies are required to provide certificates to members of the group. The individual certificate should include a summary of the essential features of the insurance coverage, including not only a description of the coverage but also an explanation about how claims are filed. The length of the certificate may vary from one page to thirty or forty pages. The length is dependent upon the benefits provided in the policy and may also be dependent on the amount of detailed information that the employer feels should be provided a group member.

Group certificates frequently are tailored to match the benefits of the group, if the group is large. Certificates may be designed to identify the employer providing the group coverage. As an example, a group certificate may contain the employer's logo as well as a message from some officer in the company. For smaller groups, standardized certificates are issued.

Dividends Some group insurance policies provide for expense refunds. The employer has the option of deciding how the refund payment will be used. Under noncontributory plans, some employers utilize the refund to reduce their costs while other employers use it to provide additional benefits. When a plan is contributory, refunds may be applied to reduce the cost of the plan to employees.

Miscellaneous Provisions Group insurance policies may contain other provisions which affect an insured. There will be provisions stipulating how an insured should file a claim. Normally, this type of provision will include statements on the maximum permissible amounts of time before (1) the insurer must be notified of the loss, (2) the insurer must forward claim forms, and (3) the insured must submit the claim forms.

The contract may contain a provision stipulating that the insurer has the right and the opportunity to have an insured examined as often as may be required reasonably to determine whether or not a claim is valid. Frequently, this provision is utilized in disability income contracts.

The contract may have a provision giving the insurer the right to have an autopsy performed in the case of death. This provision is not permitted under some state laws and therefore cannot be included in all group policies.

Finally, there may be provisions relating to the period during which an action can be brought against the insurer. Policies which contain this type of provision generally bar legal action against the insurer until at least sixty days after proof of loss has been filed in accordance with the policy requirements. There is also a maximum time after which suits cannot be filed against the insured. Frequently, this upper limit is two or three years.

Advantages and Disadvantages of Group Insurance Coverage

Group insurance coverage can be advantageous to members of a group. First, since a group rate is used, the cost of the coverage should be less expensive than if the individuals purchase individual insurance protection. Second, those who are not in good health can obtain insurance as part of a group when they might not be able to obtain insurance protection on an individual basis.

The amount of the premium paid by the employer reduces the cost to an employee. Furthermore, the employer's contribution is not treated as taxable income to the employee.

Group coverages are advantageous to an employer in at least three ways. They may give an employer a competitive edge in hiring employees. Secondly, an employer who provides an extensive group health insurance program need not be concerned about employees facing financial ruin because of extended periods of illness. An employer also may deduct any premiums paid for group insurance as a business expense.

In spite of the advantages of group insurance coverage, there are some disadvantages. If an employee should be a member of a group consisting of older employees and the group is rated on its experience, he or she may find that group coverage is more expensive than individual protection. This situation can occur in declining industries or in industries which consistently utilize older workers.

Another disadvantage of group coverage is that it cannot be

designed to meet individual needs. Thus, an employer selects those benefits which provide the best overall coverage for the group. For example, an elderly worker may not want maternity benefits protection. If this benefit is afforded under a contributory group insurance contract, then all employees are required to pay a premium for maternity benefits. The older employee is paying for a benefit that may not be utilized.

One other disadvantage of group coverage is the protection gap that can occur when an employee changes employers. The group insurance contract available from the new employer may contain a preexisting conditions clause or a waiting period that delays the effective date of coverage. The employee must retain this protection gap or utilize the conversion privilege in the prior employer's contract.

GOVERNMENTAL HEALTH INSURANCE PLANS

Medicare

Two major types of health insurance coverage are provided under the Social Security Act: disability income insurance and Medicare. The Medicare program began in 1965 when Title XVIII of the Social Security Act was passed by Congress. The program is designed to provide health insurance coverage for hospital expenses and physicians' costs incurred by individuals age sixty-five and over. The Medicare program is divided into two parts. Part A covers hospital charges while Part B is designed to pay for physicians' services. Both programs include coverage for some miscellaneous medical expenses.

Hospital Coverage Hospital insurance under Medicare pays for three types of medical expenses. Inpatient hospital care, skilled nursing facility care, and home health care are covered.[14] However, there are limitations on the amount paid for each type of medical expense incurred during a benefit period. A benefit period begins when the individual first enters the hospital and runs until he or she has not incurred medical costs for sixty consecutive days. The following example illustrates how the sixty-day period functions.

Sarah Edwards enters the hospital on October 1 for surgery. Sarah is eligible for Medicare hospital insurance benefits. On October 10, Sarah is released from the hospital. If she does not incur medical costs again until December 10, then she will have a new benefit period (i.e., her benefits will be reinstated). If she should be forced to return to the hospital before December 10, then the new period of confinement will be considered a continuation of the original benefit period.

Medicare hospital insurance pays for inpatient services only if the following conditions are met:

> ... (1) a doctor prescribes inpatient hospital care for treatment of an illness or injury, (2) you require the kind of care that can only be provided in a hospital, (3) the hospital is participating in Medicare, and (4) the Utilization Review Committee of the hospital or a Professional Standards Review Organization does not disapprove your stay.[15]

The function of the review committee is to ascertain if the care that has been prescribed is reasonable and necessary. Otherwise, Medicare will not pay for expenses incurred.

Medicare provides a broad spectrum of benefits for an individual including coverage for semiprivate rooms, meals, drugs, and other medical expenses. Figure 10-1 contains a list of some of the medical services which are and are not provided under the hospital insurance protection provided by Medicare. Although the protection is broad, an individual covered by Medicare must first pay a deductible amount in each benefit period ($124 in 1976). Thus, if an individual enters the hospital for ten days, he or she is responsible for paying the first $124 of expenses. If the individual should reenter the hospital during the same benefit period, the $124 deductible does not apply.

Nearly all of the reasonable and necessary hospital expenses incurred during the first sixty days of confinement in excess of the deductible are covered under the Medicare program. On the sixty-first day of hospital confinement, an individual again is required to share in the medical costs. From the sixty-first day to the ninetieth day, the patient is required to pay thirty-one dollars per day toward covered medical expenses. The balance of the charges is paid by Medicare.

Occasionally, an individual will be hospitalized more than ninety days. In this event, the individual can utilize some of his or her lifetime reserve days. There are sixty lifetime reserve days. When an individual utilizes a lifetime reserve day, he or she is responsible for the first seventy-two dollars per day of the hospital costs. Unlike the basic ninety days of coverage that are reinstated with each new benefit period, a lifetime reserve day that has been used can never be replaced.

Covered individuals should be aware that they are responsible for a portion of health care costs. However, the specific deductibles and participation rates will change. The Medicare law requires that the amount of an insured's participation be reevaluated every year. As the cost of medical care increases, the government will be forced to require an insured to pay more for medical services. Thus, an individual should

Figure 10-1

Types of Hospital Charges Which Are and Are Not Covered Under Medicare*

Covered
A semiprivate room (2 to 4 beds in a room)
All meals, including special diets
Regular nursing services
Costs of special care units, such as an intensive care unit, coronary care unit, etc.
Drugs furnished by a hospital during a stay
Lab test included in a hospital bill
X-rays and other radiology services, including radiation therapy, billed by a hospital
Medical supplies such as casts, surgical dressings, and splints
Use of appliances, such as a wheelchair
Operating and recovery room costs
Rehabilitation services, such as physical therapy, occupational therapy, and speech pathology services

Not Covered
Personal convenience items that are requested by a patient, such as television, radio, or telephone in the room
Private duty nurses
Any extra charges for a private room, unless a private room is required for medical reasons
The first three pints of blood received in a benefit period

*Reprinted from U.S. Department of Health, Education, and Welfare, *Your Medicare Handbook* (Washington: Superintendent of Documents, 1976), p. 13.

be concerned about understanding the basic concepts of Medicare and not concentrate on memorizing specific dollar constraints.

While Part A of the Medicare plan pays for hospital expenses, the program does not provide coverage for a physician's services even though the services are provided in a hospital. Physicians' services are covered under Part B of Medicare.

Psychiatric benefits are very limited. Each individual covered under Part A of Medicare is eligible for 190 days of coverage in a psychiatric hospital or ward. These days, like the sixty lifetime reserve days, cannot be renewed. If an individual is under psychiatric care in a hospital at the time he or she becomes eligible for Part A of Medicare, the 190 day benefit is further reduced. Any days that the individual spent in

Table 10-3

Part A Medicare Benefits for a Surgical Hospital Stay

	Charges	Medicare Pays
Hospital room	$3,750	$2,700
	($125 x 30 days)	($90 x 30 days)†
Lab tests	$ 350	$ 350
X-rays	57	57
Medical supplies	150	150
Operating room	200	200
Drugs	400	400
	$4,907	$3,857
Less deductible	—	—
Total	$4,907	$3,733

† Medicare does not pay for a private room unless a private room is medically necessary.

receiving psychiatric care in a hospital during the 150 days preceding eligibility for Medicare are subtracted from the 190 day coverage. The following example illustrates how the basic hospital benefits operate.

Thomas Daily enters the hospital on March 1, to have his gall bladder removed. Because of complications, Thomas is confined to the hospital for thirty days. His private hospital room costs $125, but the charge for a semiprivate room is $90 per day. The other hospital charges are these: (1) lab tests—$350, (2) x-ray—$57, (3) medical supplies—$150, (4) operating room fee—$200, and (5) drugs—$400. Medicare will pay the charges shown in Table 10-3.

In addition to providing basic hospital coverage, the Medicare program also affords protection for inpatient care in a skilled nursing facility for up to 100 days.[16] This coverage is reinstated with each new benefit period. Five conditions have to be met before an individual is eligible for care in a skilled nursing facility. First, an individual must have been in a hospital for at least three consecutive days before he or she is moved to a skilled nursing facility. Second, treatment in the nursing facility must be for the same condition that was treated in the hospital. Third, an individual must be admitted to a skilled nursing facility within fourteen days of being discharged from the hospital. Fourth, the doctor must state that an individual needs the skilled nursing care. And, finally, a Utilization Review Committee or a Professional Standards Review Organization has to approve the treatment.

Figure 10-2

Types of Skilled Nursing Facility Services Which Are and Are Not Covered Under Medicare*

Covered
A semiprivate room (two to four beds in a room) All meals, including special diets Regular nursing services Rehabilitation services, such as physical, occupational, and speech therapy Drugs furnished by a facility during an individual's stay Medical supplies, such as splints and casts Use of appliances such as a wheelchair
Not Covered
Personal convenience items requested such as a television, radio, or telephone in a room Private duty nurses Any extra charges for a private room, unless it is necessary for medical reasons The first three pints of blood received in a benefit period

*Reprinted from U.S. Department of Health, Education, and Welfare, *Your Medicare Handbook* (Washington: Superintendent of Documents, 1976), p. 19.

Medicare pays all costs for the first twenty days in a skilled nursing facility. After twenty days, an individual is required to pay $18.00 per day. If an individual residing in a skilled nursing facility should leave the facility and then be readmitted within fourteen days, the requirement that an insured must have been in a hospital three days before being admitted to the facility is waived. Physicians' services are not covered under the skilled nursing facility benefit. Figure 10-2 lists some of the changes which are and are not covered in a skilled nursing facility.

Part A of Medicare also pays for home health care. The full cost of up to 100 home health visits can be covered in each benefit period. For the costs of home health care visits to be covered, the following conditions must be met:

... (1) you were in a qualifying hospital for at least three days in a row (not counting the day of discharge), (2) the home health care is for further treatment of a condition which was treated in a hospital or skilled nursing facility, (3) the care you need includes part-time skilled nursing care, physical therapy, or speech therapy, (4) you are confined to your home, (5) a doctor determines you need home health care and sets up a home health care plan for you within 14 days after your discharge from a hospital or participating skilled nursing facility, and (6) the home health agency providing services is participating in Medicare.[17]

Medical Insurance Part B of Medicare, medical insurance, is designed to cover many of the expenses not covered under Part A. The medical insurance will contribute toward the cost of a physician's services in a hospital or office, outpatient hospital service, outpatient physical therapy and speech pathology services, home health services, and other miscellaneous medical services. The deductible for medical insurance is lower than for hospital insurance. Under Part B of Medicare, the first $60 of the covered reasonable medical expense are absorbed by the insured. Unlike the hospital insurance, the deductible under the medical insurance is applied to each calendar year, not each benefit period. If any portion of the deductible is met in the last three months of a calendar year, then in the subsequent calendar year, the deductible, or the portion of the deductible that has been absorbed by the insured, does not have to be satisfied a second time. For covered charges above the deductible, the insured pays 20 percent, and Medicare pays 80 percent of each dollar of loss.

A physician's charges are covered if they are provided in an office, a hospital, or a skilled nursing care facility. Figure 10-3 lists some of the typical inpatient and outpatient physicians' services that are covered. Some of the services not covered also are listed.

There are some exceptions to the 80/20 participation. For example, while an individual is an inpatient in a hospital, Part B will pay 100 percent of the charges for radiology and pathology. This 100 percent coverage applies even when an individual has not satisfied the deductible.

Payment for outpatient care for mental illness is limited to $250 in any one year, and a chiropractor's services are covered only when the, "treatment ... is manual manipulation of the spine to correct a subluxation that can be demonstrated by x-ray."[18] The services of a podiatrist are covered except for routine foot care. Dental care is available only when, "it involves surgery of the jaw or related structures or setting fractures of the jaw or facial bones."[19]

Outpatient physical therapy or speech pathology services are covered in one of three ways. When the services are provided in a doctor's office under his or her supervision, Medicare will pay 80 percent of the cost above the annual deductible. If the services are provided by a physical therapist in his or her office or in the insured's home, Medicare pays 80 percent of the cost subject to a maximum benefit of $80 per year. Finally, physical therapy or speech pathology services are covered

Figure 10-3

Type of Physicians' Services which Are and Are Not Covered Under Medicare*

Covered

Medical and surgical services
Diagnostic tests and procedures that are part of a treatment
Other services which are ordinarily furnished in a doctor's office and included in his bill, such as:
    X-rays received as part of a treatment
    Services of a doctor's office nurse
    Drugs and biologicals that cannot be self-administered
    Medical supplies
    Physical therapy and speech pathology services

Not Covered
Routine physical examinations Routine foot care Eye or hearing examinations for prescribing or fitting eyeglasses or hearing aids Immunizations (unless required because of injury or immediate risk of infection) Cosmetic surgery unless it is needed because of accidental injury or to improve the functioning of a malformed part of the body

*Reprinted from U.S. Department of Health, Education, and Welfare, *Your Medicare Handbook* (Washington: Superintendent of Documents, 1976), p. 27.

on an outpatient basis by a hospital or skilled nursing facility or if they are offered by a home health agency, clinic, rehabilitation agency, or public health agency. However, these benefits are covered only if a doctor has established a plan or routine for the provision of these services.

Outpatient coverage for the diagnosis or treatment of an injury or illness by a hospital is covered under Part B. All reasonable and necessary charges above the deductible are paid by Medicare and the insured on an 80/20 basis. Figure 10-4 shows the hospital services covered on an outpatient basis by Part B, medical insurance. Other miscellaneous services partially covered by Part B include independent laboratory services, ambulance transportation, prosthetic devices, durable medical equipment, portable diagnostic x-ray services, and medical supplies.

Like Part A, Part B provides coverage for home health care. Four

Figure 10-4

Types of Outpatient Hospital Services Which Are and Are Not Covered by Medical Insurance*

Covered
Services in an emergency room or outpatient clinic Laboratory tests billed by the hospital X-rays and other radiology services billed by the hospital Medical supplies such as splints and casts Drugs and biologicals which cannot be self-administered
Not Covered
Routine physical examinations and tests directly related to such examinations Eye or ear examinations to prescribe or fit eyeglasses or hearing aids Immunizations (unless required because of an injury or immediate risk of infection) Routine foot care

*Reprinted from U.S. Department of Health, Education, and Welfare, *Your Medicare Handbook* (Washington: Superintendent of Documents, 1976), p. 29.

conditions must be met under Part B before home health care can be afforded. These conditions are: (1) part-time skilled nursing care or physical or speech therapy is needed, (2) a doctor sets up a plan for home health care, (3) the patient is confined to his or her home, and (4) the home health agency providing services is participating in Medicare. One hundred visits are covered under Part B. The insured is not required to participate in the cost of these visits on an 80/20 basis, but must have met the annual deductible before full benefits start. The example below illustrates how Part B of Medicare provides medical insurance coverage.

On February 5, Carley Holder enters the hospital for surgery. Carley is covered under Part A and Part B of Medicare. The doctor who performs the surgery charges $1,500. The surgeon also bills Carley for the following services performed in the doctor's office during a visit by Carley prior to the operation: (1) x-rays—$75, (2) drugs—$30, and (3) diagnostic tests—$100.

Following the operation, Carley requires the services of a radiologist. Carley's radiologist charges $350.

Carley is confined to her home for two months after she leaves the hospital. During this time, she has to have ten visits from a physical therapist. Each visit costs $25. Of the medical expenses incurred by Carley, the amount paid by Medicare is shown in Table 10-4.

Table 10-4

Part *B* Medicare Benefits

Expenses Covered on a Coinsurance Basis[†]		
X-ray	$ 75	
Drugs	30	
Tests	100	
Surgery	1,500	
Total	$1,705	
Medicare pays		$1,316 [($1,705 − $60) x 0.8]
Expenses Not Covered on a Coinsurance Basis		
Radiologist	$ 350	
Home visits	250	
Total	$ 600	
Medicare Pays	$ 600	
Total Paid by Medicare		$1,916
Total Paid by Carley		389
Total Bill		$2,305

[†]The results in this example are based on the assumption that Part *A* provided coverage only if it was not available under Part *B*.

In the example, only a portion of the expense was subject to the coinsurance clause. One hundred percent of the radiologist's charges and the home visits, as discussed earlier, are covered.

Eligibility for Medicare Anyone who is age sixty-five and is eligible for retirement benefits under the social security program automatically is eligible for Part A of Medicare. No premium charge is required. The individual and his or her employer have paid for the Part A coverage through the social security tax on earned income. An individual who is not eligible for social security retirement benefits at age sixty-five may purchase Part A coverage during January, February, or March of any year without providing proof of insurability. Currently, the premium for Part A is $63 per month per insured. If an individual should elect to delay the purchase of Part A coverage beyond age sixty-five, he or she will be penalized. For every year the individual delays, the premium is increased 10 percent. The extra charge is necessary to cover the high costs that accrue because of adverse selection.

A waiting period is also used to avoid adverse selection. An individual who purchases coverage in the first three months of a year is not protected until July 1 of that year.

Part B of the Medicare program is not automatic for individuals eligible for retirement benefits under social security. Instead, it must be purchased at age sixty-five. The cost of the program is financed jointly. A person who does not purchase Part B coverage at age sixty-five can purchase it during the first three months of any subsequent year. The premium increases 10 percent every year that a person delays buying coverage. The program is funded partially by the individuals who are insured while the balance of the cost of the program is taken out of general revenues. The premium for medical insurance protection currently is $8.20 per month per person.

Operation of Medicare   Table 10-5 is a summary of the operations under the Medicare program for fiscal years 1974 and 1975. By 1975, Medicare was receiving 107.9 million billings per year. Of these billings, 26.5 million were filed under Part A, and 81.4 million under Part B.

In 1975, 23.9 million people received benefits under Part A and 23.1 million people under Part B. These individuals were paid a total of $14.2 billion.

The Social Security Administration estimates that the federal government paid 42.2 percent of the total health expenditures in this country in fiscal year 1975.[20] Medicare accounts for a substantial portion of this total. Because of the large government outlay under the Medicare program, a tremendous potential for abuse and fraud exists. During fiscal year 1975, 3,180 fraud cases and 1,363 cases of abuse involving millions of dollars were investigated.[21] The Social Security Administration is attempting at this time to develop checks on the system to eliminate these types of problems.[22]

Since its inception, Medicare has been expanded. Individuals eligible for disability benefits under the social security program have been included under Medicare. As of 1975, over 2 million disabled persons were afforded protection under Medicare.[23]

The Medicare program also has been extended to individuals who require kidney dialysis or who need kidney transplant services. A special provision extends coverage to those individuals who normally would not qualify for Medicare benefits. As of fiscal year 1975, 23,000 people were covered under Medicare's end-stage renal disease program. Of this total, "14,000 were covered under the special entitlement provision, 6,600 under the regular disability provisions of the law, and 2,400 under the regular age-65 provisions."[24] The cost of this program was $6 million per week.[25]

Table 10-5

Health Insurance Program—Fiscal Year 1975*

Claims	1974	1975	Change Since 1974
Receipts (in millions)			
Part A (fiscal intermediaries)	$22.5	$ 26.5	+16.7%
Part B (carriers)	68.0	81.4	+19.7
Total	90.5	107.9	+19.0
End-of-Year Pendings (in millions)			
Part A	$ 0.7	$ 0.7	0%
Part B	2.9	2.9	0
Total	3.6	3.6	0
Beneficiaries with Protection as of June 30 (in millions)	1974	1975	Change Since 1974
Part A	$23.3	$ 23.9	+ 2.6%
Part B	22.9	23.1	+ 0.9
Payments (in billions)			
Part A	$ 7.8	$ 10.4	+33.3%
Part B	2.9	3.8	+31.0
Total	10.7	14.2	

*Reprinted from U.S. Congress, House Committee on Ways and Means *Annual Report of the Social Security Administration for Fiscal Year 1975*, 94th Cong., 2d sess., 1976, p. 22.

Disability Income Benefits Under OASDHI

An individual who is paying social security taxes may be eligible for disability payments. Anyone over age thirty-one is qualified if he or she is fully insured (i.e., has forty quarters of coverage). An individual between the ages of twenty-four and thirty-one is qualified if he or she has one quarter of coverage for every two quarters between the time that he or she turned twenty-one and the time that he or she becomes disabled.

Anyone who is disabled before age twenty-four is eligible if he or she has six quarters of coverage out of the last twelve. The following examples illustrate the application of the disability rules.

Bruce Clark is age thirty-five. Recently, he was involved in an automobile accident and now is totally disabled. Bruce began working at age twenty-three, and he has earned four quarters of coverage every year. Disability benefits would be provided for Bruce under the social security program because he has forty quarters of coverage which qualify him as fully insured, and he has twenty quarters of coverage out of the last forty.

While skiing, Mary Lou Spencer was severely injured. Mary Lou, who is age twenty-five, is totally disabled. She began working at age twenty-three after finishing graduate school. Since that time, Mary Lou has earned six quarters of coverage. She is not eligible for disability benefits. Mary Lou turned twenty-one twenty quarters ago. Therefore, to be eligible for benefits she needs ten covered quarters. Unfortunately, she only has earned six quarters of the ten she needs.

Ronald Allison is paralyzed after falling down a flight of stairs in his home. Ronald is twenty-three. He has earned eight quarters. Since he only needs six quarters of coverage out of the last twelve to be covered, he would be eligible for disability payments.

There is a five-month waiting period before an individual can qualify for disability benefits. In addition, the expected term of the disability must be at least twelve months. If a person is disabled a second time within five years of the first disability, the five-month waiting period is not applicable, but the second period of disability also must be expected to last for at least twelve months.

If a person who has been disabled attempts to return to work, payments are continued during a trial period of nine months. If the individual is able to work after the nine-month period, benefits are provided for another three months. This affords an insured an adjustment period. If an individual is not able to return to work on a full-time basis, normal disability payments are continued.

The disability benefits payable under social security are the same as those that would be paid for retirement. Thus, payments are made to a disabled individual and to his or her dependents.

Social security benefits are integrated with any benefits available under workers' compensation. Under the social security program, the total amount that can be paid is 80 percent of the total average earnings of the disabled individual. Included in this 80 percent are any benefits that are paid by a workers' compensation plan. The next example shows the effect of this integration of benefits.

Jay Pearce's average earnings are $660 per month. While loading boxes on a truck, Jay injures his back. His workers' compensation payment is $130. Social security would pay the difference between $480 ($660 × 0.80) and $130, or the social security limit, whichever is less.

HEALTH MAINTENANCE ORGANIZATIONS

Providers of health services, insurance companies, and consumers have sought alternate methods for providing health services. The need for alternate sources has arisen because of the increasing cost of providing health insurance benefits and increasing demand for medical services. In addition, the current system is viewed as inadequate to meet the health insurance needs of some segments of the population of the United States.

One method currently being tried is the health maintenance organization (HMO). Under an HMO plan, individuals pay a periodic fixed cost for health services. For this payment, the plan participants are guaranteed specific health services. The types of services that might be afforded under a health maintenance organization plan include (1) physician services, (2) hospital services, (3) emergency health care services, (4) outpatient care services, (5) diagnostic laboratory services, (6) home health care services, and (7) preventive health services. The objective of an HMO is to reduce utilization by increasing the use of preventive health services. An HMO benefits, both financially and in terms of time, by preventing health care problems.

Most insurance plans have not stressed preventive health services. Instead, they were designed to pay for health services only after an accident or illness had occurred. Recently, many insurance companies have been working closely with HMOs in an effort to find a better way of providing health services to the public.

Although the HMO concept is just beginning to gain national acceptance, HMOs have been in existence for many years. An HMO prototype, the Ross-Loos Clinic, was developed in 1929 in Los Angeles. The Kaiser Foundation initiated a health maintenance organization type of operation in Oakland, California, in 1942. The Health Insurance Plan of Greater New York has been in operation since 1947 and functions in a way similar to an HMO.

There are two types of HMO structure. The closed panel, or group practice prepayment HMO, operates with a group or staff of professionals who provide health services. Generally, all the plan doctors are located in a common facility and are salaried employees of either the medical group or the HMO.

Under an open panel HMO (also called individual practice association), any nearby physician can participate in the HMO plan. The physician operates out of his or her office but contracts with the HMO to serve plan participants. Under the open panel concept, the physician who provides the health services is not paid a fee for each service.

Instead, he or she is paid a fee for each member of the group that is treated. This flat fee or capitation fee encourages a physician not to provide unnecessary medical treatments.

The health maintenance organization movement was given impetus by the federal government in 1973 when Congress passed an act entitled the "Health Maintenance Organization Act."[26] The act not only provides for standards under which an HMO can qualify as a federal HMO but also provides aid for the development of both profit and nonprofit HMOs. To qualify as an HMO, a plan must furnish basic health insurance services to the enrollees without any limitation on costs, health status, or time. Basic health services are defined as:

1. physician services (including consultant and referral services by a physician);
2. outpatient services and inpatient hospital services;
3. medically necessary outpatient and inpatient emergency health services;
4. short-term (not to exceed twenty visits), outpatient evaluative and crisis intervention mental health services;
5. medical treatment or referral services (including referral services to appropriate ancillary services) for the abuse of or addiction to alcohol or drugs;
6. diagnostic laboratory and diagnostic and therapeutic radiologic services;
7. home health services; and
8. preventive health services (including voluntary family planning services, services for infertility, preventive dental care for children, and children's eye examinations conducted to determine the need for vision correction).[27]

If an HMO has adequate manpower, it must offer the following additional supplementary health services:

1. services of facilities for intermediate and long-term care;
2. vision care not included as a basic health service;
3. dental services not included as a basic health service;
4. mental health services not included as a basic health service;
5. long-term physical medicine and rehabilitative services (including physical therapy); and
6. the provision of prescription drugs prescribed in the delivery of a basic health service or a supplemental health service provided by the health maintenance organization.[28]

While the federal statutes establish guidelines for HMOs, they also prohibit state laws which would inhibit their growth. Specifically, the federal law supersedes state regulations which require the approval of a medical society for the organization and operation of an HMO, membership by a specific number of physicians in the HMO governing body, participation in a delivery of services by all or a certain number of physicians in the area, or the satisfaction of the financial requirements for insurers doing business in a state respecting initial capitalization and the establishment of financial reserves against insolvency.[29] The federal law also supersedes any state law which bars a health maintenance organization while it is receiving financial assistance from the government from, "... soliciting members through advertising its services, charges, or other nonprofessional aspects of its operation."[30]

To encourage the development of HMOs, the federal government has made project grants available. Grants are available for feasibility studies, planning, initial development, and operations. Feasibility grants may be as large as $50,000. Planning grants of up to $125,000 can be utilized to establish a marketing strategy for an HMO. After planning has been completed, grants of up to $1 million are available for the initial development of an HMO. These initial development funds may be applied to the cost of implementing enrollment campaigns, developing an HMO structure, recruiting physicians and other health service personnel, and obtaining architects' and engineers' services.

Finally, up to $2.5 million may be borrowed to cover the deficits that accrue during the first three years of an HMO's operation. However, a maximum of $1 million can be borrowed during a particular fiscal year.[31]

The 1973 law propelled the HMO movement forward by requiring employers to offer HMO coverage. The law stipulates that an employer which:

> ... is required during any calendar quarter to pay its employees the minimum wage specified by section 6 of the Fair Labor Standards Act of 1938 (or would be required to pay its employees such wage but for section 13(a) of such Act), and which during such calendar quarter employed an average number of employees of not less than twenty-five, shall, in accordance with regulations which the Secretary shall prescribe, include in any health benefits plan offered to its employees in the calendar year beginning after such calendar quarter the option of membership in qualified health maintenance organizations which are engaged in the provision of basic and supplemental health services in the areas in which such employees reside.[32]

In effect, the bill has provided an automatic market for HMOs because many employers must offer employees the option of taking health maintenance coverage in lieu of other insurance protection. Where more than one type of HMO exists in the employer's area, employees must be offered the option of selecting any type.

The employer is protected from paying more for an HMO plan than he would under a health insurance program. The law stipulates that the employer is not required to pay more than he or she would for any other health insurance plan.

Health maintenance organizations do offer an alternative to group health insurance coverage. However, the future of HMOs is uncertain. The direction taken by any national health insurance program will impact directly on the development of these types of plans. Most of the national health insurance bills that have been proposed would include the use of HMOs; therefore, health maintenance organizations should be given impetus by any national health insurance bill.

BLANKET ACCIDENT AND SICKNESS INSURANCE

Union and employee groups can be covered under group insurance policies. However, they also may be covered under a blanket accident and sickness policy. A blanket policy covers an entire group, and generally no certificates are issued to individual members of the group. Members of the group are covered automatically.

As a rule, blanket coverages are more limited than group insurance coverages. For example, blanket policies provide limited forms of insurance protection, such as accidental death and dismemberment.

Most state laws stipulate the types of groups eligible for such coverage. In most states, blanket accident and sickness policies can be issued to groups:

(1) under a policy issued to any common carrier or to any operator, owner, or lessor of a means of transportation, who or which shall be deemed the policyholder, covering a group of persons who may become passengers defined by reference to their travel status on such common carrier or such means of transportation; or, under a policy issued to any automobile and/or truck leasing company, which shall be deemed the policyholder, covering a group of persons who may become either renters, lessees, or passengers defined by their travel status on such rented or leased vehicles;

(2) under a policy to an employer, who shall be deemed the policyholder, covering any group of employees, dependents, or guests, defined by reference to specified hazards incident to an activity or activities or operations of the policyholder;

(3) under a policy issued to a college, school, or other institution of learning, a school district or districts, or school jurisdictional unit, or to the head, principal, or governing board of any such education unit, who or which shall be deemed the policyholder, covering students, teachers, or employees;

(4) under a policy issued to any religious, charitable, recreational, educational, or civic organization, or branch thereof, which shall be deemed the policyholder, covering any group of members or participants defined by reference to specified hazards incident to any activity or activities or operations sponsored or supervised by such policyholder;

(5) under a policy issued to a sports team, camp, or sponsor thereof, which shall be deemed the policyholder, covering members, campers, employees, officials, or supervisors;

(6) under a policy issued to any governmental or volunteer fire department or fire company, first aid, civil defense, or other such governmental or volunteer organization, which shall be deemed the policyholder, covering any group of members or participants defined by reference to specified hazards incident to an activity or activities or operations sponsored or supervised by such policyholder;

(7) under a policy issued to a newspaper or other publisher, which shall be deemed the policyholder, covering its carriers;

(8) under a policy issued to an association, including a labor union, which shall have a constitution and bylaws and which has been organized and is maintained in good faith for purposes other than that of obtaining insurance, which shall be deemed the policyholder, covering any group of members or participants defined by reference to specified hazards incident to an activity or activities or operations sponsored or supervised by such policyholder....[33]

Since blanket policies cover an entire group and not individual members of a group, an insured may not be required to complete an enrollment card.

Some states require some standard policy provisions in blanket contracts. These provisions are confined to explaining procedures for filing a claim, conditions under which legal action can be brought, and the definition of an entire contract.

FRANCHISE ACCIDENT AND SICKNESS INSURANCE

Franchise coverage is another method of providing insurance coverage to a group. Under a franchise arrangement, coverage is issued to all members of an employer group, or an association who desire the insurance. Members are issued individual policies and are responsible for remitting the insurance premium to the employer or to the association, who in turn pays the premium to the insurance carrier.

Franchise coverage is advantageous to individuals who do not qualify for true group insurance. Even small franchise groups save the insurer some administrative costs because a single premium is remitted by the employer or association. This savings can be passed to the insureds. The cost savings is not as great, however, as it would be in a group policy, because the groups are smaller and individual policies are issued. As a result, the charge for franchise insurance protection generally is less than individual coverage but more than group insurance protection.

NATIONAL HEALTH INSURANCE

The Issues

Many issues have impacted on the increasing interest of consumers in national health insurance. A few of these issues are presented to illustrate why national health insurance is being considered.

Private Health Insurance Coverage Many critics of the current health insurance system claim that it is inefficient. Efficiency has two primary components: cost minimization and optimal utilization.

Cost minimization has not been achieved for several reasons. First, the increase in medical malpractice suits has caused doctors to perform more tests and procedures. In addition, some doctors attempt to improve their financial positions by providing unnecessary medical services. Both factors have contributed to the inflation in health insurance premiums.

Hospitals also have contributed to the cost spiral. With the advent of Medicare, many hospitals increased the cost of medical services because the government was paying the bills. Cost increases have stabilized, but they have not been eliminated.

Private insurance companies cannot have as great an impact on rising costs as Blue Cross and Blue Shield. Blue Cross and Blue Shield organizations can influence costs when negotiating contracts with the purveyors of health services. By keeping costs down for their insureds, Blue Cross and Blue Shield plans force physicians and hospitals to pass cost increases to the remainder of the public. The "artificial competitive advantages [of Blue Cross and Blue Shield] probably should be eliminated to remove one impediment to the achievement of economies of scale in the competitive process."[34]

Optimal utilization is the other component of efficiency. This problem is difficult to overcome. A general practitioner can work at an optimal level; normally, the patient load is more than adequate. However, specialists do not always function at an optimal level. Influences such as the supply of physicians in a specialized area, a physician's desire to work, and the cost of services provided by a specialist will determine how efficiently a specialist's services are utilized. Private insurers cannot impact on this vital problem. They cannot force specialists to work more or charge less.

Quality Another vital issue involves the quality of the health services that are provided consumers. The proliferation of malpractice suits has caused many persons to question whether or not the quality of health services has declined.

Increases in the number of suits may not indicate a decrease in quality. They may reflect a change in public attitude. In recent years, people have become more inclined to sue. In addition, as physicians try new techniques, the risks increase.

If quality control is a problem, it is the responsibility of the states that license purveyors of health services and the schools that graduate the personnel to provide services. Some critics of the present system contend that national health insurance would provide greater quality control.

Availability It is increasingly realized that adequate medical services are not available to everyone. Poor people and those who live in remote or rural areas often have been unable to receive the health care they require. Supposedly, national health insurance will improve health services for these groups, although Medicaid already has aided in the problem of providing medical services for the poor.

Cost Proponents of national health insurance suggest that the current system does not provide adequate protection to many individuals because they cannot afford the premium charges (i.e., some individuals cannot purchase any protection while other individuals cannot purchase enough insurance to protect against catastrophes). A national health insurance system could overcome this if at least a fraction of the costs were paid out of general revenues. While a specific individual may benefit, someone still has to provide the funds for general revenues. Most national health insurance programs would shift the cost of health services.

Cost controls are included in some national health insurance proposals. However, these are designed to control the rate of future increases, not to reduce the current costs.

Types of Insurance Plans

Several types of national health insurance programs have been considered. In the following sections some of these are discussed.

Comprehensive National Health Insurance Some of the national health insurance proposals that have been introduced in Congress would establish a comprehensive national health insurance program. The Corman-Kennedy proposal, titled the Health Security Act, calls for the provision of free medical services for all individuals residing in the United States (i.e., an insured would not be required to pay any deductible or to make any coinsurance payment).[35]

The cost of the program would be funded from three sources—employers, employees, and general revenues. A tax on wages would be paid by an employer and by an employee. Individuals that are self-employed also would pay a wage tax. Any portion of the cost of the program not funded by a tax on wages would come from general revenues.

The Corman-Kennedy bill contains some cost controls. The federal goverment only would pay for reasonable costs. In addition, a review procedure would be established to ascertain if unnecessary services were being provided by the purveyors of health services. This determination may be difficult. Supposedly, cost savings would result because Medicare would be eliminated and the role of Medicaid would be reduced.

Limited National Health Insurance While a comprehensive health care program has the support of some congressmen, others feel that a comprehensive national health insurance program is unnecessary. Two limited plans that have been suggested are the Ullman bill (the National Health Care Services Financing and Reorganizational Act) and the Burleson-McIntyre bill (the National Health Care Act).

The Burleson-McIntyre bill would provide free medical care for some individuals. The bill establishes a standard health insurance plan. An employer would provide employees with benefits at least equal to the national standard. The amount of the employee's contributions would be subject to collective bargaining. Amounts paid by employers and employees would be tax deductible.

Insureds would pay a $100 deductible and 20 percent of each dollar of loss above the deductible. No family, however, would be required to pay more than $1,000 in a single year.

Low income families would be eligible for state health insurance plans. The premium paid by a family in a state health insurance plan would be a function of a family's income. The lowest economic levels would pay no premium.

For an individual who becomes unemployed, group coverage would continue for two months. Then, the unemployed person would be eligible for coverage in a state plan.

State plans would be funded by the state and premium payments from insureds. However, a portion of a state's cost would be reimbursed by the federal government.

Medicare and Medicaid would be retained under the Burleson-McIntyre approach. Therefore, no cost savings would accrue from the elimination of any programs. The bill stipulates that services and fees would be reviewed to determine if any abuses existed.

Table 10-6

Costs of National Health Insurance
(In Billions of Dollars—Including Administrative Costs)*

	Sponsors Estimate	HEW Estimate
Corman-Kennedy	52.0	63.5
Ullman	None	10.6
Burleson-McIntyre	8.1	9.2

*Reprinted with permission from Martin S. Feldstein, et al, *New Directions in Public Health Care* (San Francisco: Institute for Contemporary Studies, 1976), p. 187.

The Ullman bill is similar to the Burleson-McIntyre bill. Employers would be required to offer benefits greater than or equal to a standard plan, but under the Ullman bill employers would pay at least 75 percent of the cost.

The Ullman bill would set a limit on the aggregate dollar loss that would have to be absorbed by a family. But, the maximum paid by a family, under the Ullman bill, would be a function of the size and income of a family. For a low income family, the maximum is less than 10 percent of the family's income. Families not in the low income category would have to pay an amount equal to 10 percent of the family's income before catastrophe coverage becomes effective.

Self-employed, low income, and unemployed individuals could purchase coverage from health insurers. The cost of the plan would be borne by the insured and the federal government.

Employers would be given a tax credit for their contributions to an approved plan. The amount of the tax credit would be equal to the cost of any new plan less 4 percent of the employer's payroll. Individuals could deduct the full cost of their health coverage from taxable income.

Health services purveyors would be reorganized. Health care corporations similar to health maintenance organizations would be established by states to provide health services. Individuals would not be required to belong to a health care corporation, but would receive an additional tax credit if they did.

The cost of any national health insurance program is important. The sponsors of the three bills that have been discussed made estimates of the cost of their programs. The Department of Health, Education, and Welfare also has estimated the cost of these plans. The results are summarized in Table 10-6. Regardless of which type of plan is implemented the cost will be a burden on the taxpayer.

Chapter Notes

1. J. E. Rhodes, *Workmen's Compensation* (New York: Macmillan Company, 1917), pp. 41-62.
2. Ibid., pp. 99-101.
3. Although a state law sets forth guidelines for unlimited medical expenses for most injuries and diseases, there may be some exceptions for one or more diseases. For example, limited medical coverage may be afforded for silicosis or asbestosis.
4. Marie Karkowiecki, "Benefit Costs Climb 23% in 2 Years, Survey Finds," *Business Insurance* 10:21 (1976): 1.
5. Blue Cross Association, "Questions and Answers About the Blue Cross Organization," mimeograph, 1976, p. 2.
6. Ibid., p. 2.
7. Ibid., p. 4.
8. Ibid., p. 10.
9. Ibid., p. 4.
10. Health Insurance Institute, *New Group Health Insurance* (New York: Health Insurance Institute, 1976), p. 14.
11. Georgia Code Annotated, Ch. 56, Sec. 3101.
12. Ibid., Sec. 3102.
13. Ibid., Sec. 2442.
14. Normally, benefits are paid only if a health care provider meets the requirements established by Medicare, i.e., is a participating unit. Benefits can be paid to a nonparticipating unit in unusual circumstances. For example, emergency treatment at a nonparticipating hospital is covered if the nonparticipating hospital is the closest hospital available with the equipment to handle the situation.
15. U.S. Department of Health, Education, and Welfare, *Your Medicare Handbook* (Washington: Superintendent of Documents, 1976), p. 12. The function of a Utilization Review Committee or a Professional Standards Review Organization is to ascertain whether unnecessary or unreasonable charges have been made. Medicare will not pay for any charges that are unnecessary or unreasonable.
16. Benefits for services rendered in a nursing facility are not paid unless the facility is a participating unit.
17. U.S. Department of Health, Education, and Welfare, *Your Medicare Handbook*, p. 36.
18. Ibid., p. 26.
19. Ibid.
20. U.S., Congress, House, Committee on Ways and Means, Annual Report of the Social Security Administration for Fiscal Year 1975, 94th Cong., 2d sess., 1976, p. 24.
21. Ibid., p. 25.

22. Ibid., pp. 25-27.
23. Ibid., p. 25.
24. Ibid.
25. Ibid.
26. Several states have enacted HMO legislation including: (1) Hawaii, (2) Michigan, (3) Minnesota, (4) New York, (5) Ohio, (6) Rhode Island, and (7) Washington.
27. 39 Federal Register 37311.
28. Ibid., 37311, 37312.
29. U.S., Statutes, vol. 87, 931.
30. Ibid.
31. Ibid., 920, 922, 923, 925.
32. Ibid., 930.
33. Texas Insurance Code, Art. 3.51-6, Sec. 2.
34. Ronald J. Vogel and Roger D. Blair, *Health Insurance Administrative Costs* (Washington: U.S. Department of Health, Education, and Welfare, 1976), p. 3.
35. When an insured pays a fixed dollar amount of each loss, he or she is making a copayment. When an insured pays a fixed percentage of each loss, coinsurance is being utilized.

CHAPTER 11

Retirement Income Planning

INTRODUCTION

It may seem incongruous to refer to the retirement "exposure." Retirement is a goal sought by many if not most people. Yet the termination of earned income associated with retirement can cause severe financial problems for many families.

Of course, retirement is not an accidental event. The real peril of retirement is the chance that the accumulated savings of the retiree may be inadequate—that is, there is always a danger that the retiree may outlive his or her savings.

Even though retirement is not an accidental event, it is almost ideally insurable, and many insurance products are designed to deal with the problems associated with it. Many of these products are intended to deal with both the premature-death exposure and the retirement exposure. These two problems, and their solutions, are intertwined.

Unlike most personal loss exposures, the retirement problem is frequently handled by noninsurance techniques. Many individuals, for example, accumulate assets through real estate, mutual funds, savings accounts, and other investment vehicles for the purpose of providing retirement income. These approaches will be treated in Chapter 13.

EXPOSURE ANALYSIS

Chances of Survival

Using a risk management approach, analysis of the retirement

Table 11-1

1958 CSO Mortality Table
(abbreviated)

Selected Ages	Number Living
0	10,000,000
20	9,664,994
30	9,480,358
40	9,241,359
50	8,762,306
60	7,698,698
65	6,800,531

exposure starts with the frequency of loss, which is equivalent to the probability of surviving to retirement. Chapter 6 showed how the probability of dying during a given time period could be computed from a mortality table. Therefore, since there are only two possible outcomes (a person either continues to live or dies), it follows that the probability of surviving to retirement age is unity (1) minus the probability of dying during that time frame. If a person, for example, has a 30 percent chance of dying before age sixty-five, the chances of reaching retirement age are 70 percent.

Perhaps an easier method of estimating the chances of survival is simply to note the number of persons living at the various ages. Consider the figures taken from the 1958 CSO Mortality Table shown in Table 11-1. The probability that a person age zero will live to age sixty-five can be determined by noting that of the 10 million people alive at age zero, 6,800,531 will reach age sixty-five. Therefore, the probability is 6,800,531 ÷ 10 million, which is about 68 percent. For a person forty years of age, the probability of living until age sixty-five would be calculated by dividing 6,800,531 by 9,241,359. This would be about a 74 percent chance of survival. At age sixty, the probability of living until age sixty-five is approximately 88 percent (6,800,531 ÷ 7,698,698).

A person's chance of surviving until age sixty-five increases with age. In other words, a person, for example, who reaches age forty has a greater chance of living to age sixty-five than a person only twenty years of age. This is a natural result of the fact that a younger person has an exposure to death that has already passed for someone who is older. Even for a young person, age twenty, there is about a 70 percent chance of reaching age sixty-five (6,800,531 ÷ 9,664,994). Of course, for a person who contemplates early retirement there is an even higher chance of surviving until retirement.

The chance of survival to retirement at any age is very high. From a theoretical point of view, it is interesting to question the utility of the insurance technique when the probability of loss is so great. After all, other lines of insurance would not be feasible with such high probabilities. Retirement is insurable even with large chances of loss because the insurance contract is written on a valued, rather than indemnity basis, and also because insurance companies can earn interest for a long period (usually many years) before losses are paid.

Estimating Financial Needs During Retirement

Using the risk management approach, the problem of estimating financial needs for retirement is equivalent to estimating loss potential. This estimation is difficult, even for a person who has just reached retirement age. For a young person, the problem is even greater. Most families have difficulty in estimating financial needs even a year or two in the future. Nevertheless, if a young person is to plan for retirement in an intelligent manner, an estimate of financial needs far into the future is required.

To estimate financial needs for retirement, an individual must make some assumptions, the most difficult of which involve future benefits from OASDHI and pension plans, investment results that will be achieved, and the standard of living required after retirement.

One financial planning company uses the form in Figure 11-1 to help individuals estimate the amount of money they will need for retirement. The steps in the far right column of the form are questions that must be answered (estimated).

The first question (Step 1) requires a person to estimate his or her retirement age. For many people, age sixty-five is appropriate. If an unrealistically low age is used in Step 1, the results obtained will be severely distorted. Step 2 requires a factual answer that presents no problems. Step 3 follows immediately from Steps 1 and 2. The amount to be inserted at Step 4 may be somewhat difficult to estimate. The problem is greatly simplified, however, by using current prices. It would be reasonable for most people to assume that no children will be living at home. Depending upon individual circumstances, it may or may not be reasonable to assume that a mortgage on the home will exist.

It may be appropriate to assume that financial needs will be lower after retirement. For example, after retirement a person may not have costs for (1) children, (2) mortgage on a home, or (3) travel expenses to and from work. However, some people may need approximately the same aftertax income as they had prior to retirement. Although some

Figure 11-1

Estimated Capital Needs for Retirement

(1) Estimated retirement age _____
(2) Present age _____
(3) Years to retirement _____

(4) Estimated monthly income needed during retirement (at today's prices) _____

(5) Less estimated monthly social security benefits (at today's prices) _____

(6) equals _____

(7) Less estimated monthly benefits from pension plans (at today's prices) _____

(8) equals _____

(9) Inflation factor _____

(10) Annual extra income required _____

Years	4 Percent Factor	6 Percent Factor	8 Percent Factor
1	1.04	1.06	1.08
2	1.08	1.12	1.17
3	1.12	1.19	1.26
4	1.17	1.26	1.36
5	1.22	1.34	1.47
6	1.27	1.42	1.59
7	1.32	1.50	1.71
8	1.37	1.59	1.71
9	1.42	1.69	2.00
10	1.48	1.79	2.15
11	1.54	1.90	2.33
12	1.60	2.01	2.52
13	1.67	2.13	2.72
14	1.73	2.26	2.94
15	1.80	2.40	3.17
16	1.87	2.54	3.43
17	1.95	2.69	3.70
18	2.03	2.85	4.00

Years	4 Percent Factor	6 Percent Factor	8 Percent Factor
19	2.11	3.03	4.32
20	2.19	3.21	4.66
21	2.28	3.40	5.03
22	2.37	3.60	5.44
23	2.46	3.82	5.87
24	2.56	4.05	6.34
25	2.67	4.29	6.84
26	2.77	4.55	7.40
27	2.88	4.82	7.99
28	3.00	5.11	8.62
29	3.12	5.42	9.31
30	3.24	5.74	10.06
31	3.37	6.09	10.87
32	3.51	6.45	11.74
33	3.65	6.84	12.68
34	3.80	7.25	13.69
35	3.95	7.68	14.79
36	4.10	8.15	15.97
37	4.27	8.64	17.25
38	4.44	9.15	18.63
39	4.62	9.70	20.11
40	4.80	10.29	21.72
41	4.99	10.90	23.46
42	5.19	11.56	25.34
43	5.40	12.25	27.37
44	5.62	13.76	29.56
45	5.84	13.76	31.92

(11) Capital needed (divide amount in step 10 by 0.08) _____

(12) Current liquid capital _____
(13) Accumulated liquid capital _____

(14) Capital that must be developed _____

expenses may decline, other costs may increase. Medical costs, for example, often are higher for older people.

Estimating OASDHI retirement benefits (for Step 5) is not as difficult as it first seems. For many people, the proper amount is the maximum retirement benefit for a husband and wife. Even if a person is not presently entitled to maximum benefits, he or she may become eligible for maximum benefits during his or her working life. (Retirement benefits under OASDHI are discussed later in this chapter.) Step 6 is the difference between Steps 4 and 5. It represents the estimated amount of monthly income, in addition to social security benefits that will be needed during retirement.

Step 7 is an attempt to recognize pension benefits. For a person near retirement, these benefits may be easily determined. For younger people, pension benefits may be extremely difficult to estimate. The appropriate figure would assume that the person will continue to participate in the pension plan until retirement, but benefits should be estimated at current prices. Suppose, for example, that a person, forty years of age, has been in a company pension plan for five years and expects to retire at age sixty-five. The proper figure for Step 7, therefore, is the amount currently being received by employees retiring with thirty years of participation in the plan.[1] Of course this figure will be an approximation, at best, because pension benefits may be increased or decreased relative to inflation.

The amount to be placed at Step 8 represents the monthly income needed at today's prices above the amount to be provided by OASDHI and a pension plan. In some cases, government and company retirement programs may provide the entire expected necessary income. Often, however, additional income is required.

Up until this point, only current prices have been considered; that is, there have been no adjustments for inflation. In years past (and even today to a large extent) financial advisors have ignored the impact of inflation. This, of course, is equivalent to assuming that prices will not rise in the future. The failure to recognize inflation has caused many individuals to reach retirement age with inadequate financial resources. Modern financial planning, therefore, requires the estimation of future rates of inflation. For Step 9, therefore, the proper procedure is to estimate the average annual rate of inflation that is likely over the individual's productive period. Suppose, for example, that an individual has twenty-five years until anticipated retirement and believes that inflation will average 6 percent during that period. If so, the monthly net income in Step 8 should be multiplied by 4.29 to adjust for inflation. This type of adjustment means that prices will be 4.29 times greater in twenty-five years if inflation continues at 6 percent per year.

The amount at Step 9 must be multiplied by twelve to determine the *annual* income needed (above OASDHI and pension benefits), and this amount should be used for Step 10.[2]

How much total capital must be accumulated to provide the annual income required at Step 10? Conceptually, there are only three basic methods used to convert a principal sum into a series of income payments. First, a person can decide to receive current income only (interest, dividends, or both) from the amount invested; the principal is not liquidated. Suppose an individual has determined a need for an annual income of $10,000 and wishes to retire using only interest earnings. If a 6 percent interest rate is assumed, the amount needed is $10,000 ÷ 0.06, or $166,666. The interest rate, 6 percent in this example, should be the rate that can be earned safely over the retirement period. Obviously this approach is suitable only when a person wants to preserve the principal amount, even after death (as an inheritance for others).

The second approach to converting a principal sum into a series of income payments is to liquidate the principal over time. This approach provides income from interest and principal, but a person cannot know how long he or she will live and how much principal can be safely withdrawn each year. Thus, with this approach there is a distinct possibility of outliving the income.

A life annuity is the third approach that may be used to convert a principal sum into a series of income payments. This approach will be described in detail later in this chapter. For purposes of estimating the amount needed for Step 11, annuity rates are needed. If a life insurer will provide an annual income of, say, 9 percent of the principal, this rate should be used to capitalize the amount at Step 10.

The amount at Step 11 is the principal sum needed to provide the desired income. Many people, however, have some investments that will appreciate and can be used toward providing the principal sum. Even if the assets are likely to be sold prior to retirement, they should be included at Step 12 if the proceeds from the sale would be reinvested and accumulated for retirement needs. Common examples of assets that should be included are equity ownership in a home, investments in real estate, stocks, bonds, and ownership in a business firm. Savings accounts should not be included unless the account will be maintained and accumulated until retirement.

The amount at Step 12 should be multiplied by the assumed rate of appreciation over the appropriate period.

If, for example, current liquid capital is $20,000 and it is believed the assets will appreciate at an average rate of 8 percent for twenty-five years, $136,800 should be used at Step 13. (This is $20,000 times the interest factor of 6.84.) A conservative approach would be to increase presently invested assets at the same rate used in Step 9 (the average inflation rate). However, it is not necessary to assume that the investment results of a given portfolio will be the same as the general increase in prices.

The difference, if any, between the figures at Steps 12 and 13 is the amount of money that needs to be accumulated prior to retirement. In many cases, the size of the financial problem will be surprising.

Although the answers derived from using the form in Figure 11-1 vary widely among individuals, many young people are surprised to learn that it may require more than $1 million to achieve financial goals that seem rather modest. On the other hand, if a person is satisfied with the amount that can be provided by OASDHI and a company pension plan, there may be little need to accumulate additional funds.[3]

There are too many assumptions in the calculation to defend the accuracy of the final amount needed. If the final amount appears unreasonable, the process might be repeated using different assumptions, particularly as to the amount of retirement income needed and the retirement age.

Although not included in Figure 11-1, the analysis can (and should) be extended in some cases to determine the annual amount that must be set aside each year prior to retirement to achieve the stated goal. This can be done easily with an interest table that shows accumulations of $1 invested periodically, as shown in Table 11-2. Notice that this table is not a mere compound interest table. It shows how $1 invested *each year* will accumulate at various interest rates.

Suppose, for example, that a person age forty needs to accumulate $200,000 for retirement at age sixty. If an annual aftertax interest rate of 8 percent can be assumed, Table 11-2 shows that about $4,370 must be invested annually. (Because $200,000 ÷ 45.762 = $4,370, approximately.) This same person would have to invest about $5,436 each year if an aftertax investment return of 6 percent is assumed. ($200,000 ÷ 36.786 = $5,436.)

Major Problems in Retirement Planning

The great majority of people are not financially prepared for retirement. The median family income for family heads age sixty-five and over in 1973 was $6,426.[4] Obviously this was at or near the poverty level. The median value of the total assets for married men age sixty-two and sixty-three (not including equity in a home) was $6,068 in 1973.[5]

Why do so many people fail to provide themselves with adequate retirement income? Clearly there are many reasons. Sound financial planning at least recognizes some of these major problems.

Table 11-2
Amount of Annuity $[(1 + i)^n - 1]/i$

Periods n	Rate i 0.01 (1%)	0.02 (2%)	0.04 (4%)	0.06 (6%)	0.08 (8%)
1	1.0000 0000	1.0000 0000	1.0000 000	1.0000 000	1.0000 000
2	2.0100 0000	2.0200 0000	2.0400 000	2.0600 000	2.0800 000
3	3.0301 0000	3.0604 0000	3.1216 000	3.1836 000	3.2464 000
4	4.0604 0100	4.1216 0800	4.2464 640	4.3746 160	4.5061 120
5	5.1010 0501	5.2040 4016	5.4163 226	5.6370 930	5.8666 010
6	6.1520 1506	6.3081 2096	6.6329 755	6.9753 185	7.3359 290
7	7.2135 3521	7.4342 8338	7.8982 945	8.3938 376	8.9228 034
8	8.2856 7056	8.5829 6905	9.2142 263	9.8974 679	10.6366 276
9	9.3685 2727	9.7546 2843	10.5827 953	11.4913 160	12.4875 578
10	10.4622 1254	10.9497 2100	12.0061 071	13.1807 949	14.4865 625
11	11.5668 3467	12.1687 1542	13.4863 514	14.9716 426	16.6454 875
12	12.6825 0301	13.4120 8973	15.0258 055	16.8699 412	18.9771 265
13	13.8093 2804	14.6803 3152	16.6268 377	18.8821 377	21.4952 966
14	14.9474 2132	15.9739 3815	18.2919 112	21.0150 659	24.2149 203
15	16.0968 9554	17.2934 1692	20.0235 876	23.2759 699	27.1521 139
16	17.2578 6449	18.6392 8525	21.8245 311	25.6725 281	30.3242 830
17	18.4304 4314	20.0120 7096	23.6975 124	28.2128 798	33.7502 257
18	19.6147 4757	21.4123 1238	25.6454 129	30.9056 525	37.4502 437
19	20.8108 9504	22.8405 5863	27.6712 294	33.7599 917	41.4462 632
20	22.0190 0399	24.2973 6980	29.7780 786	36.7855 912	45.7619 643
21	23.2391 9403	25.7833 1719	31.9692 017	39.9927 267	50.4229 214
22	24.4715 8598	27.2989 8354	34.2479 698	43.3922 903	55.4567 552
23	25.7163 0183	28.8449 6321	36.6178 886	46.9958 277	60.8932 956
24	26.9734 6485	30.4218 6247	39.0826 041	50.8155 774	66.7647 592
25	28.2431 9950	32.0302 9972	41.6459 083	54.8645 120	73.1059 400
26	29.5256 3150	33.6709 0)72	44.3117 446	59.1563 827	79.9544 151
27	30.8208 8781	35.3443 2383	47.0842 144	63.7057 657	87.3507 684
28	32.1290 9669	37.0512 1031	49.9675 830	68.5281 116	95.3388 298
29	33.4503 8766	38.7922 3451	52.9662 863	73.6397 983	103.9659 362
30	34.7848 9153	40.5680 7921	56.0849 378	79.0581 862	113.2832 111
31	36.1327 4045	42.3794 4079	59.3283 353	84.8016 774	123.3458 680
32	37.4940 6785	44.2270 2961	62.7014 687	90.8897 780	134.2135 374
33	38.8690 0853	46.1115 7020	66.2095 274	97.3431 647	145.9506 204
34	40.2576 9862	48.0338 0160	69.8579 085	104.1837 546	158.6266 701

Continued on next page

35	41.6602 7560	49.9944 7763	73.6522 249	111.4347 799	172.3168 037
36	43.0768 7836	51.9943 6719	77.5983 138	119.1208 667	187.1021 480
37	44.5076 4714	54.0342 5453	81.7022 464	127.2681 187	203.0703 198
38	45.9527 2361	56.1149 3962	85.9703 363	135.9042 058	220.3159 454
39	47.4122 5085	58.2372 3841	90.4091 497	145.0584 581	238.9412 210
40	48.8863 7336	60.4019 8318	95.0255 157	154.7619 656	259.0565 187
41	50.3752 3709	62.6100 2284	99.8265 363	165.0476 836	280.7810 402
42	51.8789 8946	64.8622 2330	104.8195 978	175.9505 446	304.2435 234
43	53.3977 7936	67.1594 6777	110.0123 817	187.5075 772	329.5830 053
44	54.9317 5715	69.5026 5712	115.4128 770	199.7580 319	356.9496 457
45	56.4810 7472	71.8927 1027	121.0293 920	212.7435 138	386.5056 174
46	58.0458 8547	74.3305 6447	126.8705 677	226.5081 246	418.4260 668
47	59.6263 4432	76.8171 7576	132.9453 904	241.0986 121	452.9001.521
48	61.2226 0777	79.3535 1928	139.2632 060	256.5645 288	490.1321 643
49	62.8348 3385	81.9405 8966	145.8337 343	272.9584 006	530.3427 374
50	64.4631 8218	84.5794 0145	152.6670 837	290.3359 046	573.7701 564

Inadequate Planning It seems probable that most people plan rather poorly, if at all, for retirement. Many people underestimate the magnitude of the problem. In many cases, a person does not become concerned about the problem until middle age or later. In these cases, often it is too late to accumulate sufficient assets to provide a meaningful income. Young people have the great advantage of having a long time to accumulate assets, but they often have lower incomes and high expenses. Furthermore, in many cases retirement is too far into the future for young people to give it a high priority.

Limited Employment Opportunities After Retirement Some people undoubtedly anticipate some type of employment after retirement from their normal occupation. The possible problems they face are formidable: age limitations on hiring new employees, poor health, out-of-date skills, and low earnings. As a result, less than one-third of the income for retired people comes from current employment.[6]

Longer Retirement Period There has been a pronounced trend for the retirement period to increase relative to the period of active employment. In other words, there is a tendency for people to work for shorter periods of time and to remain retired for longer periods. The primary reasons for shorter working lives are compulsory retirement, early retirement, and longer periods of formal education before employment is started. The main reasons is for longer retirement periods are the increase in life expectancy, and again, early retirement. As people have less time to prepare for retirement and a longer retirement period, the financial problem increases dramatically.

Inflation   Rising prices are particularly injurious for retired people who often have fixed incomes. Spiraling costs of medical care and property taxes have been especially onerous. (Investment problems caused by inflation are treated in Chapter 13.)

TECHNIQUES FOR MEETING THE EXPOSURE

Social Insurance

For many people, the OASDHI program is the most important method of dealing with the retirement problem. Sound financial planning, therefore, requires careful consideration of OASDHI retirement benefits.

Requirements for Retirement Benefits   To be entitled to retirement benefits, a person must achieve fully insured status. This status may be obtained in either of two ways: (1) receiving credit for forty quarters of coverage, or (2) receiving one quarter of coverage for each year after 1950 (or after age twenty-one, if later) up to age sixty-two. At least six quarters of coverage are required under the second criterion. If a person is credited with forty quarters of coverage, he or she is fully insured permanently. Thus, a person might work ten years in a covered employment at a young age and be entitled to retirement benefits even if no OASDHI credits were earned thereafter. Of course, the benefit so earned would be relatively modest.

In the near future many individuals will reach retirement age and achieve fully insured status with fewer than forty quarters of coverage. For persons born after 1929, forty quarters of coverage will be required.

Types of Benefits   Three basic types of retirement benefits are provided by OASDHI. The *retired worker's benefit* is most important because other benefits are not payable unless either the husband or wife qualifies for this benefit.

The spouse of a retired worker also receives a monthly retirement benefit. The full monthly benefit becomes payable when the spouse reaches age sixty-five, or as early as age sixty-two if the spouse elects a reduced benefit. This benefit is not based on the spouse's employment record. However, a spouse who has worked in covered employment may be entitled to a benefit on his or her own OASDHI account. In this case, the spouse would receive the larger of the two benefits.

A wife who has in her care a dependent child (entitled to a child's benefit, except a child receiving benefits solely because he or she is a student aged eighteen to twenty-one) also receives a monthly benefit. If the wife is under sixty-two when the child becomes ineligible for the child's benefit, her benefit temporarily ceases. She again becomes eligible for the full benefit at age sixty-five or for a reduced benefit at age sixty-two. A divorced wife of a retired worker is eligible for benefits at age sixty-two or after, provided the marriage lasted at least ten years.

Another retirement benefit is payable if the retired worker has *dependent unmarried children* under age eighteen (age twenty-two if the child is attending school). The same benefit is payable if the child is older but disabled. If the child is being supported by a grandparent, a benefit will be payable based on the grandparent's earnings.

Benefit Amounts Upon retirement at age sixty-five the retired worker's monthly income benefit is 100 percent of his or her primary insurance amount (P.I.A.). All the other retirement benefits (for wives, dependent husbands, children, and wives with children under age eighteen) are 50 percent of the retired worker's P.I.A. All these benefits may be reduced or terminated by several factors.

While there is no limit to the number of family members who may be eligible for benefits, there is a limit on the total amount of monthly benefits payable to a single family. The formula that determines the maximum family benefit is rather complex. It is weighted in favor of low-income families and is adjusted automatically for price increases. As a general rule, the maximum family benefit is between one and one-half and one and three-quarters of the P.I.A. Whenever the combined benefits payable to a single family would exceed the maximum family benefit, all benefits (except the retired worker's benefit) are reduced proportionately until the combined benefits are within the limit.

Benefits are reduced permanently if a worker retires prior to age sixty-five. A worker may retire as early as age sixty-two, but the retirement benefit will be reduced five-ninths of 1 percent for each month between the age at retirement and age sixty-five. Therefore, the benefit at age sixty-two is 80 percent of the full P.I.A.; the reduction applies for the duration of the benefit, not just until age sixty-five.

A person who retires early receives a lower monthly benefit, but of course benefits will be payable for a longer time period. All other things being equal, total benefits will be greater for a person who retires at age sixty-five (rather than sixty-two) if he or she lives past age seventy-seven. For a person in relatively poor health, the early retirement option is often attractive. Another factor that might be important is the type and amount of other benefits the family might receive. When a worker retires early, the reduced benefit he or she receives will cause dependent benefits to be less.

A worker is not forced to retire at age sixty-five since mandatory retirement before age seventy is no longer permitted. In fact, late retirement is an option that some people should consider. Even if a person is fully insured and has received maximum wage credits, he or she usually can increase the monthly retirement benefit by working past age sixty-five. This is possible for two reasons: (1) higher wage credits may be earned after age sixty-five and (2) benefits will be increased by one-fourth of 1 percent of the P.I.A. for each month after age sixty-five and up to age seventy-two that benefits are deferred. (The fraction is only one-twelfth of 1 percent for those attaining age sixty-two before 1979). At a maximum, the benefit to a retired worker can be increased 21 percent solely because of delayed retirement, not considering the possibility of higher earnings after age sixty-five. In many cases, this is not advantageous because postponing retirement reduces the period over which benefits will be paid.

In some situations, frequently because of the need for funds, a person may continue to work after age sixty-five. This practice might very well involve a problem with the so-called "retirement test." A person's retirement benefits are not reduced for any amount of earnings after age seventy-two. Prior to age seventy-two the retirement test allows an individual to earn up to a given amount without affecting the dependent's benefits. Earnings above the stipulated amount, however, may cause benefits to be reduced or terminated.

The amount of earnings allowed without affecting benefits is subject to automatic adjustments for inflation. To illustrate how the retirement test works, however, figures for 1977 will be used. In that year, a beneficiary aged sixty-five or over, but under age seventy-two, could earn $4,000 without losing any benefits. For younger beneficiaries, the amount is $3,240. Benefits are reduced $1 for every $2 of earnings are in excess of $4,000, but no benefits are lost for any month during the initial year of benefits in which the worker earns less than one-twelfth of the $4,000 amount and rendered no substantial services in self-employment.

The retirement test applies only to earnings from current employment. Income from investments, savings, insurance, pensions, or royalties is not taken into account.

Projecting Retirement Benefits   One of the important problems in financial planning is the estimation of the amount of retirement benefits that will be provided by OASDHI. This process is relatively simple for a person at or near retirement, but is much more difficult for younger workers.

For a person entering retirement, any district office of the Social Security Administration should be helpful in determining benefits. In addition, there are many published sources showing the amount of benefits available to current retirees.

For individuals who will not retire soon, the problem of estimating benefits is complex, mainly because future earnings are unknown and because benefits are automatically adjusted when prices increase. Any worker can verify his or her OASDHI earnings record by using a "Request for Statement of Earnings" form number OAR-7004, available from most social security offices.

One method of estimating future retirement benefits is to assume constant rates of increase for both prices and the OASDHI wage base. Table 11-3 shows projections made under this assumption.

Table 11-3 shows that projected retirement benefits may vary within a wide range, depending upon the assumptions used. The table shows, for example, that benefits might range between $816 and $1,639 per month under the extreme assumptions. The selection of assumptions, therefore, should be undertaken with care.

A second method of estimating the importance of OASDHI retirement benefits is to determine the amount that would be payable if a person retired immediately with maximum benefits. This approach is not as crude as it may first seem. Many people will become eligible for maximum benefits before retirement, even if they are not presently eligible for the highest benefits. And assuming that benefits keep pace with inflation, the current benefit may be taken as equivalent to the higher benefit that results from inflation. As an example, consider the case of a thirty-year-old person who has worked in covered employment for only six years. Assume the maximum benefit for a retired worker is presently $400. Although the worker is not now eligible for maximum benefits, it is probably reasonable to assume that he or she will be eligible before retirement. And $400 should be equivalent to future benefits if prices and benefits move higher at the same rates. While this approach is admittedly inexact, it may produce reasonable results with less effort than other methods. However, if present social security benefits are used in estimating retirement income needs, then the living expense, pension benefits, and other elements of the plan also should be expressed in present dollars. That is, they should not be adjusted for inflation.

Individual Annuities

One method of dealing with the retirement exposure is to purchase an annuity from an insurance company. These contracts may be purchased individually or through a group. In this section we are concerned only with individual annuities, purchased on an individual basis. Many of the concepts, however, will be applicable when pension plans are analyzed.

In the past, individual annuities have not been a particularly important method of providing retirement income. However, these contracts are gaining in popularity. More important, a sound understanding of annuities is essential for working with or understanding pension plans.

The Annuity Principle   Annuities are sometimes described as "life insurance in reverse." The primary purpose of life insurance is to accumulate an estate for the use of survivors. The insurance technique requires a large number of individuals to contribute to the plan so that losses can be paid when they occur. In life insurance, the insurer pays, or begins to pay, upon the death of the insured. Annuities are a true form of insurance because they use the insurance technique, in that a large number of individuals contribute to the plan to pay benefits (losses) when the insured event occurs. The insured event under an annuity is the survival of the insured person until a specified date or, more precisely, a series of specified dates. This is the opposite of life insurance, in which the insured event is the death of the insured person. Unlike life insurance, annuities are designed principally to liquidate, rather than accumulate, a principal sum. And annuity payments are made only while the annuitant is alive. Under a pure annuity, benefit payments stop when the annuitant dies.

The annuity principle can be illustrated by a simple example. Suppose a large number of individuals of the same age and sex each deposit the same amount of money with an insurer to purchase an annuity. Each person individually cannot know how long he or she might live. But an insurance company can use the law of large numbers to liquidate the total fund based on the expected mortality experience of the group. Furthermore, the insurer can earn interest on the funds until they are needed for benefit payments.

This type of scientific liquidation of principal is called the annuity principle, and has several significant effects. First, the annuity income can be guaranteed for life. In other words, a person cannot outlive the annuity benefits. Some people in the plan may die soon after purchasing the annuity; others, however, may live much longer than predicted by average life expectancy. Those who live longer than expected benefit at the expense of those who die early. This is the nature of sharing losses through the insurance technique.

Another significant effect of the annuity principle is that the benefit will be larger than the amount that could be provided by interest income alone. Suppose a person could earn 7 percent in a savings account and an insurance company also could earn 7 percent on invested funds. If the

Table 11-3

Estimated Effects of Automatic Adjustments to Maximum Primary Insurance Amounts Effective January 1, 1976 *

Age 65 During Calendar Year	Maximum Monthly PIA Without Automatic Adjustments	Maximum Monthly PIA With 2 percent CPI Assumptions and Wage Base Change of:			Maximum Monthly PIA With 3 percent CPI Assumptions and Wage Base Change of:			Maximum Monthly PIA With 4 percent CPI Assumptions and Wage Base Change of:			Age 65 During Calendar Year
		0%	4%	5%	0%	4%	5%	0%	4%	5%	
1976	$364.00	$ 364	$ 364	$ 364	$ 364	$ 364	$ 364	$ 364	$ 364	$ 364	1976
1977	387.80	396	396	396	400	400	400	403	403	403	1977
1978	406.30	422	423	423	430	431	431	438	439	440	1978
1979	415.00	439	442	442	452	455	456	456	468	469	1979
1980	422.20	457	461	462	475	479	481	493	498	499	1980
1981	428.70	473	479	481	496	503	505	521	528	530	1981
1982	433.50	488	498	500	517	528	530	548	559	562	1982
1983	439.50	504	517	520	539	553	557	577	592	596	1983
1984	443.10	519	536	541	561	580	585	606	626	632	1984
1985	447.80	534	556	563	583	607	614	636	663	670	1985
1986	451.50	550	577	585	606	637	645	667	701	711	1986
1987	455.10	565	599	608	629	667	677	700	741	753	1987
1988	458.60	581	621	631	653	698	710	733	783	797	1988
1989	461.00	596	642	655	677	729	744	767	827	843	1989
1990	464.70	612	665	680	702	762	780	803	873	893	1990
1991	467.00	628	688	706	727	797	818	840	921	945	1991
1992	469.40	644	713	732	753	833	856	879	973	999	1992
1993	471.80	660	738	760	779	871	897	918	1,026	1,057	1993
1994	474.30	677	763	788	806	909	939	960	1,082	1,118	1994
1995	480.20	699	796	825	841	958	993	1,011	1,151	1,192	1995

Year											Year
1996	486.00	722	831	865	877	1,009	1,050	1,064	1,224	1,272	1996
1997	491.40	744	867	906	913	1,063	1,109	1,119	1,301	1,356	1997
1998	496.80	767	905	949	951	1,119	1,172	1,176	1,382	1,444	1998
1999	502.20	791	944	994	990	1,178	1,238	1,237	1,467	1,538	1999
2000	507.60	816	985	1,042	1,031	1,240	1,308	1,300	1,557	1,639	2000
2001	513.00	841	1,028	1,092	1,073	1,304	1,382	1,366	1,652	1,744	2001
2002	517.40	865	1,072	1,144	1,115	1,371	1,458	1,434	1,705	1,855	2002
2003	521.70	890	1,117	1,198	1,159	1,440	1,538	1,504	1,853	1,972	2003
2004	525.80	914	1,163	1,254	1,201	1,511	1,622	1,575	1,960	2,095	2004
2005	528.80	939	1,211	1,313	1,246	1,586	1,710	1,649	2,073	2,225	2005
2006	532.80	964	1,262	1,375	1,292	1,665	1,803	1,727	2,193	2,362	2006
2007	536.80	990	1,315	1,441	1,340	1,747	1,902	1,808	2,318	2,508	2007
2008	539.80	1,016	1,369	1,509	1,388	1,832	2,005	1,891	2,449	2,662	2008
2009	541.80	1,040	1,425	1,579	1,435	1,920	2,112	1,974	2,585	2,823	2009
2010	542.80	1,063	1,481	1,652	1,481	2,010	2,223	2,057	2,727	2,992	2010
2011	542.80	1,085	1,539	1,728	1,527	2,104	2,340	2,142	2,875	3,169	2011
2012	542.80	1,107	1,600	1,807	1,573	2,202	2,462	2,227	3,031	3,357	2012
2013	542.80	1,129	1,662	1,890	1,620	2,304	2,590	2,317	3,194	3,555	2013
2014	542.80	1,152	1,727	1,978	1,669	2,410	2,726	2,409	3,365	3,763	2014
2015	542.80	1,175	1,795	2,069	1,719	2,521	2,868	2,506	3,545	3,984	2015

*Whenever there is a benefit adjustment for CPI changes, the monthly benefit should be increased to the next higher multiple of $.10; this was not done in these projections. Figures are for male workers and assume maximum Social Security wages for all years since 1950. Primary Insurance Amounts for females are the same as for males beginning with above calendar year of 1978, and slightly higher for prior years.

person spends $100,000 on an annuity, the annuity income will be greater than $7,000 per year. At age sixty-five a male can receive an annuity benefit of about $11,000 each year—even if the company has assumed an investment return of only 7 percent. The annuity benefit, however, is larger because it is composed of two elements: (1) interest, and (2) the partial liquidation of principal.

Table 11-4 shows the single premium payments for nonparticipating annuities available from one large life insurer. The rates in the table show two important facts: (1) annuity rates are higher for females (reflecting their longer life expectancy), and (2) annuity rates become less expensive with increasing age. This second point results from the fact that benefits will be paid for a shorter period if the annuity is purchased at an advanced age. However, there is another important, but subtle consideration. When an annuity is purchased at a young age the company can liquidate only a small portion of the principal in each benefit payment. Thus, annuity benefits at young ages will be only slightly higher than the rate of interest assumed by the insurer. Furthermore, since insurance companies tend to be conservative in their guaranteed rates, a young person might actually earn more under alternative safe investments. At the advanced ages, the insurer will be able to liquidate a larger portion of the principal in each payment and consequently, benefit payments can be substantially larger than interest earnings alone. Annuities, therefore, cannot be regarded as a suitable investment for young people if they plan to start receiving benefits before reaching an advanced age.

Types of Annuities   There are five major categories of annuities. Annuities may be classified by the (1) method of paying premiums, (2) time when benefits begin, (3) refund features, (4) number of lives covered, and (5) benefit units (i.e., fixed versus variable).

Method of Paying Premiums.   Annuities may be purchased with either a single premium or periodic (installment) premiums. The simplest arrangement is to purchase the contract at retirement with a single, lump-sum premium. Few individuals purchase annuities in this manner. However, the same result is achieved frequently when life insurance cash values or death proceeds are placed under a settlement option which is in fact an annuity. This option usually is called the "life income option" rather than an annuity, and the option is normally available at net rates. That is, there is no loading for expenses. Life insurance policies, therefore, may provide an attractive method of purchasing an annuity.

Installment premium annuities are purchased over time—usually with either annual or monthly premiums. Although many insurers use special names for their annuity contracts, the generic name for an installment premium annuity is simply the "retirement annuity." In

Table 11-4

Illustrative Annuity Rates
(Monthly Income for each $1,000)

Age of Payee	Male[†]	Female[†]
35	5.26	5.12
40	5.43	5.23
45	5.68	5.40
50	6.10	5.70
55	6.64	6.12
60	7.37	6.69
65	8.40	7.52
70	9.76	8.62
75	11.75	10.26
80	14.52	12.65

[†]For a pure annuity, i.e. one without a refund feature.

essence, these are simply plans to accumulate savings prior to retirement. Such a contract is illustrated in Figure 11-2. This figure shows only the accumulation period of the annuity, that is, the period during which premium payments are being made. The period of time when benefits are paid to the policyowner is known as the liquidation period.

Figure 11-2 is based on the assumed goal of accumulating enough funds to provide $400 each month starting at age sixty-five using the rates in Table 11-4 ($8.40).

A retirement annuity is an extremely flexible contract since, prior to maturity, the plan is basically nothing more than a method of accumulating money with an insurance company. If the annuitant wishes to discontinue premium payments, he or she may withdraw the cash value (which equals the premiums plus interest minus an expense charge) or simply elect a paid-up annuity for a smaller amount. If the entire cash value is taken, the contract is terminated. Some companies allow the policyowner to borrow against the contract. In the event of the annuitant's death prior to maturity (and with no outstanding loans) the company will pay the larger of the cash value or total premiums paid on the contract.

In most companies and contracts there is considerable flexibility in selecting the date when benefit payments commence. Thus, if a person elects early or postponed retirement, benefits can be made to coincide with the time when funds are needed.

Figure 11-2
Illustration of a Retirement Annuity

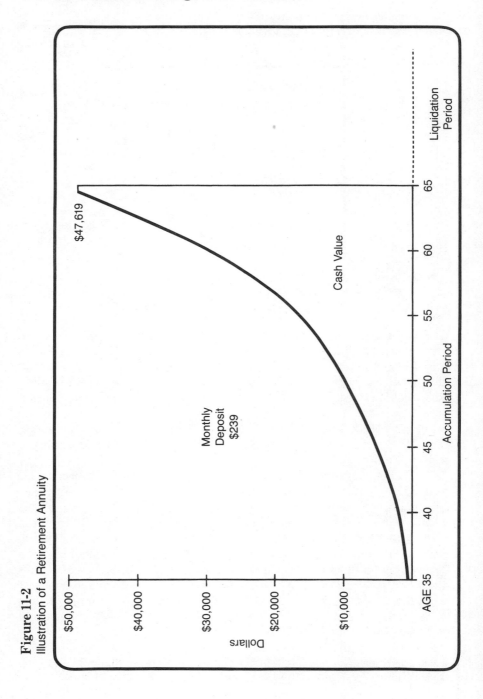

Another element of flexibility in a retirement annuity is the right to change the annuity form. This means that the refund guarantees (discussed later) may be changed. This is an important option, as will be seen, because it has a major impact on the amount of benefits that will be provided and the period of time over which they will be paid.

Almost all companies have restrictions against allowing an annuity owner to convert annuity benefits into cash. In other words, after an annuity is in the liquidation period, a person normally cannot take a lump-sum cash payment for future benefits, particularly those that are not guaranteed. If annuitants could "cash out" annuity benefits, those who are in poor health would be eager to withdraw cash, leaving the insurance company with a group that will live longer than expected. Restrictions on withdrawing cash after benefits have begun to apply to all types of annuity contracts, not only the retirement annuity.

If the retirement annuity is participating, the policyowner usually has a choice of the method of receiving dividends. The usual options are cash, application against future premiums, or accumulation with interest.

Time When Benefits Begin. Annuities can be immediate or deferred. An immediate annuity has no accumulation period. When a person buys an immediate annuity, benefits begin to accrue immediately. Actual benefit payments start one payment interval later. For example, if a person buys an immediate annuity that pays monthly benefits, the first benefit will be paid one month after the annuity is purchased.

An immediate annuity must be purchased with a single premium. An insurer will not start to pay benefits until an annuity is fully purchased.

Deferred annuities are those in which there is a period of time (greater than one payment interval) between the start of premium payments and the start of benefits. In other words, deferred annuities have an accumulation period, usually lasting for a number of years. The retirement annuity is a deferred annuity.

Refund Features. If an annuitant dies during the accumulation period, his or her beneficiaries will receive the greater of the accumulated cash value or the total premiums paid. Death during the liquidation period creates a more complex situation. Consider the case in which a person pays a sizable amount for an annuity and dies after only a few benefit payments. The annuitant may have received only a small fraction of the purchase price.

In a pure annuity, usually called a "straight life" annuity, all obligations of the insurance company cease when the annuitant dies. The entire premium is considered earned at the death of the annuitant.

Apparently many people dislike the possibility of losing all, or a large portion of their investment if death should occur in the incipient stages of the liquidation phase. The beneficiaries in such a case are likely to feel "cheated." The problem, however, is misunderstanding the nature of a straight life annuity. This type of contract provides no refund in the event of the annuitant's death, because the funds released by those who die soon are used to continue benefits to those who live longer.

Because a straight life annuity provides no refunds, it produces the greatest amount of income (benefit payments) for each dollar of purchase price. Thus, it should be preferred in cases where there are no heirs to receive a refund and perhaps when maximum benefit payments are crucial.

If the absence of a refund feature is unappealing, several types of refund annuities are available. One common type of refund annuity is a life annuity period certain contract. This plan promises benefits for the life of the annuitant or a guaranteed period, whichever is longer. The most common period certain or guaranteed period is 120 months, but other periods are available. To illustrate a life annuity with ten years (120 months) certain, consider the case of a man whose benefits under such a contract started at age sixty-five. If he should die at any time prior to age seventy-five, benefit payments would be continued to beneficiaries for the remainder of the ten-year period. If the annuitant dies at age sixty-eight, benefits would be continued for seven years. If the annuitant lives past age seventy-five, benefits under the annuity would be paid until his death.

If benefits are continued in installments for a minimum guaranteed period, the contract is known as an "installment refund" annuity. A cash refund annuity, on the other hand, pays to beneficiaries the difference between the purchase price and the total benefit payments received—if this difference is greater than zero. The main distinction between an installment refund annuity and a cash refund annuity is the method of paying the refund. In the former, benefits are continued until the full purchase price has been received. In the latter case, the refund is paid in cash in one lump sum.

A cash refund annuity is more expensive than an installment refund annuity because the insurance company cannot benefit from interest earnings if the refund is paid immediately in cash. If benefits are continued in installments, the insurance company has use of the money until the proceeds are exhausted.

At first thought, a cash refund annuity may seem puzzling. How can an insurance company afford to pay benefits to all annuitants as long as they are alive, and provide full, immediate cash refunds to the beneficiaries of those who die early? The annuity is possible because the

Table 11-5

Amount of Monthly Income per $1,000 Accumulated Under Different Kinds of Annuities (Male—Selected Ages)

†Age of Payee	No Refund	5 Yr. Certain	10 Yr. Certain	15 Yr. Certain	20 Yr. Certain	Installment Refund
35	$ 5.26	$ 5.25	$5.24	$5.22	$5.20	$5.22
40	5.43	5.42	5.40	5.37	5.33	5.37
45	5.68	5.67	5.63	5.57	5.50	5.57
50	6.10	6.07	6.00	5.90	5.79	5.92
55	6.64	6.59	6.47	6.30	6.11	6.37
60	7.37	7.28	7.07	6.77	6.44	6.96
65	8.40	8.23	7.82	7.29	6.76	7.74
70	9.76	9.40	8.60	7.69	6.92	8.66
75	11.75	10.94	9.38	7.99	7.01	9.87

† When monthly income (annuity) payments commence.

insurance company charges an additional premium for the refund feature, over and above the premium for a pure annuity. The refund feature is, in effect, decreasing term life insurance superimposed on a pure annuity.

The selection of the appropriate type of refund is important because it has a significant impact on the cost of an annuity. Stated differently, the benefit payments vary inversely with the strength of the guarantee. Table 11-5 shows this clearly.

Notice that Table 11-5 indicates that the cost of the refund feature accelerates with age. This results from the lower probability of death, and the resulting smaller chance that the refund feature will come into play at the young ages. At the advanced ages, however, the refund feature is likely to provide greater benefits.

An individual can select the most appropriate refund feature only by knowing the cost of the various annuities, his or her financial condition, and the desirability of leaving money to others. A person, for example, with no heirs and a strong need to receive maximum benefits might choose a straight life annuity. If, on the other hand, the provision of benefits to heirs is important, some type of refund annuity may be appropriate.

Two notes of caution should be recognized in selecting an annuity. First, if a person has a strong desire to leave funds to dependents, and is, therefore, inclined toward an annuity with a strong refund feature, life insurance protection should be considered carefully. As a general rule, it is a mistake to purchase an annuity unless the annuitant has a reasonable amount of life insurance. In recognition of this problem, many insurance companies allow (either contractually or optionally) an annuitant to convert an annuity into a life insurance policy. The annuitant must provide evidence of insurability at the time of the conversion, but the terms and rates of the life insurance policy will be those included in the policy when the annuity was originally purchased. Still, the conversion privilege does not solve the problem presented when a person dies owning an annuity but little or no life insurance.

A second consideration is that an annuity is almost always a poor purchase for a person in ill health. While physical examinations may be required for life insurance, they are never required for annuities. The greatest benefit from an annuity is derived by a long-lived person; the person who benefits least from an annuity is one who dies soon after buying it. It is wise, therefore, for a prospective annuitant to have a complete physical examination before buying an annuity.

Number of Lives Covered. Most annuities are based on only one life. Some annuities, however, cover two lives (usually a husband and wife), and a large number of lives may be covered by annuities in a pension plan.

Joint life annuities covering two persons provide an income as long as both annuitants are alive. Benefit payments stop when either annuitant dies. Such a plan is appropriate only when two people have an income from another source that is adequate for one person, but not for both.

The market for joint annuities is very limited and these contracts are not popular. It is important, however, to recognize the distinction between joint life annuities and more popular annuities that also cover more than one life.

A joint-and-last-survivor annuity agrees to pay an income as long as either of the two annuitants is alive. Since the insurance company is assuming the obligation of paying benefits for a longer period of time than under a single life annuity, joint-and-last-survivor annuities are more expensive than most other annuities. Still, the contract is appealing to many couples who need an income as long as either is alive. The cost can be kept reasonably low by two features. First, most joint-and-last-survivor annuities do not include any refund feature. Usually a refund feature is not needed because benefit payments will continue for the surviving annuitant. Second, many joint-and-last-survivor annuities provide a reduction in income when one of the annuitants dies. A popular plan is known as the joint-and-two-thirds annuity. With this contract, benefits are reduced by one-third when the first annuitant dies. The surviving annuitant continues to receive two-thirds of the previous benefit for life. The cost can be decreased even further (or larger benefits can be provided) if the survivor receives only one-half of the joint benefit.

A joint-and-last-survivor form is frequently made available as a life insurance settlement option. They also are used widely in pension plans.

Benefit Units (Fixed Versus Variable). Most annuities agree to pay fixed dollar benefits. For example, a person may buy an annuity with a monthly benefit of $300 per month. If prices rise, and therefore the purchasing power of the benefits decreases, there can be a serious erosion of values. A benefit of $300 each month might have been a valuable supplement to other sources of retirement income when the annuity was purchased, but with inflation, $300 per month may lose much of its purchasing power.

The variable annuity was developed as a method of protecting the purchasing power of annuitants. The basic mechanism for achieving this goal is to provide benefits that are expressed in units, rather than dollars. In a variable annuity, when an annuitant enters the liquidation period, he or she is guaranteed to receive the value of a stipulated number of units. The value of the units may change, but the number of units does not. If the value of the units increases, the dollar benefits increase—perhaps enough to offset inflation or even to increase purchasing power.

An annuity may have one or more characteristics from each type of annuity described above. For example, a given annuity may be purchased with installment premiums, have deferred benefits, and cover two lives. Another may be bought with a single premium, provide immediate benefits, and cover only one life. In either example, benefits may be fixed or variable.

Major Characteristics of Variable Annuities. There are some differences among the variable annuities issued by different insurers. However, all of those issued in this country share some important characteristics. Among these characteristics are: (1) equity funding and valuation, (2) dollar cost averaging, (3) diversification, and (4) the annuity principle.

EQUITY FUNDING. According to the variable annuity concept, the real income of annuitants can be maintained (or even improved) during periods of inflation if the value of the underlying portfolio of common stocks increases. In other words, in a variable annuity plan, the premiums paid by policyholders are invested in common stocks. Of course, stock prices do not always increase during periods of inflation, as shown in Figure 11-3.

Over the long run common stock prices have provided an effective hedge against inflation. In recent years, they have not done so. Consequently many people currently believe that variable annuities are

Figure 11-3

Consumer Prices and Stock Prices—1900–1974*

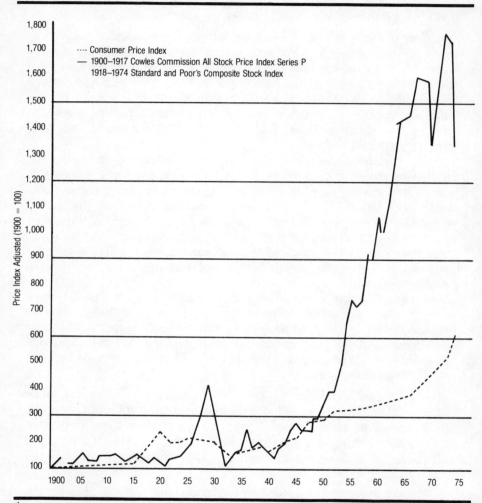

* Reprinted with permission from Glenn L. Wood, J. Finley Lee, and Margaret A. Kelley, "Retirement Income Planning," The Variable Annuity Approach" (Bryn Mawr, PA: The American College of Life Underwriters, 1975), p. 4.

not as effective against inflation as was once thought. Others, however, feel this trend is short-lived, and that stock prices will in the future parallel inflation.

Although variable annuities can be purchased with a single premium to provide immediate benefits, the variable annuity approach is best illustrated by deferred, installment premium contracts. In these plans, when an annuitant makes a deposit (premium), he or she is credited with a certain number of accumulation units. As an example, suppose a person pays $106 to the insurer and $6 is deducted immediately for expenses. The net premium invested on behalf of the annuitant, therefore, is $100. Suppose the current value of an accumulation unit at the time of the net deposit is $10. If so, the annuitant would be credited with ten units (i.e., $100 ÷ $10). When the next $100 *net* deposit is made, suppose the accumulation units are valued at $12. In this case, the annuitant would be credited with 8.333 new units (i.e., $100 ÷ $12). This would mean the annuitant would then have a total of 18.333 (accumulated from both premiums). If the value of the unit falls at the time the next $100 net deposit is made, say to $8, the annuitant would receive 12.5 new units (i.e., $100 ÷ $8) and would then have a total of 30.833 units.

Accumulation units are revalued frequently (often twice a day). The revaluation can be illustrated by the following simple formula:

$$V = v \left(1 + d + i + c\right)$$

where V = value of an accumulation unit, v = previous value of an accumulation unit, d = rate of dividends received, i = rate of interest received, and c = rate of realized and unrealized capital gains (or losses).

Following the given example, suppose the previous value of an accumulation unit was $8, the variable annuity plan has total assets of $10 million, dividends amount to $128,000, interest income is zero, and capital appreciation amounts to $800,000. The accumulation unit would be revalued as follows:

$$V = v \left(1 + d + i + c\right)$$

$$= \$8 \left(1 + 0.0128 + 0 + 0.08\right)$$

$$= \$8 \left(1.0928\right)$$

$$= \$8.7424$$

Notice that the valuation formula recognizes both realized and unrealized capital gains and losses. Some plans use slightly different formulas. Investment expenses, for example, may be treated differently. Another common variation is to account for dividends at less frequent intervals.

When an annuitant begins to receive benefits (enters the liquidation period), the accumulation units are exchanged for *annuity* units. As the name implies, accumulation units accumulate prior to retirement. When the accumulation units are converted into annuity units, the number of annuity units remains fixed for the lifetime of the annuitant. As the

Table 11-6

Illustration of Dollar Cost Averaging

Month	1	2	3	4
Stock Price	$10	8	13	6
Number of Shares Purchased	10	12.5	7.70	16.67

Average stock price = $10 + $8 + $13 + $6 ÷ 4 = $9.25
Average price paid = amount invested, or $400, divided by total number of shares acquired (46.87) = $8.53

value of the units changes, the dollar amount of the monthly benefit would also change.

DOLLAR COST AVERAGING. Another important characteristic of most variable annuities is the dollar cost averaging concept which involves the investment of equal amounts at regular intervals. When this is done, the average cost of securities will be lower than the average of stock prices prevailing during the period.

As a simplified example, suppose an investor (or variable annuity owner) invests $100 (net) each month and stock prices are as shown in Table 11-6.

In the Table 11-6 example, the average cost of the securities is $8.53 while the average stock price during the period is $9.25. This results because more shares are purchased when stock prices are lower and fewer shares are purchased when stock prices increase.

Dollar cost averaging is no panacea for investors. Still, it is beneficial to variable annuity owners. If contributions to the fund are made over a long period of time, the accumulated amount is not unduly affected by common stock prices that exist at any point in time. The dollar cost averaging concept usually is stated in terms of *purchasing* securities, but the concept applies also to the liquidation of annuity benefits.

DIVERSIFICATION. Individuals who invest directly in common stocks often cannot obtain a high degree of diversification. A variable annuity owner, however, achieves the practical result of sharing in a portfolio of common stocks. A variable annuity owner does not *legally* own the securities in the plan. Legal ownership is held by the plan itself. Often, a variable annuity plan will own thirty, forty, or more individual common stocks. Adverse experience of a few stocks, therefore, is likely to be offset by the superior performance of other stocks.

Advantages and Disadvantages of Variable Annuities. The pros and cons of variable annuities have been debated frequently in the 1960s and 1970s. Many of the controversial points are now interesting only from an historical point of view and will not concern us. However, in advising individuals about the merits or problems of variable annuities, several points should be considered.

As a long-range investment for the purpose of accumulating a retirement income, variable annuities provide a unique combination of advantages. A variable annuity offers an equity investment, dollar cost averaging, diversification, and the annuity principle. Variable annuity owners cannot outlive their annuity incomes, and the gradual liquidation of principal makes larger benefits possible. These are major advantages over many investment alternatives, especially because they are available in a single form of investment.

There are, however, a few drawbacks. Some people have negative psychological reactions to variable annuities. One of these reactions concerns the correlation of stock prices and consumer prices. In periods of high inflation when the stock market is not performing well, variable annuities are more difficult to sell. In the 1960s many variable annuities were purchased (both individual and group, i.e., pension plans) but a large number of people voiced dissatisfaction when many stock prices declined in the early 1970s.

A person who purchases a variable annuity should realize that annuity benefits will not be perfectly correlated with consumer prices. In fact, based on historical evidence, there may be times when stock prices do not keep pace with inflation for several years. It is impossible to know whether variable annuity benefits will maintain an individual's purchasing power in the future or even over the long term. However, it is clear that variable annuities should be regarded as a *long-range* method of dealing with the retirement problem. They should not be judged on the basis of results over a period of only a few years.

There are other reasons why variable annuities should be regarded only as long-range investments. One reason is the federal income tax treatment. Consider an individual variable annuity that does not qualify for the favorable income tax treatment afforded a qualified pension plan. (Qualified pension plans are treated later in this chapter.) The owner of this plan incurs no federal income tax liability during the accumulation period, even if the value of the accumulation units is appreciating rapidly. It would be a mistake, however, to conclude that taxes are not paid during the accumulation period. A life insurer is required to pay taxes (at capital gains rates) on all realized capital gains on funds invested on behalf of nonqualified variable annuity owners. Moreover, in about one-half of the states, premium taxes are paid by an insurance company on premiums received for such plans. Naturally, these taxes must be paid indirectly by variable annuity owners.

After retirement, variable annuity benefits are taxed in essentially the same manner as conventional annuities. Basically, the intent of the tax law is to tax the appreciation (the investment gain) but not the portion of the annuity benefit representing return of capital. The taxation is on a level basis, over the entire period of the benefits.[7] This means that variable annuity owners are in effect taxed twice: once indirectly through the company, and again when benefits are received.

If a nonqualified variable annuity is surrendered for cash prior to retirement, the investment gain (if any) is taxed as ordinary income in the year received. This can present a major income tax problem.

Pension Plans

Basically, a pension plan is nothing more than the application of the group technique to the retirement exposure. The group technique allows administrative economies to be achieved and produces several other advantages for both employers and employees.

From an employer's point of view, a pension plan may (1) enable a company to attract and retain employees (because many of them expect pension benefits), (2) allow a company to meet union demands, and (3) encourage greater employee productivity. From an employee's point of view, a pension plan may be a convenient, efficient, tax-advantageous method of accumulating funds for retirement.

Because of these reasons, pension plans have had dramatic growth since World War II. Approximately 44 percent of all employed persons are now covered by pension plans.

Pension plans can be classified according to several important characteristics. For our purposes, it is helpful to distinguish between: (1) formal and informal plans, (2) funded and unfunded plans, (3) insured and uninsured plans, and (4) qualified and nonqualified plans.

A *formal* pension plan is one that includes specific rules to define the important features of the plan. The established rules provide a basis for employees to plan for pension benefits. An *informal* pension plan is basically no plan at all. It operates at the discretion of the employer, and as a result, often cannot be used by employees to plan for future benefits. In an informal arrangement, an employer provides benefits to selected employees and the benefits are individually determined.

Data are not available to indicate the importance of informal plans. They may be quite numerous, but their relative significance in terms of dollar amounts is undoubtedly small.

In a *funded* pension plan, the employer sets aside funds in advance of the time when benefits will be paid. An *unfunded* plan is basically a pay-as-you-go system. Money is not set aside in advance of actual payment of benefits.

Most informal plans are not funded. Most formal plans are funded, but a significant number of formal plans are unfunded. Some funded plans are also less than fully funded. A pension plan may be funded with an insurance company (an *insured* plan) or with a trustee (an *uninsured* plan). Some plans are funded in both ways, and are known as *split funded* plans. In a funded, uninsured plan, the employer establishes a trust fund for employees, and actuarial assumptions are used as the basis for contributions to the plan. The trustee is responsible for investing the funds and distributing benefits. In a trusteed (uninsured) plan the investment results, mortality experience, and administrative expenses generally are not averaged with other pension plans. The actuarial assumptions (for mortality, disability, turnover, salary, retirement ages, and so on) used in an uninsured plan usually are developed by an actuarial firm, and the employer has considerable flexibility in determining the degree of conservatism in the estimates.

In a *fully insured* plan, the actuarial assumptions are guaranteed by the insurance company. One reason this is possible is that the insurance company generally pools the investment, mortality, and expense results of such plans with others the company insures. The insurance company normally handles much (or all) of the administrative responsibilities.

The characteristics of uninsured plans usually make this approach inappropriate for small plans. Insured plans may be appropriate for large or small groups. However, in terms of assets and number of workers covered, uninsured plans are about twice as important as insured plans. A *qualified plan* meets the requirements established by the Internal Revenue Service for favorable income tax treatment. Most employers are unwilling to forgo the tax benefits, and therefore, qualified plans are much more popular. In some cases, however, an employer wishes to have greater flexibility than allowed for qualified plans, and nonqualified plans are used.

Qualification Requirements The federal income tax advantages of qualified plans are important. Basically, the major advantages are as follows:

1. Contributions to the plan by the employer (within limits) are deductible as a business expense.
2. Investment earnings generally are not subject to federal income taxation until benefits are paid.
3. Employees are not considered to have taxable income for federal income tax purposes until benefits are received.

4. Distributions from the plan may receive favorable income tax treatment.
5. Death benefits paid in installments are not included in an employee's estate for federal estate tax purposes (to the extent they are financed by employer contributions).

In order to qualify for this favorable tax treatment, a pension plan must meet a number of requirements. The most important of these requirements are discussed below.

1. The plan must be for the exclusive benefit of employees and their beneficiaries, and cannot discriminate in favor of officers, stockholders, or highly paid employees. To qualify, a plan must meet *either* of two requirements—often called the 70 percent rule and the discretionary rule. The 70 percent rule requires that at least 70 percent of all employees be covered, or, if the plan requires contributions from employees and if at least 70 percent of all employees are eligible, that at least 80 percent of those eligible participate in the plan. Thus, a contributory plan might qualify if as few as 56 percent of all employees participate (assuming 70 percent are eligible and 80 percent elect coverage, i.e., 80 percent x 70 percent = 56 percent).

   The discretionary rule allows an employer to set up some other coverage system, as long as it does not discriminate in favor of the prohibited group—officers, stockholders, and highly paid employees. The coverage rules must be approved by the Internal Revenue Service.

   It is possible to qualify a plan that covers salaried personnel only, as opposed to hourly workers. However, the Internal Revenue Service is likely to object to such a plan if all, or virtually all, of the salaried employees earn more than hourly workers. This arrangement would discriminate in favor of the more highly paid employees.

2. A qualified plan cannot discriminate in favor of officers, stockholders, or highly compensated employees in contributions or benefits. In interpreting this requirement, the Internal Revenue Service will consider all aspects of contributions and benefits.

   A plan can be qualified even if it excludes persons whose earnings are less than the OASDHI wage base or if it provides larger benefits to those who earn more than the taxable wage base. In either case, however, the plan benefits must be properly integrated with OASDHI benefits. Many benefit formulas, in fact, are integrated with social security benefits. Benefits from a private pension plan must be dovetailed, i.e., integrated, with

OASDHI benefits such that the total benefits received from both sources (the pension plan and OASDHI) are not proportionately greater for highly paid employees than for those who earn less. In other words, OASDHI benefits discriminate against higher paid employees, so pension plan benefits are allowed to pay higher benefits for highly paid employees, as long as the combined benefits are not proportionately greater.

3. A qualified plan must be in writing and must be communicated to employees.

4. Contributions to the plan cannot be diverted for other purposes. An employer generally cannot receive any funds from the plan unless all the liabilities of the plan have been met.

5. The plan must provide definitely determinable benefits. A plan is considered to have satisfied this requirement even if benefits cannot be known, as long as the employer's contribution is specified. Variable annuity plans must also meet this requirement.

   Because of this requirement, the forfeitures of terminating employees cannot be used to provide larger benefits for other employees in the plan. They must be used to reduce future employer contributions.

6. The plan must be intended to be permanent. Most employers reserve the right to terminate or modify the plan at any time and the Internal Revenue Service permits a plan to be terminated for reasons of "business necessity" without involving tax problems. However, if a plan is terminated within a few years after adoption, the Internal Revenue Service is likely to rule that the plan was not intended to be permanent. This would lead to unfavorable tax consequences.

7. A qualified plan must provide full vesting for employees at the normal retirement age and when a plan is terminated. In addition, the plan must fulfill one of the vesting requirements of the Employee Retirement Income Security Act of 1974 (ERISA). Vesting requirements (and ERISA) are covered later in this chapter.

8. A substantial amount of death benefits cannot be included. The Internal Revenue Service permits life insurance in a plan, but the death benefits must be incidental. Death benefits in pension plans are treated later in this chapter.

9. A large number of requirements for qualification are embodied in ERISA. It is inappropriate even to summarize these requirements here, but some of them will be treated later in this chapter.

Qualification requirements, especially since the enactment of ERISA, are extremely detailed and complex. Therefore, it is customary (although not legally required) for an employer to submit a plan to the Internal Revenue Service in advance to determine whether or not the plan will achieve qualified status. The Internal Revenue Service, in such cases, issues an advance determination letter. Retroactive changes in a plan are permitted if the changes are made before the due date of the employer's federal income tax return.

Basic Features of Pension Plans The detailed provisions of pension plans vary considerably. However, most plans incorporate certain basic features. Qualified plans are required to include specified features in order to comply with the Internal Revenue Code, the regulations of the Internal Revenue Service, the Employee Retirement Income Security Act and other state and federal laws and regulations. The paragraphs that follow will discuss some of the important features.

Eligibility Requirements. Within the limits permitted for qualified plans by the Internal Revenue Service, employers generally establish eligibility requirements to determine who may participate in the plan. Often certain employees are excluded, either on a temporary or permanent basis, in order to reduce pension costs. Eligibility requirements may be influenced by the employer's overall pension objectives and by union pressures.

YEARS OF SERVICE AND MINIMUM AGE. The most common eligibility requirements are based on years of service, minimum age, or both. ERISA prohibits eligibility requirements that set the minimum age above twenty-five or service requirements longer than one year. Generally, an employee must be given credit for one year of service if he or she works at least 1,000 hours in a twelve-month period.

MAXIMUM AGE. The cost of providing benefits to employees who become eligible for the plan at an advanced age may be extremely high. If the plan provides defined benefits, a specified benefit will be established for each employee; contributions will be calculated so as to be sufficient to provide the stated benefit. A critical factor in the determination of contributions is the length of time between initial participation and retirement. For individuals retiring shortly after initiation into the pension plan, contributions must be sizable. In a defined contribution plan, the pension plan has no obligation to provide benefits of any stated amount. Contributions are made for each employee according to a method stated in the pension plan. The benefits to be received are dependent upon the investment performance of the plan. The size of the contribution does not necessarily vary directly with the length of time between initial participation and retirement. Consequently, ERISA will not allow any employees to be excluded from a plan by means of a maximum age requirement. In defined contribution plans, employees who become eligible at advanced ages may not accumulate a sizable pension benefit, but they cannot be excluded. Normal retirement ages under age sixty-five are uncommon because the cost is often prohibitive. According to ERISA regulations, the normal retirement cannot be later than age sixty-five, except for employees who have participated in the plan for less than ten years.

Most plans contain provisions for early retirement. Usually, the employee need not obtain the employer's consent but must meet certain requirements in order to retire before the normal retirement age. Frequently, for example, early retirement is permitted only if an employee is disabled (after a certain age) or has reached a specified age (such as age fifty-five) and has participated in the pension plan for a minimum period of time (often ten years).

Employees who retire early usually receive reduced benefits. There is a shorter period of time for benefits to accrue and the benefits must be paid over a longer period. The reduction factor that is applied to determine the early retirement benefit depends primarily upon the employee's age and sex, the amount of accrued benefits, and the type of annuity to be received. The reduction is often 10 to 15 percent if the employee retires at age sixty-three, but retirement at age sixty may cause benefits to be reduced as much as 35 or 40 percent.

Retirement Benefits. In planning retirement benefits, it is customary to assume that retirement income (from OASDHI and a pension plan) should be equal to 50 or 60 percent of an employee's average earnings prior to retirement. The goal may be relatively lower for highly paid employees, perhaps 45 to 50 percent of previous earnings; for lower paid employees the desired percentage may be 65 to 70 percent.

There are two basic types of benefit formulas. In one type, known as a defined contribution or money-purchase plan, the contribution is fixed and the benefit is the amount that can be provided by the contributions. In these plans, the cost to the employer is known, but benefits can only be estimated. The more popular type of benefit formula is referred to as a defined benefit or annuity purchase plan. These plans specify the benefits, and contributions are computed as the amount required to generate the specified benefits.

Under either type of formula it is important to define employees' earnings precisely. This is not always easy. In most plans, bonuses and other types of unusual compensation are normally not considered. Commissions pose a special problem because they often fluctuate considerably. If employees receive a salary plus a commission, some plans recognize only the basic salary for benefit purposes. In other plans

Table 11-7

Illustration of a Defined Contribution Pension Formula

Age at Entry	Normal Retirement Age	Sex	Compensation[†]
25	65	M	$12,000
30	65	M	14,000
35	65	F	15,000
35	65	M	15,000
45	65	M	8,000
55	65	M	20,000

Total Contribution	Fund At Retirement	Monthly Benefit
$1440	$173,952	$1,359
1680	111,552	871
1800	119,590	845
1800	119,590	935
960	31,743	247
2400	30,187	235

[†]This table assumes that (1) employee contribution is 8 percent of compensation and employer contribution is 4 percent of compensation, and (2) contributions accumulate at 5 percent.

commissions may be averaged over several years. When commissions represent a large portion of an employee's income, a defined contribution may be much preferable to a defined benefit formula.

DEFINED CONTRIBUTION FORMULAS. Many defined contribution plans are contributory. The employer's contribution is often set at the same rate as that paid by employees, but it may be larger or smaller. Table 11-7 shows an example of a defined contribution formula.

Several aspects of Table 11-7 are worth noting. A defined contribution formula generally produces a wide variation in benefits among employees. Those who participate in the plan for long periods tend to generate much larger benefits. However, employees who enter the plan at an advanced age may not have enough time to accumulate adequate pension benefits.

The most common criticism of defined contribution plans is that actual retirement benefits cannot be predetermined. Of course, projections can be made, but there are too many uncertainties involved to make them reliable for an individual employee. Notice that the projected benefits in Table 11-7 are predicted on the assumption that the earnings of an individual will not change. Normally, an employee's compensation will increase, contributions will be larger, and resulting benefits will be greater. On the other hand, inflation is likely to destroy much (or all) of the increased benefits, so the net result is indeterminate. A person's real income (adjusted for inflation) may or may not increase beyond the benefits projected in Table 11-7.

DEFINED BENEFIT FORMULAS.   There are four basic types of defined benefit formulas, but sometimes a plan will provide benefits based on a combination of these approaches. The basic formulas are (1) flat amount, (2) flat percentage of earnings, (3) flat amount for each year of service, and (4) fixed percentage of earnings for each year of service.

A flat amount formula provides the same dollar benefit to all employees—regardless of age, earnings, or length of service. All retired employees, for example, might be paid $150 per month.

It is common for flat amount formulas to include a service requirement. To achieve the full benefit an employee may be required to participate in the plan for a stated number of years. If this requirement applies, employees with fewer years of service normally receive reduced benefits. Thus, in effect, even a flat amount formula might indirectly recognize years of service.

Flat amount formulas are not common, but they are used in some union plans. More often, a flat amount formula is used in conjunction with another formula.

A flat percentage of earnings formula is used in many pension plans. Usually this approach is designed to provide 20 to 40 percent of an employee's earnings. The percentage may apply to an employee's average earnings while participating in the plan (called "career average" earnings) or it may apply to average earnings over the last few years prior to retirement (called "final average" plans). Final average earnings may be computed in a variety of ways. For example, earnings may be based on the last five years before retirement, or they may be computed by using the five consecutive years of highest earnings in the ten-year period prior to retirement. Of course the purpose of any type of final average plan is to relate benefits more closely to the cost of living. Career earnings formulas are likely to provide inadequate benefits during a period of sustained inflation.

Most flat percentage of earnings formulas are not based precisely on an employee's earnings. Instead, many plans use earnings brackets to determine benefits. For example, if the plan calls for 40 percent of earnings, the benefits shown in Table 11-8 might be provided.

Again, a flat percentage of earnings formula does not consider an

Table 11-8

Benefits Based on Earnings

Monthly Earnings	Monthly Retirement Benefit
$ 800— 879	$336
880— 959	368
960—1,039	400
1,040—1,119	432

employee's length of service, except indirectly. If the service requirement for full benefits is long and benefits are reduced for less service, the effect is to recognize years of service.

A flat amount for each year of service provides a benefit of a stated amount, such as $10 or $12 per month, multiplied by the number of years of service. With a benefit of $10 per month and twenty-five years of service, the monthly retirement benefit would be $250.

These plans specify a minimum number of hours that must be worked in a twelve-month period to receive full credit for a year's service. It is common to require 1,600 to 1,800 hours to meet the requirement. According to ERISA, proportionate credit must be granted to an employee who worked at least 1,000 hours in the twelve-month period.

Generally, credit is given to employees for service prior to adoption of the pension plan. This is known as past service credit. While the objective is to treat all employees fairly, granting credit for past service causes a number of problems—not the least of which is a funding difficulty.

A formula that determines benefits as a percentage of earnings for each year of service is also called a unit credit or past and future service approach. In its simplest form, the retirement benefit is equal to a fixed percentage of earnings multiplied by the number of years of credited service. For example, if a plan provides for a 1 percent benefit, an employee who has twenty-eight years of credited service and average monthly earnings of $1,000 would receive a monthly retirement benefit of $280 (0.01 × $1,000 × 28). In practice, the computation may be complicated somewhat by credit for past service.

When the percentage of earnings for each year of service formula is used with a plan using career earnings, it is common to distinguish between past and future service. Future service is defined as service after the effective date of the plan. Usually past service credit earns a lower percentage benefit than future service. The earnings level during the past service period is usually taken as the earnings of the employee at the time the plan was adopted. This makes it unnecessary to verify an employee's earnings before the effective date of the plan. In other words, past service credit is simply based on earnings when the plan is implemented. This figure is, in all probability, higher than the employee's average earnings during the past service period. Thus the reduction in the formula is mitigated by the use of an unrealistically high earnings figure.

A simple example will clarify these rules. Suppose a plan provided a benefit of one-half of 1 percent for each year of past service and 1 percent for future service. An employee with credit for ten years of past service and twenty-five years of future service had monthly earnings of $800 when the plan was implemented, and career average earnings of $1,500. The monthly retirement benefit would be computed as follows:

Past service 10 years × $800 × 0.005   = $ 40
Future service 25 years × $1,500 × 0.01   = 375
Total Benefit   = $415

The number of years of past service credited to an employee does not always equal the total number of years he or she has worked prior to adoption of the plan. First, it is common to deduct the time required to become eligible for participation. If, for example, the plan requires one year of service for eligibility, one year would be subtracted from the employee's total past service. Also, as a cost control measure, it is usual to place a limit on the number of years of past service credit that can be granted.

Withdrawal Benefits. If a fully vested employee terminates employment, he or she must receive at least the value in the fund that is attributable to his or her contributions; however, the employee does not necessarily receive the total value of his or her contributions. Investment losses, which are not rare, may cause the value of an employee's contributions to decrease. In these cases, the employee is entitled only to the decreased value that is attributable to his or her contributions.

The vesting rules for contributions made by an employer have been made more complex by ERISA. ERISA requires the vesting of employer contributions to be at least as favorable to employees as one of the following rules:

1. One hundred percent vesting after ten years of service.
2. Twenty-five percent vesting at the end of five years of service, increasing 5 percent each year for the next five years, and 10 percent each year for the next ten years. This produces 50

percent vesting after ten years and 100 percent vesting after fifteen years.

3. Fifty percent vesting for employees who have five years or more of service when age and service total forty-five, increasing by 10 percent each year for the next five years. However, all employees, regardless of age, must be 50 percent vested after ten years of service, increasing by 10 percent each year for the next five years.

ERISA is very specific about the accrual of vested benefits. The law specifies (1) the minimum number of hours per year an employee must work to receive credit for a year's service (generally 1,000 hours), (2) what constitutes an hour of service, and (3) periods that may be disregarded.

The rate at which vested benefits accrue is also subject to the requirements of ERISA. Benefits must meet one of the following tests:

1. The employee's accrued benefit must be at least 3 percent per year of the final, projected normal retirement benefit.
2. The employee's accrued benefit may be the benefit earned to date; however, the accrual rate for any subsequent year cannot be more than 133 percent of the rate for the current year (except for amendments to the plan's benefits).
3. The accrued benefit must be a pro rata portion of the employee's projected normal retirement benefit.

Vested benefits to terminating employees may be paid in several forms. Even if a plan provides full, immediate vesting of employer contributions, the employer is not necessarily required to pay cash to a terminating employee. In some plans the employee is entitled to an immediate cash payment, but in other plans, payment is deferred until the normal retirement age. When the benefit is deferred, a person may have a choice of receiving cash or some type of annuity.

Death Benefits. In virtually all pension plans, if a person dies prior to retirement, the beneficiaries of the deceased are entitled to a return of the employee's contributions, usually accrued at some rate of interest. In addition, ERISA requires that an employer must provide a "preretirement spouse death benefit." This is an optional benefit, effective only for those employees eligible for early retirement who elect the benefit and are willing to pay the premiums. It must be made available to all employees who have been married at least one year and are within ten years of the normal retirement age. The benefit must be available as a life income to the spouse and must amount to at least one-half of the actuarially reduced benefit the employee would receive if he or she selected early retirement with a joint and one-half survivorship annuity.

An employer is not required to provide a death benefit prior to retirement other than those mentioned above. Many employers, however, provide additional death benefits. This can be accomplished by individual life policies, a group life insurance plan, or by cash distributions from the pension plan itself. If a group life insurance plan is used, it is often issued directly to the employer. If this is done, the life insurance is not considered part of the pension plan for federal tax purposes, even if the two plans are closely related (e.g., death benefits might be based on pension benefits).

If preretirement death benefits are financed by the plan directly, the death benefits must be "incidental." This test is met in a defined benefit plan if the death benefit is not greater than 100 times the expected monthly pension benefit (or the reserve for the pension benefit if greater).

After retirement, death benefits depend primarily upon the type of annuity that is provided to the employee. According to ERISA, retirement benefits must be available as a joint and one-half survivorship annuity, provided the employee is married and has been married for at least one year. Of course, some employees will not have a spouse, and others elect a different form of annuity. Other available annuities include pure annuities (with no death benefits for beneficiaries), annuities with a ten-year guarantee, and modified cash refund annuities. Under a modified cash refund annuity the death benefit equals the total contributions made by the employee, with or without interest, less benefits received before death. In other words, a modified cash refund annuity guarantees that the retired worker or the beneficiaries will receive at least the amount that has been contributed by the employee.

Disability Benefits. Many employers provide disability benefits separate from any such benefits that might be included in a pension plan. These include wage continuation plans, health insurance plans, and in recent years, group long-term disability plans.

However, a large number of pension plans provide additional disability benefits. For example, full vesting of all contributions (employer and employee) might be provided to employees who become totally and permanently disabled. Another approach treats a total and permanent disability as an early retirement. With this approach, an employee usually must be beyond a certain age (age fifty, for example) and must have worked a minimum period of time to be eligible for disability benefits. Separate disability benefits may also be found in a pension plan. These benefits can be paid from disability riders attached to life insurance contracts (if the pension plan is funded with a life insurance product) or from assets in the pension plan itself.

Employee Contributions. In recent years most new pension plans have been noncontributory, i.e., financed entirely by employers. The major reasons for this trend might be summarized as follows:

1. There is a tax advantage associated with noncontributory plans. If employee contributions are required, an employee must contribute to the plan with aftertax dollars. Contributions to a qualified pension plan are deductible for income tax purposes by an employer.
2. A noncontributory plan requires less administration. Fewer records are needed, employees do not have to be asked to participate, and there are no problems arising from employees who retire without participating in the plan.
3. A noncontributory plan contributes to better employee morale.
4. There could be an estate tax advantage with noncontributory plans. In a contributory plan, that part of the death benefit attributable to employee contributions must be included in an employee's estate for purposes of the federal estate tax.

Contributory plans also have advantages to both employers and employees. Either larger benefits or a smaller contribution from the employer must result from implementation of employee contributions. Although some employees may appreciate a noncontributory plan, a contributory plan may have the benefit of constantly reminding employees that their company is helping to develop retirement benefits for them. Another advantage of contributory plans is the provision of benefits for employees who terminate employment. In a noncontributory plan withdrawing employees may receive little or no benefits depending upon their vesting status.

Types of Funding Instruments At the time a pension plan is implemented, a funding agency and a funding instrument must be selected. A funding agency is an organization (or individual) used to accumulate funds and administer the pension plan. Important funding agencies for pension plans include life insurance companies, banks and other financial institutions, and individual trustees.

The types of contracts used by funding agencies to provide pension benefits are known as funding instruments. The selection of the funding instrument often has important implications for the types of benefits, contribution rates, and the security of benefits promised in the plan.

Individual Policy Plans. There are more individual policy plans in existence than any other kind of pension plan. Since these plans are usually used to cover very small groups, the number of employees covered by such plans is relatively small. Because a trustee is commonly used, these plans are sometimes called individual policy pension trusts, or simply pension trusts. Unfortunately, the term pension trust can be misleading, because trustees are used by other funding instruments. The term "individual policy plans" may also be confusing because such plans are classified as pension plans. However, it is appropriate because individual policies are issued to a number of employees who work for the same employer.

In most individual policy plans, one or more separate insurance contracts are purchased for each employee and a trust arrangement is established. Usually, the trustee then applies for individual insurance or annuity contracts for those employees designated by the employer. Contributions are made to the trustee, who in turn pays the premiums on the contracts.

The trust agreement, as a legal document, should be drafted or reviewed by the employer's attorney or legal staff. As a practical matter, however, most life insurers provide sample trust agreements for guidance. In fact, many insurance companies have submitted prototype trusts to the Internal Revenue Service for approval, and if these forms are used, approval of a specific plan is much easier. In recent years some life insurers have developed plans that make a trust agreement or trustee unnecessary. In these cases, the insurance company itself handles the functions that otherwise would have been performed by a trustee.

An important consideration with individual policy plans is that the Internal Revenue Service will not permit the plan to provide life insurance benefits that are more than "incidental." Most whole life policies (by themselves) cannot be used to fund the pension benefits because the death benefits are too large in relation to the cash values the policy will develop. To satisfy the IRS requirement, a policy must generate relatively large cash values. Generally the only two types of policies that meet the requirement are the retirement annuity and a retirement income contract. However, the combination of a whole life policy and a separate trust fund may meet the requirement.

The retirement annuity has been described previously. A retirement income contract differs from a retirement annuity, in that it contains decreasing term insurance. This type of plan is illustrated in Figure 11-4.

Because a retirement income policy contains an insurance element, the cash values tend to build more slowly for given premium outlay as compared to a retirement annuity. The difference in cash values, however, may not be large. As a practical matter, there is often a more important distinction between a retirement annuity and a retirement income contract. The former requires no evidence of insurability, since

Figure 11-4

Illustration of a Retirement Income Contract

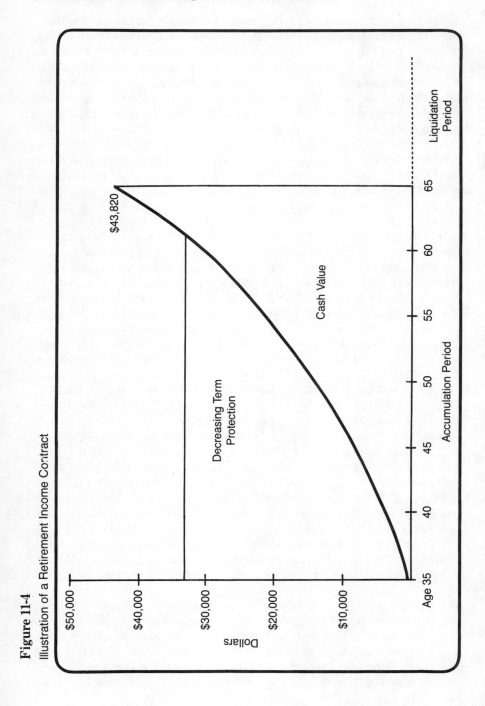

no life insurance is involved. A retirement income contract, however, includes pure insurance protection, and evidence of insurability may be required. However, some companies issue these contracts up to a specified amount without evidence of insurability. Also, some plans may be issued on a substandard basis, with a higher premium charge for persons who do not qualify under normal underwriting requirements.

In some companies, the retirement annuities and retirement income policies issued to participants in an individual policy pension plan are identical to those issued to persons who purchase individual contracts apart from a pension plan. Other insurers, however, have developed special contracts that may be more adaptable to a pension arrangement.

RETIREMENT BENEFITS. In a retirement income or retirement annuity contract, the size of the annuity payments often bears a simple relationship to the face amount of the policy. For example, a retirement income contract typically pays $10 each month as an annuity benefit (after age sixty-five) for each $1,000 of face amount. Suppose an employee is earning $1,200 per month and is entitled to a retirement benefit of 45 percent of earnings. The anticipated benefit, therefore, would be $540 per month (0.45 × $1,200). A retirement income policy in the amount of $54,000 would be sufficient to provide this income.

When an employee becomes entitled to a larger retirement benefit, an additional retirement income contract might be purchased to fund the increase in the benefit. Employees usually accumulate a number of policies in an individual policy plan. Evidence of insurability for a few additional retirement income contracts usually is not required. In the event that an employee becomes entitled to smaller benefits, the amount of the retirement income contracts held for that employee is reduced.

An individual policy pension plan is not equally well-suited to all types of benefit formulas. Defined contribution formulas are easily adapted to individual policy plans. Basic problems, however, are created in defined benefit plans if the retirement benefit cannnot be predicted with reasonable accuracy. Consider the situation in which benefits are based on final average earnings. It is impossible to know precisely the level of annuity benefits which should be purchased. While salary projections may be used, they are not reliable over long periods of time. The same type of problem exists, but to a slightly lesser degree, when benefits are based on career average earnings.

DEATH BENEFITS. Although retirement annuities do not have an insurance element, these contracts return the total premiums paid or the reserve under the contract, whichever is larger, if an employee dies before retirement. Typically, this amount is paid to the beneficiary of an employee as a death benefit.

When retirement income policies are used, the death benefit

payable to the beneficiary of the deceased employee usually is the greater of the face amount of the policy or the cash value. As illustrated in Figure 11-4, the cash value in a retirement income annuity exceeds the face value at some point in time, usually a few years before retirement.

DISABILITY BENEFITS.   The waiver of premium benefit for disabled employees is routinely added to policies in an individual policy plan. This benefit allows full pension benefits to accumulate even after an employee is totally and permanently disabled.

Disability income benefits usually are not included in individual policy plans. These benefits would often be desirable, especially if the employer does not have a group health insurance policy plan. Apparently disability income is not commonly provided because of cost and the underwriting consideration.

WITHDRAWAL BENEFITS.   The benefits paid to terminating employees depend upon the vesting provisions in the plan. When a terminating employee is entitled to all the cash values of the policies purchased on his or her behalf, ownership of the contract may be transferred to the employee, who can then either surrender it or maintain it by paying the required premiums.

If the cash values are only partially vested, the employee is usually allowed to choose either a paid-up life insurance policy or a paid-up deferred annuity. In some plans, the latter option is made mandatory.

When the cash value is greater than the amount to which a terminating employee is entitled, the difference is credited to the plan trustee. This amount, then, is used to reduce the employer's future contributions.

Combination Plans.   A combination plan is a plan that combines an insurance approach with an unallocated funding instrument. An unallocated funding instrument does not allocate funds to individual employees prior to retirement. The unallocated fund is called an auxiliary fund, side fund, or conversion fund.

A combination plan is used to obtain the advantages of both the individual policy plan and an unallocated fund. One of the major advantages of an individual policy plan is the guarantee available from an insurance company. Because insurance companies pool the experience of a large number of individuals, they can guarantee mortality, interest and expenses. As a result, an employer can be assured that the cost of the plan will not exceed the premiums required for the contracts. Another advantage is that it allows an employer to use the administrative experience and expertise of an insurance company.

The major advantage of an unallocated fund is its flexibility. An unallocated fund generally permits a wide latitude in benefit formulas, investment media, types of benefits, and contributions.

A combination plan always uses a trustee. The trustee normally owns the life insurance contracts and may administer the conversion fund. In many cases, however, the administration of the conversion fund is handled by a life insurance company.

The types of life insurance policies used in a combination plan are not as limited as in an individual policy plan. Basically, the type of contract selected depends upon the balance that is sought between the individual policies and the conversion fund. If benefits are to be paid primarily from the unallocated fund, life insurance policies that generate relatively low cash values (straight life contracts, for example) might be used. If life insurance cash values are the primary source of benefits, a policy that generates larger values (an endowment at age sixty-five, for example) could be used. If retirement annuities or retirement income contracts are purchased, a relatively smaller portion of retirement benefits will be provided by the conversion fund. Evidence of insurability may be required for policies containing larger elements of protection. Most insurers, however, do not require evidence of insurability for life insurance policies, up to a specified face amount, when used as part of a combination plan.

Almost any type of benefit formula may be used readily in a combination plan, including final pay formulas. If an employee's benefit is larger than the amount that can be financed by the life insurance policies, the deficiency is paid by the conversion fund. This is possible because money in the conversion fund is not allocated to specific individuals until retirement.

A plan may incur difficulty if withdrawals from the conversion fund are larger than anticipated. In this event, larger contributions to the conversion fund may be required.

One of the major advantages of a combination plan is that employer contributions to the conversion fund need not be constant. To be deductible, the contributions must be within limits established by the Internal Revenue Service. These limits, however, permit considerable flexibility. If an employer has large profits and adequate cash, relatively large contributions can be made to the pension plan. When financial experience is poor, an employer might make smaller contributions. This type of flexibility in contributions is not possible under an individual policy plan because predetermined premiums must be paid annually.

If contributions to the conversion fund are determined by the employer, there may be less assurance that the fund will be adequate to provide the promised benefits. This is true even when a life insurance company holds the assets in the conversion fund. However, if the conversion fund is placed with an insurance company, the company assumes responsibility for maintaining the fund intact and guarantees a minimum rate of investment earnings. If the fund is handled completely by an insurer, the annuity rates are guaranteed. This guarantee pertains not only to amounts taken from the conversion fund but also to funds accumulated in the life insurance policies.

If the conversion fund is to be managed by an insurance company, the employer may choose between a fixed dollar account or a variable dollar account. In a fixed dollar account, the fund is pooled with other investments and the plan receives a guaranteed return. A variable annuity account has no such guarantee. Often, however, variable annuity accounts yield higher returns.

There may be even greater investment flexibility if the conversion fund is not managed by an insurance company. This enhanced flexibility probably was more important in the past than it is now. According to ERISA, fiduciaries of the plan must use the care, skill, and prudence in investments that a prudent person would use under the same circumstances. In addition, a large number of more specific requirements for trust investments are contained in ERISA.

The death benefit in a combination plan normally is smaller than that of a fully insured plan. In most combination plans, only the face amount of the life insurance contract is paid if an employee dies before retirement. The death benefit can be made larger, however, if the employer is willing to allow withdrawals from the conversion fund to supplement the life insurance contract death benefits.

Disability benefits in combination plans are similar to those in individual policy plans. The waiver of premium benefit is common, while disability income is not often provided. Most combination plans allow employees who are permanently and totally disabled to withdraw their shares of the conversion fund. Verification of disability is made by a licensed physician, not by the insurance company.

An employee who withdraws from a combination plan (for reasons other than death, disability, or retirement) usually has a vested interest in the cash values of the life insurance contracts on his or her life. The withdrawing employee may or may not have a vested interest in the conversion fund. Again, however, the vesting provisions must at least meet the requirements of ERISA.

Group Permanent. The group permanent approach arose from one of the major problems in most group life insurance programs. Almost all group life insurance is one-year, renewable term insurance. This is an economical method of providing life insurance benefits, but term policies contain no cash values that can be used to fund a retirement income. A group permanent pension plan attempts to provide both life insurance and retirement income at the reduced cost resulting from use of the group insurance concept.

Theoretically, any life insurance policy generating a cash value at advanced ages might be used in a group permanent plan. In practice, most group permanent plans use retirement income contracts, although other policies are utilized. When retirement income contracts are used, the plan can provide substantial death benefits and use the cash values to provide monthly income during retirement. In essence, the accumulated cash value at retirement age is used to purchase an annuity.

The principal characteristic of a group permanent plan that distinguishes it from an individual policy plan is the advantage of group underwriting. That is, it is true group insurance and must qualify as such under state laws. When the number of covered employees is sufficient to qualify as a group plan, a group permanent plan might be preferable to an individual policy plan. Group underwriting produces economies in commissions and other expenses and does not require evidence of insurability from individual employees. Furthermore, a trust arrangement is not necessary.

The benefits in a group permanent plan are essentially the same as those in individual policy plans. Since both types of plans are allocated funding instruments and fully insured, guaranteed benefits are easily obtained. Funding problems, however, arise under defined benefit formulas if the retirement benefit is not known in advance.

In recent years, combination plans using a conversion fund with group permanent contracts have become more popular than pure group permanent plans. The advantages and limitations of this type of combination plan are the same as those described previously for individual policy plans.

Group Deferred Annuities. In its basic form, a group deferred annuity uses single premiums to purchase annually a fully paid-up annuity for each employee in the plan. The amount of annuity purchased each year depends upon the credit earned by the employee during the year. To illustrate, assume that a covered employee earns $15,000 and the formula calls for a 1 percent pension credit. A paid-up annuity will be purchased with a single premium to provide an income of $150 ($15,000 x 0.01) per year to begin at the normal retirement age. This, of course, is not a large annual income, but a deferred annuity will be purchased for the employee each year. Over time, the annuity benefit will increase. When the employee retires, the monthly benefit will be the sum of the benefits provided by all the annuities that have been purchased for that employee.

The very nature of a deferred annuity contract makes certain benefit formulas seem appropriate. Therefore, most group deferred annuity plans use a benefit formula that creates a unit of accrued benefit for each year of service. This means that the usual benefit formulas are those that provide either a percentage of career earnings or a flat dollar amount per year of service. Deferred annuity plans generally are not satisfactory for final pay plans.

Benefits earned for past service pose somewhat of a problem. If many employees receive past service benefits, it usually is impossible to purchase all the required annuities when the plan is adopted. In this situation, the common procedure is to purchase annuities for older employees first. This can be done as each employee reaches retirement, or the past service liability may be funded in advance by an unallocated instrument.

A group deferred annuity plan does not utilize contracts containing an insurance element. If an employee dies prior to retirement, the death benefit usually is a return of the employee's contributions, possibly with interest. Some employers provide larger death benefits, but the deferred annuity funding instrument does not inherently provide such benefits.

Disability benefits usually are not provided in a group deferred annuity program. Again, they can be added separately, but deferred annuities are not designed to accommodate disability benefits.

Benefits for withdrawing employees are determined by the plan provisions (and requirements of ERISA). The total amount of employee contributions usually may be taken in cash or as a paid-up deferred annuity. The amount of employer's contributions that has been vested usually is payable as a deferred annuity, with benefits beginning at the normal retirement age.

Group deferred annuities are appropriate whenever the employer wants the security provided by a fully insured plan, plans to cover a sufficiently large group to qualify under the group underwriting rules of an insurer, and is less interested in large death benefits for employees. It is worth noting that premium rates in a group deferred annuity are provided with strong guarantees. Typically, the master contract for the group plan contains a guaranteed rate that applies to annuities purchased in the first five years of the program. Moreover, after a paid-up annuity is purchased on behalf of an employee, the premiums and annuity values cannot be changed. Of course, these guarantees do not apply to deferred annuities yet to be purchased for an employee.

Group Deposit Administration Contracts. A deposit administration pension plan is an insured plan using an unallocated funding instrument. Funds are transferred from the unallocated fund to purchase an annuity for an employee only upon retirement.

The unallocated fund in a deposit administration plan is called by a number of names, such as the "active life" fund or annuity purchase fund. The unallocated fund may be commingled with the other assets of the insurance company; a minimum rate of interest is guaranteed. If interest in excess of the guaranteed minimum rate is earned by the insurer, a part of it may be credited to the plan's account as a dividend or experience credit. In most cases, not all of the excess interest is credited to the plan's account. Part of it is withheld as a contingency reserve to compensate the insurer for the obligation assumed under the minimum interest guarantee. An alternative is to use a separate account. The fund is segregated from the other funds of the insurer, and each separate account is invested independently. The flexibility available with separate accounts is a major reason for the rapid growth of deposit administration plans in recent years.

A separate account may be invested in fixed dollar assets, in equity investments, or in some combination of these. If a combination of fixed and variable dollar investments is desired, the employer can choose the proportions to be invested in each. As a general rule, an employer can transfer funds from the fixed account to the equity account or vice versa. Although there is considerable flexibility in transferring funds, most life insurers impose restrictions in order to minimize expenses and to prohibit a company from interfering excessively with the insurance company's investments.

Virtually any type of benefit formula is compatible with a deposit administration plan. Final-pay formulas cause no major problems. Early or late retirements can also be handled rather easily. This flexibility in choice of benefit formula is a direct result of the fact that deposit administration plans are unallocated funding instruments.

If separate account funds have been invested in equities, employees may be given the option of receiving a group variable annuity as the retirement benefit. In some plans, employees may be given the choice between fixed and variable investments, either before or after retirement, or both.

Death benefits prior to retirement usually are limited to the benefits attributable to an employee's contributions. If a separate account has been used, it is possible for investment losses to cause the death proceeds to be less than the employee paid into the plan. Larger death benefits can be provided in the plan provisions. In this event, death proceeds would simply be paid from the unallocated fund.

Annuity purchase rates are guaranteed, usually for contributions made during the first five years, for annuities purchased from a fixed dollar account. There is considerable variation among insurance companies with regard to the annuity rate guarantees for contracts purchased from an equity account.

If a deposit administration plan (or other unallocated funding instrument) is used, the unallocated fund is distributed among active employees if the plan is discontinued. This provision is required by the Internal Revenue Service. In a deposit administration plan, retired employees have highly secure benefits because annuities have been purchased for them. However, if the plan is discontinued, the funds may not be adequate to provide the promised benefits to active employees.

In the past, deposit administration plans were considered appropriate only for large cases. In recent years, however, many insurance companies have provided these plans for relatively small groups. It is not uncommon, for example, to require only thirty-five or forty individuals and a minimum annual deposit of only $10,000.

Group Immediate Participation Guarantee Contracts. These plans, generally referred to as I.P.G. contracts, actually are a form of deposit administration program. In the usual deposit administration arrangement, the insurer accumulates a contingency reserve and calculates dividend payments. In effect, the company retains funds to protect its guarantees of future interest earnings.

In a large pension plan, employers may object to the contingency charges provided in a deposit administration plan. With an I.P.G. plan, there is no interest guarantee, and therefore, no charge is made to build up a contingency reserve. Only actual benefits and expenses are charged to the unallocated fund, and no dividends are paid to employers. An I.P.G. plan, in other words, operates on a less conservative basis, but the status of the unallocated fund at any time should be an accurate measure of the amounts available for benefits and expenses.

Except for these major differences, I.P.G. plans are essentially the same as deposit administration contracts.

Trust Fund Plans. A trustee is generally required even in insured plans that are not issued on a group basis. A trusteed, or trust fund plan, however, is one in which a trustee is responsible for the investment of pension funds.

A trust agreement stipulates the responsibilities of the trustee. Generally, these include requirements the trustee must satisfy in the receipt, investment, and disbursement of funds. In most cases, the trust agreement is a separate document from the provisions of the pension plan itself. By keeping plan provisions separate from the trust agreement, changes in the provisions of the plan do not directly involve the trustee.

As a general rule, the record-keeping investment functions of the employer and the trustee are stated explicitly in the trust agreement. Normally, records for employee contributions, earnings, and credited service are handled by the employer, not the trustee. Trustees are held responsible for full accounting of investments and all transactions involving assets in the plan. In other words, employers usually perform the administrative record keeping, while trustees handle investment record keeping.

The investment powers granted to the trustee are set forth in the trust agreement. While the trustee may have considerable investment flexibility, ERISA contains a large number of requirements for the investment of funds in a trusteed plan.

Under the common law, a trustee is required to keep the assets in a trust segregated from other funds. This presents a major problem for small trust fund plans. If a fund is not large enough for adequate diversification, the adverse experience of one or two investments may cause sizable losses. In response to this problem, common trust funds have been developed. These plans allow trustees with statutory permission to commingle their assets with other trusts. Thus, a common trust fund permits a small trust fund to join with others to obtain the advantages of diversification and economies that result from the larger size.

As a trust fund is unallocated, any type of benefit formula may be used. Preretirement death benefits usually are provided in large trust fund plans, and many of these plans provide disability benefits. ERISA regulations concerning vesting apply equally to trust fund plans as to other plans.

Chapter Notes

1. Through Step 8, all figures are based on current prices. This means there is an important, but implicit, assumption that both OASDHI and pension benefits will keep pace with inflation. This is a simplification, but it seems reasonable as a planning technique.
2. Of course, a person's income is likely to increase over his or her working years—because of increases in productivity, promotions, and inflation. These increases in income, however, are not relevant to the problem at hand. We are concerned with estimating income needs after retirement. Increases in income prior to retirement should make it easier for a person to accumulate the amount needed (which is considered in Step 11).
3. For people in lower income brackets, even a modest pension plan, coupled with OASDHI, often replaces almost 100 percent of their preretirement, aftertax income. Many studies, however, have indicated that young people tend to have aspirations of higher incomes than they actually achieve. Figure 11-1 is a method of helping a person set goals.
4. U.S. Bureau of the Census, *Current Population Reports*, Series P-60, No. 93, "Money Income in 1973 of Families and Persons in the United States," (Washington, D.C.: U.S. Government Printing Office, July 1974), p. 9, Table 6.
5. Sally R. Sherman, "Assets on the Threshold of Retirement," *Social Security Bulletin*, Vol. 36, No. 8 (August 1973) p. 9.
6. Lenore Bixby, "Income of People Aged 65 and Older," *Social Security Bulletin*, Vol. 33, No. 4 (April 1970).
7. The taxation of annuity benefits is beyond the scope of this text, but is described in detail in many other publications. See, for example, "Tax Facts on Life Insurance" (published annually), National Underwriter Company, Cincinnati, Ohio.

CHAPTER 12

Retirement Income Planning (Continued)

INTRODUCTION

For some people, techniques other than pension plans and social security retirement benefits may be necessary to enable them to meet their financial needs during retirement. This chapter analyzes some of these other techniques; specifically, profit sharing plans, thrift and savings plans, retirement plans for the self-employed, individual retirement savings programs, tax deferred annuities, employee stock ownership plans, and deferred compensation arrangements. Subsequent chapters cover other topics which are closely related to retirement income planning, such as personal investments, business insurance, and estate planning.

PROFIT SHARING PLANS

Profit sharing plans have long been an important method of providing employee benefits. And in recent years, with more stringent ERISA requirements for many types of pension plans, profit sharing plans have become increasingly popular.[1]

Broadly defined, the concept of "profit sharing" encompasses any plan by which a company's profits (or a portion of profits) are distributed to employees. According to this broad definition, wage supplement programs must be considered as profit sharing plans. For example, a cash bonus plan is a method of distributing profits to employees. Since many of these plans have little to do with the loss exposures analyzed here, a narrower definition of profit sharing will be adopted.

In this text, a profit sharing plan refers to a qualified plan in which an employer makes contributions to a trust fund for deferred payments to participating employees. These plans are in many respects similar to pension plans; indeed, many companies establish both a pension plan and a profit sharing plan. However, the two types of plans are not perfect substitutes for each other, as will be seen.

Eligibility Provisions

The income tax advantages of a qualified profit sharing plan are essentially the same as those for a qualified pension plan. In both cases the employer's contributions are deductible, amounts contributed are not currently taxable to employees, and the funds accumulate tax free until distributed. To obtain these tax benefits, both types of plans must meet the same general requirements. That is, they must be written, communicated to employees, designed for the exclusive benefit of employees, intended to be permanent, and cannot be discriminatory in favor of highly paid employees (officers, stockholders, and highly paid employees are commonly referred to as the "prohibited group").

The specific requirements for an employee to participate generally are not as restrictive in profit sharing plans as they are in pension plans. Profit sharing plans, for example, seldom impose a minimum age or a minimum earnings requirement, and employees may not be excluded from a profit sharing plan because they are older than some maximum age requirement. Most profit sharing plans include all full-time employees after they have worked for one year. Part-time employees must be included, according to ERISA, if they meet the service requirement. Generally this means that all employees who have worked the equivalent of more than one year must be included in the plan.

Even though the eligibility requirements under ERISA are the same for pension and profit sharing plans, employers generally choose more liberal standards in their profit sharing plans for several reasons. First, the purpose of a profit sharing plan is to encourage all, not just the long-term, employees to work as efficiently as possible. Secondly, the employer's cost normally is a function of company profits and is not affected by either the age or the number of employees as it is in the case of a pension plan. Only the allocation of profits among employees is affected. Third, an employer (or stockholder-employee) may benefit personally by liberal eligibility requirements. When an employee terminates employment, the invested profits that have been allocated to the employee are typically reallocated to the remaining participants in the plan. As a result, the benefits for officers and stockholder-employees are increased.

Employer Contributions[2]

One of the major differences between a profit sharing plan and a pension plan is the employer's flexibility in making contributions. In the case of a pension plan, the employer must make annual contributions at least equal to the normal cost of benefit credits accrued that year.

In a profit sharing plan, the employer has greater flexibility with respect to making contributions. First, contributions must be "substantial and recurring" if the plan does not contain a specific contribution formula. The other requirement is that contributions cannot be adjusted (in the amount or time) such that discrimination will result in favor of the prohibited group (the highly paid employees).

Within these general restrictions, an employer may use any method to determine the amount to be contributed to a profit sharing plan. One method for determining contributions is to leave the decision to the discretion of the company's board of directors annually. Another commonly used approach is to contribute a predetermined percentage of company profits to the plan annually. Some companies contribute a flat percentage of profits while others contribute a flat percentage of profits in excess of a stipulated amount. For example, if a plan requires a 10 percent contribution of profits above $500,000 and the company earns $800,000, the contribution would be $30,000 ($800,000 − $500,000 × 0.10). Another commonly used formula provides for increasing percentage contributions as profits increase. For example, 10 percent may be contributed when profits are less than $100,000, but contributions will be 12 percent when profits are between $100,000 and $200,000, 14 percent when profits are between $200,000 and $300,000, and so on. Some people believe this type of formula is the most effective in encouraging maximum productivity from employees.

Some companies use a combination of the discretionary and formula approaches. For example, a formula may establish a broad range for the contributions, but the exact amount may be left to the discretion of the board of directors. This discretion is desirable if the formula may call for a larger contribution than that legally permitted (15 percent annually).

The primary advantage of the discretionary approach is that it provides the employer with greater flexibility. The board of directors can consider a number of factors that cannot be taken into account by a single formula, such as the company's budget for the coming year and the level of expected profits.

From an employee's point of view, a definite formula usually is preferable to a discretionary contribution. When employees know that their efforts will be rewarded by a definite amount, they are likely to place greater value on the profit sharing plan which, in turn, is advantageous to the employer.

Employer contributions to a qualified profit sharing plan are deductible up to an average of 15 percent of the annual compensation of participants. To accomplish this, the Internal Revenue Code contains carry-over provisions that enable an employer to deduct an average of 15 percent. For example, a 10 percent contribution in one year can be followed by a 20 percent contribution in the subsequent year. If 20 percent is contributed one year, up to 5 percent of the excess can be written off in a subsequent year when the contribution is less than 15 percent.

Allocation Formulas

The contributions must be apportioned to individual participants by means of a nondiscriminatory allocation formula. Normally, contributions are transferred to a trustee, who invests and administers the funds on a "pooled basis," i.e., as a common trust fund. Each person has an individual account in the common fund for record keeping purposes. The ultimate disposition of the individual's share of the fund depends upon the benefit provisions of the plan.

The most popular method of allocating profits is based on an employee's compensation as a percentage of the aggregate compensation. For example, assume that the total compensation for all participants during the year was $500,000 and A earned $25,000. In this case A would be credited with 5 percent ($25,000 divided by $500,000) of the employer's contribution since A earned 5 percent of the total compensation.

Another common type of allocation formula gives credit for both earnings and length of service. For example, points can be awarded for each $100 of income and for each year of service. To illustrate, a plan may give one point for each $100 of income and two points for each year of service. A ten-year employee who earns $20,000 would receive 200 points for compensation and 20 points for service, or a total of 220 points. The employee's share of the employer's contribution would then be divided by the total number of points credited to all participants. This type of arrangement may encounter problems with the Internal Revenue Service if it discriminates in favor of the highly paid employees.

Few profit sharing plans allocate profits on the basis of service only. This method rewards long-term employees under any system because employees receive an allocation every year in which a contribution is made. Moreover, an allocation formula based only on service might tend to favor the prohibited group, since they often are long-term employees. Such a result would, of course, be unlawful.

Benefits

Retirement Benefits The amount accumulated in a participant's account at retirement depends upon the number of years of participation, the amount allocated each year, the investment experience of the fund, and reallocated nonvested forfeitures. Thus, employees with long service tend to accumulate larger amounts than those who have worked a shorter period of time. Consequently, many profit sharing plans generate a satisfactory level of retirement income only for the employees who work a long period, perhaps twenty years or longer.

Some profit sharing plans pay retirement benefits only for a fixed period, such as ten years. It is increasingly common, however, for trust funds to purchase an annuity for an individual upon retirement. In some plans the person has a choice of a fixed annuity, a variable annuity, or a combination of the two. Retirement benefits under a profit sharing plan are taxed to the recipient the same as retirement benefits from a qualified pension plan.

Death Benefits Profit sharing plans usually provide a death benefit equal to the amount accumulated in a participant's account. The benefit is smaller in the early years of participation than in later years, which is inconsistent with a person's life insurance needs. Young employees normally have a greater need for life insurance than older employees.

In a pension plan, life insurance must be limited to an amount considered "incidental" to the projected retirement benefit. Although limitations also exist in profit sharing plans, it may be possible to acquire a larger amount of protection than that permitted through a pension plan. A profit sharing participant may authorize the trustee to purchase life insurance for him or her on an individual basis. Not all of the participants need to be insured so long as all employees have the opportunity for insurance. If the funds used to pay the premiums have been accumulated for two years or longer, or if a retirement income or endorsement contract is purchased, there are no limits on the amount of insurance that can be purchased (other than the practical limit imposed by the amount of funds in the employee's account). Otherwise the premiums cannot be greater than 50 percent of the employee's account. As a practical matter, the life insurance premium should not be greater than one-third of the amount an employee can expect to be allocated each year because the premium is fixed, but the employer's contribution may vary. The value (determined by the government's one-year term insurance rates) of the insurance protection (i.e., the face amount less the cash value) must be included in the participant's gross income in the year in which the premium is paid. The proceeds, if not paid in a lump sum, may be excluded from the employee's estate for federal estate tax purposes.

The trustee should be the applicant, owner, and premium payer of the policy. Normally, the employee designates his or her own personal beneficiary.

Severance Benefits The vesting requirements of ERISA apply to profit sharing plans as well as to pension plans. In a pension plan, nonvested forfeitures cannot be used to increase benefits. Forfeitures by terminating employees in a profit sharing plan, however, can be reallocated among remaining participants on the basis of a participant's compensation as a proportion of the total compensation of all continuing participants.

Other Benefits One major difference between profit sharing plans and pension plans is that the former often provides benefits for a wider variety of purposes. A pension plan may provide death, disability, and termination, as well as retirement benefits. In addition to these benefits, a profit sharing plan may provide funds to educate children, pay medical expenses, or meet other unusual expenses.

An employee's right to withdraw funds from a profit sharing plan depends upon the actual provisions in the plan. Some plans do not allow withdrawals prior to separation from employment. Others permit the withdrawal of vested funds that have been deposited with the trustee for more than two years. Amounts withdrawn must be included as ordinary income in the year of withdrawal.

The disadvantage of allowing withdrawals before termination of employment is that it may prevent the accumulation of funds for retirement. To offset this, some profit sharing plans include a loan provision which allows a participant to borrow a certain percentage of the vested funds, at a stated interest rate, for a specified period. To obtain the approval of the Internal Revenue Service, a repayment schedule is required.

Loan provisions have several advantages over withdrawal provisions. First, a loan is likely to be repaid so that the retirement objective has a greater chance of success. Secondly, funds obtained by loan are not taxable as income, and interest on the loan is deductible.

Investment of Profit Sharing Funds Pension plans and profit sharing plans must conform to the investment regulations imposed by

ERISA. In general, acceptable investments include mutual funds, real estate (and real estate mortgages), common stocks, bonds, and insurance company products.

There are several significant differences in the investment portfolios for profit sharing and pension plans. First, the former usually cover a smaller number of employees than pension plans.[3] To the extent that the asset value is also smaller, the trustee must be more concerned with safety of principal. In larger plans, investment may be diversified among conservative and aggressive assets, and the effect of diversification will eliminate some of the investment risk. This is an important consideration because an employee bears the investment risk in a profit sharing plan (and also in a defined contribution pension plan). If the invested assets decrease in value, the employee's account suffers. In a defined benefit pension plan, the employer bears the investment risk.

Second, profit sharing plans frequently make two types of investments that are not common in pension plans. One of these is investment in the employer's common stock, bonds, or real estate. Most profit sharing plans are subject to a 10 percent limitation on the amount of plan assets that may be invested in the employer's real estate or securities. However, this limitation can be changed (increased without limit) if the plan contains a specific provision to do so.

Profit sharing funds may also be invested in key employee life insurance. If the profitability of the company is largely dependent upon the efforts of an extraordinary employee, all the participants in the plan benefit from that employee's efforts. Obviously the death of that person represents a loss to the employees as well as to the employer because profits will be smaller. To protect itself against this loss, the trust itself may purchase life insurance on the key employee's life. The usual requirement that insurance must be "incidental" does not apply to insurance purchased for key employee purposes in a profit sharing plan.

Comparison of Pension and Profit Sharing Plans

The decision as to whether a company should establish a pension plan or a profit sharing plan (or perhaps a combination of the two) is not always easy. Both provide retirement income to employees without increasing their current income tax liabilities; both can provide life insurance and annuity benefits; finally, either can be used to help attract and retain employees. Despite these similarities, there are several important differences between them.

If the primary goal of the employee benefit plan is to provide retirement income (particularly if the plan contains older employees), a defined benefit pension plan is probably preferable to a profit sharing plan. The size of benefits in a profit sharing plan increases with participation. This is also true in most pension plans, but pension benefit formulas can be used that place little or no weight on the length of participation in the plan. Older employees, as a result, can achieve a substantial retirement benefit in a short time in a pension plan but not in a profit sharing plan.

If the retirement income objective is not considered paramount, a profit sharing plan may be preferable since it can provide emergency funds to employees prior to retirement. A profit sharing plan can be designed so that employees can withdraw funds while they are actively employed. Withdrawals are not allowed by active employees in a pension plan.

If one of the objectives of the plan is to stimulate employee productivity, a profit sharing plan might be preferable since it provides a more direct stimulus than does a pension plan.

Death benefits may differ in pension and profit sharing plans. The death benefit in a pension plan may be up to 100 times the projected monthly pension plan benefit payment. In a profit sharing plan, the practical limitation is the amount of coverage that can be purchased with about one-third of the employee's annual share of the profits. Consequently, the death benefits will be larger in a pension plan, particularly for older employees, than in a profit sharing plan.

Funding flexibility is often a major consideration in choosing between a pension and profit sharing plan. Companies that have volatile profits may be ill-advised to assume the relatively fixed obligations of a pension plan. There is more contribution flexibility in profit sharing plans since contributions must only be "recurring and substantial."

The relative cost of each type of plan also must be considered. The maximum amount of employer contributions that may be deducted is higher in a pension plan than in a profit sharing plan. An employer can deduct an average of only 15 percent of total compensation in a profit sharing plan, but there are no percentage limitations on the deductibility of contributions in a defined benefit pension plan and $25,000 or 25 percent of compensation adjusted for cost of living change in a defined contribution pension plan. Contributions, however, must be actuarially justifiable and reasonable.

For a given amount of retirement benefits, the aftertax cost to an employer tends to be higher for profit sharing plans than for deferred benefit pension plans because investment experience is credited to participants. In a deferred benefit pension plan, investment gains reduce the employer's costs. Furthermore, in a profit sharing plan, employee forfeitures usually are reallocated to the remaining participants. In a pension plan, forfeitures reduce future employer contributions.

SAVINGS PLANS

Savings plans, which have been gaining popularity, closely resemble profit sharing plans. They are also known as "thrift plans," "thrift savings plans," and "investment savings plans."

A savings plan is a formal method used to encourage employees to save regularly. These plans offer employees a systematic, tax advantageous method of accumulating funds that may be used for a variety of purposes. Because employer contributions are contingent upon voluntary employee contributions, these plans are relatively inexpensive from the employer's viewpoint. Not only are contributions not made unless the employee elects to contribute, but the maximum allowable employer contribution is 6 percent of any particular employee's earnings.

Eligibility Provisions

Eligibility requirements in a qualified savings plan cannot be more stringent than those allowed by ERISA. For example, the minimum age can be no higher than twenty-five and an otherwise eligible employee must be allowed to participate once one year of service (three years is allowed if the plan has full and immediate vesting) has been completed. Furthermore, a savings plan cannot exclude anyone because of advanced age nor can the plan discriminate in favor of members of the prohibited group.

Many savings plans exclude part-time, seasonal, and short-term (i.e., less than one-year) employees. Some plans exclude executives and other highly paid employees, especially if the company has other benefit plans for these people. Savings plans that are supplemental to a pension or profit sharing plan (which is usually the case) often use the same eligibility requirements in both plans.

Contributions

Most savings plans are contributory, and employee contributions are collected by means of payroll deductions.

The amount of the employee's contribution may be determined in a variety of ways. One simple approach is to have all participating employees contribute a specified percentage (e.g., 4 percent) of their earnings. Other plans establish different contribution rates based on the earnings of the employees. For example, employees earning less than $10,000 may contribute 2 percent, those earning between $10,000 and

$16,000 may contribute 3 percent, and those earning more than $16,000 may contribute 4 percent. The IRS has indicated that 6 percent is generally the maximum employee contribution that can be matched by an employer contribution. If there were no such limitation, highly paid employees who could better afford to contribute a large percentage of their income to the plan, could thereby gain a large matching contribution from the company. The most common method of determining the employee's contribution is to allow each individual employee to select the contribution rate that is most appropriate for his or her own circumstances. Generally, companies place some restrictions on an employee's right to make frequent changes in the contribution rate.

Although the IRS generally will not approve matching contributions from the employer for contributions in excess of 6 percent, employees may make additional voluntary contributions—up to a limit of 10 percent of compensation. Investment earnings on all accumulated employee contributions are not taxed until actually distributed to the employee.

Employer contributions to a savings plan typically are defined as a percentage (25, 50, or 100) of the employee's contribution up to 6 percent of the employee's earnings. The IRS has approved plans that restrict employer contributions to a $.25 employer contribution for each employee contribution of $1. In these cases employer contributions are limited to 3 percent and employee contributions cannot exceed 13 percent of earnings.

In many plans the employer's contribution increases as the employee's length of service increases. For example, a plan may call for employer contributions of $.25 for each $1 of employee contributions for employees with less than two years of service, $.40 for each $1 of employee contributions for employees who have worked more than two years but less than five years, and $.60 for each $1 of employee contributions for employees who have more than five years of service.

Another common variation is for the employer to contribute a certain rate, and each year make additional contributions depending upon the earnings pattern of the company. Whichever contribution approach is used, it cannot discriminate in favor of the prohibited group.

Investment of Funds

In most plans, the employer's contribution is allocated to an additional account maintained for each employee, and the account is increased by employee contributions, asset earnings, and reallocated forfeitures of nonvested assets by terminating employees.

An employee may be allowed to specify how the account balances will be invested. For example, there may be four separate investment vehicles: (1) a fixed dollar investment account (such as a bank savings account); (2) an equity fund (composed either of individual common stocks or a mutual fund); (3) a balanced account (combining equity and fixed dollar investments); and (4) an employee stock fund. In some plans, an employee may use a portion of the account to purchase life insurance or an annuity.

When a plan offers investment alternatives, employees generally are given the right to split the account into two (or more) funds and to change from one fund to another periodically. Changes may be permitted only on certain dates (such as the end of each quarter), and the aggregate number of changes may be limited in any one- or two-year period. These restrictions are designed to discourage employees from "playing the stock market" and to minimize administrative costs.

In most small plans, the funds are invested in a single trust fund and are placed into one investment vehicle. Each participant, then, is credited with a proportionate share of the investment results.

Benefits

Upon retirement, an employee normally may receive a lump sum or may receive periodic payments for a fixed period or for life (as an annuity).

Death and disability benefits depend upon the provisions in the plan. Most savings plans provide no death or disability benefits, other than a vesting of the employer's contribution on behalf of the employee.

If employment is terminated, an employee is entitled to the value of his or her contributions plus all vested employer contributions. The vesting provisions generally are much more liberal than the minimum requirements imposed by ERISA.

Many savings plans allow employees to withdraw funds that have accumulated for at least two years while actively employed. In some plans, an employee may withdraw up to a stated percentage (e.g., 25, 50, or 100) of his or her contributions. Withdrawals of a portion of vested employer contributions may be allowed. Withdrawals are permitted only in cases of financial hardship or important financial needs (e.g., purchasing a house).

Many plans limit the number and amount of withdrawals an employee may make in a certain period to minimize administrative expenses. Withdrawal rights normally are restricted to ensure that employees are not found to be in "constructive receipt" of the annual employer contributions. If an employee may withdraw funds at any time without penalty, he or she will have to include the amounts placed in the account as current income, even if the funds are not withdrawn. Therefore, many plans impose some form of restriction or penalty on employees' withdrawal rights. A common approach is to suspend employee participation in the plan for a certain period after an unapproved withdrawal. The penalty is the loss of matching employer contributions during the period of nonparticipation.

In lieu of withdrawal provisions, some savings plans allow a participant to borrow a percentage of his or her account. These loans are similar, in purpose and design, to those in profit sharing plans.

Comparison of Savings Plans and Profit Sharing Plans

The federal tax law does not recognize savings plans. For purposes of tax treatment and regulation, they are considered to be equivalent to profit sharing plans. Thus, the qualification requirements that apply to profit sharing plans apply as well to savings plans.

From a practical point of view, the objectives, benefits, eligibility requirements, and investment policies of savings plans are very similar to those of profit sharing plans. However, there are important differences. One obvious distinction is that a savings plan is contributory and a profit sharing plan is not. And, unlike profit sharing plans, savings plans rarely are used as the sole retirement vehicle. In most cases they are supplemental to a basic pension plan.

The other distinctions between savings plans and profit sharing plans are more subtle. From an employer's point of view, an important difference might be the cost of the plans. A savings plan normally will be less expensive for an employer. In part, this is because employees help pay the cost, but the total contributions (of employers and employees) usually are lower in a savings plan.

A profit sharing plan appears to provide greater motivation for employees to increase their productivity than a savings plan. The former is recognized by employees as something the employer is doing for them, while the latter is seen as a plan in which the employees are helping themselves. Despite this, many employees apparently do recognize that a savings plan is a tax favored, convenient, inexpensive, and regular method of savings.

PENSION AND PROFIT SHARING PLANS FOR THE SELF-EMPLOYED

Until the passage of the "Self-Employed Individuals Tax Retirement Act of 1962," the tax advantages associated with a qualified

.pension or profit sharing plan were not available to the self-employed. Subject to certain limitations and restrictions, "Keogh" or HR-10 plans enjoy tax advantages that resemble those of qualified corporate plans.

Eligibility and Coverage Requirements

Generally the principal motivation for establishing an HR-10 plan is to provide retirement benefits for the businessowner rather than for the employees. Therefore, the law contains a number of restrictions that protect the interests of employees.

If a self-employed person establishes an HR-10 plan for the employees while excluding the owners, the HR-10 rules do not apply. These plans may be treated as corporate pension plans.

The HR-10 rules apply only when a self-employed person is included in the plan. All sole proprietors and partners are considered self-employed individuals, but not all self-employed individuals are regarded as owner-employees. In particular, an owner-employee is a sole proprietor or any partner who owns more than 10 percent of the organization (measured either by capital contribution or share of the profits). The distinction between a self-employed person and an owner-employee is important because the law contains a number of provisions that are more restrictive when an owner-employee is included in the plan.

Only two factors may be considered in setting the eligibility requirements for the plan: (1) length of service, and (2) whether the employee is full- or part-time. A full-time employee is defined by ERISA as one who works 1,000 hours or more during any consecutive twelve-month period. If an owner-employee is covered, all full-time employees who have worked at least three years must also be covered. If the plan or company is new, every employee who has as much service as the owner-employee (not to exceed three years) must be covered. Part-time employees can be included at the option of the owner-employee, as can employees with less than three years of service.

These requirements mean that an owner-employee cannot use age or earnings (or any other factor) in determining eligibility. In fact, an owner-employee cannot exclude an employee who refuses to make contributions to a contributory plan.

If a plan covers only self-employed individuals who are *not* owner-employees, the eligibility requirements may conform to the rules for corporate pension or profit sharing plans.

In order to qualify for coverage, a self-employed person must contribute personal services and derive earned income from the business. Earned income does not include rental or investment income, such as dividends, interest, and royalties.

An HR-10 plan may be established by a person who is self-employed on a part-time basis. For example, an accountant might be employed in a full-time position (and may be covered in a corporate pension plan) but may earn additional income on a part-time, self-employed basis. Such a person may establish a Keogh plan for the self-employment income.

If the spouse is a bona fide employee, he or she may be included in the plan. In fact, the spouse must be included if he or she has worked three years, or as long as the owner-employee.

Contributions

The amount of the contribution to a Keogh plan is deductible for income tax purposes, subject to several limitations. An owner-employee may deduct the lesser of 15 percent of his or her income up to $7,500 each year.[4] If earned income exceeds $50,000, the $7,500 limitation means that the amount deducted will be less than 15 percent. Amounts of annual income in excess of $100,000 cannot be considered.[5]

Most HR-10 plans operate on a defined contribution (e.g., a percentage of income) basis. However, some plans operate on a defined benefit principle. The benefit is fixed (i.e., defined) and the contributions are computed as the amount necessary to provide that amount. In this case, the 15 percent and $7,500 limits do not apply. Instead, the information shown in Table 12-1 must be used to determine the maximum benefit that may be accrued for a self-employed person for each year of participation.[6]

These percentages are applied only to the first $50,000 of annual earned income, and the IRS may change the percentages to adjust for prevailing interest and mortality rates.

To illustrate, a thirty-five-year-old entrant who earns $40,000 would be entitled to purchase a life annuity of $2,160 for each year of service ($40,000 × 0.054 = $2,160) or $64,800 (65 – 35 × $2,160). Approximately $590,000 must be accumulated by age sixty-five to purchase an annuity of this amount. The required annual contribution exceeds $10,000, assuming an investment return of 4 percent. Higher or lower yields will change this calculation.

An HR-10 is nondiscriminatory even though the deposits made on behalf of employees, other than the owner, may be a smaller percentage of their salary than the contribution made on behalf of the owner-employee.

For example, assume that a business owner and her two employees have three or more years of service. The plan objective is to provide 25

Table 12-1

Maximum Benefit for Self-Employed
Persons

Age†	Applicable Percentage
30 or less	6.5
35	5.4
40	4.4
45	3.6
50	3.0
55	2.5
60 or over	2.0

† When participation started.

Table 12-2

ABC Company HR-10 Plan

Phyllis Owner	Age 48 Female	$40,000 income
Sue Secretary	Age 31 Female	$10,000 salary
Carrie Clerk	Age 25 Female	$ 6,000 salary

			Results	

Name	Retirement Income	Required Accumulation	Required Annual Deposit at 4 percent	Annual Deposit as percent of Current Salary
Phyllis	$10,000	$98,503	$3,997	10%
Sue	$ 2,500	$24,646	$ 339	3.39%
Carrie	$ 1,500	$14,775	$ 150	2.50%
			Total $4,486	

percent of salary at age sixty-five. The results of such a plan are shown in Table 12-2.

In the ABC plan, 89 percent of the deposit goes to the owner-employee account to reflect her higher pay and the shorter number of years to age sixty-five. This arrangement is not considered to be discriminatory because each participant will receive the same retire-

Table 12-3

ABC Company HR-10 Plan with Defined Contribution Formula

Name	Deposit as Percent of Current Salary	Annual Deposit	Accumulation at 4 Percent	Retirement Income at Age 65	Retirement Income as Percent of Salary
Phyllis	10%	$3,997	$98,503	$10,000	25%
Sue	10%	$1,000	$72,652	$ 7,376	74%
Carrie	10%	$ 600	$59,296	$ 6,020	100%
	Total	$5,597			

ment income. In the case shown in Table 12-2, if a defined contribution formula had been used, the result would be as shown in Table 12-3. Obviously the plan shown in Table 12-3 is much less favorable to the owner-employee than the previous example.

Most owner-employees limit their contributions to the maximum amount that can be deducted. Voluntary additional contributions are permitted if another participating employee also has the right to make additional contributions. The amount is limited to 10 percent of earned income, or $2,500, whichever is less. Tax deductions are not permitted on additional voluntary contributions, but the contributions accumulate on a tax deferred basis until they are distributed.

Voluntary additional contributions should not be confused with excess contributions which are above the allowable contribution. Voluntary additional contributions qualify for favorable tax treatment, but there is a 6 percent cumulative excise tax on excess contributions.[7]

An owner-employee in a defined contribution plan cannot contribute a larger percentage of his or her salary than the percentage contributed on behalf of the other employees. For example, if an owner-employee contributes 8 percent of his or her account, the contribution made for employees must be at least 8 percent. Contributions made on behalf of employees are nonforfeitable since they vest immediately and fully. An employer can postpone the payment of the benefits until the employee's normal retirement age, or death, but the benefits cannot be taken from the employee.

Funding Instruments

Contributions to a Keogh plan can be invested in a variety of ways.

First, HR-10 plans may be funded through contributions to a trust. Most HR-10 trustees are financial institutions—banks, savings and loan associations, and credit unions. The funds are invested according to the terms of the trust agreement. However, the investments may not violate state law, and the trustee is subject to strict fiduciary rules. The trust instrument may give a self-employed person the right to select or to disapprove investments proposed by the trustee.

Second, a custodial account, similar to a trust, may be used. The same rules that apply to trustees generally apply to custodians, and most custodians are financial institutions. Custodial account assets may be invested only in life insurance or annuity contracts or in mutual fund shares. It is possible to achieve greater investment flexibility by using both a trustee and a custodian for a single HR-10 plan.

Third, HR-10 plans may be funded by United States Retirement Plan bonds, designed especially for qualified plans. They must be issued in the name of the concerned individual, and they are nontransferable. Consequently, they cannot be sold, discounted, or used for collateral to secure a loan. They can be converted into cash only in the event of death, disability, or upon attaining age fifty-nine and one-half.

These bonds are issued at par in denominations of $50, $100, $500, and $1,000. The redemption value of the bonds increases at six-month intervals to reflect the accrual of interest. When the bonds are redeemed at retirement, the increase in value (the excess of the redemption value over par) is taxed at ordinary rates. The ten-year averaging rule is not permitted.

Fourth, HR-10 plans can be funded by means of face amount certificates. These are investment contracts in which the buyer receives the face amount at maturity in exchange for a lump sum or periodic payments. The law treats this type of funding instrument as an annuity.

Fifth, variable or fixed-dollar annuities are frequently used as funding instruments for HR-10 plans. To qualify for favorable tax treatment, annuities must either be nontransferable or owned by a qualified trust. A trust is not necessary if the annuities are purchased directly from an insurance company and are nontransferable. Furthermore they cannot contain more than an "incidental" amount of life insurance. Specifically, life insurance benefits are regarded as "incidental" if they do not exceed 100 times the monthly benefit at retirement. Thus, a typical retirement income contract is permissible.

A self-employed person may combine several funding instruments in one HR-10 plan. For example, it is possible to use a trust and annuity plan, a trust and bond plan, or a bond and annuity plan.

Benefits

Since HR-10 plans are retirement vehicles, distributions cannot be made to owner-employees prior to age fifty-nine and one-half except for reasons of death or total and permanent disability. This age limitation applies only to "owner-employees"; it does not apply to regular employees or self-employed individuals who are not owner-employees. A distribution to an owner-employee prior to age fifty-nine and one-half is treated as a "premature distribution." This type of distribution incurs a 10 percent penalty tax (10 percent of the amount of the distribution) in addition to the ordinary income tax liability.

An owner-employee may receive a premature distribution by (1) obtaining a loan from an insurance or annuity contract, (2) using trust assets as collateral to obtain a loan, and (3) transferring funds from one funding instrument to another if the money is even temporarily placed with an owner-employee.

A dividend on a participating insurance or annuity contract is not considered a premature distribution unless the dividend is actually received in cash.

Retirement benefits to an owner-employee must start before the end of the taxable year in which the owner-employee reaches age seventy and one-half. This rule applies even if the owner-employee is not retired. In this case, benefits must begin, but the owner-employee may continue contributions to the plan. Other employees are not required to draw benefits until they retire, regardless of age.

Upon retirement, distributions received as annuity income will be taxed according to the usual tax rules pertaining to annuities. A portion of a lump-sum distribution is subject to long-term capital gains treatment and the ten-year averaging rule may be used.

If a self-employed person dies before retirement, any death benefit is considered taxable income with the exception of that portion of the benefit which represents pure insurance (i.e., the death benefit in excess of the cash value). It is received income tax free. For the portion that is taxable, the beneficiary's gain is taxed the same as it would have been taxed if the self-employed person had lived and taken a cash distribution.[8]

Arranging an HR-10 Plan

Insurance companies, banks, savings and loan associations, and professional associations have master or prototype plans that have been approved by the IRS. A *master plan* is one that is standardized and administered by a financial institution or association. A *prototype plan* is also standardized, but it is administered by the self-employed individual—not the sponsoring organization.

Even though the sponsoring organization obtains original approval for a master or prototype plan from the IRS, it does not necessarily guarantee that contributions to the plan will be deductible. The approval of deductions comes about only when a self-employed person's tax return is examined.

When a self-employed person adopts a previously approved master or prototype plan, individual approval is not necessary. The plan will be deemed to meet the qualification requirements so long as it is not modified by the self-employed individual. A self-employed individual may "tailor make" his or her own plan, but the qualification procedure is detailed and time consuming, and may cost a considerable sum relative to the first-year tax deduction.

If an owner-employee (or group of owner-employees) controls (i.e., owns more than 50 percent of the business) more than one business, the employees of all the businesses must be covered (subject to the full-time, three-year rule). Furthermore, if an owner-employee participates in an HR-10 plan that he or she does not control, the benefits contributions for employees in a plan that is under the owner-employee's control must be at least as favorable as those in the plan outside the owner-employee's control.

Two examples should clarify these rules. Smith works for a corporation and also owns two businesses. Smith is the only employee of Company X, while Company Y has three other employees. If Smith establishes an HR-10 plan for Company X, he must include all the employees of Company Y who are full-time employees and who have worked for more than three years. In other words, all the businesses under Smith's control will be regarded as one by the IRS.

To illustrate the second part of the above rule, assume Wallace owns 40 percent of Company A which has a very liberal HR-10 plan. If Wallace establishes an HR-10 plan for Company B (which she controls), she must provide contributions and benefits to Company B employees that are as liberal as those in Company A.

An owner-employee cannot contribute any type of property other than money to an HR-10 plan. This prohibits transferring an existing life insurance or annuity contract to the plan, or to a trustee who is administering the program.

Other "prohibited transactions" include (1) lending funds from the assets in the plan to an owner-employee, (2) paying an owner-employee for any services provided to the plan, and (3) acquiring property from or selling property to an owner-employee.

The owner-employee must file certain disclosure forms with the IRS each year. One form is a financial report for the assets in the plan. Another form describes the status of the owner-employee in the plan (or, if an owner-employee is not included, a different form describes the status of employees). An additional form is required for any year in which an owner-employee (or his or her beneficiaries) receives a cash distribution.

INDIVIDUAL RETIREMENT SAVINGS PROGRAMS

Despite the widespread popularity of pension and profit sharing plans, many individuals are not covered by a qualified retirement plan. According to one estimate, before 1974 only about 50 percent of the labor force was eligible to participate in a qualified retirement program.[9]

To remedy this, ERISA includes provisions designed to allow individuals to establish their own tax sheltered retirement programs. These plans are known as Individual Retirement Accounts, Individual Retirement Annuities, or simply "IRAs."

Eligibility Requirements

To establish an IRA, a person must meet three fundamental requirements. First, the individual must receive compensation for personal services. Investment income is not regarded as compensation for purposes of the IRA requirements. Second, the person must be younger than seventy and one-half. Contributions to the plan are not allowed beyond that age. Third, the individual cannot be an active participant in a qualified pension, profit sharing, stock bonus, bond purchase, HR-10, tax deferred annuity, or government pension plan. A person may establish an IRA if he or she is eligible to participate in a qualified plan but does not actually participate. Such a person, in other words, has a choice between an IRA and the other qualified plans.

If a person has an IRA and decides to participate in some other qualified plan, the IRA is not terminated, but contributions are simply discontinued. Upon retirement, benefits would be paid from the IRA. However, if the person receives accrued benefits in the qualified plan for years when IRA contributions were made, the IRA plan may be disqualified retroactively.

Contributions and Deductions

A person may deduct 15 percent of earned income contributed to an IRA subject to a maximum of $1,500 each year. These contributions are deductible from gross income, even if a person does not itemize deductions. To be deductible, contributions must be made in cash.

If a husband and wife each have earned income, each may establish their own IRAs. In cases where only one spouse has earned income, the couple may establish two IRAs (one in each name) and contribute (and deduct) up to 7½ percent of earned income with a maximum of $875 for each account. Or the couple may set up one account and contribute (and deduct) up to 15 percent of the earned income subject to a maximum of $1,750.

Excess contributions are subject to a nondeductible excise tax of 6 percent. If the funds from the excess contributions remain in the plan, the 6 percent tax is imposed on the funds each year. One method of eliminating the penalty tax is to reduce contributions in the year following the excess contribution. For example, if a person contributes $1,800 in one year and is entitled to a deduction of only $1,500, the contribution in the following year should be $1,200.

The most common cause of excess contributions is joining a qualified plan. When a person makes an IRA contribution and joins a qualified plan during the same year, the contribution to the IRA is considered to be an excess contribution. If the excess contribution is refunded before the taxpayer's filing date, there will be no penalty tax.

A person who has contributed less than the amount allowed in previous years cannot make an excess contribution to take advantage of the lost deductions since IRA programs do not have a "carryback" provision.

Funding

An IRA may be funded by (1) an individual retirement account, (2) an individual retirement annuity, or (3) an individual retirement bond.

The most flexible method is the individual retirement account. A person creates a trust or custodial agreement, and the administrator may invest the funds in a wide variety of assets with the exception of life insurance.

Many types of financial institutions including banks, savings and loan (S&L) associations, life insurance companies, mutual funds, and credit unions offer IRAs. These organizations normally have pre-approved prototype plans involving minimal administrative detail.

Individual retirement accounts are usually invested in one or more of the following: (1) bank savings accounts, (2) bank certificates of deposit, (3) bank pooled funds, (4) savings and loan shares, (5) savings and loan certificates of deposit, (6) credit union accounts, (7) mutual fund shares, (8) individual retirement annuity contracts, (9) individual retirement income contracts, or (10) real estate investment trust shares.

If the plan is funded with annuities only, a trustee or custodian is not necessary. Contributions may be placed with a life insurance company to purchase a retirement annuity, a retirement income, or endowment contract. Straight life insurance is not permitted.

If an IRA is funded with any insurance product, only the portion of the premiums that are allocated to the savings element is deductible.

If a person wishes to take the maximum deduction and the plan is funded with an insurance contract, a second plan will have to be established since the annual premium for the insurance or annuity contract cannot be greater than $1,500. The second account contribution can equal the charge for the insurance element of the first contract. A person can establish any number of plans; only the amount of deductible contributions is limited, not the number of plans.

This approach is not as cumbersome as it may seem. Insurance companies have prototype plans and specialized contracts that are adapted to the IRA market. Some of these plans allow flexible premiums so the annual premiums do not need to be level. Participating or nonparticipating contracts may be used, and dividends may be used to decrease future premiums or to increase benefits. The latter choice is preferable because a reduction in the premiums may reduce the tax advantage of the plan.

Insurance company products may be advantageous for several reasons. First, only an insurance company can guarantee an income *for life* at retirement. Furthermore, the annuity is purchased initially rather than at retirement, and the expense load factor is charged as a percentage of the deposits rather than as a percentage of the entire fund. Also, if the annuity is purchased initially, the annuity rate is guaranteed which is advantageous since longevity increases in the future.

Second, only insurance companies can offer waiver of the deposit if the participant is disabled. Consequently, the participant will receive the originally planned amount—even if he or she is unable to make the periodic payments during the period of disability.

Another funding alternative for an IRA is a special edition of U.S. government bonds. No trust or custodial agreement is necessary and there is no need for a special plan. A person simply purchases the bonds, and deducts the contributions from his or her gross income. These bonds are issued in denominations of $50, $100, and $500. A maximum of $1,500 may be purchased each year. They are nontransferable and cease to earn interest when the buyer reaches age seventy and one-half. Interest is payable only upon redemption.

In selecting the funding instrument, a person should consider investment risks, expected returns, flexibility, simplicity, and special services that may be provided. No matter which funding instrument is chosen, the funds must be nontransferable and nonforfeitable. Furthermore, the assets in the plan cannot be used to obtain credit, and the individual for whom the plan is intended cannot sell, exchange, or lease plan assets.

Distributions

Distributions made after age fifty-nine and one-half or as a result of total disability or death escape penalty taxes, but are taxed as ordinary income. In general, lump-sum retirement benefits from qualified plans receive favorable tax treatment, but in the case of an IRA, lump-sum distributions are not taxed at favorable capital gain rates, and they are not eligible for the special ten-year averaging rules.

A premature distribution occurs whenever an individual under age fifty-nine and one-half receives benefits unless disabled or dead. The distribution is taxable income in the year received, and in addition, a penalty tax of 10 percent of the distribution is imposed. A premature distribution occurs if the individual borrows from the plan or uses the assets as security for a loan.

In order to provide portability of pension benefits, a person may make a tax-free transfer known as a "rollover" of assets from one plan or one investment instrument to another under certain circumstances. The requirements for a rollover are as follows:

1. The full amount taken from the previous IRA must be placed in the new IRA within sixty days.
2. The new IRA cannot have any assets before the exchange takes place.
3. Property, other than money, taken from the previous IRA must be reinvested in the new account.
4. Rollovers between the IRAs cannot be more frequent than once every three years.
5. IRA bonds may not be exchanged for different IRA bonds.

When funds are taken from an IRA and then used to fund a new IRA with a funding instrument that contains an insurance element, the amount used to buy pure insurance must be included in the person's gross income. (This amount, however, is not regarded as a premature distribution and does not incur the 10 percent penalty tax.)

Comparison of IRAs and Other Plans

IRAs are similar to HR-10 plans, but they are not interchangeable. People who participate in a qualified plan and who also earn income from self-employment may establish an HR-10 plan, but they are ineligible for an IRA. Self-employed individuals who do not participate in a qualified plan may choose between an IRA and an HR-10 plan.

The amount that may be deducted each year will be greater in an HR-10 plan ($7,500) than in an IRA ($1,500). Furthermore, an HR-10 plan must include all full-time employees who have more than three years of service. There is no such requirement for an IRA.

Third, IRA-funded retirement benefits are taxed at ordinary income tax rates. Lump-sum distributions after retirement in an HR-10 plan receive favorable tax treatment, being taxed under the ten-year averaging rules. An employer, association, or union may establish an IRA in lieu of a qualified pension or profit sharing plan.

The main advantages of an employer sponsored IRA are: (1) they may be simpler and less costly to administer than a regular retirement program, and (2) an employer may select the employees who will be eligible for the plan, and contributions also may discriminate among employees. The principal limitation is that contributions are limited to relatively low amounts ($1,500 annually).

TAX DEFERRED ANNUITIES

Historically, employees of nonprofit organizations often were not given an opportunity to participate in an employer sponsored retirement plan. Nonprofit organizations, being tax exempt, had no tax incentives to provide a qualified plan. Since these organizations pay no income tax, the deductibility of employer contributions is of no consequence, and many nonprofit organizations simply had insufficient funds for this purpose.

This problem was recognized officially in 1942 when the Internal Revenue Code was amended to give employees of tax-exempt organizations the opportunity to establish a tax sheltered retirement plan. Specifically, amounts contributed by employees (within limits) are excluded from gross income.

Because of the tax advantages and because only annuities could be used to fund these plans when they originated, they have come to be

known as "tax sheltered," "tax favored," or "tax deferred" annuities
(TDA's); these are now misnomers since funding instruments other than
annuities may be used.

Eligibility Requirements

Only organizations that qualify under the terms of Section
501(C)(3) of the Internal Revenue Code and public schools may offer tax
deferred annuities to their employees. More specifically, they are
nonprofit corporations, funds, community chests, and foundations that
are organized and operated exclusively for religious, charitable,
scientific, testing for public safety, literary, or educational purposes, or
for the prevention of cruelty to children or animals. To qualify, an
organization may not (1) divert any of its net earnings to an individual,
(2) devote a substantial part of its activities to political purposes, or (3)
participate in political campaigns.

Most, but not all, churches and private schools may qualify as
501(C)(3) organizations. State colleges and universities also may qualify,
as well as employees of certain units of local, county, or state
governments.

Not all nonprofit organizations, or even all tax-exempt organizations qualify as 501(C)(3) employers. To qualify, an organization must
receive a determination letter from the Internal Revenue Service
stating that it is tax exempt under Section 501(C)(3).

To be eligible for a deferred annuity plan, a person must be a bona
fide employee—not an independent contractor. Furthermore, an individual in an elected or appointed position is not an employee (for purposes
of the deferred annuity plan laws) unless he or she has been trained or is
experienced in that field. For example, an attorney who is elected to the
local school board would not be considered an employee.

If a person is an employee of a qualified organization, he or she is
eligible for a tax deferred annuity plan. It makes no difference if the
person is only a part-time employee. Seasonal employees also are
eligible. The level of income is irrelevant.

Contributions

Contributions to a tax deferred annuity plan are not taxable income
to the employee as long as the amounts contributed are within the
maximum limits established by the law.[10] There are basically two types
of limitations on the amount of allowable contributions to a tax deferred
annuity plan. The first limitation is the "exclusion allowance," which is

the amount that may be excluded from an employee's gross income. The second limitation was added by ERISA. It applies to all defined contribution plans including tax deferred annuities.

The basic formula for determining the exclusion allowance is:

1. twenty percent of the employee's "includable compensation"
2. multiplied by the employee's "years of service"
3. minus the total "annuity premiums" paid in previous years

An employee's "includable compensation" is *reportable* income. Since this is taxable income, it does not include contributions to the tax deferred annuity plan or contributions to a qualified plan made during the taxable year.

To illustrate, consider Mr. A whose annual earnings are $26,200. He can contribute 20 percent of his taxable earnings, but the contribution itself will be deducted from his gross earnings to arrive at taxable income. How much can he deduct? The answer is simply one-sixth of his gross income. One-sixth of a person's gross income will always be exactly equal to 20 percent of his or her taxable income (income after subtracting the contribution). In this case, one-sixth of $26,200 is $4,366, which is the maximum deduction.

The phrase "years of service" refers to the number of years the employee has worked full time for the present employer. If a person worked eight years for a school system, and then accepted a position in a different school system and worked three years, the "years of service" would be three.

The exclusion allowance for a part-time employee will be less than it would be if the person were employed on a full-time basis because the "years of service" is interpreted to mean the equivalent of full-time service. For example, suppose a person works twenty hours each week in a position where forty hours is considered full time. This person must work twice as many years as a full-time employee to receive the same number of "years of service."

The third phrase "annuity premiums" is the total of all previous excludable amounts paid into any retirement plans of the employer. This means that contributions to a qualified pension plan, for example, as well as amounts paid into the tax deferred annuity plan must be included.

Again, consider Mr. A, who has gross annual earnings of $26,200. If he has been employed for four years and has participated in the company's regular pension plan for the past two years (with contributions of $1,152 each year), his maximum contribution to a tax deferred annuity would be as shown in Table 12-4.

Obviously a person may be entitled to make large contributions if he or she has worked for the organization for a long time, has not

Table 12-4

Mr. A's Maximum Contribution

Gross Income	$26,200
⅙ of gross income	4,366
Years of service	x 4
	$17,464
Less previous	−2,304
contributions	
(2 x $1,152)	
Exclusion allowance	$15,160

previously had a tax deferred annuity, or has not participated in a regular pension program. If a person has built up a large maximum exclusion allowance, he or she may wish to purchase a single premium annuity. With this approach, the maximum exclusion allowance for subsequent years becomes 20 percent of current earned income.

Many employees cannot afford to make a lump-sum contribution that is large enough to "use up" accumulated credits but would like to maximize their contributions over time. Normally, a person may deduct up to 20 percent of his or her taxable income (to all retirement programs), but this percentage may be increased if a person has built up unused credits.

However, ERISA also limits a person's deductible contributions to a tax deferred annuity plan. Generally, these rules limit annual deductions to $25,000 or 25 percent of the person's yearly compensation, whichever is smaller. ERISA contains some special rules for employees of certain types of 501(C)(3) organizations.[11]

Two facets of the deductible contribution rules are important. One is that large amounts may be deducted (large in comparison to other retirement plans). Secondly, "catch up" contributions are permitted since a person is allowed to deduct contributions for years when he or she did not have a tax deferred annuity plan.

Contributions to a TDA must be made by means of a payroll deduction by the employer. More realistically, contributions may be financed either by the employer, employee, or both. For example, the contributions may be paid by the employer in addition to the employee's salary, or the employee may agree to a salary reduction. At this point it is important to avoid income taxation under the rule of constructive receipt. The IRS takes the position that taxable income for an employee includes amounts actually or constructively received (that is, amounts which the employee receives in effect).

Constructive receipt can be avoided if the employee's salary is reduced by means of a written agreement. The reduction can then be used to fund the tax deferred annuity plan, and the employee does not incur a current income tax liability on the contributions. The IRS provisions allow only one salary-reduction agreement per year.

In a tax deferred annuity, funds withdrawn are not subject to a 10 percent penalty tax as they are under an IRA, but they are added to taxable income in the year withdrawn. This makes them convenient tools to finance, for example, a sabbatical leave by reducing taxable income while working, sheltering the earnings, then drawing against it while on leave. This ability to adjust income has many applications. It makes it possible for an individual to finance a leave of absence to complete a thesis or obtain further education, or it can provide cash flow while writing a book or starting a business. Many persons eligible for tax deferred annuities think of them only as a retirement vehicle, and thereby pass up what could be a most flexible financial arrangement.

Funding Instruments

TDAs may be funded with annuities or mutual funds. Any type of annuity may be used including single or annual premium, immediate or deferred, and fixed or variable contracts. The annuity must be nontransferable and must not contain more than an "incidental" amount of life insurance. The IRS uses the general rule that death benefits cannot be greater than 100 times the monthly retirement benefit. If the contract contains a greater amount, the excess allocated to pure insurance is taxable income. Also, premiums paid for waiver of premium or disability income benefits represent taxable income.

Distributions

A TDA participant may select any age to start benefits. The amounts received are taxed as ordinary income regardless of whether they are paid over time or in a lump sum.

TDA death benefits are taxed the same as if the participant had lived to receive the benefits. In most cases, however, a $5,000 death benefit exclusion is available that permits a beneficiary to exclude the first $5,000 of death benefits from income taxation.

NONQUALIFIED DEFERRED COMPENSATION

A qualified pension or profit sharing plan has substantial tax advantages to both the employer and the employee. In return for these advantages, a plan must not discriminate in favor of members of the prohibited group. Consequently, a qualified plan normally provides relatively small benefits to highly paid employees.

One method of providing larger benefits to highly paid employees is through the establishment of a nonqualified deferred compensation plan.

A nonqualified deferred compensation plan may provide significant tax advantages to an employee by postponing the payment of income and tax liability until the employee is in a lower tax bracket. Consider an employee, age fifty, who is in a high tax bracket. A raise may have marginal appeal because of the large tax liability. Moreover, the person may be more concerned about retirement income than about additional current income. A deferred compensation plan would postpone earnings and taxes until retirement when the employee's tax bracket is likely to be lower than it is currently. Furthermore, such a plan would provide additional income to the executive when it is needed—after retirement.

Types of Deferred Compensation Plans

Nonqualified deferred compensation plans may be classified according to who is responsible for initiating the plan and how the employees' rights to the postponed earnings are defined. They may be initiated either by the employer or the employee. When the plan is requested by an employee, it is sometimes known as a "deferred-oriented" or "savings-type" plan. In these plans, the employee voluntarily suggests that a portion of income be deferred.

Plans that are initiated by an employer are called "benefit-oriented" or "inducement-to-stay" plans since they may be used as a method of attracting and retaining valuable employees. These plans, in other words, may be used as an employee benefit for selected individuals.

Obviously a plan must appeal to both parties if it is to be established. Still, the plan design is strongly influenced by the motivations of the party who initiates it. Variations among plans depend upon the relative bargaining positions of the employer and the employee.

The doctrine of constructive receipt is an important consideration in a deferred compensation plan. According to this concept, a taxpayer is taxed on income to which the taxpayer has access. For example, funds deposited with a trustee to which an employee has a nonforfeitable right (e.g., allows the employee to withdraw funds at any time), will be considered constructively received by the employee when they are placed with a trustee. To avoid the rule of constructive receipt, the employee's rights to the funds must be subject to substantial limitations or restrictions. The employee should not have the right to withdraw the funds except at certain events—retirement, death, disability, or dismissal. This places "substantial limitations or restrictions" on an employee's ability to receive the funds.

The "economic-benefit" theory is a greater threat for deferred compensation plans. Under this concept, a person is taxed whenever a monetary value can be attached to the compensation. Since the present value of future income can be determined readily, the mere postponement of income does not allow it to escape current taxation. Consequently a person may not have actual or constructive receipt of income, but may still be taxed on the basis of its economic benefit. For example, an employee clearly has not actually or constructively received funds placed with a trustee in 1978 to be paid to an employee starting in 1980. Even so, the employee might be taxed in 1978 on the theory of the economic benefit received at that time.

A deferred compensation plan should be funded in one sense, but unfunded in another. Plans are funded if assets are set aside to provide benefits at a later date. In this sense, a plan can be funded even if assets are not allocated to specific individuals (e.g., deposit administration pension plan). Funding is desirable because it provides greater security for the employee.

For purposes of analyzing nonqualified deferred compensation plans, the IRS has developed a more specific meaning for "funding." In this sense a funded plan is one in which specific assets have been set aside and the employee is given a current beneficial interest in the assets. For example, if an employer buys an annuity and gives the employee ownership rights to it, the plan is funded.

An unfunded plan in which an employer simply promises to pay income in the future is not affected by the constructive receipt rule. Furthermore, if the plan is not secured (i.e., it is unfunded) the employee has not received an economic benefit.

An unfunded deferred compensation plan should promise a postponed income to which the employee has nonforfeitable, unconditional, and vested rights. Furthermore, an employer may earmark assets to pay the promised benefits so long as the employee has no specific claim against the assets. This is sometimes described as being "informally funded," but for tax purposes, it is regarded as an unfunded plan.

The important distinction between a funded plan and an unfunded (or informally funded) plan is that in the latter case the employee is given no rights to specific assets. In an unfunded plan, the employee is a general creditor if the employer fails to honor its promises and is not a secured creditor, with rights to specific assets.

As an example, assume an employer promises to pay $800 per month to an employee after retirement. To fund the plan, the employer purchases an annuity but gives the employee no rights in the contract. This plan is considered unfunded by the IRS and informally funded by others. The employee is not taxed currently on the premiums paid for the annuity. If the employer becomes insolvent or fails to deliver on its contractual promise to pay retirement benefits, the employee may sue the employer as a general creditor. The employee cannot look to the annuity for the benefits.

It is much more difficult for a funded plan to postpone taxation. If an employee is given rights to specific assets, the employee will escape current taxation only if there is a "substantial risk of forfeiture" both before and after retirement. Forfeiture provisions such as the following are frequently used: (1) an employee may be required to provide consulting services after retirement, and (2) he or she might be required to sign a noncompeting agreement (stating that the employee will not compete with the employer). Generally, funded deferred compensation plans are not considered advisable. The employer is not entitled to an income tax deduction for contributions to a nonqualified deferred compensation arrangement until benefits are distributed to the employee. When the plan is unfunded, the employer merely gives an unsecured promise to pay benefits at a later time, and is not entitled to an income tax deduction before the employee begins to receive benefits. Even in an informally funded plan, there is no current income tax deduction since the funds are still within the sole control of the employer. Contributions to a funded deferred compensation plan follow the same rule. The employer is not entitled to a tax deduction until the income is taxable to the employee. In a funded plan, the funds set aside may very well be taxable to the employee while he or she is still working. In this case, the employer would receive an income tax deduction, but of course, the objective of deferring taxes for the employer has been defeated.

To be deductible by the employer when the benefits are taxable to the employee, the benefits must qualify as ordinary and necessary business expenses which means that they must represent "reasonable" compensation. They cannot be deducted if they are unreasonable—that is, excessive. If the IRS determines that the compensation is excessive, the portion of the benefit that is unreasonable will be regarded as a dividend. This means it will be taxable to the individual at ordinary rates but no deduction will be allowed to the employer.

In determining whether compensation is reasonable or not, it is not necessary for the compensation to be reasonable for personal services in the year that the benefit is received. Otherwise a retired person might be considered to be receiving excessive income for the personal services actually provided. Instead, the test is applied on an overall basis. The personal services provided to the company in all prior years (as well as the current year) will be compared to the compensation paid to the employee in all those years.

In considering a deferred compensation plan, an employer must weigh the advantages obtained against the loss of the current income tax deduction. To bring this decision into focus, consider the situation where an employer is choosing between a $10,000 raise and a contribution to an informally unfunded plan. If the company provides the raise, the aftertax cost will be less than $10,000 because salaries are a deductible expense. For example, a $10,000 raise would cost an employer in the 48 percent tax bracket $5,200 ($10,000 × 1–0.48). Many companies contribute an amount to the deferred compensation plan that is equivalent to the aftertax cost of the alternative salary increase. In the above example, the contribution could be $5,200 rather than $10,000. The current cost to the employer is the same under either approach, and the employee defers taxes. Futhermore, the total amount available to the employee may be greater (even disregarding the income tax savings) if the funds accumulate at interest.

Arranging a Deferred Compensation Plan

A deferred compensation agreement is a legal contract that should be drafted by an attorney. It should specify the purposes of the instrument, the consideration given by each party, the benefit amounts and circumstances under which they are payable, and a description of how the agreement may be modified or terminated.

There is disagreement over whether or not the deferred compensation agreement should be separate from any funding instrument. The agreement should make it clear that the employee has no rights to the assets embodied in the funding instrument.

Normally, deferred compensation agreements have contained a number of forfeiture provisions. Now, with additional clarification by the IRS, these provisions are not necessary in unfunded (or informally funded) plans. For funded plans, strong forfeiture provisions are necessary for tax purposes, but few employees will place much value on the plan if the benefits are highly uncertain.

Vesting Provisions Some deferred compensation agreements provide that all benefits will be forfeited if the employee voluntarily terminates employment before normal retirement age. In other words, benefits do not vest. This approach generally is used with employer-initiated plans. If the plan is suggested by an employee in lieu of a salary increase, he or she will probably insist on full and immediate vesting.

In between these extremes, a plan may call for delayed or graded vesting. For example, a plan may provide no vesting for three years with 10 percent increments thereafter. This provides complete vesting after the twelfth year. Vesting in these cases is not subject to ERISA requirements and is determined by the wishes and bargaining power of the parties involved.

Consulting Services Many agreements stipulate that the employee must provide consulting services to the company after retirement in order to strengthen the case for tax purposes. This is unnecessary in unfunded (and informally funded) plans, but might alleviate problems of excessive compensation. If the plan is funded, a stronger case can be made for requiring consulting services, but funded plans should be avoided if at all possible.

There are several major problems that may occur when consulting services are required. First, the benefits may be regarded as wages and consequently subject to full taxation. More important, the benefits might decrease the individual's social security benefits since social security benefits are reduced when a person earns more than a certain amount ($3,000 in 1977). Third, the retiree may still be considered an employee if wages (deferred compensation benefits) are being paid. Therefore, a lump-sum distribution from a qualified pension plan would be taxed as ordinary income rather than at capital gains rates and ordinary income subject to a ten-year averaging rule.

Noncompeting Agreements Many unfunded deferred compensation agreements contain a provision that prohibits the employee from competing with the employer within a specified geographical area for a stipulated time period. If the restrictions are very broad in terms of time and place, the provisions may be invalid as an unreasonable violation of an individual's right to work.

Noncompeting agreements generally are not necessary for tax reasons. If they are well drafted, however, they may protect an employer who is concerned about the competitive environment.

Funding Deferred Compensation Plans

An unfunded or informally funded plan is more desirable than a funded arrangement (as defined by the IRS) from an employee's point of view. Therefore, the following discussion deals only with informally funded arrangements. In effect, these are funded for practical purposes, but unfunded for tax purposes.

A deferred compensation plan may be funded with any type of asset including common stock, real estate, mutual funds, or deposits in a savings account. In selecting the funding instrument, the parties should consider (1) the safety of the investment, (2) how well the investment matches the promised benefits, and (3) any special benefits or services provided by the investment medium. In most cases, life insurance is an ideal funding instrument for a deferred compensation plan. Generally, speculation instruments are not employed due to the risk involved.

In terms of matching benefits with the funding instrument, life insurance is often better suited than any other choice since many deferred compensation agreements provide death benefits and disability benefits. If any other funding instrument is used and a death benefit is promised, there is no assurance that the fund will be large enough to provide the benefit.

Disability benefits can be provided by means of a waiver of premium provision. In the event of the employee's disability, the premiums will be waived and the policy will be maintained in full force. The amount of the premiums can then be continued by the employer, not as a premium payment to the insurance company, but as disability income to the employee. If a larger disability income benefit is desired, the policy can include a disability income benefit.

Because the premium payments have not been deducted for tax purposes when paid to the insurance company, the employer can make payments to the disabled employee equal to the premium plus the tax savings and have the same net outlay. See Table 12-5.

In both examples shown in Table 12-5, the corporate, before-tax earnings required to pay the insurance premium are equal to those required to pay the disability income. The formula for this result is:

Step 1. 100% minus tax bracket % = A

Step 2. Insurance premium divided by A = earnings required to pay premiums

This formula, illustrated by the Corporation B example shown in Table 12-5, would produce the following results:

Step 1. $(1.00 - 0.25 = 0.75)$

Step 2. $\left(\dfrac{\$100}{0.75} = \$133.33. \right)$

Life insurance offers several other advantages as a funding instrument. First is the tax free accumulation of the cash value which is

Table 12-5

Examples of Disability Income Payments

Corporation A	
$100 monthly premium	
50% combined federal and state income tax	
$200 monthly disability income	
(1) Corporate, before-tax earnings required to pay premiums	= $200 monthly
(2) (a) Premiums waived by insurance company	= 100 monthly
(b) Tax savings due to $200 monthly payment to disabled employee	= 100 monthly
(c) Corporate earnings required to pay disability income	= $200 monthly
Corporation B	
$100 monthly premium	
25% combined federal and state income tax	
$134 monthly disability income	
(1) Corporate, before-tax earnings required to pay premiums	= $134 monthly
(2) (a) Premium waived by insurance company	= 100 monthly
(b) Tax savings due to $134 monthly payment to disabled employee	= 34 monthly
(c) Corporate earnings required to pay disability income	= $134 monthly

not currently taxable to the employer (or employee). Second is the availability of the settlement options to make benefit payments during the retired employee's benefit period. This is particularly valuable when the benefits are promised as a life income. If this approach is used, the benefits should be payable to the employer, who in turn, can remit the payments to the individual. This avoids the tax problems involved if the benefit payments are made directly to the retired employee.[12]

Arranging life insurance for an informally funded deferred compensation agreement is simple. The employer is the applicant, premium payer, beneficiary, and owner of the policy. The employee is the insured only. The use of life insurance as a funding instrument does not change the tax effects at all. Premiums are not tax deductible and death proceeds are excluded from the employer's gross income. The other tax rules, for surrender and annuity (life income) benefits, are the same as they are in an individual situation.

Figure 12-1

Illustration of an ESOP

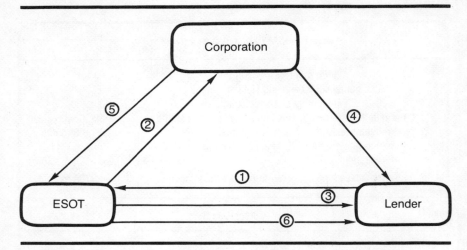

EMPLOYEE STOCK OWNERSHIP PLANS

In recent years employee stock ownership plans (ESOPs) have attracted enormous attention. Although the number of these plans is relatively small compared to the number of other plans that provide retirement benefits, their use is increasing rapidly.[13]

Some believe that ESOPs are the most useful and flexible employee retirement system available, while others believe the merits of ESOPs are greatly overrated, the plans are often misused, and serious problems may be encountered after these plans are installed.

An ESOP is an employee stock bonus, qualified retirement plan. It provides a method by which employees receive employer stock, and the employer obtains a method of raising funds. Thus, most ESOPs are two things: (1) a corporate financing technique, and (2) an employee benefit system.

ESOP as a Financing Technique

Most ESOPs are leveraged, which means that the ESOP borrows money from a financial institution and that cash is traded for stock which is issued by the company. To understand how this may provide funds to a company, consider Figure 12-1.

First, notice that three organizations are involved in a typical

ESOP—a corporation (the employer), a lender (which may be a bank or another type of financial institution), and the ESOT (an employee stock ownership *trust*).

Line 1 in the illustration depicts a loan made by the lender to the ESOT. The trustee invests the amount borrowed in newly issued corporate stock (at its fair market value). (See Line 2.) At this stage, the company has raised funds by selling new common stock, and the ESOT has invested in the company's securities.

Line 3 indicates that a note is given to the lender. Line 4 represents that the company guarantees the satisfactory fulfillment of the provisions of the note in the event that the ESOT fails to fulfill its obligation.

The annual contributions to the ESOT (Line 5) may be used by the ESOT to pay the installment payments on the debt (Line 6). Subject to the limits in the law, these payments are tax deductible by the corporation as contributions to a qualified trust.

The results of these transactions can be attractive to all parties. The lender makes a loan that is guaranteed by a corporation with earning power as well as by a note from the ESOT. The employees accumulate common stock in the company on a tax favored basis. The corporation raises funds in an efficient and relatively inexpensive manner, and the payments to the ESOT (for both principal and interest) are tax deductible. Furthermore, employees are likely to become more productive and dedicated as they gain an equity position in the company.

Not all ESOPs use debt. Plans that do not use debt (often called "basic" or "ordinary" ESOPs) operate in much the same way as described above. The employer contributes funds to the ESOT which invests in the common stock of the employer.

Contrary to common belief, the tax advantage of a leveraged ESOP over its nonleveraged counterpart is an illusion. While the payments are deductible, an unleveraged ESOP combined with conventional borrowing can produce the same net profits and the same cash flow. Therefore, it is misleading to conclude that a leveraged ESOP has a financial advantage over an unleveraged plan.[14]

ESOP as an Employee Benefit

As an employee benefit, ESOPs closely resemble profit sharing plans. The ERISA rules for employee participation and vesting apply to ESOPs and the requirements concerning the allocation of funds to employees are the same. The same is true concerning the limits imposed on the maximum amounts that may be deducted by the employer.

One important difference between ESOPs and profit sharing plans is that ESOPs may invest exclusively (or primarily) in the securities of the employer. A profit sharing plan is permitted to invest up to 50 percent of the plan assets in company stock under certain circumstances, but it is unusual. ESOPs, however, are not exempt from the rules regarding prudent investments, and the trustee(s) must act solely for the benefit of employees and their beneficiaries.

Confining investments to the employer's securities may have advantages and disadvantages for employees. If the company prospers, the stock may appreciate. If the company does not perform well, an employee could lose his or her job at the same time the invested funds are declining in value. According to some authorities, an ESOP increases the chances that a company will not perform well because of the dilution factor. When a company issues new stock, the increasing number of shares may cause earnings per share to decline, which can lead to lower stock prices.

Closely related to this problem is the increased risk associated with leveraging. A leveraged ESOP involves debt, and debt has the effect of magnifying changes in earnings. When a company is earning more than the debt costs, leverage is favorable and earnings increase. The leverage effect is unfavorable when a company earns a lower rate than the debt costs.

A problem of special concern to ESOPs (and a general difference from profit sharing plans) concerns valuation of the employer's stock. ERISA stipulates that the price paid for company stock cannot exceed "fair market value." When securities are purchased in an active market, there is little problem. ESOPs, however, have special appeal to small- and medium-sized companies. If the stock is not actively traded, it may be difficult to determine the fair market value.

The allocation of benefits to employees in an ESOP usually is based on compensation, as it is in a profit sharing plan. However, employees may not be entitled to receive shares that are pledged as collateral for a loan. If an employee retires, for example, and becomes entitled to a distribution, only the unencumbered shares may be available. At a later date, when the stock is released from the assignment, the additional shares become available.

Chapter Notes

1. Everett T. Allen, Joseph J. Melone, and Jerry S. Rosenbloom, *Pension Planning* (Homewood, IL: Richard D. Irwin, 1976), p. 287.
2. If employees make contributions, the plan is known as a "thrift" plan. These plans are discussed in a subsequent section.
3. *Life Insurance in Profit Sharing Plans*, Information Bulletin No. 23C, The Bankers Life, Des Moines, Iowa.
4. If a person is self-employed on a part-time basis, the amount that can legitimately be deductible may be greater than 15 percent. The deductible amount is not 100 percent with a maximum of $750 each year, as many people believe. For a discussion of this problem, see Advanced Underwriting Service, Research and Review Service of America, Indianapolis, Indiana, Vol. 3, p. 17-214.
5. In calculating the earned income of a self-employed person, any contributions made on behalf of employees must be subtracted from the owner's income. In other words, earned income is defined as net income after contributions for employees.
6. These figures apply only if the benefit is a pure life annuity starting at age sixty-five. Other figures must be used if the benefit is payable in some other form.
7. For a definition of these tax rules, see Advanced Underwriting Service, Vol. 3, p. 17-224, Research and Review Service of America, Inc., Indianapolis, Indiana.
8. The $5,000 employee death benefit exclusion available with qualified corporate plans is not allowed for a self-employed person's beneficiary.
9. Advanced Underwriting Service, Research and Review Service of America, Indianapolis, Indiana, Vol. 3, p. 17-189.
10. In complex cases it may be wise to have the funding agency calculate the maximum allowable contribution. For an excellent source that contains sufficient detail for most cases, see Advanced Underwriting Service, Research and Review Service of America, Inc., Indianapolis, Indiana, Vol. 3, p. 17-239.
11. In general, these are educational institutions, hospitals, and some health service agencies. Employees of these organizations are allowed even larger deductions for "catch up" contributions.
12. If payments are made directly to the employee, the IRS is likely to conclude that the policy has been transferred to the employee and, as a result, the full value of the contract would be taxable in the year of the transfer.
13. Ronald M. Bushman, "ESOPs: A Closer Look," *C.L.U. Journal*, April, 1977, p. 33.
14. For a careful analysis of the financial effects of an ESOP, see Harry A. Lund, Walter J. Casey, and Phillip K. Chamberlain, "A Financial Analysis of the ESOT," *Financial Analysts Journal*, Jan.-Feb., 1976, p. 55.

CHAPTER 13

Investment Risks and Returns

INTRODUCTION

Traditionally, most personal insurance decisions have been approached without reference to the broader financial goals and plans of an individual or family. There is increasing recognition, however, that personal insurance and risk management decisions should be considered within the broader context and perspectives of a family's overall financial objectives and plans.

When an insurance advisor understands an individual's or family's financial goals, he or she can provide a more complete and appropriate risk management and insurance service. Indeed, the true risk management approach to personal financial problems requires a careful consideration of several alternative methods of treating loss exposures. For example, in dealing with the problem of providing retirement income, a financial advisor would be shortsighted to suggest insurance products as the only solution to the exposure. Many individuals believe that common stocks, real estate, or other investments can provide a more substantial retirement income. A modern insurance advisor, therefore, should recognize that alternative investment vehicles are available, and that each vehicle has its own peculiar advantages and limitations.

Of course, a financial advisor cannot be an expert in all aspects of financial planning. Still, financial advisors should be familiar with the risk/return and other characteristics of the various investment alternatives and with several techniques for using each alternative toward the ultimate goal of providing financial security.

FACTORS INVOLVED IN THE SELECTION OF
SAVINGS AND INVESTMENT VEHICLES[1]

In developing a financial security program, an individual should consider many factors. While investment return and the degree of risk generally are of overriding importance, other elements such as marketability, convenience, tax treatment, and special services should also be considered.

For most individuals, several factors play a changing role in a well-designed investment strategy. Informed investment counselors frequently advocate a balanced investment policy. For example, individuals should first satisfy the safety need by acquiring highly liquid, safe assets equal to approximately six months of their disposable income. Once this need is met, less liquid investments which offer a higher rate of return should be purchased. Then, more speculative investments which emphasize capital appreciation may be considered. Lastly, highly speculative ventures can be considered without the possibility of destroying the investor's financial security.

The point to be remembered is that of the following characteristics, no one of them should dominate the entire investment portfolio. A wise investor probably will need to acquire several investment instruments, each of which emphasizes a different factor (or factors). Only in this way will the individual's investment portfolio be properly balanced to ensure that the investor's long-term goals have the best chance of being met.

Investment Returns

All assets held by an individual or family that are not being used for current consumption are expected to yield some type of investment return. Basically, this return takes the form of periodic income, capital appreciation, or both. Income is normally in the form of either periodic interest payments or dividends. Capital gains occur when an investment is sold at a price higher than its purchase price.[2] Generally investors seek to maximize their investment return subject to their personal investment objectives and other constraints. For many investors, achievement of the highest rate of current income (for a given risk level) is the principal objective, while others place little value in current income and, instead, seek to maximize their capital gains. Of course, some investors desire a balanced portfolio yielding both types of return.

The investment objective of an investor should be primary in the selection of appropriate investment vehicles. If current income is the investor's chief goal, savings accounts, bonds, or preferred stock may be indicated. Investments providing only the opportunity for capital gains include some common stocks, some investment companies, and certain speculative investments such as options and warrants. An investor seeking both current income and capital appreciation might choose from many common stocks, bonds, investment companies, and real estate.

Investment Risks

Whenever the future value of an investment is uncertain, there is investment risk. It is common in everyday language to speak of "risky" assets and "safe" assets. Investments should not be placed into one category or the other because investments have varying degrees of risk. That is, some risky investments are more risky than others. More importantly, it is sometimes misleading to refer to investment risk without specifying the exact type of risk under consideration. Each type of investment is subject to several types of investment risk. It follows, therefore, that there is no perfectly safe investment. An asset can be safe only with regard to certain types of risk.

Interest Rate Risk This type of investment risk refers to the uncertainty of future values caused by changes in interest rates. Although changes in interest rates affect the prices of all assets, the interest rate risk usually is associated with fixed income securities, particularly those with a long duration to maturity.

To understand the interest rate risk, it may be helpful to consider a bond investor's most useful measure of total yield, the yield to maturity. Suppose that an investor is considering the purchase of a twenty-year bond carrying a coupon rate of 6 percent which has been on the market for ten years. Assume that the bond has a face value of $1,000 but can be purchased *at 80* (which means $800, since bond prices are quoted in percents of face value). If the market price of a bond is less that its face value, the bond is said to be selling at a "discount." In our example, the discount is $200.

When a bond is purchased at a discount, the total investment return will consist of two parts: (1) the bond interest ($60 each year in our example), and (2) appreciation in the value of the bond—all bond prices will move toward the face value as the maturity date approaches, since the company issuing the bond must pay the full face value when it matures. Assuming there will be no default on the bond, the bond in our example is selling at $800 now, but will be worth $1,000 in ten years.

This means that our potential investor could expect to receive $60 each year in bond interest and $200 appreciation in the value of the bond. Since the bond has ten years until maturity, the average amount of appreciation each year will be $20 (i.e., $200 divided by ten years).

How much would our investor have invested in the bond if he or she buys it at $800 and it appreciates to $1,000? At the beginning, the investment would be $800. But as time passes, the investor would have more invested because the value of the bond will increase. On the average, the investment would be $900 (i.e., $800 + $1,000 ÷ 2). The yield to maturity is the annual return, or $80 ($60 of interest plus $20 of appreciation) divided by the average amount invested, or $900. This is a yield to maturity of $80/$900, or approximately 8.9 percent.

A simple formula (which is nothing more than another way to state the same relationships described above) to figure the approximate yield to maturity is:

$$Y = \frac{C + \dfrac{F - M}{N}}{\dfrac{F + M}{2}}$$

Where Y = yield to maturity, C = coupon yield (in dollars per year), F = face value of bond, M = market value of bond, and N = Number of years to maturity.

Using the figures assumed in our example:

$$Y = \frac{\$60 + \dfrac{\$1,000 - \$800}{10}}{\dfrac{\$1,000 + \$800}{2}}$$

$$= \frac{\$60 + \dfrac{\$200}{\$10}}{\dfrac{\$1,800}{2}} = \frac{\$80}{\$900} = 8.9 \text{ percent}$$

Not all bonds sell at a discount. In some cases the market price of a bond will be higher than the face amount, and the bond is said to sell at a *premium*. Suppose that the bond previously discussed could not be purchased at $800, but instead, is selling at 120 (i.e., $1,200). With these facts, an investor would not benefit from the appreciation in the value of the bond because the $1,200 market price will move toward $1,000 at maturity. The premium, therefore, will be gradually lost by a new investor. (This loss must be subtracted from the current interest to determine the true yield.) When a bond sells at a premium, the yield formula must be modified to compensate for this loss:

$$Y = \frac{C - \dfrac{M - F}{N}}{\dfrac{F + M}{2}}$$

In our example, the yield to maturity would be:

$$Y = \frac{\$60 - \dfrac{\$1,200 - \$1,000}{10}}{\dfrac{\$1,000 + \$1,200}{2}}$$

$$= \frac{\$60 - \dfrac{\$200}{10}}{\dfrac{\$2,200}{2}} = \frac{\$40}{\$1,100} = 3.6 \text{ percent}$$

It should be clear that the true yield (yield to maturity) is equal to the coupon rate on a bond only when a bond is purchased at its maturity value. In cases where a bond is purchased at a discount, the true yield will be greater than the coupon rate. Conversely, if a bond is purchased at a premium, the true rate will be less than the coupon rate.

What causes the market prices of bonds (and therefore, their true yields) to change? The answer should be suggested by our previous discussion and the yield formulas. Perhaps a simple example will clarify the answer. Assume that you purchased a twenty-year $1,000 bond when it was first issued ten years ago. At the time of your purchase, bonds of that quality carried an interest rate of 6 percent, and therefore, your coupon rate was the same. If you want to sell the bond now, but interest rates have increased to 8 percent on new bonds similar to yours, how much could you receive for your bond? Clearly a new buyer would not pay $1,000 for your bond in order to receive 6 percent interest when equal quality bonds can be purchased that return 8 percent. If you are willing to drop the price of your bond, however, the new investor might be interested. If the price is decreased to the point where the yield to maturity is 8 percent, you can sell the bond. Specifically, the yield to maturity will be approximately 8 percent to the new investor if you sell it at a price of $857.

If interest rates have decreased from the time the bond was originally purchased, the market price of the bond must increase because new investors will prefer the higher coupon yield on the old bonds. As a result, they will bid up the prices on outstanding bonds to

Figure 13-1

Relationship Between Bond Prices and Interest Rates

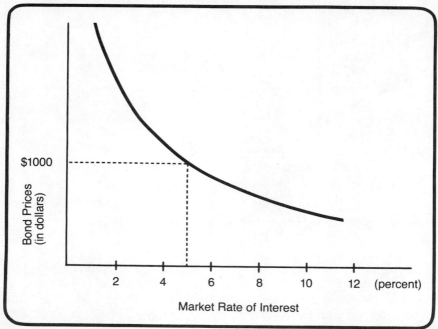

the point where the yield to maturity is equivalent to the yield on new bonds. In short, there is an inverse relationship between bond prices and interest rates, as shown in Figure 13-1. This relationship is called the interest rate risk.

Losses from the interest rate risk can be substantial—sometimes even over short periods. As evidence, some professional speculators are able to achieve short-term profits by buying bonds when they expect interest rates to fall, or by selling bonds when they forecast an increase in interest rates. For the nonprofessional investor, it comes as quite a surprise to purchase a bond "for its safety" and then watch the market price fall significantly. Of course, bonds that sell at a large discount will appreciate to the full face value at maturity, but an investor might be unable to hold bonds until maturity.

Some investors believe they can avoid the interest rate risk (or at least minimize it), by buying short-term bonds. It is true that short-term bonds do not fluctuate as much in price (principal) as long-term bonds because short-term bonds are nearer to maturity (when they must equal the face value). This solution to the problem, however, is more imaginary than real. Investors who buy short-term bonds are faced with a series of short-term reinvestments at changing yields.

Financial Risk Financial risk is the uncertainty of future market values that result from changes in the financial condition of the organization that issued the security. Many factors can cause the financial health of an organization to deteriorate. Some of the more important sources of financial risk are: the use of excessive debt by the issuing company, high operating expenses, uninsured property and liability losses, and changes in the economic, political, and social environment.

Financial risk may be applicable to almost any type of investment, but it is associated most closely with common stocks. Normally, holders of common stock are in a position to gain the most if business is profitable, but they also usually lose the most if the business is unsuccessful.

Market Risk Many changes in security values must be attributed to general market conditions. A company may be in excellent financial health but its securities may be dropping in price because of the overall market conditions. This is market risk. More specifically, market risk is the uncertainty that results from changes in the securities market.

Market risk affects common stocks more than most other investments. This is because it is more difficult to determine stock values. Even changes in investors' attitudes can have a large impact on stock prices.

Losses from market risk can be substantial. During the depression of the 1930s, common stock prices declined approximately 86 percent. Even since World War II, common stock prices (measured by commonly used market indexes) have declined 20 percent or more six times (1946, 1961-62, 1966, 1968-70, 1973-74, 1977).[3]

An important aspect of market risk is that diversification within the same market is not a solution to the problem. A well-diversified group of common stocks, for example, is not protected against market risk when the stock market falls.

Purchasing Power Risk Purchasing power risk refers to the uncertainty of future values caused by changes in the price level. Inflation has been a serious problem for investors, particularly in recent years. Table 13-1 indicates the "cost of living" compared to the base year, 1967.

Although the data in Table 13-1 may seem to indicate that an investor would lose 70.5 percent on his or her fixed income investment between 1967 and 1976, this is not correct. To determine the loss caused by inflation, it is necessary to convert current dollars received by the investor into constant or real dollars. This conversion from current dollars to constant dollars removes the effect of price level changes. To do this, divide the amount in question (in current dollars) by the Consumer Price Index divided by 100.

Table 13-1

Consumer Price Index (1967 = 100)*

Period	Index
1967	100.0
1968	104.2
1969	109.8
1970	116.3
1971	121.3
1972	125.3
1973	133.1
1974	147.7
1975	161.2
1976	170.5

*Reprinted from Social Security Bulletin, October 1977, Vol. 40, No. 10, Table M-41. The Consumer Price Index is based on a weighted average of the prices of a wide variety of goods and services, compiled by the U.S. Department of Labor.

Suppose, for example, that an investor bought a bond in 1967 for $1,000 and held it until 1974 when it was sold for the same amount. The value in 1967 dollars of the $1,000 received in 1974 can be determined by dividing $1,000 by 1.554 (the index of prices in 1974). This shows that the $1,000 received is actually worth only $644 (that is, $1,000 divided by 1.554). With these figures the investor would lose purchasing power of $356 (i.e., $1,000 - $644). This is a loss of 36 percent of the value of the original investment. This is a sizable loss—especially in an investment that was probably purchased because it was "safe."

Although investment and insurance advisors occasionally will point out that prices do not necessarily always increase, the historical evidence is very one-sided. The Consumer Price Index has declined in only one year since 1950. In the past seventy-five years, prices have decreased in three or more consecutive years only once (1930-1933). Clearly, purchasing power risk has been a major problem for investors.

Marketability

An investment that can be converted to cash promptly and easily at a reasonable price is said to have a high degree of liquidity or marketability. Assets that can only be sold after a large price concession has been made are not regarded as highly marketable.

As a general rule, assets that are not very marketable command a lower market price than they would carry if they were highly marketable. Alternatively, the expected return is higher for investments that have poor marketability. Therefore, it is not necessarily unreasonable for an investor to possess nonliquid assets.

Most investors believe it is desirable to hold at least a portion of their assets in highly marketable investments. The proportion of such investments depends upon the financial requirements and circumstances of the investor. A person may have minimal need for marketable assets if he or she has:

1. a secure source of income,
2. a comfortable margin between income and expenses,
3. an excellent health insurance program, and
4. easy access to credit.

To the extent that these criteria are *not* met, a strong case can be made for holding at least some highly liquid assets.

Divisible Amounts

Some investments are not available to many investors simply because the size of the required investment is excessive and the investor does not have the option of buying a portion of the asset. For example, an investor may view a large apartment complex as an excellent investment but may be unable to raise the down payment. Normally it is impossible to purchase only a portion of an apartment complex.

Some investments are easily divisible into convenient investment amounts. Common stock, for instance, can be purchased in a wide variety of amounts. An investor can buy 10, 100, 1,000, or more shares of stock, depending upon his or her financial resources.

An investment that can be divided into manageable units to suit an investor's buying preferences can also be liquidated in units for another buyer. Thus, there is a close relationship between divisible amounts and marketability. Generally an asset that can be easily divided into units is also highly marketable.

Tax Considerations

There is considerable variation in the tax treatment accorded different kinds of investments. Since investors seek to maximize aftertax returns, taxes can be a significant influence in an investor's decisions. Because of their tax-exempt status, municipal bonds are attractive to investors in higher income brackets despite their relatively modest yields.

Another well-known tax consideration is the advantageous tax treatment of capital gains compared to ordinary income taxation. This leads some investors to prefer investments such as common stocks that do not pay dividends over stocks having a high dividend yield. A taxpayer may exclude $100 of dividend income from taxation each year, but above this amount, dividend income is taxed as ordinary income.

Some types of investments have the effect of postponing income taxation. Pension plans are perhaps the best example of this advantage.

A tax shelter is an investment that produces real economic income (or gains) but because of the tax accounting treatment provides tax losses (or deductions) which can be deducted from income derived from other sources. Tax shelters are increasingly popular, but their advantages have been mitigated somewhat by changes in the tax laws in 1976.

Financial Leverage

Some investors consider leverage to be a leading factor in the selection of an investment. Generally, financial leverage results whenever an investor has a fixed cost as a part of, or associated with, an asset. A simple approach to leverage is involved when a person borrows to invest. If an investor borrows money, his or her cost (the interest expense) is fixed, and if the rate of return on the investment is greater than the fixed cost, the investor's profits are magnified. Consider this simple example. An investor has $5,000 of his or her own money to invest, but can borrow another $5,000 for investment purposes. Assume that the interest rate on the debt is 10 percent. Table 13-2 shows the results if the investment return on the asset is 5 percent, 10 percent, 15 percent, and 20 percent, respectively.

Notice that the figures in the table indicate that the investor would earn the same amount ($500) under either approach (borrowing or not borrowing) if the return on the asset is exactly the same as the cost of the debt. However, the use of debt increases the net return if the investor earns a higher rate than the cost of the debt. In fact, profits are magnified. With no borrowing, an increase in the return from 10 percent to 15 percent will produce an increase in profits of 50 percent. But if debt is used and the return increases from 10 to 15 percent, profits will double.

Financial leverage also magnifies losses when earnings are at a lower rate than the fixed interest expense. This can be seen by considering the net results in Table 13-2 when a rate of 5 percent is earned on the asset.

Table 13-2

Illustration of Financial Leverage

	Investment Returns			
	5 percent	10 percent	15 percent	20 percent
With no borrowing (amount invested is $5,000)	$250	$500	$750	$1,000
With borrowing (amount invested is $10,000)	$500	$1,000	$1,500	$2,000
Minus interest cost	−500	−500	−500	−500
Net return	0	$500	$1,000	$1,500

An investor may add leverage to an asset (or a group of assets, i.e., a portfolio) by borrowing. This is sometimes called *external* leverage. Some types of assets, however, require no borrowing to have a leverage effect. These assets have *inherent* leverage. Investments with inherent leverage may not have a fixed cost in the form of interest expense but contain an element involving a fixed cost. If, for example, an investor has a contractual right to buy an asset at a fixed price, profits will be magnified if the value of the asset increases above the cost.

The leverage factor becomes a consideration in the selection of investments because it is practically impossible to obtain leverage with some assets, extremely easy to obtain leverage with other assets, and some investments contain inherent leverage.

TYPES OF SAVINGS AND INVESTMENT VEHICLES

Savings Accounts

Savings accounts of various types are offered by commercial banks, savings and loan associations, mutual savings banks, credit unions, and other types of institutions. Many differences exist among these various types of savings institutions. The legal nature of the organization is one such difference. Commercial banks are corporations, owned and controlled by stockholders. Mutual savings banks, on the other hand, are owned by depositors and controlled by an independent board of directors. Most savings and loan associations are mutual companies, but some are owned by stockholders. Credit unions are usually organized and operated by a nonprofit association that is related to some other entity (such as an employer, church, or fraternity).

Another basic difference among the various financial institutions that offer savings accounts pertains to the type of accounts available. The variety in types of accounts seems greater than it is, primarily because of differences in terminology. Many institutions use different names for accounts that are essentially the same. Still, there are some genuine differences in the types of accounts offered by the various organizations. Some accounts may be liquidated upon notice while others may be withdrawn only after a specified period or withdrawn before maturity only with a financial penalty.

There is nothing inherent in the legal form of organization that generally affects the risk, return, and other investment characteristics. A saver should not select a certain type of financial institution on the assumption that the highest returns can be obtained from that type of organization. And no type of financial institution can demonstrate conclusively that it provides the "safest" form of savings account. In other words, *some* credit unions may provide a higher return for a saver than certain other organizations, and vice versa. And *some* commercial banks have less financial risk than *some* savings and loan associations, but the reverse may be true also.

A person who is interested in selecting a savings vehicle should not begin by determining the legal type of organization that he or she believes is preferable. This would be analogous to starting an insurance decision by choosing between stock and mutual insurance companies. Instead, an individual should examine the factors that are relevant in the selection of any savings or investment vehicle, such as return, risks, marketability, taxes, special services, and so on as they apply to each savings institution under consideration.

Investment Risks in Savings Accounts Most savings accounts are insured. The preponderance of deposits in commercial banks and mutual banks is insured by the Federal Deposit Insurance Corporation (FDIC). Most deposits in savings and loan associations are insured by the Federal Savings and Loan Insurance Corporation (FSLIC), and many credit union accounts are insured by the National Credit Union Administration.

Although each insurance plan operates a little differently than the others, the basic plan is essentially the same. At present, each depositor is protected against loss of savings, up to a maximum of $40,000. In practice, a person who needs more than $40,000 of protection can obtain it by opening additional accounts. The $40,000 maximum applies to each account in a single institution. A person can open additional accounts in other institutions, open an account under the name of a spouse, open a joint account with a spouse, and open accounts with others, such as a trustee.

Assuming that the financial institution has insurance for savings account depositors (and that accounts are split if necessary to obtain adequate protection) there is no financial risk for the depositor. Not all financial institutions are insured, however. About 98 or 99 percent of all commercial banks have insurance, but a sizable percentage of mutual banks, savings and loan associations, and credit unions are not insured. It can be argued that insurance is not necessary to protect savers because virtually all financial institutions are subject to extensive regulations. However, losses and even failures among financial institutions do occur on occasion.

The concept of market risk does not apply to savings accounts. Savings accounts are not sold but redeemed by the issuing institution which eliminates the need of any type of secondary market.

The relationship between savings accounts and interest rates (the interest rate risk) is an interesting one. Changes in interest rates cannot affect the principal that has been saved. Therefore, there is no interest rate risk to the principal in a savings account. Changes in interest rates, however, affect the interest that will be paid in the future. The risk to interest earnings, however, is a problem when interest rates decrease. When interest rates decline, financial institutions have the legal right to decrease the rate of interest paid on savings accounts.

The most serious investment risk for insured savings accounts is the purchasing power risk. Although a financial institution may raise interest rates during an inflationary period, increases in savings account yields have tended not to keep pace with inflation. At any point in time, the yield to an investor is defined by the interest rate offered to depositors, while the return on some other investments may have no such limit.

Investment Returns on Savings Accounts Because there are virtually no financial, market, or interest rate risks with savings accounts, the yield to the saver is relatively low. In effect, the yield is just slightly above the return that could be expected with a "risk-free" asset. However, higher interest rates can often be obtained if the individual is willing to leave his or her savings in the account for several years.

Other Factors The most popular kind of savings account is one from which savings can be withdrawn upon notice. Certain time deposits, of various maturities, cannot be liquidated prior to a specified date, but others can be liquidated with an interest penalty. For example, some time deposits pay a one-fourth to one-half percent higher rate of return than conventional day-in, day-out accounts, but the investor cannot withdraw his or her savings except at the end of each quarter without forfeiture of the accrued interest.

A certificate of deposit (CD) is an investment instrument issued by commercial banks which has gained popularity in recent years. CDs are relatively long-term instruments which mature one, five, or more years in the future. They also may require a minimum deposit of $1,000 or more. The primary advantage of CDs is the high rate of interest that they earn with the rate being 1 to 4 percent higher than passbook accounts depending on the minimum deposit and contract term. A significant amount of interest is forfeited if the CDs are redeemed prematurely.

Most savings accounts rank high in terms of convenience. In most locations they are geographically accessible and transactions (opening, additions, withdrawals, and closing) are easy. One of the major attractions of savings accounts is that a wide variety of other financial services (such as checking accounts, safe deposit boxes, bill paying service, etc.) are often available with them. As a result, many savers accumulate savings at the same institution where they use other financial services.

U.S. Government Securities

Securities issued by the U.S. government can be classified into savings bonds, Treasury bills, Treasury certificates of deposit, Treasury bonds, and agency issues (which are issued by agencies of the federal government, such as the Federal National Mortgage Association).

Savings Bonds Although ten different series of savings bonds have been issued, only Series E and H are now important. The yield on Series E bonds is received by an investor in the form of appreciation in the value of the bond rather than through bond interest. These bonds are purchased at 75 percent of their maturity value. Series E bonds now being issued mature in five years but may be extended for an additional ten years. If the bond is held for at least five years, the appreciation in the value of the bond will be equivalent to a 6 percent investment return. These bonds may be redeemed at any financial institution that is an authorized paying agent, but redemption before maturity will sharply decrease the investment return. The true annual percentage return is very low if the bond is redeemed shortly after it is purchased, but the return increases (to a maximum of 6 percent) with the length the bond is held.

Unlike Series E bonds, Series H bonds are sold at face value. The return of Series H bonds is paid semiannually and the yield amounts to 5 percent the first year, 5.8 percent annually for the next four years and 6.5 percent annually for the second five years. Over the entire life of the bond, the average return is 6 percent (6.06).

Unlike most bonds, both series of savings bonds are noncallable. The U.S. government cannot "call" the bonds, that is, force the investor to submit the bonds for redemption.

Government bonds have no financial risk. Savings bonds have no market risk because they are nonmarketable. Interest rate changes do not affect the principal or interest of savings bonds, except the U.S. government has increased the interest rates on savings bonds (even on outstanding bonds). The purchasing power risk is the major investment risk for savings bonds. In general, savings bonds are affected adversely by inflation to about the same extent as savings accounts. In fact, if the return on savings bonds is less than that earned in a savings account (which is often the case) savings bonds are hurt even more by inflation.

Savings bonds enjoy perfect liquidity because they may be redeemed at any time (after two months from the issue date).

An individual can purchase United States savings bonds without paying any commission. These bonds are sold and redeemed by many banks without any charge.

Series E bonds offer the possibility of a unique tax advantage. The investor has a choice between current taxation or deferred taxation. The annual increase in the value of the bond can be treated as interest income and taxed each year, or the saver may wait until the bond is redeemed to report the appreciation in the value of the bond. If a person expects to be in a lower income tax bracket in the future, it may be worthwhile to postpone taxation.

Table 13-3 summarizes the relevant characteristics of Series E and Series H bonds.

Treasury Bills Treasury bills are short-term debt instruments issued by the federal government. The maturity may be as long as one year, but most Treasury bills are issued for periods between three and six months.

The return on Treasury bills fluctuates with conditions in the short-term money market. Since 1970, yields have been as low as 3 percent and as high as 9.5 percent. Treasury bills offer the lowest return of any marketable security because they involve little risk. There is no financial risk, and essentially no purchasing power risk or interest rate risk, although reinvestment problems may result from changes in interest rates.

The minimum denomination for Treasury bills is $10,000. Although all of these investments are purchased at a discount and do not pay interest (they are redeemed at face value), the income on Treasury bills

Table 13-3

Comparison of Series E and Series H Bonds

Characteristic	Series E	Series H
Denominations	$25, 50, 75, 100 200, 500, 1,000	$500, 1,000, 1,500
Purchase price	75% of denomination	Denomination value
Interest rate	6% to maturity 4½% the first year with gradually increasing rate to maturity	6% to maturity 5% the first year 5.8% for years 2 to 5 6.5% for years 6 to 10
Maturity	5 years	10 years
Payment of interest	Increase in the redemption value	By semiannual check to the bondholder
Tax status of interest	Taxed as current income or may be deferred until redemption	Taxed as current income
Redemption	Any time after two months from issue date	Any time after six months from issue date
Exchange provision	May be exchanged for Series H bond; $500 minimum	None

is not taxed as a capital gain. Suppose, for example, that an investor pays 98 for a Treasury bill and a few months later collects the full face amount. The appreciation is treated as ordinary income for taxation purposes.

Treasury bills are appropriately used only when an investor has temporary excess cash and alternative investments are paying a lower rate of return.

Treasury Notes and Bonds Treasury notes have maturities ranging from one to seven years. Treasury bonds have maturities beyond five years. Many of those bonds are callable.

As a generalization, the investment returns on Treasury bonds are higher than the yields on Treasury notes, which in turn are higher than those on Treasury bills. In other words, the longer the maturity, the higher the yield.

Investment risks, other than financial risk which is absent, are minimal on the shorter-term issues. As the maturity increases, the purchasing power risk and the interest rate risk become more serious problems.

Corporate Bonds

A corporate bond is a debt instrument arising from a corporation's long-term borrowing. With the issuance of a bond, a company assumes the legal obligations to pay periodic bond interest and to redeem the bond for its full face value at maturity. As creditors, bondholders are legally entitled to receive bond interest before dividends are paid to common and preferred stockholders. Moreover, in the event of failure, reorganization, or liquidation of the company, bondholders have a prior claim to assets (that is, ahead of the claims of stockholders).

The legal status of bondholders places them in a fixed income position. While this provides a high assurance of income, it places a limit on the income bondholders receive.

Types of Bonds   Many bonds are known by the type of security (collateral) they provide. *Mortgage bonds* are backed by the issuing company's real property—either land, buildings, or both. If the company defaults on an interest payment (or fails to redeem the bonds at maturity) the bond trustee can safeguard the rights of bondholders by foreclosing the mortgage.

Collateral trust bonds are secured by specific securities, usually the bonds or common stocks of other companies. *Equipment trust bonds* or certificates are backed by personal property, usually heavy equipment. These bonds are popular with railroads (and other transportation companies) because their "rolling stock," e.g., freight cars, locomotives, buses, etc. can easily be repositioned, moved, and sold or leased.

Bonds that have no specific assets for collateral are known as *debentures*. Sometimes the point is made that these bonds are secured, but only by the general credit rating of the issuing company. Some companies issue *subordinated debentures* which rank below ordinary debentures in terms of priorities (to income and assets). In a sense, the type of bond that has the lowest priority is known as an *income bond*. These are debt instruments, but the borrowing company has a legal obligation to pay interest only if the company has earnings from which the interest can be paid.

In the past, the type of security behind a bond was considered extremely important. Today, there is much less emphasis on collateral and more emphasis on the earning power of the borrowing company. This is recognition of the fact that it is better to avoid bankruptcy than to pursue claims against a financially distressed organization. As a result, it is not uncommon for the debentures of a financially strong company to have a higher quality rating than the first mortgage bond of a weaker organization.

Sometimes it is convenient to classify bonds according to the repayment method. *Sinking fund bonds* require a corporation to set aside a specific sum periodically for the purpose of retiring the securities. In some cases the company places an amount annually in escrow to retire the whole bond issue at the maturity date; in other cases bonds selected at random are redeemed each year and the sinking fund payment is used to pay the bondholders. This latter case is very similar to serial bonds. With these obligations, a portion of the bonds are scheduled to mature each year. For example, a company may borrow $20 million through a bond issue, which consists of $1 million in bonds maturing in one year, and the same amount maturing each year for the next nineteen years. With these bonds, an investor knows when the issuing corporation will redeem each bond, which is not always the case with sinking fund bonds.

Most bonds (including sinking fund bonds) are callable. This, of course, is an undesirable feature from the investor's point of view. One consolation to the investor is the *call premium*, which is the amount by which the call price exceeds the face or maturity value. Often the call premium is equal, or close to, one year's interest on the bond. In many cases the call price declines gradually as the maturity date approaches.

Convertible bonds give the owner the option of exchanging the bonds for another type of security, usually common stock, of the issuing corporation. The bond indenture specifies the terms of conversion, the ratio at which each bond can be converted, and safeguards for the rights of bondholders.

To demonstrate how bonds may be converted, assume that a bond may be converted *at 50*. This conversion price ($50) divided into the face amount ($1,000) shows that twenty shares of common stock are obtainable for the bond. If the common stock is selling at a very low price, say $20 per share, a bondholder could obtain only twenty shares worth $20 each, or a total value of only $400 if the bonds were converted. Obviously there would be no reason to convert the bonds. However, if the common stock appreciates, it may be worthwhile to exchange the bonds for stock. At a price of, say, $60 per share for the common stock, the value is $1,200 (that is, 20 × $60 = $1,200). The market will force the market price of the bonds to follow the price of the common stock. Thus, convertible bonds offer investors an interesting security that behaves like a bond (when the price of the common stock is low) but provides advantages similar to those associated with common stock (if the common stock price rises).

Investment Returns on Corporate Bonds The yield for corporate bonds fluctuates, depending upon interest rate conditions in the economy. In recent years high quality bonds generally have been issued at an interest rate of approximately 8 to 9 percent. This means that existing bonds (of high quality) could also be purchased in the market to provide a similar yield. Table 13-4 shows the history of annual yield rates on high quality bonds from 1925 to 1969.

In addition to the interest return, corporate bonds offer the possibility of capital gains (and losses). As explained earlier, interest rate changes affect the market price of bonds. As a result, an investor can sometimes buy a bond in the market and later sell it (prior to maturity) at a price higher (or lower) than was paid for it.

Risks of Corporate Bonds The interest rate risk is one of the prime concerns of bond investors. As explained previously, interest rate changes can cause the price of bonds to fall. If an investor is forced to sell at a time when bond prices have decreased, a loss may result. Even if an investor holds the bond to maturity, changes in interest rates may still cause a loss. This may happen when the bond is called by the corporation. One of the main reasons why a company calls bonds is to refinance at a lower interest cost. But from an investor's point of view, this causes a reinvestment problem because interest rates are lower. In these circumstances the investor can buy new bonds that carry lower rates or buy existing bonds that have had their prices driven up by the decrease in interest rates. It is easy, therefore, to see that the interest rate risk is a significant problem for bond investors.

Since bonds represent fixed income investments, the purchasing power risk is another major concern for bond investors. Even when a bond returns 8 or 9 percent, the true return may be extremely low or negative if inflation has been running at a high rate.

The financial risk for corporate bonds is generally low. For specific bonds, the financial risk is rather accurately estimated by bond ratings. Several investment services, such as Standard & Poor's and Moody's, provide objective ratings for the bonds of most large companies. These ratings are made by committees that attempt to evaluate all the factors that may have a significant impact on the quality of a bond.

Bonds with a Triple A or Double A rating are considered to have a small chance of default and usually are referred to as "high quality" bonds. Bonds with a Single A or Triple B rating are often called "medium quality" securities. Bonds with lower ratings are regarded as speculative. A study of investor experience during the period of 1900 to 1943 provided good evidence that bond ratings are reasonably reliable in estimating the chances for default. The figures in Table 13-5 show the

Table 13-4

Annual Returns from a High-Quality Bond Portfolio*

											From									
To	12/25	12/26	12/27	12/28	12/29	12/30	12/31	12/32	12/33	12/34	12/35	12/36	12/37	12/38	12/39	12/40	12/41	12/42	12/43	12/44
12/26	7.2																			
12/27	7.0	6.7																		
12/28	5.4	4.5	2.3																	
12/29	4.4	3.5	1.9	1.6																
12/30	5.6	5.2	4.7	5.9	10.4															
12/31	4.7	4.2	3.5	3.9	5.1	0.1														
12/32	4.7	4.3	3.8	4.1	5.0	2.4	4.8													
12/33	5.1	4.9	4.6	5.0	5.9	4.4	6.7	8.6												
12/34	6.2	6.1	6.0	6.7	7.7	7.0	9.5	11.9	15.3											
12/35	6.6	6.5	6.5	7.1	8.1	7.6	9.6	11.3	12.6	9.9										
12/36	6.7	6.7	6.6	7.2	8.0	7.6	9.2	10.4	11.0	8.8	7.7									
12/37	6.3	6.3	6.2	6.7	7.3	6.9	8.1	8.7	8.8	6.6	5.0	2.4								
12/38	6.3	6.2	6.2	6.6	7.1	6.7	7.7	8.2	8.2	6.4	5.3	4.1	5.8							
12/39	6.2	6.1	6.1	6.4	6.9	6.5	7.4	7.7	7.8	6.1	5.2	4.3	5.3	4.8						
12/40	6.1	6.0	6.0	6.3	6.7	6.3	7.1	7.4	7.2	5.9	5.1	4.4	5.1	4.8	4.8					
12/41	5.9	5.8	5.7	6.0	6.4	6.0	6.6	6.8	6.6	5.4	4.7	4.1	4.5	4.1	3.7	2.6				
12/42	5.7	5.6	5.5	5.8	6.1	5.7	6.3	6.4	6.2	5.1	4.4	3.9	4.2	3.8	3.4	2.7	2.9			
12/43	5.0	5.5	5.4	5.6	5.9	5.5	6.0	6.1	5.9	4.9	4.3	3.8	4.0	3.7	3.4	2.9	3.1	3.3		
12/44	5.5	5.4	5.3	5.5	5.8	5.4	5.9	6.0	5.7	4.8	4.3	3.8	4.0	3.8	3.6	3.2	3.5	3.7	4.2	
12/45	5.5	5.4	5.3	5.5	5.7	5.4	5.8	5.9	5.7	4.8	4.3	3.9	4.1	3.9	3.8	3.6	3.8	4.1	4.5	4.8

12/46	5.3	5.2	5.1	5.3	5.5	5.2	5.6	5.8	5.4	4.6	4.2	3.8	4.0	3.7	3.6	3.4	3.6	3.7	3.9	3.7
12/47	5.0	4.9	4.8	5.0	5.2	4.9	5.2	5.2	5.0	4.2	3.7	3.4	3.5	3.2	3.0	2.8	2.8	2.8	2.7	2.1
12/48	5.0	4.9	4.8	4.9	5.1	4.8	5.1	5.1	4.9	4.2	3.7	3.4	3.5	3.3	3.1	2.9	3.0	3.0	2.9	2.6
12/49	5.0	4.9	4.8	5.9	5.1	4.9	5.1	5.2	4.9	4.3	3.9	3.6	3.7	3.5	3.4	3.2	3.3	3.4	3.4	3.2
12/50	4.9	4.8	4.7	4.8	5.0	4.7	4.9	4.9	4.7	4.1	3.7	3.5	3.5	3.3	3.2	3.1	3.1	3.1	3.1	2.9
12/51	4.6	4.4	4.4	4.4	4.6	4.3	4.5	4.5	4.3	3.7	3.3	3.0	3.0	2.8	2.7	2.5	2.5	2.4	2.3	2.1
12/52	4.5	4.4	4.3	4.4	4.5	4.3	4.5	4.5	4.3	3.7	3.3	3.1	3.1	2.9	2.8	2.6	2.6	2.6	2.5	2.3
12/53	4.4	4.3	4.2	4.3	4.4	4.2	4.4	4.4	4.1	3.6	3.2	3.0	3.0	2.8	2.7	2.5	2.5	2.5	2.4	2.2
12/54	4.5	4.4	4.3	4.4	4.5	4.2	4.4	4.4	4.2	3.7	3.4	3.1	3.2	3.0	2.9	2.8	2.8	2.8	2.7	2.6
12/55	4.3	4.2	4.1	4.2	4.3	4.0	4.2	4.2	4.0	3.5	3.2	2.9	3.0	2.8	2.7	2.5	2.5	2.5	2.4	2.3
12/56	4.0	3.9	3.8	3.8	3.9	3.6	3.8	3.8	3.6	3.0	2.7	2.5	2.5	3.3	2.2	2.0	2.0	1.9	1.8	1.6
12/57	4.0	3.9	3.6	3.9	4.0	3.7	3.9	3.9	3.7	3.2	2.9	2.7	2.7	2.5	2.4	2.3	2.2	2.2	2.1	1.9
12/58	3.8	3.7	3.6	3.7	3.8	3.5	3.7	3.6	3.4	3.0	2.7	2.4	2.4	2.3	2.1	2.0	2.0	1.9	1.8	1.6
12/59	3.7	3.6	3.5	3.5	3.6	3.3	3.4	3.4	3.2	2.7	2.5	2.2	2.2	2.1	1.9	1.8	1.7	1.7	1.6	1.4
12/60	3.8	3.7	3.6	3.6	3.7	3.5	3.6	3.6	3.4	2.9	2.7	2.5	2.5	2.3	2.2	2.1	2.0	2.0	1.9	1.8
12/61	3.8	3.7	3.6	3.6	3.7	3.5	3.6	3.6	3.4	3.0	2.7	2.5	2.5	2.4	2.3	2.1	2.1	2.1	2.0	1.9
12/62	3.9	3.8	3.7	3.7	3.8	3.6	3.7	3.7	3.5	3.1	2.9	2.7	2.7	2.6	2.5	2.4	2.4	2.4	2.3	2.2
12/63	3.8	3.7	3.7	3.7	3.8	3.6	3.7	3.8	3.5	3.1	2.9	2.7	2.7	2.6	2.5	2.4	2.4	2.3	2.3	2.2
12/64	3.8	3.8	3.7	3.7	3.8	3.6	3.7	3.7	3.5	3.1	2.9	2.7	2.8	2.6	2.6	2.5	2.5	2.5	2.4	2.3
12/65	3.7	3.7	3.6	3.6	3.7	3.5	3.6	3.5	3.4	3.0	2.8	2.6	2.6	2.5	2.4	2.4	2.3	2.3	2.3	2.2
12/66	3.6	3.5	3.4	3.4	3.5	3.3	3.4	3.3	3.2	2.8	2.6	2.4	2.4	2.3	2.2	2.1	2.1	2.1	2.0	1.9
12/67	3.4	3.3	3.2	3.2	3.3	3.1	3.2	3.1	3.0	2.8	2.4	2.2	2.2	2.1	2.0	1.9	1.9	1.8	1.8	1.7
12/68	3.3	3.3	3.2	3.2	3.2	3.1	3.1	3.1	2.9	2.6	2.4	2.2	2.2	2.1	2.0	1.9	1.9	1.8	1.8	1.7
12/69	3.3	3.2	3.1	3.2	3.2	3.0	3.1	3.1	2.9	2.6	2.4	2.2	2.2	2.1	2.0	1.9	1.9	1.8	1.8	1.7

Continued on next page

To \ From	12/45	12/46	12/47	12/48	12/49	12/50	12/51	12/52	12/53	12/54	12/55	12/56	12/57	12/58	12/59	12/60	12/61	12/62	12/63	12/64	12/65	12/66	12/67	12/68
12/46	2.6																							
12/47	0.8	-0.9																						
12/48	1.8	1.4	3.9																					
12/49	2.8	2.9	4.9	5.9																				
12/50	2.6	2.5	3.7	3.7	1.5																			
12/51	1.6	1.4	2.0	1.4	-0.8	-3.1																		
12/52	1.9	1.8	2.4	2.0	0.7	0.3	3.9																	
12/53	1.9	1.8	2.3	2.0	1.0	0.8	2.9	1.8																
12/54	2.3	2.3	2.8	2.6	1.9	2.0	3.8	3.8	5.7															
12/55	2.0	2.0	2.3	2.1	1.5	1.5	2.7	2.3	2.5	-0.7														
12/56	1.3	1.2	1.4	1.1	0.4	0.3	0.9	0.2	-0.3	-3.2	-5.7													
12/57	1.7	1.6	1.9	1.7	1.2	1.1	1.8	1.4	1.3	-0.1	0.2	5.4												
12/58	1.4	1.3	1.5	1.3	0.8	0.7	1.2	0.8	0.6	-0.6	-0.6	2.0	-2.2											
12/59	1.1	1.0	1.2	1.0	0.5	0.4	0.8	0.4	0.1	-1.0	-1.0	0.6	-2.2	-2.2										
12/60	1.6	1.5	1.7	1.5	1.1	1.1	1.6	1.3	1.2	0.5	0.7	2.4	1.1	2.7	7.9									
12/61	1.7	1.8	1.8	1.7	1.3	1.3	1.8	1.5	1.5	0.9	1.2	2.6	1.7	3.0	5.7	3.6								
12/62	2.1	2.0	2.2	2.1	1.8	1.8	2.3	2.1	2.2	1.7	2.1	3.4	2.9	4.2	6.4	5.6	7.7							
12/63	2.1	2.0	2.2	2.1	1.8	1.9	2.3	2.1	2.2	1.8	2.1	3.2	2.7	3.7	5.3	4.4	4.9	2.1						
12/64	2.2	2.2	2.3	2.2	2.0	2.0	2.4	2.3	2.4	2.0	2.3	3.4	3.0	3.9	5.1	4.4	4.7	3.3	4.5					
12/65	2.1	2.0	2.2	2.1	1.9	1.9	2.2	2.1	2.1	1.8	2.1	3.0	2.6	3.3	4.2	3.5	3.4	2.1	2.1	-0.3				
12/66	1.8	1.7	1.9	1.8	1.5	1.5	1.9	1.7	1.7	1.4	1.6	2.3	1.9	2.3	3.1	2.3	2.0	0.7	0.2	-1.9	-3.5			
12/67	1.5	1.5	1.6	1.5	1.3	1.2	1.5	1.4	1.3	1.0	1.1	1.8	1.3	1.7	2.2	1.5	1.1	-0.2	-0.7	-2.4	-3.4	-3.4		
12/68	1.5	1.5	1.6	1.5	1.3	1.3	1.5	1.4	1.3	1.0	1.2	1.8	1.4	1.7	2.2	1.5	1.2	0.1	-0.3	-1.4	-1.8	-0.9	1.5	
12/69	1.6	1.5	1.6	1.5	1.3	1.3	1.5	1.4	1.4	1.1	1.2	1.8	1.4	1.7	2.1	1.5	1.2	0.3	0.1	-0.8	-0.9	-0.1	1.6	1.7

*Reprinted with permission from Lawrence Fisher and Roman L. Weil, "Coping with the Risk of Internal Rate Fluctuations: Returns to Bond Holders from Naive and Optimal Strategies," *Journal of Business*, October 1971, pp. 425–426.

Table 13-5

Percentage of Bonds

Rating Category	Rate of Default
1	6%
2	6
3	13
4	19
5—9	42
Composite of rating of various agencies	

percentage of bonds in each rating classification (at the issue date) that have defaulted.

The figures cover a period of more than forty years and include two major wars and a severe depression. Therefore, the default rates may be higher than those of recent years. Still, the default rates are closely correlated with the original ratings of the bonds. It is also worthwhile to note the high percentage of low-rated bonds (in the 5 to 9 category) that defaulted. Thus, it is not accurate to conclude that all bonds are generally safe in terms of financial risk.

Market risk is not a problem for bond investors. Changes in general market conditions do not cause the prices of bonds to change. Bond prices are determined by interest rates and by the financial ability of the issuing corporation.

Other Factors A large, efficient market exists for corporate bonds. Thus, liquidity or marketability for these bonds is not a problem. Nor is divisibility a concern, since corporate bonds can be purchased in various amounts. Although most bonds have a face or maturity value of $1,000, the smallest amount usually traded is $5,000, and most bond orders are taken in multiples of that amount. Corporate bonds can be purchased "on margin," but this is a questionable approach for a small investor who wants to invest $15,000 to $20,000 but has only a few thousand in available resources. (Margin buying is discussed later with common stocks.)

Municipal Bonds

There are basically three types of bonds issued by state and local governments—*full faith and credit bonds* (also called *general obligations*), *revenue bonds*, and *assessment bonds*. Full faith and credit bonds are unconditionally backed by the total taxing power of the issuer. Revenue bonds are backed only by specific revenues, usually only those obtained from the assets constructed with the bond proceeds. For example, a state government may issue revenue bonds to finance a bridge and pay interest (and provide security) from the tolls collected. Assessment bonds finance improvements such as streets, sidewalks, and sewers.

In most respects, the analysis of municipal bonds parallels that of other bonds. Rating services provide ratings for municipals so it is rather easy, in most cases, to determine the quality of a municipal bond. In analyzing the quality of a municipal, analysts necessarily look to different financial ratios than those used for corporate bonds. For example, with general obligation municipal bonds, analysts study the amount of debt as a percentage of assessed property values, debt per capita, debt service costs (interest and debt retirement obligations) as a percentage of the issuer's operating budget, and sociological measures.

Because municipal bonds are debt obligations, they are subject to purchasing power risk and interest rate risk. In terms of financial risk, almost all municipal bonds are of high quality. General obligation bonds, of course, have less financial risk than revenue bonds. However, even revenue and assessment bonds have enjoyed high ratings from the rating services and few have defaulted.

Undoubtedly, the best known feature of municipal bonds is their tax status. Interest income received from a municipal bond is exempt from federal income taxes. Most states also provide a tax exemption for interest received from their own bonds and from bonds issued by local governmental units within the state.

The importance of the tax exemption can best be seen by the following simple formula:

$$\text{Tax equivalent yield} = \text{Taxable yield} \times (1 - \text{Tax rate})$$

Suppose, for example, that an investor, who is in the 40 percent income tax bracket, can buy a corporate (taxable) bond that pays 8 percent. The formula shows that the same investor would achieve an equivalent yield by buying a municipal bond that provided only a 4.8 percent return. The corporate bond would pay 8 percent, but 40 percent (or 3.2 percent) would be required to pay taxes, and 8 percent minus 3.2 equals 4.8 percent.

This explains why investors in high income tax brackets are attracted to municipal bonds. By using the formula, it is apparent that municipal bonds become more attractive as a person's tax bracket rises. Similarly, municipal bonds might not be attractive to investors in low

Table 13-6
After-Tax Yield

	Pre-Tax Yield	Tax Rate	After-Tax Yield
Coupon income	5.00	0	5.00
Capital gain	1.00	25[†]	0.75
		Total	5.75

[†] Taken as one-half the gain on regular rates.

tax brackets. High income investors bid up the price of municipal bonds, sometimes to the point where the yield to lower income investors is inadequate, even with the tax advantage.

A seldom discussed but important point about the tax treatment of municipal bonds is that there is no tax advantage for the capital gains on these investments. Consider the situation where a 5 percent municipal bond can be purchased at a discount to yield 6 percent. If the investor is in the 50 percent tax bracket, the aftertax yield would be as shown in Table 13-6.

Under these assumptions, the aftertax return on the corporate bond is more than the aftertax return on the municipal—even if the coupon rates are the same. This is because the capital gain is larger on the corporate bond and the tax rates (on the capital gains) are the same. Admittedly, the facts in the example are contrived and may not be realistic for many cases. Still, the example does show the importance of examining the tax situation with care.

Annuities

In recent years, life insurance companies have begun to issue single-premium, fixed-dollar annuities that possess many of the characteristics of municipal bonds. These annuities provide an interest-free buildup at an interest rate comparable to that paid by commercial banks on CDs (discussed earlier).

These annuities may be sold with a front-end charge of 5 to 6 percent or may subject the investor to a similar charge in the event of withdrawal in less than a minimum number of years (e.g., five years). Frequently, modest amounts (e.g., 7 percent of the initial investment) may be withdrawn even during the early years without penalty.

Any withdrawals up to the amount of the initial deposit are considered to be a return of principal and no tax liability is incurred until that amount has been received by the investor. For example, an investor depositing $5,000 could receive $500 annually for ten years without incurring a tax liability. Future withdrawals would be treated as ordinary income and would be taxed accordingly.

This type of investment can be liquidated without ever converting to an annuity arrangement involving mortality considerations. Consequently, it probably is an investment instrument worthy of an investor's consideration.

Common Stocks

Although accurate figures are not available, an enormous number of individuals own common stocks. Many people own common stocks indirectly through mutual funds, pension funds, insurance companies, and other financial institutions; but the New York Stock Exchange has estimated that there are about twenty-five million direct shareholders of public corporations. Of course, the number of individual common stock owners changes dramatically. When the market is high, more individuals are interested in owning common stocks. In any event, common stocks are widely accepted by individuals, and any financial advisor should have a sound understanding of the legal and investment characteristics of common stocks.

There is wide variety among common stocks. Some are known as "blue chip," but others are highly speculative. Between these two extremes, stocks may be classified as growth stocks, income stocks, cyclical stocks, or defensive stocks. Depending upon the classification system, other types of stocks can be identified.

From a potential investor's point of view, the type of stock under consideration is a question of practical significance. This is because the investment characteristics of the various types of common stocks are substantially different. Nevertheless, it is not always easy to classify a given stock.

Blue chip common stocks are usually defined as high grade issues of major companies that have had a long, uninterrupted history of earnings and dividends to stockholders. In general, these are the stocks of companies that are large, mature, and well established. The qualifications for a company to earn the blue chip label do not change much; however, the list of blue chip stocks changes over time. Thus, an investor who buys a blue chip stock has no assurance that the stock will continue to qualify as a blue chip.

Growth stocks are defined in a number of different ways. According to one authority, a growth company must possess these characteristics:[4]

1. a leading position in an attractive business,
2. top-notch proprietary products, services, or skills,
3. good pricing flexibility,
4. ability to develop new products and markets,
5. low labor costs,
6. high return on equity,
7. strong financial position,
8. high flow-back ratio,
9. conservative, sensible accounting,
10. limited exposure to environmental, social, and political pressures, and
11. relative freedom from import competition.

Obviously, the above list contains many subjective evaluations. Furthermore, there is no generally accepted concensus that all the characteristics in the list are necessary to define a growth stock. Other authorities may define a growth stock as one that has had a rate of growth (in sales, earnings, or in stock prices) that is higher than the growth rate for the economy.

Interest in growth stocks seems to rise and fall. The prevailing attitude in the mid-seventies was less optimistic than it had been in the 1960s. One of the primary reasons was the fact that a number of research studies showed that high growth in one period was not necessarily a reliable sign of high growth in a subsequent period.[5]

Income stocks are those that pay reliable, high dividends. In other words, the dividends are high enough to provide a high rate of current income, and the payment of the dividends is reasonably assured. Many companies have a policy of paying a fixed dividend, and if the price of the stock falls substantially, the fixed dollar dividend may well represent a high current rate of income. Most of these stocks would not be considered income stocks by the majority of common stock authorities. More often, income stocks are thought of as securities that can be purchased for their high current income. To a large extent, income stocks overlap with blue chips; i.e., many blue chip stocks are also income stocks.

Cyclical stocks are those in which earnings tend to fluctuate with the business cycle. Often these are the securities of companies producing materials basic to the economy, such as steel, cement, paper, and building materials. It is important to realize that the stock prices for cyclical securities do not necessarily follow the business cycle. One of the primary reasons why this is so is that investors who can identify cyclical stock prices can make profits by buying when stock prices are depressed.

This type of buying pressure bids up the prices of the stocks and therefore tends to eliminate the natural cyclical fluctuation.

When general business conditions are worsening, some companies tend to fare very well, or at least better than most other companies. The common stocks of these companies are known as defensive stocks. Generally, sales and profits of these companies compare less favorably to others when business is improving. As in the case of cyclical stocks, the actual stock prices may not follow the sales and profits of the company for the reasons given above.

Defensive stocks are generally found among companies making products that are insensitive to recessions. Often these are companies selling necessities such as food, utilities, and drugs.

Speculative stocks, of course, are those characterized by extreme price fluctuations. These are often associated with young, small companies, particularly those selling new, untested products.

Legal Characteristics of Common Stocks   Holders of common stock are the owners of a corporation. As such, their financial welfare is tied directly to the degree of success the company experiences. Because common stockholders are the *residual* owners of a corporation, the value of their ownership is likely to fluctuate more than other financial interests in a company.

One of the common-law rights of a common stockholder is the right to vote on important corporate matters. Normally, each share of common stock carries one vote. As a practical matter, most stockholders (at least in large corporations) never exercise their voting rights unless they vote by *proxy*. Voting by proxy is a method of legally designating another person to vote the shares.

Some companies (generally smaller organizations) issue two classes of common stock. The purpose of this approach is to establish a nonvoting category of corporate owners, usually to maintain control over the corporation. (Nonvoting common stock cannot be listed on the New York Stock Exchange.)

Another important common-law right of holders of common stock is the right to receive an equal dividend per share if dividends are declared. Some stockholders believe they have a legal right to dividends, but this is not true. The declaration of a dividend is under the control of the company's board of directors and in normal circumstances, it is virtually impossible to legally force the declaration of a dividend.

Under the common law, owners of common stock must be allowed to maintain their proportionate interest in the corporation if the company issues new common stock. Thus, if a corporation issues new common stock, existing common shareowners must be offered an opportunity to purchase the number of shares that are necessary to protect them against dilution of their interests. This right is known as the *preemptive right*.

As a practical matter, the common law has been modified to allow companies to exclude the preemptive right from stockholders. Accordingly, many companies (in their corporate charter or bylaws) specify that they shall not be required to provide preemptive rights. If this approach is used, a company may still offer new common stocks to existing stockholders, but the company is under no legal compulsion to do so. Actually, the preemptive right is not especially valuable to a stockholder in a large corporation because the proportionate interest of any single owner is usually minute. Furthermore, when new stock is sold, the value of each share is likely to drop. As a result, the gain from the preemptive right will probably be offset by the decline in the per share price of the stock.

Another legal right of common stockholders is the right to receive a pro rata share of the value of the company if it is dissolved. As a practical matter, a bankrupt organization seldom contains any value for common stockholders after the claims of all creditors are satisfied.

Investment Characteristics of Common Stocks For many types of investments a potential investor can determine with reasonable accuracy the future income that will be derived from the investment. With a savings account or a bond, for instance, a buyer can be reasonably assured of the amount of periodic income and future value of the asset. It is relatively easy, therefore, to determine the value of these assets at any given point in time. The returns from common stock, however, generally are very unpredictable. This means the valuation of common stock is a difficult problem.

The *price* of a share of common stock is easy to obtain (if there is an active market for the shares). The *value* of the stock refers to the real, or intrinsic, or true worth of the asset. If price and value were always the same, there could be no "overpriced" or "underpriced" stocks. Therefore, stock valuation, essentially, is the process of estimating "true" values which are independent of stock prices. If, for example, an investor can discover a stock that has a value of $20 per share but is currently selling for only $12 per share, he or she has discovered a "bargain." This is based on the presumption that stock prices tend to move to their "true" values. In fact, this presumption appears valid. If a stock is attractively priced (that is, the price is lower than the value), other investors are likely to discover this discrepancy and bid up the price of the stock.

Common stock valuation is a difficult subject and largely beyond the scope of this text. However, it is worthwhile to recognize that some valuation method is essential; if a potential investor has no method of estimating value, it is not reasonable to expect investment profits.

On the surface, it would appear that *book value* could be used to estimate a stock's worth. Book value (or net asset value) can be determined by examining a company's balance sheet, subtracting liabilities from assets, and dividing the net worth of the company by the number of common shares outstanding. The problem with this method is that almost all financial analysts agree that book value has very little relevance to true value, except in relatively few types of companies. Book value is an unreliable measure of a stock's worth for many reasons, but some of the more important reasons are: (1) book value is not directly related to a firm's future earnings; (2) the values shown on the balance sheet may not be realistic (for example, assets generally are carried at their original cost less depreciation rather than their present value); and (3) the balance sheet may not include some of the firm's most productive assets ("human capital," i.e., a company's investment in manpower, for example, is not shown).

Because the value of common stock depends heavily upon investor's expectations about the future, most valuation techniques are based upon the estimation of expected future earnings and the calculation of the present value of these earnings. In other words, earnings can be capitalized to arrive at an estimated value. The simplest, and most popular valuation technique is through the price/earnings (P/E) ratio. The P/E is simply the price of a share of common stock divided by the earnings per share. For example, a stock that has earnings (per share) of $1 and sells for $10 per share has a P/E ratio of 10/1. In effect, this means the investor is getting a benefit of 10 percent. If the stock appreciates to $20 but earnings per share stay at $1, the P/E ratio would be 20/1, implying a capitalization rate of 5 percent. A P/E ratio of 30/1 implies a capitalization rate of 3.3 percent.

Some financial analysts use much more sophisticated methods of estimating a stock's value. Some, for example, make adjustments for different rates of growth in earnings or dividends. Although some adjustments can become extremely complicated, there is no assurance that a more complicated technique produces better answers.

Investment Returns. In a monumental study of investment returns on common stocks, the actual returns (dividends plus stock price appreciation) on the stocks listed on the New York Stock Exchange were computed. The study covered a thirty-four year period and average returns over any set of consecutive years were developed. Table 13-7 shows these results.

The Fisher-Lorie study was significant because it provided hard evidence of the average actual rates of return for a large number of common stocks. The figure most often quoted from the study is the 9.3 percent annual rate of return earned on the stocks over the entire period (1926 to 1965). The figures are also illuminating in that the yearly returns are highly variable. Another significant aspect of the study was the fact that the returns over any extended period of time (ten years or longer) are generally quite high. Compared to the returns for high quality bonds (shown in Table 13-4), common stock investment returns have almost always been higher.

Despite the value of the Fisher-Lorie study, the limitations in the data are substantial. For example, it is clearly inappropriate for any investor to rely upon the 9.3 percent average annual return or any other figure in the study. The rates shown in Table 13-7 were historical averages, and thus may not apply to the future at all.

Another limitation is that the returns are not categorized by type of stock. For example, it is impossible to determine (from the study) if blue chip stocks outperformed the growth stocks or vice versa. However, in recent years there have been a number of studies that generally confirm the accepted notion that higher returns are associated with higher risk stocks. Therefore, it is reasonable to assume that, in general, stocks with greater risk (e.g., growth stocks) should outperform "safer" stocks (e.g., defensive stocks).

Knowledgeable authorities sometimes publish their views as to the rate of return that could reasonably be expected from various categories of common stock. One authority, for example, studied historical returns over a long period and believes the following expected returns are reasonable:[6]

1. Income Stocks—4.8 to 6.4 percent
2. Income/Growth Stocks—7.2 to 8.8 percent
3. Growth Stocks—9.6 to 12.8 percent
4. Speculative Growth Stocks—13.6 to 17.6 percent

Despite the accuracy in the above figures, other authorities have predicted different returns for the same categories of stocks.

As a result, we must conclude that investment returns in common stocks are largely unpredictable. Historically, investors who have owned a large group of diversified stocks and have held them for long periods have generally received a rate of return somewhat higher than that obtainable from investments carrying less financial and market risk. Although it is tempting to expect history to repeat itself, there have been many periods when common stocks have not performed well.

Investment Risks. As a category, common stocks generally are low-grade investments in terms of financial risk and market risk. Because common stock prices are affected greatly by investors'

Table 13-7

Rates of Return on Investment in Common Stocks Listed on the New York Stock Exchange with Reinvestment of Dividends (percent per annum compounded annually)*

To	1/26	12/26	12/27	12/28	12/29	12/30	12/31	12/32	12/33	12/34	12/35	12/36	12/37	12/38	12/39	12/40	12/41	12/42	12/43	12/44
12/26	-1.6																			
12/27	15.3	30.0																		
12/28	23.9	37.7	45.5																	
12/29	7.8	9.6	0.1	-30.0																
12/30	-2.3	-3.5	-13.0	-31.7	-37.2															
12/31	-11.1	-13.5	-21.7	-36.3	-40.8	-47.8	-11.1													
12/32	-11.0	-12.7	-19.0	-30.3	-32.1	-31.0														
12/33	-2.7	-3.2	-7.7	-15.6	-11.8	-1.3	36.9	108.4												
12/34	-1.2	-1.6	-5.2	-11.3	-7.0	2.4	28.2	55.0	13.8											
12/35	2.2	2.1	-0.8	-5.7	-0.5	9.3	32.9	53.5	31.2	50.4										
12/36	6.6	5.5	3.1	-0.4	5.3	15.3	37.5	54.5	40.9	56.8	63.9									
12/37	0.5	0.1	-2.3	-6.2	-2.8	3.3	16.1	23.1	8.2	6.6	-10.9	-46.0								
12/38	2.8	2.5	0.4	-2.9	0.9	7.0	18.7	25.1	12.9	12.4	1.1	-16.2	30.7							
12/39	2.6	2.3	0.3	-2.6	0.9	6.0	15.7	20.5	10.1	9.0	0.4	-11.2	12.9	-3.3						
12/40	1.9	1.6	-0.2	-3.0	0.2	4.7	13.0	16.9	7.9	6.4	-1.1	-9.8	6.3	-5.0	-9.9					
12/41	1.2	0.9	-0.8	-3.3	-0.5	3.5	10.8	13.8	5.8	4.2	-1.9	-9.2	2.6	-5.5	-9.0	-10.2				
12/42	2.0	1.9	0.4	-1.9	0.9	4.8	11.6	14.3	7.2	6.0	0.9	-4.9	6.1	0.6	1.1	7.6	31.1			
12/43	3.5	3.6	2.2	0.2	3.1	7.2	13.8	16.5	10.2	9.7	5.5	0.9	12.3	9.4	12.1	22.2	47.1	56.7		
12/44	4.6	4.7	3.5	1.7	4.7	8.7	15.2	17.9	12.3	12.0	8.4	4.6	15.7	13.7	17.1	26.8	45.6	49.3	38.1	
12/45	6.3	6.5	5.5	3.9	7.0	11.3	17.6	20.4	15.4	15.5	12.4	9.3	20.3	19.4	23.7	33.6	51.4	55.4	50.1	59.8

Continued on next page

12/46	12/47	12/48	12/49	12/50	12/51	12/52	12/53	12/54	12/55	12/56	12/57	12/58	12/59	12/60	12/61	12/62	12/63	12/64	12/65
20.2	13.2	9.1	11.4	15.0	15.2	14.5	12.5	16.4	16.9	16.4	13.6	16.0	15.8	14.6	15.4	13.5	13.9	14.0	14.4
26.0	18.9	14.2	15.2	17.9	17.7	16.8	14.8	18.2	18.6	17.9	15.1	17.3	17.1	15.9	16.5	14.6	14.9	15.0	15.4
34.5	26.3	20.8	20.8	22.4	21.6	20.4	18.1	21.0	21.1	20.2	17.5	19.4	19.1	17.9	18.5	16.5	16.7	16.7	16.9
34.8	27.5	22.5	22.2	23.5	22.6	21.5	19.3	21.9	21.8	20.8	18.3	20.2	19.9	18.7	19.3	17.3	17.4	17.4	17.5
24.2	20.3	17.0	17.3	19.0	18.6	17.9	16.1	18.7	18.8	18.2	15.9	17.8	17.6	16.6	17.3	15.6	15.8	15.8	16.0
17.8	15.5	13.3	13.9	15.6	15.6	15.1	13.7	16.2	16.6	16.2	14.2	16.0	16.0	15.1	15.8	14.3	14.6	14.7	14.9
15.0	13.6	11.7	12.3	14.1	14.1	13.8	12.5	14.8	15.2	15.1	13.2	15.0	15.0	14.2	15.0	13.5	13.8	14.0	14.2
16.3	14.7	12.7	13.3	14.8	14.8	14.5	13.3	15.5	15.9	15.6	13.9	15.5	15.6	14.8	15.4	14.0	14.3	14.4	14.6
7.2	6.7	5.8	6.8	8.5	9.0	9.0	8.3	10.5	11.1	11.1	9.7	11.3	11.5	11.1	11.8	10.7	11.0	11.3	11.6
10.2	9.4	8.4	9.1	10.6	11.0	11.0	10.2	12.2	12.7	12.6	11.2	12.7	12.8	12.3	13.0	11.8	12.2	12.4	12.6
13.1	12.1	11.0	11.5	12.8	13.1	13.0	12.1	14.1	14.6	14.4	12.9	14.4	14.5	13.9	14.5	13.3	13.6	13.7	14.0
13.3	12.4	11.3	11.7	12.9	13.1	13.0	12.2	14.0	14.5	14.4	12.9	14.3	14.4	13.9	14.4	13.2	13.5	13.6	13.9
18.0	16.8	15.5	15.7	16.7	16.7	16.4	15.3	17.0	17.4	17.1	15.5	16.7	16.8	16.1	16.6	15.3	15.6	15.6	15.9
15.6	14.6	13.5	13.8	14.9	15.1	14.8	13.9	15.5	15.9	15.7	14.3	15.5	15.6	14.9	15.4	14.3	14.6	14.5	14.9
9.9	9.3	8.5	9.1	10.2	10.6	10.5	9.8	11.4	11.9	11.8	10.7	11.9	12.1	11.6	12.2	11.2	11.6	11.6	12.0
6.0	5.8	5.2	6.0	7.0	7.5	7.6	7.1	8.7	9.2	9.2	8.3	9.5	9.7	9.4	9.9	9.1	9.5	9.6	10.0
3.2	3.1	2.8	3.6	4.6	5.1	5.3	5.0	6.4	6.9	7.0	6.3	7.5	7.6	7.5	8.1	7.3	7.7	7.9	8.2
4.7	4.6	4.2	4.9	5.9	6.4	6.5	6.1	7.6	8.0	8.1	7.3	8.4	8.5	8.3	8.9	8.2	8.5	8.8	9.0
5.7	5.6	5.2	5.8	6.7	7.1	7.2	6.8	8.2	8.6	8.7	7.9	9.0	9.1	9.0	9.5	8.8	9.1	9.3	9.5
5.5	5.3	5.1	5.7	6.5	6.9	7.0	6.6	6.1	8.4	8.5	7.8	8.8	8.9	8.8	9.3	8.6	8.9	9.1	9.3

To	From 12/45	12/46	12/47	12/48	12/49	12/50	12/51	12/52	12/53	12/54	12/55	12/56	12/57	12/58	12/59	12/60	12/61	12/62	12/63	12/64
12/46	-9.9																			
12/47	-4.4	-0.5																		
12/48	-3.5	-1.0	-2.9																	
12/49	1.9	5.4	8.2	19.3																
12/50	7.8	12.4	16.6	27.0	35.8															
12/51	9.4	13.3	16.4	23.1	25.2	14.9														
12/52	9.4	12.9	15.2	19.7	19.8	12.4	8.9													
12/53	7.9	10.5	12.1	15.0	13.7	7.5	3.5	-3.1												
12/54	12.5	15.5	17.7	21.3	21.6	17.9	18.5	22.8	54.8											
12/55	13.4	16.2	18.2	21.4	21.7	18.5	19.1	22.2	37.2	19.0										
12/56	13.3	15.6	17.2	19.8	20.0	17.0	16.9	18.6	26.7	13.3	6.5									
12/57	10.5	12.3	13.5	15.3	14.8	12.0	11.1	11.1	14.5	3.4	-3.7	-12.9								
12/58	13.2	15.2	16.7	18.7	18.6	16.5	16.5	17.5	21.9	14.5	13.0	17.4	57.9							
12/59	13.3	15.3	16.6	18.6	18.6	16.6	16.6	17.6	21.2	15.0	14.0	17.6	36.0	14.4						
12/60	12.2	14.0	15.2	16.8	16.5	14.9	14.8	15.3	17.8	12.4	11.2	13.1	21.9	6.4	-1.9					
12/61	13.2	14.9	16.0	17.5	17.3	16.0	16.0	16.6	19.0	14.6	13.9	16.1	23.7	13.6	12.9	27.6				
12/62	11.3	12.8	13.7	14.9	14.5	13.1	12.8	13.0	14.7	10.5	9.4	10.4	15.1	6.3	3.8	5.9	-13.3			
12/63	11.8	13.2	14.0	15.2	14.9	13.5	13.3	13.5	15.0	11.3	10.4	11.5	15.7	8.7	7.4	10.4	2.0	17.7		
12/64	12.1	13.4	14.2	15.3	15.0	13.7	13.5	13.8	15.3	11.9	11.2	12.3	16.2	10.4	9.7	12.8	7.6	18.5	16.3	
12/65	12.6	14.1	14.9	15.9	15.8	14.5	14.3	14.7	16.2	13.1	12.5	13.6	17.7	12.7	12.4	15.9	12.9	22.6	23.4	28.3

*Reprinted with permission from James H. Lorie and Mary T. Hamilton, *The Stock Market: Theories and Evidence* (Homewood, IL: Richard D. Irwin, 1973), pp. 32–33. Note: Part A—Cash-to-portfolio, tax exempt.

expectations about the future, the stock market is subject to extreme fluctuations. Most authorities agree that there is some type of "mass psychology" at work that produces overreactions in the market in both directions. Bad news is likely to have a depressing effect on the market that is greater than seems justified. And the market is likely to make a major advance with good news—again, a larger advance than appears reasonable. The net effect, of course, is violent swings in the market.

When the stock market undergoes a major shift, most stocks are pulled in the same direction. Indeed, the purpose of the segregation of market risk from financial risk is to indicate that security prices may be adversely affected when the market turns downward even if a company is enjoying its best, most profitable years.

The financial risk associated with many common stocks is also great. If a company is not large, well established, and growing at a reasonable rate, the financial risk may be an important consideration for an investor. For those companies where financial risk is not important, another type of risk may come into consideration. Some companies are so large, well established, and financially secure that even their common stocks are regarded as "income" securities. With investments of this type, the interest rate risk assumes greater importance. An increase in interest rates is likely to have an adverse impact on these common stock prices.

For many years common stocks were regarded as an effective hedge against inflation. In the past ten to fifteen years, however, common stock prices have often not been reliable in this function. In other words, the purchasing power risk has been affecting common stocks. Table 13-8 compares the nominal rate of return with the real rate of return for selected periods.

The risks and returns available on common stocks can be influenced greatly by buying on margin. When stocks are purchased on margin, the buyer puts up only a portion of the purchase price and borrows the difference from the brokerage house. The percentage of the purchase price that must be paid by the buyer is not a matter of negotiation. It is determined by the Federal Reserve Board and is changed periodically.

Suppose, for example, that the initial margin requirement has been set at 80 percent and an investor has $8,000 cash to invest. The investor has a choice: to purchase $8,000 in securities on a cash transaction basis or to purchase $10,000 in securities on a margin basis. The investor is able to acquire a greater number of shares on a margin basis by borrowing part of the purchase price ($2,000 in the example), thus leveraging the account. If the stock appreciates, the investor will earn a larger profit than he or she would have earned on a smaller number of shares.

Despite the appeal of margin buying, it has several potential

Table 13-8

Common Stocks as Inflation Hedges*

Time Period		Nominal Market Rate of Return†	Real Rate of Return (nominal rate adjusted for inflation)
From	12/31/65	7.7	3.9
To	12/31/68		
From	3/31/56	−6.2	−9.5
To	3/31/58		
From	3/31/50	31.5	23.1
To	12/31/51		
From	3/31/46	−0.7	−11.7
To	9/30/48		

† As measured by Standard and Poor's Industrial Stock Index.

* Reprinted with permission from R. K. Reilly, G. L. Johnson, and R. E. Smith, "Inflation, Inflation Hedges and Common Stocks," *Financial Analysts Journal*, January—February, 1970, pp. 104-110.

disadvantages. Just as margin buying magnifies profits if the stock price increases, it also magnifies losses if the stock price declines. In other words, buying on margin increases risk. Another potential disadvantage is the possibility of a margin call (a request for more money, an amount which will bring the investor's equity up to the required margin percentage). When stock is purchased on margin, the brokerage firm maintains a computerized record which, among other things, calculates periodically the margin in the account. The margin is equal to:

$$\frac{\text{Value of the collateral} - \text{Debit balance}}{\text{Value of the collateral}}$$

The value of the collateral is the current value of the stock and the debit balance is the amount owed to the broker. To follow the previous example, suppose the investor buys 200 shares at $50 per share when the initial margin requirement is 80 percent. Immediately after the purchase, the margin would be:

$$\frac{\$10,000 - \$2,000}{\$10,000} = 80 \text{ percent}$$

After the purchase, the margin call requirement is not based on the initial margin requirement, but on the "maintenance margin requirement." The maintenance margin requirement is set by the stock exchange. The current maintenance margin requirement on the New York Stock Exchange is 25 percent.

Suppose the stock price in the previous example fell to $45 per share. The margin in the account then would be (ignoring interest on the debit balance):

$$\frac{\$9,000 - \$2,000}{\$9,000} \text{ or about } 78 \text{ percent}$$

This is below the initial requirement but well above the maintenance requirement of 25 percent, so there would not be a margin call. But suppose the stock falls to $13 per share. Ignoring interest on the debit balance, the margin would be:

$$\frac{\$2,600 - \$2,000}{\$2,600} \text{ or about } 23 \text{ percent}$$

Under these circumstances a margin call would be made. The investor would be asked for additional cash (enough usually to bring the margin up to 35 percent). If the investor is unable or unwilling to pay the additional amount, the broker will sell the stock, recover the amount owed to the firm, and remit the remaining amount to the investor.

Another disadvantage of margin buying is the interest charge. Although the interest rate usually is fairly low because the broker has the stock as collateral, the interest builds up the debit balance and this varies the margin in the account.

Margin buying may be appropraite for short-term speculators but it generally is not appropriate for other investors. Margin increases risk, and when used for long-term investments the growing interest cost may make it difficult to earn a net profit.

The Modern Approach.   In recent years there has been extensive research on the relationship between risk and return for common stocks. While much of this research has been rather theoretical, the main ideas in the theory have been well supported and more investment counselors are making practical use of the basic concepts.

Previously, we divided investment risk into four types (interest rate risk, purchasing power risk, market risk, and financial risk). According to a newer classification system, risks associated with common stocks can be divided into *systematic* and *unsystematic* risks. Systematic risk is that portion of risk which arises from factors that affect the prices of all securities simultaneously. For example, changes in the economic, political, and sociological environment may affect all common stocks. Unsystematic risk arises from factors that are unique to a firm or industry. These are factors such as labor strikes, changes in consumer

Figure 13-2

Rates of Return For a Stock and the Stock Market

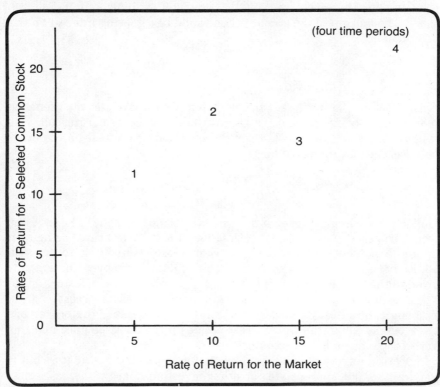

attitudes towards a product, and management mistakes. Therefore, in this approach:

$$\text{Systematic risk} + \text{Unsystematic risk} = \text{Total risk}$$

If a person were to follow the stock market and the price of a selected common stock, it would be possible to prepare a chart such as the one in Figure 13-2.

Point 1 in Figure 13-2 shows that the stock had a rate of return of 10 percent when the market had a return of 5 percent. Point 2 shows a return on the stock of 15 percent when the market return was 10 percent. Each point in the figure simply shows how the rates of return were related at any point in the past.

If a larger number of observations were made (pairing the rates of return), it would be possible to draw a line that represents the average relationship between the two rates of return. This type of relationship is called a stock's *characteristic* line and is shown in Figure 13-3.

Figure 13-3
A Stock's Characteristic Line

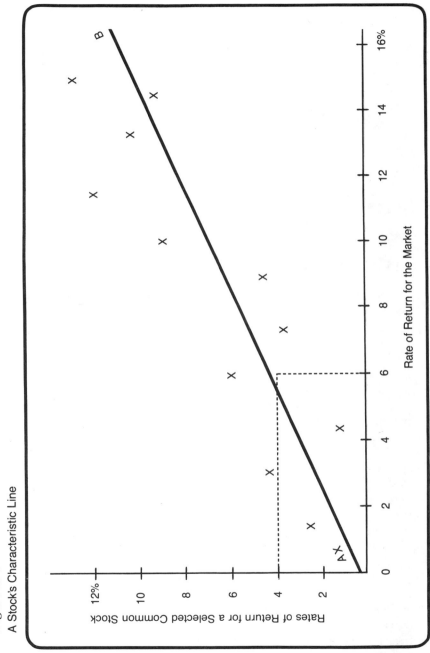

Figure 13-4

Stock A

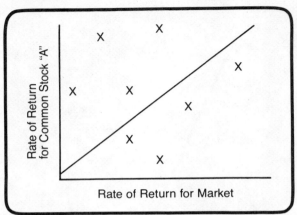

The characteristic line $(A-B)$ is extremely useful because it may be helpful in predicting the rate of return on a common stock under various market conditions. For example, if the market is expected to have a 6 percent return, what rate of return could be expected for the stock? If the average relationship holds, the stock's return could be predicted at 4 percent.

Of course, there is never a perfect correlation between a stock's rate of return and the market return. This is shown in Figure 13-3 by the fact that the points do not all fall exactly on the characteristic line. Consider Figures 13-4 and 13-5, which show two different stocks.

In Figure 13-4, the points are widely scattered around the characteristic line. Therefore, any expectations (predictions) based on this line would not be highly reliable. The case is different in Figure 13-5. In this case, the points all fall close to the characteristic line. Thus the expected return can be predicted with greater confidence.

Two other aspects of the characteristic line are extremely important. The point at which the characteristic line cuts the vertical axis is called *alpha*. It is an estimate of the stock's rate of return when the market return is zero. For most common stocks this rate of return is very low (close to zero in most cases).

The slope of the characteristic line is very important. If the line is very steep, it shows that a stock typically advances strongly when the market increases, but the common stock price tends to fall rapidly when the market declines. The steepness or slope of the characteristic line is called *beta*. Stocks with a beta greater than 1 are called aggressive stocks. Those with a beta less than one are called defensive stocks. If a stock has a beta of 1 its rate of return should, on the average, move

Figure 13-5

Stock B

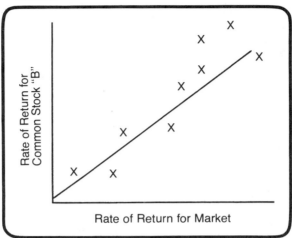

Rate of Return for Market

exactly with the market return. It has been shown that, in general, common stocks with greater betas (higher systematic risk) provide higher rates of return.[7] This is what a person would expect based on the previous discussion of types of stocks and rates of return.

Preferred Stocks

Preferred stocks are a hybrid security. In many respects they resemble common stock, and in other ways they are similar to bonds.

Characteristics of Preferred Stocks Legally, preferred stock represents an ownership interest in a corporation. In the event of liquidation of the company, claims of creditors (including bondholders) must be satisfied before payments can be made to preferred stockholders. The same priority exists with regard to the payment of income. That is, bond interest must be paid before dividend payments to preferred stockholders. Like dividends on common stock, preferred dividends are paid only after approval of a company's board of directors. Another similarity between most preferred stocks and common stock is that neither has a maturity date. Again, this reflects the legal position of preferred stockholders. For taxation purposes preferred dividends are treated as distributions of income to corporate owners. As a result, preferred dividends represent taxable income to preferred stockholders and are not a deductible expense for a corporation.

In a less legalistic and more practical sense, preferred stocks share many characteristics with bonds. Dividends on preferred stock are usually stated as a percentage of par value (normally $100) and are fixed. Therefore, 6 percent preferred stock would pay a dividend of $6 each year. Although the board of directors may legally elect to omit one or more dividend payments, most preferred stocks are *cumulative*. This means that dividends that have been missed on the preferred stock must be paid before the corporation is allowed to pay dividends to common stockholders.

Like bonds, preferred stocks may be callable by the issuing corporation; the call provisions are similar to those of bonds. For example, a call premium (often equal to one year's dividend) may be required. Sinking funds may be associated with preferred stocks. Another similarity is that preferred stocks may be convertible into common stocks.

Most companies restrict the voting rights for preferred stockholders. As a rule, preferred stockholders cannot vote unless dividends have been missed. With regard to voting rights, then, preferred stocks are similar to bonds.

Because preferred stocks generally provide a fixed dividend income to the investor, the interest rate risk is substantial for most preferred stocks. The principal invested, therefore, is not always stable and an investor can sustain losses if interest rates have increased since the time of issue of the stock.

The purchasing power risk for preferred stocks is also a substantial problem. The dividend income from a preferred stock will not increase over a long period even if inflation persists. An investor's real income, therefore, is likely to be eroded by price increases.

Investment Characteristics of Preferred Stocks The rating services that evaluate the quality of bonds also rate preferred stocks. These ratings, in effect, provide a good estimate of the financial risk associated with a preferred stock issue. As in the case of bonds, the ratings vary from high quality (Triple A or Double A) to speculative.

In general, holders of preferred stock are in a less secure position than bondholders. Compared to preferred stocks, bonds have prior claims to both dividends and assets upon liquidation. In a company with both preferred stock and bonds outstanding, preferred stockholders will assume greater risk. In this situation, it would be logical to assume that investors, preferring the more secure position of bonds, would bid up bond prices relative to the prices of preferred stocks. The interest return for bonds, then, should be lower than the dividend return from preferred stock. While this is a logical line of reasoning, it is not followed in practice. As a general rule, interest on a company's bonds will provide a greater income than will its preferred dividends. This apparent anomaly is a result of the federal income tax law. In order to avoid double taxation, the Internal Revenue Service allows corporations to exclude from their taxable income 85 percent of dividend income received from other corporations. This tax advantage is not provided to individual investors. Thus, preferred stocks are more attractive to corporate investors than to individuals. As a result, corporations have bid up the prices of preferred stocks to the point where the aftertax yield to individual investors is less than the yield generally available from high quality corporate bonds. Preferred stocks, therefore, generally are unwise investments for individuals. In some exceptional cases the dividend income from a preferred stock will be higher than that provided by bonds, but this is almost always an indication that the preferred stock is of poor quality.

Investment Companies

Investment companies are corporations (or in some cases, trusts) which invest shareholders' funds in securities. Investors are considered to be shareholders and as such, are the legal owners of the assets of the company. The assets, of course, consist almost entirely of investments— usually stocks and bonds of other companies. The effect, therefore, is to provide investors with an indirect means of owning stocks, bonds, and other assets.

An investment company has three basic functions. These are: (1) investment advice, (2) marketing, and (3) administration. The "management" company or "investment advisor" typically is a corporation separate from the corporation owning the securities, although it need not be. In its investment advisory function, the company selects securities for the portfolio of assets held by the investment company. The marketing function may be handled by employees of the investment company corporation or it may be handled by one or more securities brokers. The administrative function involves the overall management and operation of the investment company.

Types of Investment Companies

Closed End Investment Company. A *closed end investment company* begins operations by selling its common stock (and possibly preferred stock and bonds). Although a closed end company may legally change its size by issuing new securities, retiring existing securities, or retaining earnings, in practice this is rarely done. The capital structure of the organization, therefore, is relatively fixed; thus, the name "closed end."

The common stock of a closed end company is not redeemable by the company. If an investor wishes to sell his or her shares, the shares can only be sold to parties outside the investment company itself. In other words, shares of closed end companies are actively traded in the securities markets, just as the shares of other companies are bought and sold. The price of the shares in a closed end company, therefore, is determined by the forces of supply and demand in the market. As a result, the shares may sell at prices that are higher or lower than the net asset value, which is the net worth divided by the number of shares outstanding.

Open End Investment Company (Mutual Fund). In contrast to closed end companies, open end companies (also known as mutual funds) are much more important in terms of assets. While the assets of mutual funds have declined in recent years, these companies have enjoyed tremendous growth in most years since the 1940s. Closed end companies, on the other hand, have had a slower but gradually steady growth since the 1940s. They are somewhat less popular than mutual funds.

Upon a shareholder's request, a mutual fund will redeem any outstanding shares at the current net asset value. And new shares may be offered for sale continuously.

Many types of mutual funds are available in the market owing to their differences in terms of investment objectives. *Income funds* have an investment objective of providing liberal current income to investors. These funds, therefore, often purchase fixed income securities (bonds and preferred stocks) that provide high current yields. Common stocks are found in the portfolios of income funds but are not usually emphasized.

A *balanced mutual fund* strives for both capital appreciation and current income and usually owns bonds, preferred stocks, and common stocks. Although most balanced funds avoid inflexible rules, they normally attempt to maintain a fairly constant proportion of their assets invested in each of the major types of securities.

In recent years, *liquidity funds* or *money market funds* have become very popular. As their name suggests, these funds emphasize short-term investments such as Treasury bills, commercial paper, and other short-term assets. The basic objective is to provide investors with an alternative to savings accounts.

Common stock funds invest almost exclusively in common stocks and convertible securities. Often they are classified according to their principal investment objective—growth, growth and income, or capital gains. The distinction between growth funds and capital gains funds is not always clear. However, funds that seek maximum capital gains often invest in speculative assets.

Most mutual funds are "load" funds. These companies charge a

Table 13-9

Sliding Rate of Scales

Amount Purchased	Sales Charge
Less than $20,000	8.75%
$20,000— 30,000	7.00
30,000— 40,000	6.00
40,000— 50,000	4.00
50,000 or more	3.50

sales commission to an investor when shares are purchased. Usually there is no sales commission or redemption fee when shares are sold, but some companies charge a modest redemption fee.

The sales load for most companies is determined by a sliding scale of rates. For example, a company may impose charges as shown in Table 13-9.

Because there is considerable variation among companies in sales charges, the figures quoted above should be taken as illustrative only. Still, two features are worth noting. First, most load funds charge a commission that is approximately 8.5 percent for small purchases. Depending upon the scale, "small" purchases often are defined such that most individual investors pay the maximum rate. Second, the figure quoted may be misleading because sales charges are stated as a percentage of the offering price. For example, suppose an investor makes a $1,000 investment and the quoted sales charge is 8.5 percent. This is $85. However, when it is expressed as a percentage of the amount actually invested (which seems more appropriate) the sales charge is $85 divided by $915 (i.e. $1,000 – $85 = $915) or 9.3 percent.

An increasing number of mutual funds, known as "no-load" funds, do not charge a sales commission. These companies sell directly to the investor and therefore incur no sales commission. However, no-load funds often charge a small (½, 1, or 2 percent) redemption fee.

Both load and no-load funds charge investors for operating expenses on an annual basis. While these charges vary by company, a rate of three-fourths of 1 percent per year is fairly typical.

In addition to the loading charge (if any) and the charge for operating expenses, there is an annual fee for investment advice (the advisory fee). Often this charge is related directly to the performance of the fund. If performance is good, the investment advisor earns a higher percentage. The advisory fee is also frequently related to the size of the fund, with smaller percentage charges as the fund becomes larger. Thus, it is difficult to generalize about the amount of the advisory fee. However, to provide a general perspective, the fee is usually about one-half of 1 percent per year.

Investment Characteristics of Investment Companies The investment performance of mutual funds (and closed end companies) has been a subject of much debate and study in recent years. Much of the controversy has been generated by studies that have shown that the past performance of investment companies has not been better than that represented by general market measures. One major study, for example, computed the average annual return for each of forty mutual funds over the period 1951 to 1960.[8] The median annual return was 14.5 percent for the mutual funds, while the average return on all stocks on the New York Stock Exchange for the same period was 14.7 percent. A number of other studies have shown essentially the same results. In general, mutual funds have not been able to outperform the market.

Several studies have been undertaken comparing performance between load and no-load funds. Most of these studies have concluded that no-load funds have performed at least as well as load funds. [9] This is probably one of the main reasons for the increased interest among investors in no-load investment companies.

In recent years there has been more recognition of the fact that an investor's main interest should be focused on the performance of a specific fund, rather than on the performance of types of funds. An investor should be careful to compare a mutual fund's historical performance against the proper standards. One such standard is the company's stated investment objectives. Although some investment companies have followed investment policies that are inconsistent with their stated objectives, most companies adhere to their objectives reasonably well. By comparing actual performance to stated objectives, an investor has a better measure of meaningful results. For example, an income fund should not be expected to appreciate in value as rapidly as a growth fund.

Another standard by which a mutual fund's past performance may be measured is the Dow Jones Industrial Average (which measures the overall performance of stocks listed on the New York Stock Exchange) or some other market index. It may also be helpful to compare a specific mutual fund's performance to the performance of other investment companies.[10] In recent years there has been increasing recognition that the amount of risk assumed by a mutual fund should be a consideration in the measurement of the fund's performance. For example, aggressive funds should outperform more conservative funds, at least during periods when the stock market is advancing.

Table 13-10

Fund Performance

From 1970 to 1975	
The fund has an average annual rate of return of:	10%
During the period the average rate on Treasury bills was:	5%
Beta for the fund was:	1.5
From 1975 to 1980	
The fund had an average annual rate of return of:	12%
During the period the average rate on Treasury bills was:	8%
Beta (same as above) was:	1.5

To relate a mutal fund's performance to risk, the following simple formula has been developed and is being used extensively:

$$\text{Portfolio Performance} = \frac{\text{Risk Premium}}{\text{Systematic Risk Index}}$$

The numerator in the formula, the risk premium, is the average rate of return on the portfolio above the risk free rate (which is the rate earned on Treasury bills). The systematic risk index is the beta of the fund's characteristic line. The risk premium is used rather than the rate earned by the fund because it is desirable to eliminate the effects of changing interest rates. Or, stated differently, a fund should not be given credit for better investment performance that is a direct result of an increase in interest rates. Two examples will clarify this measure of performance.

Example One. Notice that in Table 13-10 the fund's risk level was unchanged and the average rate of return increased from 10 percent to 12 percent. But did the fund improve its performance?

$$1970-75: \frac{0.10 - 0.05}{1.50} = \frac{0.05}{1.50} = 0.033$$

$$1975-80: \frac{0.12 - 0.08}{1.50} = \frac{0.04}{1.50} = 0.027$$

Actually, the performance of the fund was worse in the second period. Superficially the performance improved, but the apparent improvement was caused by higher interest rates, not better fund management.

Table 13-11

Comparative Fund Performance

	Mutual Fund A	Mutual Fund B
Risk-free rate (rate on Treasury bills):	0.05	0.05
Average annual rate earned on the portfolio:	0.10	0.10
Beta:	1.50	0.50

Example Two. Note that in Table 13-11, during the same time period, the two mutual funds earned the same average annual rate of return (10 percent) but Fund A was an aggressive fund (beta = 1.5) while Fund B was conservative (beta = 0.5). Which represents better performance?

$$\text{Fund A: } \frac{0.10 - 0.05}{1.50} = \frac{0.05}{1.50} = 0.033$$

$$\text{Fund B: } \frac{0.10 - 0.05}{0.50} = \frac{0.05}{0.50} = 0.10$$

Fund B shows better performance even though the actual rates of return were identical. The performance measure, however, is logical because Fund A assumed high risk to achieve the return while Fund B did as well without high risk. Fund B, therefore, deserves a higher rating.

Because there is such a wide variety of investment companies, it is difficult to generalize about investment risks. Basically the types and degrees of investment risk depend upon the types of securities in the investment company's portfolio. An income fund consisting almost entirely of bonds, for example, would be subject to interest rate risk and purchasing power risk, but probably not subject to much financial risk (assuming high quality bonds) and virtually no market risk. Mutual funds composed mostly of common stocks, however, would be subject to the investment risks of those assets.

As an exception to the foregoing, there is one important type of risk that affects an investment company. Financial risk is often a major problem if an investor owns only a small number of common stocks. However, if an investor owns a larger number of similar investments, this type of risk is largely eliminated by diversification. Several studies have demonstrated that a portfolio of approximately between eight and sixteen common stocks selected at random will have investment returns close to those in the stock market as a whole.[11] This means, therefore, the financial risk (more accurately, unsystematic risk) has been largely eliminated. Consequently, investors who purchase investment company shares benefit because diversification practically avoids financial risk. Some of the companies in the portfolio may be financially weak, but other companies probably will experience above-average results. With several stocks in the portfolio, the good and bad effects of financial risk tend to cancel each other.

Compared with buying stocks or bonds individually, investment companies offer investors a number of "special" or convenient features. Not all investment companies provide all the services described below, but most are available from a number of companies.

Automatic dividend reinvestment is commonly available. If an investor chooses this option, all dividends provided by the fund are automatically invested in additional shares of the investment company. In some cases this approach allows an investor to escape commission charges on reinvested amounts.

Life insurance benefits are available with many plans. Some investment companies provide life insurance in the amount of shares purchased to date, but others offer "completion plan" insurance, which provides sufficient insurance to complete an investment program if the investor dies.

If an investor wishes to liquidate his or her investment over time, a *withdrawal account* may be appropriate. Under this arrangement, the fund makes payments to the investor of a specified amount usually at regular intervals. Payments are made first from dividend income (if available), but if dividends are inadequate, a suffucent number of shares are automatically redeemed. Obviously a withdrawal plan might be convenient for an individual, but usually an investor cannot determine very well how long the payments will be continued.

Investment companies that have associations (usually ownership connections) with other investment companies often provide shareholders an *exchange privilege*. This allows an investor to switch from one fund to another in the "family" with little or no charge. Since different funds in the group usually have different investment objectives, the exchange privilege may provide a worthwhile benefit. Consider the situation of an investor who has owned a growth fund and would like to change to an income fund, for example. Without the exchange privilege, the investor would have to sell the shares in the growth fund, perhaps incurring an income tax liability and then probably paying sales commissions in order to buy shares in the income fund.

An interesting aspect of a small but increasing number of mutual funds is the option of buying *mutual fund insurance*. This type of insurance insures investors against losses in their accounts. Basically, the insurance plan guarantees that investors will receive at least the amount they paid for their shares. However, policy periods are from ten to fifteen years and the guarantee is applicable only at the end of the policy period. In other words, the insurance policy must be held for the entire policy period before compensation for loss can be made. In effect, this type of insurance is intended to eliminate the financial risk from this type of investment and possibly some market risk. The elimination of financial risk is a benefit of little value because diversification should have effectively removed this type of risk.

Undoubtedly, two of the major attractions for mutual fund investors are (1) the ability to purchase shares in almost any amounts, thus permitting investors to gradually build up an investment program; and (2) the professional management of the investment company. While many observers question whether the management services are worth their cost, the fact remains that mutual funds allow an investor to almost completely turn over his or her investment problems to others.

Speculative Stock Market Investments

Warrants Common stock warrants are an interesting type of investment that has been gaining in popularity since the mid-1960s. Not long ago they could not be traded on the New York Stock Exchange but now they are traded in all the important security markets.

A warrant is an option that gives the owner the right to buy from a company a specific number of shares of a security (usually common stock) at a stated price during a certain period of time. For example, the ABC Company may raise funds by selling warrants (after the warrants are sold they may be traded among investors in the market). Assume that each warrant allows the owner to buy one share of common stock from the company (not from another investor) at a price of $80. If the common stock of the ABC Company is selling at a price much below $80, the warrants will sell at a low price. Suppose, for example, that the ABC common stock is selling for $40 per share. Obviously it would not benefit an investor to pay $80 for the stock by exercising the warrant when the stock can be purchased in the market at one-half of that price. Still, the warrant will command some price in the market if there is a period of time remaining before the warrant expires and there is some chance that the common stock price will appreciate to $80 or more in the future.

To follow the example of the ABC Company, suppose the warrants will not expire for another five years and are selling for $2 each. If the common stock price moves upward, say to $50, investors will see a greater likelihood that the common stock price will exceed the exercise price (of $80) and they will bid up the price of the warrants. The warrants might go up to $4, for example. With these (hypothetical) figures the common stock appreciated from $40 to $50, or an increase of 25 percent. The percentage increase in the value of the warrant, however, was 100 percent (from $2 to $4).

The leverage inherent in warrants results from the fixed exercise price. The percentage price changes in warrants will be greater than corresponding changes in common stock. The exact amount of the price movement in warrants depends upon several factors, but the most important are (1) the time remaining before the warrant expires, (2) the relationship between the warrant price and the common stock price, (3) investor's expectations about the future common stock prices, and (4) the dividend return on the common stock.

The preceding example of the ABC Company was simplified to show the principle of leverage. In practice, warrants may contain other features. Often warrants are exercisable into more or less than one share of common stock. Some warrants have an exercise price that changes over time. A similar feature allows an investor to use either cash or debt of the company to exercise the warrant.

Warrants offer the possibility of sizable financial rewards and, of course, the possibility of substantial losses. The investment risks associated with warrants are exactly the same as those that apply to common stocks. In fact, the investment risks inherent in a specific warrant are derived from the risks of the common stock of the same company. In essence, both the investment returns and investment risks for a warrant are the same as those for the common stock except both (returns and risks) are magnified by the purchase of warrants.

Options Basically, options are very similar to warrants. One type of option, a *call*, gives the owner of the option the right to buy a certain number of shares of a stock at a specified price during a given period of time. However, there are two major differences between a call and a warrant. First, a call gives the right to purchase the stock from another investor, rather than solely from the issuing company, as in the case of warrants. Second, call options are exercisable over a much shorter period of time. Warrants may not expire for many years. Options, however, usually expire in one year or less. Naturally, since a call expires in a few months, the call price (which is equivalent to the exercise price) is normally set very close to the market price of the common stock. A six-month call, for example, might involve a spread of only $5 on a stock selling for $70. That is, if the stock is selling at $70, a call might be bought that will allow the option buyer to acquire the stock at $75. If the stock does not appreciate, obviously the call will expire without value.

Another important option is known as a *put*. A put gives the owner of the option the right to sell a certain number of shares of a stock at a stated price during a given period of time. Basically, it is a contract between investors in which an investor agrees to buy on demand a security from the owner of the put.[12]

The description of investment risks and returns for warrants applies generally to options. The returns and risks attached to the common stock are magnified when a person buys a put or call option.

Real Estate

Types of Real Estate Investments   Real estate offers a wide spectrum of opportunities to investors. Investments in real estate may be classified in numerous ways, but for purposes of examining risks and returns, three methods of classification are helpful. These classification methods are: (1) lender versus equity owner positions, (2) forms of ownership, and (3) uses of the property.

Lender Versus Equity Owner.   A real estate investor may decide to assume a creditor position (by owning mortgages) rather than actually owning real estate. For individuals as opposed to financial institutions, the most common method of becoming a real estate creditor involves junior mortgages.[13] Generally, a junior mortgage (which is subordinate to the primary or first mortgage on the property) arises when a buyer does not have sufficient cash to purchase a home.[14] In some of the cases, the seller may be willing to accept a second mortgage as part of the down payment. The terms of the second mortgage obviously must be acceptable to both parties, but it is common for a second mortgage to run for five or ten years at an interest rate that is 1 or 2 percent higher than the rate on the first mortgage. If a home seller accepts a junior mortgage, he or she has invested in a fixed dollar investment. Often the home seller is interested in receiving cash and may, therefore, sell the junior mortgage. Although the market for junior mortgages is not a well developed, efficient one, most localities have firms or individuals who periodically purchase junior mortgages. Often real estate brokers are helpful in establishing and maintaining such a market.

Forms of Ownership.   Although real estate may be owned legally by a variety of methods, there are four forms that may have special appeal to individual investors. These are limited partnerships, joint ventures, syndicates, and real estate investment trusts (popularly known as "REITs").

Limited partnerships developed in the real estate investment field to provide a mechanism for combining the financial resources of a number of individuals. The limited partnership arrangement avoids the tax problems of a corporation because a partnership is not a taxable entity. At the same time, a limited partnership offers some advantages over a general partnership. For example, the participants in a limited partnership may have limited liability and control over the business. Furthermore, the death of a limited partner does not require the dissolution of the business. These advantages may be particularly important for an organization involved in real estate investments.

In recent years the IRS has been more frequently challenging real estate limited partnerships on the basis that they may be, in substance, corporations rather than partnerships, and therefore should be taxed as corporations. If a limited partnership is large (some have as many as 200 or more limited partners) and has a number of corporate characteristics, the IRS is likely to question the tax treatment. On the other hand, if a small number of investors organize a limited partnership and are careful to avoid corporate characteristics, this form of ownership may be reasonably safe from corporate income taxes.

A joint venture is simply a partnership formed for a single purpose. Often a joint venture will be set up as a limited partnership. In many cases a joint venture is established by a promoter who contributes administrative and management expertise, while limited partners provide the funds for the investment.

A real estate syndicate is a group of individuals who combine to invest in one or more properties. Notice that this definition overlaps with the definitions of limited partnerships and joint ventures. In other words, a syndicate is a broader concept. A syndicate may be owned in several ways, including a partnership, corporation or trust, or it may be a joint venture.

The financial advantages that result from syndication may be substantial. First, if established properly, the tax advantages associated with real estate investments (described later) will flow directly to the individual participants in the syndication. Second, a person may participate in a syndication in units with minimum amounts from $1,000 to $10,000. Not only does this provide opportunities for small investors, it also allows an individual to diversify his or her real estate investments by participating in more than one syndicate. A third major advantage of syndication is that most plans provide expert management, thus freeing individual investors from real estate management problems. Of course one of the most important advantages of syndication is that it provides a means for combining the funds of investors in order to invest in large projects and take advantage of economies of large scale operations.

Real estate syndicates, of course, are not free of problems. A potential syndicate member must have some understanding of the real estate investments to be undertaken. It is also vitally important to evaluate the sponsor of the syndicate. This individual (or firm) must have a good record of achievement, high credit rating, and administrative and managerial ability. Another factor that should be analyzed carefully is the legal agreement between investors and the sponsor (or promoter). A well-designed agreement will be very specific about possible assessments of participants, compensation of the sponsor, possible conflicts of interest, broker's fees, and the allocation of profits and expenses.

Real estate investment trusts (REITs) enjoyed enormous growth in the 1960s and early 1970s. While many of them have had financial troubles in recent years, they still offer individuals an interesting method of investing in real estate.

Basically, a REIT is very similar to a closed end investment company. A REIT has trustees, shareholders, and investment advisors. Usually, a REIT is established by an organization (often a financial institution) of individuals. Shares are sold very similarly to those of investment companies. The shares in REITs usually have a secondary market where investors may trade shares with other investors (but not with the REIT itself). In fact, some REITs are listed on the major stock exchanges.

Most REITs can be classified into one of the three following types: equity trusts, mortgage trusts, and construction trusts. Equity trusts own real estate; whereas mortgage trusts invest primarily in real estate mortgages. With a mortgage trust, the investor has an ownership interest in the trust but because of the debt instruments in the portfolio, the investor's basic position is that of a creditor rather than owner. Construction trusts specialize in the development of real estate projects.

The basic advantages and possible problems to an investor in a REIT are the same as those described before for real estate syndicates. The image of REITs was tarnished in the mid-1970s when a number of plans had financial difficulties and some failed. Most of the problems were related to the excessive use of debt and overly aggressive (risky) investment projects. As a result, many REITs have not performed well in recent years, even though many of these plans have been managed effectively and conservatively.

Uses of Property. When real estate investments are classified according to uses of the property, a wide assortment of investments are available. For example, real estate investments may be classified as:

1. owner-occupied residences,
2. individual rental homes,
3. apartment houses (new and existing),
4. agricultural and undeveloped land,
5. predeveloped land,

6. hotel and motel,
7. office buildings (small and large),
8. shopping centers, and
9. industrial buildings.

Other classifications by use of property are possible. The significant point, however, is that the risk-return relationships vary considerably with the use of the property.

Investment Characteristics of Real Estate Investments

Investment Returns. The yield on real estate investments can take one or more of three forms: cash income, tax shelter, and capital gains.

While tax considerations are important in many types of investments, they are often critical for investments in real property. The two major aspects of real estate investments that generate tax advantages for investors are leverage and depreciation. Leverage is associated with most real estate investments simply because it has become accepted practice to finance a real estate purchase by borrowing most of the purchase price. The tax advantage arises because interest is a deductible expense when computing the federal income tax liability. In the early years of an amortized mortgage the bulk of the total payment consists of interest. This makes a large part of the total payment deductible.

Even though a real estate investment often is made primarily from borrowed funds, the tax laws allow an investor to depreciate the total investment. Depreciation is often misunderstood. It is a genuine cost (otherwise you could be assured that the IRS would not allow it as a deduction), but does not require the owner of an asset to make a physical payment. That is, a check is never written for depreciation. Therefore, depreciation is succinctly viewed as a noncash expense. Depreciation reduces taxable income but does not reduce the cash inflow from a real estate investment.

Consider the example in Table 13-12. Both columns of the table represent the same investment, but the left column shows cash flow and the right column shows taxable income.

With this example a person would actually receive $200 each period but would show a loss for tax purposes of $300. Of course, not all real estate investments provide depreciation charges large enough to offset net income after interest charges. The amount of depreciation that can be charged against net income depends upon the method of depreciation used and the asset's depreciable life.

With only a few exceptions there are no reliable statistics that show the rates of return earned by real estate investors. At least there is no convenient index comparable to the Dow Jones Industrial Average, for example, that might indicate investors' experiences in real estate. However, two noted authorities have written that, "Those involved in

Table 13-12

Comparison of Cash Flow and Taxable Income for a Real Estate Investment

	Cash Flow	Taxable Income
Revenue	$4,000	$4,000
Expenses	−1,600	−1,600
Net income	2,400	2,400
Mortgage payments:		
Interest	−2,000	−2,000
Principal	− 200	
Cash flow	$ 200	
Depreciation		1,800
Taxable income		$−1,600

the real estate business, especially those in selling positions, tend to make unrealistic claims about returns that can reasonably be achieved from real estate investments."[15]

The interest rate for original owners on second mortgages normally is 1 or 2 percent higher than the interest rate on new home mortgages. However, this does not mean that these investors earn these rates. Very often second mortgages are sold by the original owners and when they are, they almost invariably sell at a substantial discount. The amount of the discount varies but is usually 20 or 30 percent. If a second mortgage pays 10 percent but is later sold at a discount of, say, 25 percent, it is hardly accurate to claim a true 10 percent investment return.

Those who buy second mortgages at a substantial discount may earn returns of 20 percent per year or more, but these rates are unadjusted for losses and expenses that are commonplace with second mortgages.

The ratings given to the investment returns of various types of real estate investments are shown in Table 13-13. Several aspects of Table 13-13 are interesting. First, only Hotels and Motels and Industrial Property have received high grades for cash flow. Second, only New Apartments and Hotels and Motels seem to function well as tax shelters. Third, all forms of property (except Small Offices and Industrial Property) apparently provide good appreciation. Another interesting facet of Table 13-13 is that none of the investments (except Hotels and Motels) receives high ratings or even good ratings on all three sources of investment returns.

Table 13-13
Investment Returns on Various Forms of Real Estate*

Type of Property

Investment Returns	Agricultural and Undeveloped Land	Predeveloped Land	New Apartments	Existing Apartments	Hotel and Motel	Small Office Properties	Shopping Centers	Office Buildings	Industrial Property
Cash Income	Low (or Negative)	Negative	Low to Medium	Reasonable	Possibly High	Average to Good	Average to Good	Average	Average to High
Tax Shelter	Low	Low	High	Low to Medium	Medium to High	Low to Medium	Low to Medium	Low	Low
Appreciation	Good	Good	Good	Good	Good	Low	Average	Average	Poor

*Reprinted with permission from Sherman J. Maisel and Stephen E. Roulac, *Real Estate Investment and Finance*, (New York: McGraw-Hill Book Co., 1976), p. 470.

Investment Risks. In general, most types of real estate investments provide a good hedge against inflation. In fact, real estate may be as effective a hedge against inflation as any other major category of investments. Thus, comparatively, the purchasing power risk is not generally a problem with real estate investments.

Interest rate changes certainly affect real estate values. The relationship between asset values and interest rates, however, is much less clear than it is with fixed income securities such as bonds.[16] In theory, property values should tend to move inversely with interest rates. In practice, interest rates do not seem to be *directly* connected to property values. During periods of extremely high interest rates, fewer buyers may be able to finance real estate purchases and property values may not rise as fast because of the lower demand. On the other hand, it can be argued that high interest rates make new mortgages prohibitive for many buyers, and as a result, existing properties become more valuable. In short, the effect of changes in interest rates upon property values is indeterminate.

Legal and political risks may be a major problem in some real estate investments. Perhaps the most common example of these risks with real estate is property rezoning. A real estate buyer may rely on existing zoning regulations or may assume incorrectly that the zoning may be changed after property is purchased. Other possible legal problems may result from titles that are not perfectly clear.

Natural hazards pose an important risk to some types of real estate. Most buildings are insured, but many for inadequate amounts and against relatively few "named" perils. More important, land is often subject to perils that frequently are uninsured, such as earthquakes and flood.

Marketability is one of the major problems for many real estate investors. The real estate market, as active as it is at times, is simply not as efficient as the markets for many other investments. Thus, the investment return on real estate should be higher than the return on highly marketable assets.

Required investment amounts for real estate purchases are often a problem for investors without substantial wealth. Some form of syndication might provide more convenient investment amounts but, as noted before, syndications also create problems. In some cases, investors possess sufficient resources to arrange a real estate purchase, but the property acquired may be too small to operate efficiently. Owners of small farms, ranches, motels, or office buildings, for example, may have difficulty competing against larger investors.

Perhaps the most unrecognized problem for inexperienced real estate investors is the degree of expertise and management time that may be required of them. Even investing in undeveloped land requires

Table 13-14

Changes in Antique Prices

	Percentage Change In:	
	Antique Index	Stock Prices [†]
1925—1968	785%	801%
1950—1968	562	225
1960—1968	486	160

[†] Measured by the Standard and Poor's Stock Index.

some current knowledge about political and economic trends. Apartment buildings, which also require a relatively small amount of time and expertise, often requires a resident manager. The management of commercial property requires a high degree of expertise in tenant selection, lease negotiation, and other areas.

Art and Antiques

Placing a value on paintings is an exceedingly difficult, largely subjective judgment. Even for recognized masterpieces, experts often differ considerably in their valuations.

Despite numerous problems, indexes that show changes in prices of paintings are available. One authority conducted an extremely careful study and calculated rates of return for valuable paintings over a long period of time, 1925 to 1960.[17] Over this period, the rate of return on the art price index compared favorably with returns on common stocks. Another respected index showed that most categories of art had a higher investment return than the average mutual fund over the 1950 to 1970 period.[18]

Returns on antiques have been impressive, especially in recent years. According to one index, antique prices have changed as shown in Table 13-14.[19]

Despite the attractive investment returns that have been associated with art and antiques, experts warn investors against several possible problems. For example, market risk may be substantial. Both art and antique prices have shown declines during recessions. Another possible problem is that investments in these assets are relatively nonmarketable. Of course buyers can always be found, but the markets for art and antiques are not nearly as developed and as efficient as are markets for many other securities.

Not only do valuable art and antiques fail to produce a current income, but also there is usually a maintenance expense. High quality investment paintings and antiques may well cost over $5,000 and these assets normally should be insured.

Another possible problem, or limitation, of paintings and antiques is that a high degree of expertise is required. A potential investor who is not at least as knowledgeable as the average art or antique investor will be operating at a significant disadvantage.

Precious Metals[20]

Gold has intrigued investors for centuries, and gold bullion became a legal investment in the U.S. in 1975. Basically, an investor can invest in gold in five ways: (1) gold bullion, (2) gold coins, (3) gold futures, (4) investment companies that specialize in gold, and (5) common stock of gold mining companies.

The price of gold is determined by supply and demand factors in a worldwide market. Historically, the world price of gold has shown wide swings, indicating that investors have had opportunities for large investment profits and large losses.

The ownership of gold bullion in this country has been legal for such a short period of time that it is impossible to develop a meaningful price trend. One of the major attractions of gold is that it reputedly provides an effective hedge against poor business conditions. The possible disadvantages are numerous. Gold bullion provides no current income, and indeed, requires maintenance expenses in the form of assay fees, insurance, and fees for safekeeping. In addition, there are commissions and sales taxes on gold transactions. Fraudulent gold bars are uncommon, but investors should conduct gold investments only through highly reputable bullion dealers.

Investments in gold coins are similar to investments in gold bullion, with few exceptions. Numismatic expertise is highly desirable for investing in coins. Also, counterfeiting may be a problem because it is not illegal in some foreign countries to replicate U.S. coins.

The common stocks of gold mining companies are closely associated with the price of gold. That is, their prices tend to move together. One of the important practical implications of this fact is that the common stock prices of gold mining companies *do not* closely correlate with the stock market. For this reason, investors seeking diversification and protection against market risk are often interested in these stocks. The stocks of most gold mining companies appreciated greatly in 1973 and

1974 in anticipation of the legalization of gold ownership. Although it is much too soon to evaluate their performance, gold mining company stocks generally have been declining since 1975.

Coin Collecting

Little is known about investor experience in coin collecting. Occasionally an article will appear that provides some evidence of investment returns, but the evidence is sketchy at best.

It is clear that coin collecting for investment purposes should be delineated from coin collecting as a hobby. As an investment, expert knowledge is necessary. If coins are collected for their metallic content, the investor should be aware that the prices of most precious metals are subject to wide fluctuations.

Stamp Collecting

Investing in postage stamps (as opposed to collecting stamps as a hobby) is said to be a good inflation hedge. Stevenson and Jennings, however, conclude that, "Although recent rates of return have been very high, the long-term historical rates of return are not especially high relative to the return earned on common stocks during the same period."[21]

Stamp collectors must be knowledgeable about the condition of the stamp, type of paper the stamp is printed on, watermarks, type of separation, and method of printing. Clearly, stamps as an investment do not provide a good arena for the novice.

COMBINING VARIOUS INVESTMENT VEHICLES

The beneficial effects of diversification have long been recognized. Only in recent years, however, have investment advisors begun to realize that the benefits of diversification depend greatly upon the investment risks of the individual assets in a portfolio. Consider the situation where a widow is advised to invest in several "safe" common stock investments. Following this advice, the widow might purchase some preferred stocks of a company, some stock of a public utility, and several very high quality (blue chip) stocks. Despite the fact that she has bought three different kinds of stock, her portfolio is not very well diversified. The investment risks of the securities are similar and the investment returns may be highly correlated with each other. If interest rates increase, for example, the prices of all the securities are likely to decline. If the prices of the investments tend to move together (that is, they are highly correlated with each other), there may be little benefit from the attempt to diversify.

Now consider the situation where an investor acquires investments in which the returns are fairly independent. In this case, some investments may be adversely affected by certain factors (for example, rising interest rates) but other investments may be experiencing high returns. In fact, the same factors that hurt one investment may be beneficial to another.

Thus, there are basically two types of diversification. Naive diversification simply relies on a number of different investments. However, if the investment returns are highly correlated, this type of diversification may be very ineffective. Effective diversification relies on combining assets that have returns which are not correlated (at least not highly correlated) with each other. With effective diversification, an investor is able to lower the overall level of risk and still achieve the same rate of return. Alternatively, effective diversification allows an investor to maintain the same level of risk (as someone who is not effectively diversified) and achieve higher rates of return.

The practical implications of effective diversification are significant, even for individuals who are not sizable investors. The concept of diversification applies to *all* forms of investments—not just stocks and bonds. Therefore, if an individual owns a home, has cash value life insurance, maintains a savings account, and owns several stocks (or a mutual fund), there may be a substantial degree of effective diversification. However, as previously noted, it requires, as a rule of thumb, eight to sixteen different investments to be effectively diversified. This means that a wise investor who already owns several types of assets and is considering other investments should look for different types of investments. Conversely, the person who uses only one investment vehicle (other than a home, savings account, and life insurance) to accumulate assets may not be effectively diversified.

Chapter Notes

1. Some authorities make a distinction between savings and investments. In this chapter, the words "savings" and "investment" are used interchangeably, although the word traditionally used with the various vehicles discussed will be used.
2. For federal income tax purposes, an asset must have been owned for one year to qualify for favorable capital gains tax treatment.
3. See, for example: Douglas H. Bellemore and John C. Ritchie, *Investments* 4th ed. (Cincinnati, OH: South-Western Publishing Company, 1974), pp. 104-110.
4. Jerome B. Cohen, "Common Stocks," *Financial Analysts Handbook* (Homewood, IL: Richard D. Irwin, 1975).
5. See, for example: Jesse Levin, "Growth Rates—The Bigger They Come the Harder They Fall," *Financial Analysts Journal* (November-December 1972), Vol. 28, No. 6, pp. 71-77.
6. John R. Holmes, "Anticipated Growth is the Prime Measure of Potential Risk, Hence Potential Reward," *Financial Analysts Journal*, Vol. 32, no. 3, (May-June 1976), p. 47.
7. See, for example: W. F. Sharpe and G. Cooper, "Risk-Return Classes of NYSE Common Stocks, 1931-67," *Financial Analysts Journal* (March- April 1972).
8. Eugene F. Fama, "The Behavior of Stock Prices," *Journal of Business* (January 1965), p. 93.
9. See, for example: Robert S. Carlson, "Aggregate Performance of Mutual Funds, 1948-67," *Journal of Financial and Quantitative Analysis* (March 1970), p. 1. Also, Irwin Friend, Marshall Blume and Jean Crockett, *Mutual Funds and Other Institutional Investors* (New York: McGraw-Hill, 1970), p. 157.
10. Several companies publish this type of information. One popular source is *Investment Companies: Mutual Funds and Other Types* (New York: Arthur Wiesenberger Financial Services) published annually.
11. For example, see John L. Evans and Stephen H. Archer, "Diversification and the Reduction of Dispersion: An Empirical Analysis," *Journal of Finance* (December 1968), p. 761.
12. The investment opportunities with options are not limited to buying options. Some investors prefer to write or sell options to others. This may be done when the individual owns the security (a "covered" position) or when the individual does not own it (a "naked" position). See, for example, Jack C. Francis, *Investments: Analysis and Management* (New York: McGraw-Hill, 1976), Chapter 13.
13. It is possible to have mortgages that are subordinated to a second mortgage. These would be third, or even fourth mortgages.
14. Junior mortgages also originate often from home improvement loans.

15. Sherman J. Maisel and Stephen E. Roulac, *Real Estate Investment and Finance* (New York: McGraw-Hill, 1976) p. 420.
16. Of course, the interest rate risk is a major problem for fixed income real estate investments such as mortgages.
17. Richard H. Rush, *Art as an Investment* (New York: Bonanza Books, 1958).
18. Richard Stevenson and Edward Jennings, *Fundamentals of Investments* (St. Paul, MN: West Publishing Company, 1976), p. 456.
19. Richard H. Rush, *Antiques as an Investment* (Englewood Cliffs, NJ: Prentice-Hall, 1968) p. 536.
20. The discussion focuses on gold as an investment, but the concepts apply to other precious metals.
21. Stevenson and Jennings, p. 454.

CHAPTER 14

Business Uses of Life Insurance and Estate Planning

INTRODUCTION

In property and liability insurance a clear distinction exists between "personal lines" and "commercial lines." In life and health insurance a similar distinction can be made. Most life and health exposures can be classified as personal or commercial, but this terminology is not common. More often, the "commercial lines" in life and health insurance are called the "business uses of life and health insurance."

One of the reasons for the different terminology is that the distinction between "personal" and "business" is more blurred in life and health insurance. The owner of a small business, for example, may have difficulty in distinguishing between personal and business needs for life insurance in the estate planning process.

It is difficult for a property-liability insurance advisor to be an expert in estate planning. However, he or she should be able to recognize the various personal exposures, and be able to make informed recommendations in basic situations.

There is a close parallel between estate planning and risk management. Estate planning attempts to view financial problems in a broad perspective, and the solutions are not limited to insurance. Thus, estate planning is to life insurance what risk management is to traditional property-liability insurance.

KEY EMPLOYEE INSURANCE

The most valuable asset possessed by many business firms is not shown on a company's balance sheet. Companies list their inventory, accounts receivable, buildings, and other assets, but they do not show the value of the contributions made by employees to the organization. Yet many business firms would have substantial financial problems if one or more of their important or "key" employees died or became disabled.

Astute management should recognize the importance of the contributions made by key employees to the company's financial welfare. The impact of their loss to the company as a result of premature death or disability can be minimized by the purchase of "key employee insurance."

Identifying Key Employees

There are at least three different definitions of a "key employee." According to one concept, a key employee is an individual whose death or disability would have an adverse financial impact on the business. The trouble with this concept is that the death or disability of *any* employee normally causes a financial loss in some amount. In most cases the losses are small, even insignificant, involving only minor expenses of replacing and training a new employee.

According to a second definition, a key employee is an individual who is important to an organization. Thus, it is common to speak of a vice-president, for example, as a "key" employee. For risk management purposes it is important to distinguish between "important" employees and those who represent a key-employee exposure. As explained below, the death of an important employee often causes only an insignificant loss to the company.

Since the concern here is only with significant exposures, a key employee will be defined as a person who possesses an unusual skill, talent, or ability and whose death or disability would probably cause a substantial financial loss to the company.

A number of factors must be considered to identify key employees. These factors include a person's title and position, decision-making authority, and salary. However, none of these factors provides a reliable guideline for identifying key employees. In fact, all these measures taken together might be misleading. Consider, for example, a vice-president who has considerable authority and a large salary. If this person could be replaced with few problems and at little or no cost (as is often the case), he or she should not be regarded as a key employee.

Some people are considered key employees because they have developed personal contacts which bring the company business that might be lost if these key individuals die or become disabled. Others are key employees because they provide a source of capital not otherwise available. Small businesses particularly have difficulty selling stock and bond issues inexpensively and in securing loans at favorable rates on acceptable terms.

Individuals who possess special talents, such as being the company's inventor of new products or the person responsible for the company's efficient operations, may be key employees.

Certain types of businesses are more apt to have key employees than others. They are common in companies where:

1. the business has been built or is being developed by a small number of people;
2. the company does not have many individuals who can move quickly to a higher position;
3. the company is growing rapidly, does not have abundant working capital, and debt is obtained through personal contacts; and
4. the product or service offered by the company is unique or at least unusual.

Although few companies have all these features, they generally describe small firms that are successful *because* of key employees. Large companies may have many executives and other important employees, but as a general rule, these people can be replaced with relative ease, and, consequently, the firms have few key employees.

Estimating Key Employee Losses

Even when a company knows that an individual is a key employee, it is difficult to estimate the loss value associated with his or her death or disability. When a key employee is lost, the company must decide whether or not a replacement is necessary. If replacement is not practical, the loss may be relatively easy to estimate. Suppose, for example, that a key employee has been in charge of a project which must now be discontinued since he or she is irreplaceable. The loss is the amount invested in the project that cannot be recovered. The amount of the exposure increases to the point where other employees could manage the project.

As a second example, assume that a company has annual sales of

$10 million and one salesperson produces 25 percent of the business ($2.5 million). If the profit margin is 6 percent, the company derives annually a profit of $150,000 from the salesperson's efforts. If the salesperson's contacts are nontransferable and his or her business will likely be lost when retirement occurs in eight years, his or her value to the company is the present value of $150,000 per year for eight years. If other salespeople could obtain and maintain 60 percent of the sales level of this salesperson, the proper discount would be 40 percent of $150,000 ($60,000 annually) since this is the profit the company would lose if the key employee died or became disabled.

In situations in which key employees are replaceable, expenses may be incurred, profits lost, or both. In determining replacement expenses, only the additional costs of replacing the key employee should be considered. These expenses include any fees paid to an employment agency the new employee's moving expenses, and the difference between the new and old employee's salaries assuming the new employee is paid more than his or her predecessor.

If profits also are adversely affected, estimates must be made for the size and duration of this decline. Some life insurance companies provide formulas for estimating the value of a key employee. Some formulas are too simple to be reliable while others, more technically correct, are difficult to use. Consequently, many companies simply use a subjective estimate that gives lip service to the factors previously mentioned. Another approach is simply to use some multiple of the key employee's annual salary or an estimate of his or her value since many life insurers have underwriting rules that restrict the amount of key employee insurance to a multiple such as five times the employee's salary.

Key Employee Life Insurance Arrangements

Key employee life insurance does not require any special type of policy. Moreover, unlike most other business life insurance plans, no formal agreement is required between the company and the key employee.

Term insurance normally is purchased if the purpose of the arrangement is to reimburse the company for losses caused by the key employee's death. A policy that accumulates a cash value is appropriate if the arrangement is also used to fund a nonqualified, deferred compensation plan for the key employee.

A company has an insurable interest in the lives of key employees and, consequently, can buy life insurance on their lives if their deaths would be detrimental financially to the company. An insured key employee must consent to the purchase and must affirm the information contained in the application. As a further underwriting safeguard, many insurers require that the board of directors of a corporate applicant pass a resolution which states the purpose of the insurance and attach the resolution to the application. Normally, the company is the applicant, the owner, the premium payer, and the beneficiary since the insurance protects the company.

Insurable interest is required in life insurance only at policy inception. When a key employee's employment is terminated, the firm may continue to pay the premiums and keep the insurance in force, surrender the policy for its cash surrender value, or sell the policy to the insured. This approach is particularly advantageous to otherwise uninsurable individuals.

Tax Aspects of Key Employee Life Insurance

The Internal Revenue Code prohibits an income tax deduction for key employee life insurance premiums since they are not considered to be necessary and reasonable business expenditures. Deductions are disallowed for life insurance premiums paid on "any officer, employee, or any person financially interested in any trade or business carried on by the taxpayer when the taxpayer is directly or indirectly a beneficiary under the policy." Thus, even if the proceeds are payable to a key employee's personal beneficiaries, the business firm is considered an "indirect" beneficiary and the premiums are not deductible. On the other hand, premium payments are not treated as taxable income to the key employee.

If a cash value policy is carried on the life of a key employee, the annual increase in the cash value is not subject to taxation—either to the company or to the key employee. If the company surrenders the policy and the cash value exceeds the total premiums paid, the gain is taxable as ordinary income to the company.

As a general rule, life insurance death proceeds received by a company are not subject to federal income taxes. This rule is valid whether the beneficiary is an individual or an unincorporated business. However, when proceeds are paid to a corporation and are then paid to stockholders, they may be treated as dividends subject to taxation as ordinary income, and the distribution is not deductible by the corporation.

An exception to the above occurs when an existing life insurance policy is purchased from an individual or another business. The death proceeds are taxed (subject to certain exceptions) to the extent that the proceeds exceed the purchase price of the policy and the subsequent premiums paid.[1] This is known as the "transfer for value" rule.

Key Employee Health Insurance

The impact on the firm is the same regardless of whether a key employee's services are lost by death or by disability. Even though disabilities (even total and permanent) occur more frequently during the working ages than death, key employee disability income insurance (designed to reimburse the employer for the employee's services) is not as prevalent as key employee life insurance. Frequently the waiver of premium rider is purchased on a key employee life insurance policy which provides the company with a limited form of disability protection since the company ultimately will receive indemnification for the loss of the employee's services by means of the death proceeds.

This relative lack of interest in key employee disability income insurance does not stem from any adverse tax situation since it is the same as it is with key employee life insurance, i.e., premiums paid are not deductible, but benefits are tax-exempt. Rather, this type of coverage suffers from several underwriting limitations not found in the case of life insurance. For example, most insurers limit coverage to 40 to 70 percent of the insured's salary subject to a stated monetary limit such as $2,000. Consequently, the benefit may be a small portion of the individual's predisability income. To illustrate, assume that an insurer has a monthly limit of $2,500 and a maximum percentage of 50 percent. The annual benefit paid in the event of the disability of an $80,000 per-year insured would be $2,500 per month ($30,000 per year) which may be inadequate to protect the firm for its losses.

Secondly, this coverage may interfere with the employee's ability to purchase a reasonable amount of personal disability income insurance due to the potential moral hazard involved. This would be particularly true if the key employee is also a part-owner of the business.

Limited disability income protection is afforded by means of "business overhead" insurance. It pays (up to a specified limit) office overhead expenses such as rent, utility bills, employees' salaries, and depreciation that continue when an insured is disabled. The insured's lost income is not covered. This coverage generally is limited to proprietors and partners; a key employee might not be eligible for this coverage.

Table 14-1

Illustration of a Basic Split Dollar Plan

Policy Year	Annual Premium	Cash Value	Annual Increase In Cash Value	Amount Paid By Employee	Face Amount Less Cash Value
1	$1830	0	0	$1830	$100,000
2	1830	$ 300	$ 300	$1530	99,700
3	1830	1900	1600	230	98,100
4	1830	3100	1700	130	96,400
5	1830	5200	1600	230	94,800
6	1830	6900	1700	130	93,100
7	1830	8700	1800	30	91,300
8	1830	10,400	1700	130	89,600
9	1830	12,200	1800	30	87,800
10	1830	14,000	1800	30	86,000
11	1830	15,900	1900	0	84,100
12	1830	17,700	1800	30	82,300
13	1830	19,600	1900	0	80,400
14	1830	21,500	1900	0	78,500
15	1830	23,500	2000	0	76,500
16	1830	25,400	1900	0	74,600
17	1830	27,400	2000	0	72,600
18	1830	29,400	2000	0	70,600
19	1830	31,400	2000	0	68,600
20	1830	33,400	2000	0	66,600
Age 60	1830	42,800	1900	0	57,200
Age 65	1830	51,600	1900	0	48,400

SPLIT DOLLAR LIFE INSURANCE

Just as a business suffers a financial loss when a key person dies or becomes disabled, it also incurs a loss if a key employee voluntarily leaves the business. One method used to retain and attract key employees is by means of a split dollar life insurance plan. It is a method of sharing the costs and benefits of a life insurance policy.

In the basic split dollar arrangement, the employer pays a portion of each premium equal to the annual increase in cash value, and the employee pays the remainder. For example, assume that A is thirty-five years of age, and the plan under consideration is a $100,000 straight life, nonparticipating contract with an annual premium of $1,830. Table 14-1 shows how the policy can be purchased as a split dollar plan.

In the first year of the plan, A pays the entire premium of $1,830. In the second year the increase in the cash value (column 3) is $300.

Therefore, the company would pay $300, and A would pay $1,530. Each year thereafter the company pays an amount equal to the increase in cash value, and A pays the rest. Over time, A's payments would decline to zero over the first twelve policy years.

The death proceeds will be divided between the employer and A's beneficiary. The company will receive an amount equal to the cash value at the insured's death, and the employee's beneficiary will receive the remainder. Suppose A died in the tenth year. The amount payable to the company would be $14,000, and A's beneficiary would receive $86,000.

The death proceeds payable to A's beneficiary decrease over time. In effect, the employee's protection is similar to a decreasing term policy. The cost of the protection to the employee, however, is quite low.

While an employer recovers the total premiums paid, there is a cost to the company, i.e., the loss of the use of the money tied up in the contract. The true cost (and the out-of-pocket expense) can be quite low if the employer uses policy loans to help pay the company's share of the premiums. If the company deducts the policy loan interest for income tax purposes, the cost will be even lower.

Variations of the Basic Split Dollar Plan

Although it is impossible to describe all the variations in split dollar plans, it is important to consider some of the common modifications. Some of these variations ameliorate certain problems that are involved in the basic plan.

Types of Policies Used   A split dollar plan can use any policy that accumulates a cash value. Straight life policies are perhaps most often used, but limited payment plans (especially life paid-up at age sixty-five) are also common.

Policies that slowly develop cash values require the employee to bear a larger portion of the cost in the early policy years (unless the premium sharing between the employer and employee is modified). Therefore, policies that develop relatively large cash values in the early policy years (known as "high cash value" policies) are often used since the employee's cost may be reduced to zero in four or five years. Unless the sharing of the premium is modified, however, the employee may still have to make large cash outlays in the first few years.

Normally it is not practical to use an existing policy owned by the employee since little or nothing would be gained by allowing the employer to pay part of the cost and become entitled to part of the proceeds. If the existing policy is owned by the firm, the company normally would have other purposes for the contract.

Dividends Participating policies offer several methods of achieving flexibility in split dollar plans. One approach is to use dividends to reduce the premiums which initially reduces the employee's annual cost and later reduces the employer's annual out-of-pocket expense. In the early years the net premium (the premium minus the dividend) is greater than the annual increase in the cash value. The dividend, therefore, reduces the employee's obligation because the employer's contribution is limited to the cash value increase. Thus, the employee's cost is reduced rapidly because two factors are at work: (1) the dividends (which are increasing) reduce the cost, and (2) the employer is paying a larger share of the premium because the cash value is increasing.

Dividends also may be used to purchase one-year term insurance. This approach, known as the "fifth dividend option," quickly generates dividends large enough to purchase an amount of term insurance that offsets the annual increase in cash value. If the dividend is sufficient to purchase an amount that exactly offsets the cash value increase, the death proceeds payable to the employee's beneficiary will remain level. As a practical matter most policies generate dividends (after a few years) that are larger than the amount needed, so the excess is usually applied to reduce the premium.

The other dividend options (purchase paid-up additional insurance and accumulate at interest) seldom are used in split dollar plans. Under the paid-up additions option, the usual procedure is to split the death benefit in the same manner as the basic policy—with the cash value going to the employer. However, the plan can be designed so that the full death benefits of the paid-up additions are paid to the employee's beneficiary.

Allocation of Cost A common objection to the basic split dollar plan is that the employee's cost in the early years is high. This problem may be handled in several ways. One popular approach has been for the employer to pay the entire premium. Another approach is for the employer to lend the employee funds to finance the early premiums.

A third method is for the employer and employee to pay a level amount over a designated number of years. As an example, the employer's contribution can be determined by dividing the cash value at age sixty-five by the number of years that will elapse to that age. Using the figures in Table 14-1, an employer would pay $1,720 ($51,600 divided by thirty years) and the employee then would pay $110 ($1,830 minus $1,720) annually.

Tax Aspects The "economic benefit" of a split dollar plan must be included each year in the employee's taxable income.[2] For income tax purposes this benefit is measured as the one-year term insurance cost of the amount of life insurance protection provided to the employee, minus

Table 14-2

Table of P.S. 58 One-Year Term Rates

Age	Rate	Age	Rate	Age	Rate
15	$1.27	37	$ 3.63	59	$ 19.08
16	1.38	38	3.87	60	20.73
17	1.48	39	4.14	61	22.53
18	1.52	40	4.42	62	24.50
19	1.56	41	4.73	63	26.63
20	1.61	42	5.07	64	28.98
21	1.67	43	5.44	65	31.51
22	1.73	44	5.85	66	34.28
23	1.79	45	6.30	67	37.31
24	1.86	46	6.78	68	40.59
25	1.93	47	7.32	69	44.17
26	2.02	48	7.89	70	48.06
27	2.11	49	8.53	71	52.29
28	2.20	50	9.22	72	56.89
29	2.31	51	9.97	73	61.89
30	2.43	52	10.79	74	67.33
31	2.57	53	11.69	75	73.23
32	2.70	54	12.67	76	79.63
33	2.86	55	13.74	77	86.57
34	3.02	56	14.91	78	94.01
35	3.21	57	16.18	79	102.23
36	3.41	58	17.56	80	111.04
				81	120.57

any portion of the premium paid by the employee. In calculating the cost of the life insurance protection, the federal government's P.S. 58 Rate Table may be used (or the actual rates used by the life insurer may be used if they are lower).[3] The government's rates are shown in Table 14-2.

These rules can be clarified by returning to the example involving A. The death proceeds payable to A's beneficiary in the first year are $100,000. Using the term rate in Table 14-2, at age thirty-five ($3.21) the value of the insurance protection is $321. The value taxable to A is found by subtracting A's portion of the premium ($1,830). Since A will pay more than the value of the protection received, A will have no income tax consequences in the first year. The same is true in the second year; but in the third year, the amount of the protection is $98,100 which is valued at $356 ($3.63 × $98,100). Subtracting the amount A pays ($230), A's taxable income is $126. In a split dollar plan where the employee's contribution decreases, there will almost always be increases in taxable income. There are no provisions that allow an employee to "carry over" the excess cost in the early years to later years.

Dividends that are distributed to an employee, accumulated at interest for the employee, or used to purchase one-year term insurance are considered part of the employee's "economic benefit" and are taxable. An employer cannot deduct for tax purposes the premium payments paid for a split dollar plan.

An exception to this concept is a "private plan," i.e., one where there is no employment relationship between the parties involved. Plans between family members, for example, are private plans. These plans normally do not create taxable income for the insured.

Death proceeds are received free of income tax, both by the employer and the employee's beneficiary.

Implementation

The first step in implementing a split dollar plan is to decide whether to use an endorsement assignment or a collateral assignment.

Under the endorsement system the employer is the applicant and the policyowner. However, the policy includes an ownership endorsement which gives the insured employee the right to name (and change) the beneficiary for the proceeds in excess of the cash value. As the owner of the policy, the employer is primarily responsible for the payment of premiums.

Under the collateral assignment system the insured applies for the policy and becomes responsible for the premium payments. As the owner of the policy, the employee designates the beneficiary. By separate agreement, the employer agrees to "lend" the employee (normally at zero interest) the amount of the annual increase in the cash value (or whatever amount on which the parties have decided). In order to protect the employer, the policy is assigned to the employer with a collateral assignment form which protects the employer to the extent of the "loan." As a collateral assignee, the employer receives the death proceeds but is obligated to pay the employee's beneficiary the amount by which the death proceeds exceed the cash value. Also, the employer is given the right to surrender the policy and to make policy loans. Usually, however, the employer agrees not to surrender the policy unless the employee fails to pay the appropriate portion of the premium. Any agreeable assignment form may be used, but it is preferable to use a standard collateral assignment form, such as the one developed by the American Bankers Association. A copy of the assignment should be sent to the life insurance company because a life insurer is not bound by the terms of the assignment unless the company has written notice of the assignment.

Although the distinctions between endorsement and collateral assignments are largely technical, there are several important, practical differences. First, some state laws prohibit corporations from making loans to directors, officers, and shareholders of the corporation. Consequently, a collateral assignment should not be used in those states.

An endorsement assignment provides an employer with greater control which is an important consideration if the employer desires to obtain a policy loan since this right may be restricted in a collateral assignment system. Greater control is also important if the employer wants to combine the split dollar plan with some other plan, such as a deferred compensation agreement, since dual purpose plans can be managed better if the company owns the policy.

The main advantage of the collateral assignment system is its simplicity, since the employee owns the policy and assigns it as security for a loan. Furthermore, this type of assignment is simpler to use if the dividends belong to the employee. Third, it is easier to arrange a plan where the cost split is not determined by the cash value increase with a collateral assignment. Finally, this type of assignment inherently involves loans and it is easy to schedule the loans to fit the desires of the employer and employee.

The second major step in implementing a split dollar plan is to execute an agreement which sets forth the obligations of each party, the cost allocation, the disposition of policy dividends (if any), the rights to obtain policy loans, the circumstances which will terminate the plan, and the rights of the parties when the plan is terminated. Many plans stipulate that the employee may purchase the policy when the employment relationship terminates.

BUSINESS CONTINUATION
SOLE PROPRIETORSHIP INSURANCE[4]

There are more sole proprietorships than any other form of business enterprise despite the fact that they are particularly vulnerable to major losses caused by the death or disability of the owner.[5]

Types of Losses

When a sole proprietor dies or becomes disabled, the business normally loses its most valuable asset since it has been built around the talents and contributions of the owner. A serious problem is the loss of valuable management ability which may be only partially replaceable. If the deceased's spouse assumes the responsibility, the company may suffer if the spouse is not fully trained in the business and cannot manage the company as well as it was managed previously. Even if a capable manager is hired, the cost will be an additional financial drain on the business.

Typically, the morale of employees is adversely affected by the loss of the owner due to concern over the fate of the company and their own job security. If they question the ability of the owner's replacement, some (or all) employees may seek employment elsewhere, which compounds the problems facing the business.

When a sole proprietor dies, there is often a need for liquidity which arises due to the lack of legal distinction between the owner's business and personal assets. All assets, regardless of type, are subject to the claim of creditors immediately to offset obligations regardless of due date. Moreover, funds may be needed to pay estate administration expenses and taxes. Finally, cash may be needed to "buy out" the business interest of one or more of the deceased's heirs in order to continue the business.

The loss of credit is frequently another important type of loss when a sole proprietor dies. Even long-time creditors may refuse to lend additional money due to the company's uncertain future.

The owner's disability may be a worse threat to the company's survival than death. This may be due to the medical expenses incurred and the continuation of personal maintenance expenses. Furthermore, if the services of the spouse are needed to care for the disabled proprietor, they will be unavailable to the business.

The value of a business forced to liquidate due to the problems described above normally is significantly diminished. In addition to the uncertainty of survival confronting the business, potential buyers normally are in short supply which strengthens their bargaining position. Consequently, sellers may receive much less for the business than they think is fair.

Most business assets are liquidated for less than their value in an ongoing situation. Due to collection difficulties, accounts receivable normally bring 20 to 40 percent of their previous value. Inventory often loses value because some items may be unseasonal or out of style by the time the assets are sold. Used furniture and fixtures normally have little value in a forced sale. "Goodwill," based on the owner's efforts, may have evaporated with the loss of the owner. Fixed assets, such as a building, may or may not decline in value, but they usually are not a major item on the balance sheet of sole proprietorships.

Plans to Avoid or Minimize Losses

Generally, financial losses will be minimized by continuing the business after the sole proprietor's death or disability, assuming expected profits are sufficient to warrant that course of action. This business can be continued after the proprietor's death by:

1. someone without proper authority,
2. a court order,
3. the proprietor initiating action alone prior to death (that is, without developing an agreement with others),
4. a trust agreement, or
5. a buy-sell agreement.

Continuation of the Business Without Proper Authority In many situations a sole proprietor dies without having given express authority to someone to continue the business. The proprietor may have had no plans for business continuation, or may have assumed or agreed orally that a son, daughter, or someone else would take over the business. Under these circumstances it is very likely that the person who assumes control will be doing so without proper legal authority.

Unless specific plans have been made to the contrary, all assets and liabilities (including business assets and liabilities) must pass through the estate administration process. In the usual situation the executor (administrator) of the estate must settle the estate as quickly as possible. This normally involves selling estate assets to pay debts, taxes, and estate administrative expenses, and distributing the remainder of the estate to the heirs. The distribution may be made according to the terms of the deceased's will or by the laws of descent. Therefore, anyone else who continues the business without proper authority is inviting legal problems. The general rule of law is that losses from the business will be borne by the person assuming control, but profits will benefit the estate and heirs. Obviously this is a personally risky and thankless position, especially since the business may be much more difficult to operate profitably after the sole proprietor's death.

An heir who attempts to gain authority to continue the business by obtaining the consent of the other heirs probably will have difficulties. First, the consent of all heirs is required and it may be difficult to identify and locate all of them. Secondly, minors are not legally competent to give their consent. Finally, any heir can withdraw consent at any time.

In short, an informal or oral plan to continue a sole proprietor's business is an ineffective arrangement and should never be used.

Generally, heirs should liquidate the estate regardless of the losses incurred.

Continuation of the Business by Court Order   Most states have enacted laws that give the executor (administrator) the authority to continue a business temporarily. These statutes are designed to avoid or minimize the losses to heirs.

These laws can be classified into several types. Some statutes allow continuation until the inventory is sold in the ordinary course of business. Others permit continuation for a "reasonable" period until the business can be sold as a going concern. However, the definition of "reasonable" is not left solely to the discretion of the executor (administrator). These statutes do not solve all problems since they are not designed to handle unique or specific situations.

Continuaton of the Business by Proprietor-Initiated Action   While a sole proprietor's oral statements directing someone to continue the business are not effective, it is possible to bequeath the business by will. This approach can eliminate the problems concerning the authority of the legatee to continue the business and may also alleviate some of the financial problems that follow the owner's death. The existence of a trained and legally designated successor should eliminate the uncertainty in the minds of employees and creditors over the future success of the business. Liquidity problems may arise because of the need to settle the estate, but in most cases this need can be met by life insurance on the life of the sole proprietor. Consequently, it may not be necessary to liquidate the business.

It is important for the success of the business that the will provide for all heirs at least according to the minimum state distribution requirements. If a widow, for example, is not provided with the minimum portion of the estate that is legally required, all plans may fail and the business may have to be sold. This again is a problem that can be handled by life insurance. The business can be given to whomever the proprietor chooses, and other assets (including life insurance) can be given to other family members.

It may still be wise to arrange the will in such a manner that an heir will have at least temporary ownership of the business. With the proper will provisions, an heir might be able to avoid liquidation losses by continuing the business until it can be sold as a going concern. If so, life insurance would normally be needed to meet the liquidity needs that will arise.

Trust Agreements   Business insurance trusts are not infrequently used in conjunction with business continuation agreements. Such trusts require that the business entity's stock be placed with the trustee upon the death or disability of one of the owners. The trustee is empowered to negotiate for the purchase of the deceased's stock and to see that this is done promptly so that the business does not suffer. The trust will also hold any insurance policies if they are to be the funding instrument. The trustee is usually compensated for these services—being an outside objective arbitrator—on a percentage of value handled. The subject of trusts in general is dealt with more fully later in this chapter.

Buy-Sell Agreements Many businessowners use a buy-sell agreement to handle the financial losses and legal problems that accompany death. This approach requires that a person (or persons), such as a relative, employee, or even business competitor, must be found who is interested in buying the business when the proprietor dies. The next step is to develop a legally binding agreement that obligates the owner to sell and the buyer to purchase the company when the sole proprietor dies. By having a formal, written agreement each party can be assured that the transaction will occur and each can plan accordingly. The buy-sell agreement should be drafted by an attorney to ensure that it conforms to the wishes of the parties involved.

Most buy-sell agreements are funded by life insurance owned by the purchaser on the life of the owner. This is the ideal funding instrument since it automatically supplies the needed funds at the time they are needed.

Important Provisions in a Buy-Sell Agreement. A buy-sell agreement should carefully identify the parties to the agreement and their commitment to buy and sell at a mutually operable price. Often it is desirable to set up a trust so that a trustee will receive the life insurance proceeds and make sure that the business is transferred properly.

Most buy-sell agreements include a "first offer" provision. Therefore, if a sole proprietor decides to sell the business while still alive, it must first be offered to the other party. If the sole proprietor receives an offer from another party, the purchaser (in the buy-sell agreement) must be given an opportunity to buy the business under the same terms and price as the other person.

Because a sole proprietor's business assets are not legally separate from personal assets, it is important to describe the assets and liabilities (if any) that will be transferred to the buyer. Usually the business will be purchased on a "net" basis (that is, net of the liabilities), but the business can be bought on a "gross" basis (including the liabilities).

A valuation clause should always be included in a buy-sell agreement because:

1. without an agreed price or method of determining the price, neither party could regard the agreement as reliable;

2. with a previously agreed upon valuation method, the heirs of the sole proprietor will not be placed in a difficult bargaining position after the sole proprietor's death; and

3. if the valuation is reasonable and proper (i.e., it is an "arm's length" transaction), the Internal Revenue Service will accept it for estate tax purposes.

The price can be determined by negotiation, and the agreed dollar value can be used in the agreement. The advantage of this approach is that the parties involved are in the best position to place a value on the business.

Normally the value should be recomputed (at least) annually to reflect changing conditions. Most agreements that use this approach state that the value will be determined by some other method if the business has not been revalued within a certain period, such as two or three years.

A second valuation approach is to use appraisers after the sole proprietor's death. Often the sole proprietor's heirs select one appraiser, the buyer selects another, and the two appraisers select a third. The value they decide upon is then binding on the parties to the buy-sell agreement. In general, this approach is unsatisfactory because the purchase price is not established prior to the proprietor's death. This makes it difficult for the buyer to fund the agreement, and the uncertain purchase price may cause estate planning problems for the proprietor.

A third valuation method sometimes used due to its simplicity is to set the purchase price at the company's book value, i.e., the excess of assets over liabilities. Normally this approach is inappropriate because the book value may be far different from the company's market value. For example, book value is based on historical (uninflated) cost and ignores the company's profitability as a going concern.

A fourth valuation method employs the use of a formula to value the business at the time of the proprietor's death. Although the actual valuation is not known until the proprietor dies, it can be approximated by applying the formula while the proprietor is alive.

One common formula approach is to adjust book value to reflect goodwill. This can be done by determining the book value and net profits of the company, perhaps as an average over the previous five years. A reasonable percentage of the net profits can be attributed to earnings on book value and the remainder can be attributed to goodwill. The amount traceable to goodwill can then be capitalized (by multiplying by a multiple such as two, three, or four), and the capitalized goodwill is added to the company's book value.

To illustrate, assume that a company has a book value of $100,000 and average net profits of $30,000. If 12 percent earnings on book value

Table 14-3

Hypothetical Adjustment of Book Value to Reflect Goodwill Value of Firm

Facts:	
1. Book value	$100,000
2. Average net profits	30,000
3. Capitalization Multiple:	3
Average net profits	30,000
Less: 12% on book value	12,000
Difference attributable to goodwill	18,000
	x 3
Capitalized goodwill	54,000
Plus book value	100,000
Value of the company	$154,000

is reasonable and the goodwill should be capitalized at a multiple of three, the value of the company would be as shown in Table 14-3.

The adjusted book value formula suffers from two major disadvantages. First, book value may not accurately value the company's assets and liabilities. Second, the formula does not account for future changes in the value of the company. One approach to overcome this disadvantage is to assume that net profits will continue to increase at the same rate that occurred during some past period.

Other Provisions in a Buy-Sell Agreement. The buy-sell agreement should include a provision that makes it clear that the sole proprietor's heirs and the buyer are bound by the agreement. Furthermore, the buyer should be given the power of attorney to continue the business immediately after the proprietor's death until the transfer in ownership is formally made.

A clause should be included that stipulates how the agreement can be changed or terminated. It is common, for example, to state that only the buyer and seller have the power to alter the agreement. Usually the agreement is terminated if either party becomes bankrupt, if the buyer dies or becomes permanently disabled, or if the buyer voluntarily terminates his or her employment with the company.

Benefits of an Insured Buy-Sell Agreement.

ADVANTAGES TO THE PROPRIETOR. The proprietor (and family) is assured of receiving the full, going-concern value of the company which eliminates the losses that result from forced liquidation. Secondly, the proprietor's estate can be settled promptly. Without an agreement, business problems may delay the settlement of the estate for years. Furthermore, negotiations with the IRS over the value of the business are avoided.

The advantages to the proprietor are not limited to those occurring after death. If an agreement is in force, the proprietor's business will have added solidity. Creditors, suppliers, and customers may be more inclined toward long-term relationships. Employees, too, are likely to feel more secure and dedicated to the company. Furthermore, the proprietor's business responsibilities might be less if the buyer is eager to work closely with the owner.

ADVANTAGES TO THE BUYER. An insured buy-sell agreement provides the buyer with more job security and a better idea of what to expect in the future. This helps the buyer plan his or her business and personal estate with more certainty. Even before the business is purchased legally, the buyer will begin to feel more like an owner than an employee.

Arranging Proprietorship Insurance

Two types of insurance needs have been identified in the previous sections. One is for estate liquidity (described later in this chapter). The second is concerned with funding a business continuation (buy-sell) agreement.

Type and Amount of Insurance   The plan of insurance must be consistent with the terms of the buy-sell agreement. Ordinarily this means that term insurance is inappropriate because it may not provide protection as long as it is needed. If the proprietor intends to work until a certain age (usually sixty-five) and then retire, a policy should be used that accumulates a cash value sufficient at that time to purchase the business. This might be a paid-up at sixty-five policy, an endowment at age sixty-five, or a straight life policy. If the proprietor plans to work as long as possible or until death, the face amount and not the cash value of the policy would dictate the most appropriate type of policy.

In many situations the proceeds (or cash value) will differ from the purchase price, especially if the price is determined by formula. Most agreements stipulate that if the price is less than the proceeds, the price will be increased to equal the proceeds. This makes the amount of insurance the minimum purchase price.

Normally when the proceeds are inadequate to purchase the company, the difference is financed by a series of interest bearing notes from the buyer who therefore pays for the deficiency in installments. With this approach it is better to fix the periodic amount of the payments rather than setting the duration and letting the amount vary to ensure that the payments are not too large for the new business operator to handle.[6]

Ownership and Premium Payments Either the person buying the business or a trustee should be the owner of the life insurance policy. Since the buyer is purchasing the compny, it is logical for the buyer to pay for the insurance. This may present a financial problem for the buyer unless the proprietor either loans the employee money or increases the employee's salary enough to pay for all or part of the premiums. A split dollar arrangement with the proprietor being the insured may be desirable if the proprietor pays a portion of the premium since it provides the needed insurance protection while securing the loan to the purchaser.

Beneficiary Designation Many authorities believe that a trustee should be named as the beneficiary of buy-sell insurance so the trustee can collect the proceeds and can promptly and efficiently arrange the transfer of the company. This type of transfer is likely to be facilitated by using a trustee since a trustee is unbiased and is usually experienced in these matters.

An alternative is to name the purchasing party as the beneficiary since the buyer has paid the premiums and must have proceeds to discharge his or her obligation to buy the company. Furthermore, to gain legal ownership of the company, the proceeds must be paid to the proprietor's heirs.

It is unwise to designate the proprietor's estate as the beneficiary since this approach may cause delays and estate tax problems. Also, when the estate has the proceeds and the legal ownership of the company, the parties are not in equal positions. The buyer has a legally enforceable right to purchase the company, but legally enforceable rights are not as valuable as cash.

Disposition of Policies

Since it is possible that the buyer might die before the sole proprietor, the buy-sell agreement should give the proprietor the option to buy the insurance policy should that contingency occur. This not only provides a method for the proprietor to obtain insurance, it also provides cash for the heirs of the deceased. The policy may be an attractive purchase for the proprietor, particularly if he or she is uninsurable.

Tax Aspects

The insurance premiums used to fund a buy-sell agreement are not deductible for federal income tax purposes. If a sole proprietor increases an employee's salary to pay the premiums, the salary is deductible by the employer but is taxable income to the employee. However, the proceeds will be received by the employee free of federal income taxation.

Naturally the value of the business is included in the estate of a deceased proprietor and is subject to federal estate taxation. If the purchase price determined in a buy-sell agreement is an "arm's length" transaction, that price will be the valuation of the business that will be included in the deceased's estate.

PARTNERSHIP INSURANCE

Business partners are more likely than sole proprietors to understand the types of losses that can occur when one of the partners dies, since they can see the contributions of the other(s) and can easily imagine the problems created by the death of one of them. Thus, partnership insurance for business continuation purposes is more popular than proprietorship insurance.

Since the continuation problems confronting partnerships are similar to those facing proprietorships, this discussion will be brief. Emphasis will be given to how partnership exposures and solutions differ from those in a proprietorship.

Types of Losses

A partnership is automatically dissolved when a partner dies, since it is a voluntary, contractual relationship in which each partner's actions impose unlimited liability on the other partners. Accordingly, no person can choose a partner for someone else, and a person cannot be obligated to become a partner of another.

Unless the partners have an agreement to the contrary, the death of a partner terminates the survivors' authority to continue the partnership except to wind up the company's business. They become "liquidating trustees" obligated to complete outstanding obligations, collect the assets and liabilities of the company, and pay the amount owed to the deceased partner's estate. They cannot enter into new business contracts on behalf of the partnership.

In general, the types of losses that occur when a partner dies are the same as those involved when a sole proprietor dies. In both cases the company may (1) lose management talent, (2) have problems with employees, (3) have acute liquidity needs, (4) suffer from a loss of credit, and (5) be forced to liquidate the business.

Of course, some of the losses have a different impact in the case of a partnership. For example, a surviving partner may very well be liquidating his or her own job as the partnership is dissolved. Moreover, the survivor will be required to pay the firm's debts if the estate of the deceased partner becomes insolvent.

Problems in Reorganizing a Partnership

Although a partnership is dissolved when a partner dies, it can be reorganized. One method of reorganizing and continuing the business is for the surviving partners to accept the heirs of the deceased as partners. Normally, this is not desirable if the heirs are not experienced and are less able to contribute to the company. Furthermore, the surviving partners and the heirs may have different business goals. For example, the former may want growth and expansion, while the latter favor current income. One possibility is to accept the heirs as limited partners who do not participate in the operations of the company. This is normally impractical because they will receive their share of company profits without contributing to the business. Further, if there are minor heirs, generally the court will require that their interest must be liquidated.

A second approach is to accept the buyer of the heir's interest as a partner. This provides the heirs with cash and allows the partners to continue the business. However, it may be difficult to find someone with the requisite experience who will pay a reasonable price for the partnership interest.

Third, the survivors could sell their interests to the heirs if they are interested and financially capable to buy the business. However, this is seldom done since in almost all cases, heirs normally need cash and surviving partners usually want to continue the business.

Normally the survivors purchase the interest of the heirs unless one or more of the following problems is insurmountable:

1. The surviving partners may not have the cash needed to buy the deceased's portion of the business.
2. A purchase price acceptable to all parties cannot be agreed to.

3. The purchase of the interest in question may be difficult to arrange through the deceased's executor or administrator who would normally be unfamiliar with the business.

All of these problems are eliminated if there is an insured buy-sell agreement. The buy-sell agreement, the insurance to fund the plan, and the benefits of such a plan are basically the same for a partnership as they are for a proprietorship. Actually, buy-sell agreements are easier to arrange for a partnership because there is no need to search for a buyer. Partners usually are anxious to buy the share of the business previously owned by a deceased partner.

Arranging Partnership Insurance

Types of Partnership Buy-Sell Agreements   The most common type of partnership buy-sell agreement is the "cross-purchase" plan. Under this arrangement each partner must purchase the interest of the deceased partner and the deceased partner's estate must sell the business interest to the surviving partners. The partnership itself is not a party to the plan since each partner is the owner, premium payer, and beneficiary of the life insurance on the other partners.

To illustrate the cross-purchase plan, assume that partners A and B each own 50 percent of the $200,000 partnership. Each partner insures the life of the other for $100,000. When one of the partners dies, the surviving partner receives $100,000 in cash to purchase the deceased partner's share of the business.

If there are four equal partners, A, B, C, and D, and the business is worth $200,000, there must be $50,000 of life insurance on each partner. A should have $16,667 of insurance on B, C, and $D;$ B should have $16,667 on A, C, and $D;$ and so on. When one partner dies, the other three receive $16,667 each (a total of $50,000), and the deceased's share of the business can be purchased.

When a partner dies the policies owned by the deceased partners can be handled in two ways. The policy can be purchased by the surviving partner or the policy can be surrendered. In either case, the cash value is included in the estate of the deceased partner.

In some cases the "entity" plan is preferable to a cross-purchase arrangement. In an entity plan the partnership is the owner, premium payer, and beneficiary of the life insurance policies. When a partner dies the partnership receives the cash needed to purchase the deceased's share of the business. The partnership then distributes the interests in the company in any desired proportion.

To illustrate, assume that a business is worth $200,000 and A owns

50 percent of the company, B and C each own 20 percent, and D owns 10 percent. The partnership will purchase \$100,000 on the life of A, \$40,000 each on B and C, and \$20,000 on D. If B dies the partnership receives \$40,000 which is used to buy B's interest. Since the company is still worth \$200,000, B's \$40,000 interest must be divided among the three remaining partners. If the same proportions of ownership are maintained, A will own 62.5 percent of the company, C will own 25 percent, and D will own 12.5 percent. The amount of insurance on each partner must now be increased after one of the partners dies to ensure that sufficient funds are available to buy out a deceased's interest.

In choosing between a cross-purchase and an entity plan, several factors should be considered. First, the cross-purchase plan becomes awkward as the number of partners increases. With four partners, twelve policies are required; when there are six partners, thirty policies are necessary.[7] Another factor to consider is the fairness or equity between the premium burden and the benefits of the plan. In a cross-purchase plan each person purchases insurance in the amount of the business he or she will buy. Consider the case where A, who is fifty-five years of age, owns 70 percent of the company, and B, only thirty years of age, owns 30 percent. If the business is worth \$200,000, A will buy a policy on B's life in the amount of \$60,000. Since B is young, the premium should not be too burdensome. On the other hand, B must buy a \$140,000 policy on a relatively old person. This heavy financial burden is a common problem associated with cross-purchase plans. B must pay a larger premium, but B has a better chance than A of acquiring the business and B stands to gain a larger portion of ownership than A.

An entity plan generally is not as equitable as a cross-purchase arrangement. If there are wide differences in ages or large variations in the proportions owned, an entity plan favors the younger partners and those who have smaller interests. Since the partnership pays the premiums, they are paid by the partners in proportion to their ownership. If, for example, a person owns 50 percent of the partnership and five others own 10 percent each, the first partner pays 50 percent of the premiums. One solution to this inequity is to adjust the purchase price of the various interests. An older partner who owns a relatively large portion of the company may be willing to bear some inequity if the other partners are willing to increase the amount paid to the older partner's heirs.

Often the best procedure to follow at plan inception is to purchase term insurance on the older (and usually major) partner and permanent insurance on the younger (and usually minor) partners. The advantages are:

1. The premiums paid by each insured are closer to the same size.

2. The cash value on all policies owned by the partnership are partially owned by the senior partners. For the ownership interests set forth above, the senior partners would own 50 percent of the cash value on all policies owned by the partnership.

3. The cash values of the life insurance on the junior partners can be used to make the down payment on a "during life" purchase of the senior's interest.

4. If the senior partner dies first, his or her interest can be purchased with the death benefit from his or her policy and the cash value from the other policies.

Other Aspects of Partnership Insurance   After a decision is made between a cross-purchase or entity plan, most of the other decisions are analogous to those previously discussed in a sole proprietorship situation. Two problems, however, are especially important in partnership insurance. One is the problem of the uninsurable partner, and the other pertains to the beneficiary designation.

If one of the partners is uninsurable (i.e., cannot obtain life insurance at any reasonable price), some other funding arrangement must be employed to ensure that sufficient funds are available when that partner dies. One solution is to establish a sinking fund to cover the uninsurable partner's interest. In many cases the fund will be large enough to continue the business even if the fund is less than the full amount needed at the uninsurable partner's death. If the uninsurable partner lives long enough, the fund will build up to the full amount needed.

One method of building a sinking fund is to purchase an annuity on the life of the uninsurable individual. Since this approach has a tax advantage, the accumulation is not taxable until dispensed by the insurance company.

Another procedure is to increase the coverage on the insurable partners enough to cover the insurance not purchased on the uninsurable partner. The additional cash values will provide a sinking fund which can be used to purchase a portion of the uninsurable individual's interest or which can be used as collateral to finance the purchase. This may even be an "interest only" loan until the death of (one of) the other partner(s) or until the cash values are sufficient to pay off the bank loan.

Regardless of which approach is used, it may be desirable to name a trustee as the beneficiary of the policies. This places the execution of the buy-sell agreement in the hands of an experienced, unbiased party. It is also reasonable to name the other partners as beneficiaries in a cross-purchase plan or to designate the partnership as the beneficiary in an entity plan. One approach that should be avoided is to name a widow or other named heirs as the beneficiary since she (they) may misunderstand the intent of the buy-sell agreement and claim both the insurance proceeds and the deceased's share of the business. If the buy-sell agreement is not "ironclad," the beneficiary may be successful. Another possible problem with this beneficiary designation is that creditors of the estate may interfere with the desired use of the proceeds. If the assets in the estate are inadequate to meet the creditors' claims, they may be able to satisfy their claims from the insurance proceeds.

CORPORATION INSURANCE

Corporations can be classified into two categories: (1) publicly held, and (2) closely held. In the former, ownership of company stock is open to the public. Generally these are large organizations owned by a large number of stockholders who do not participate in the management of the company.

A closely held corporation typically is smaller and company stock is not frequently or widely traded. These companies are owned and controlled by a small group of stockholders. In many respects these corporations are more similar to a partnership than to a public corporation.

Normally there are no adverse financial consequences to a publicly held corporation when a stockholder dies. Consequently, insurance for business continuation purposes is unnecessary. It is also unnecessary for the heirs since there is a ready market for their shares if they need or desire to sell them.

The situation is entirely different when a stockholder in a closely held corporation dies. Since these organizations usually are small and managed by the stockholders, the income provided by the business is normally all (or a large portion) of their income. Furthermore, the stockholders are likely to have a large part of their wealth tied up in the company. Therefore, their death has adverse financial consequences for both the corporation and their heirs.

Types of Losses

The death of a stockholder of a closely held corporation does not dissolve the firm as does a death in the case of a partnership. The company continues to exist and the interest of the deceased stockholder is transferred to the estate of the deceased and from the estate to the heirs. However, the company normally does lose a valuable member of the management team which may affect employee morale, credit, or confidence. Furthermore, both the firm and the heirs of the deceased stockholder usually have great liquidity needs. Thus, the basic problems are the same as those encountered when a sole proprietor or partner dies.

Problems in Reorganizing a Closely Held Corporation

Heirs of a deceased stockholder have three alternatives: (1) to take an active role in the corporation, (2) to remain inactive and hope the business will meet their needs, or (3) to sell their interest in the business.

Heirs who own a minority interest have limited rights. They can attend meetings, vote, and receive their share of dividends. In some instances minority stockholders have been successful in suits to force the company to pay larger dividends. However, in general, the majority stockholders control the firm and their interests are usually different from those of the heirs; namely, heirs generally are interested in receiving large dividends, while surviving stockholders are more interested in growth.

If the heirs are majority stockholders, they can control corporate policy which may be detrimental to the health of the company if they are inexperienced and incompetent. If the heirs and surviving stockholders own equal interests, each stockholder has equal rights so that neither actually controls the corporation. Disputes, therefore, often cannot be reconciled. One solution to this dilemma is for the heirs to stay out of the active operations of the company. If their predecessors actively participated in company operations, the surviving stockholders may feel inclined to reduce payments (dividends) while increasing the salaries of the active stockholders. This may lead to a conflict since heirs may not understand why their income should not be as large as before.

The third alternative is for the heirs to sell their shares in the organization. If there are no prearranged plans for selling the stock, problems are likely to exist. The heirs are likely to need quick cash, but the other stockholders may not have immediate access to the necessary funds since credit sources may not be available. Moreover, it may be difficult to determine a price that is acceptable to both the heirs and the surviving stockholders since stock of a closely held corporation is not actively traded. This is especially true if the stockholders and heirs are in an unequal bargaining position. The heirs might search for other buyers, but they may be scarce or nonexistent if the shares represent a minority interest. A majority interest is more marketable, but then the surviving stockholders (and probably the employees) would be in a vulnerable position.

Most, if not all, of these problems can be solved by a buy-sell agreement similar to those used for sole proprietorships and partnerships. Each stockholder enters into a legally binding agreement to sell his or her shares at death, and the corporation (or other stockholders) is bound to purchase them. The heirs are assured of receiving a fair price without delay, and the surviving stockholders are assured of maintaining (and perhaps gaining) ownership and control of the corporation. The funds needed are provided automatically by life insurance proceeds. There is no haggling over the price to be paid and all parties can plan their futures with more certainty.

Arranging Closely Held Corporation Insurance

Types of Buy-Sell Agreements   A stock purchase plan may be established on a cross-purchase or a stock redemption basis. With the former approach, the stockholders individually agree to buy the stock of the deceased, and each stockholder agrees that his or her interest in the corporation will be sold in the event of his or her death. This is the same arrangement as that used with unincorporated businesses.

If the agreement is between each stockholder and the corporation, it is known as a stock redemption or stock retirement plan. Here, the stockholders agree to sell their shares to the corporation which is obligated to buy the shares.

The factors that should be considered in deciding between a cross-purchase plan and a stock retirement plan are somewhat different than those involved in a partnership case. The first factor to consider is whether the corporation has the ability to buy its own stock. Some states have restrictions or prohibitions which prohibit a corporation from buying company stock. In these states there may be no choice except to use a cross-purchase plan.[8]

A second factor to consider is the impact of federal income taxes. This is not a factor for a partnership since it is not a taxable entity and all taxes are paid by the partners. However, in the case of a corporation, which is a taxable entity, the tax question might be an important consideration. Since life insurance premiums are not tax deductible, the effective tax rates of the corporation should be compared to the tax rates of the stockholders. If the corporation is in a higher tax bracket than the stockholders, the stockholders should pay the premiums (i.e., use a cross-purchase plan). If, on the other hand, the stockholders are in a higher tax bracket, it would be less expensive to use a stock retirement approach.

A stock retirement plan may involve special income tax problems. Therefore, the tax consequences of a stock redemption plan should be analyzed carefully by tax counsel before it is used.

If it is desirable to have the cash values of the insurance policies shown as an asset on the corporation's financial statements, a stock redemption plan may be desirable.

If there are many stockholders, a stock retirement plan will be simpler and more practical. Only one life insurance policy on each stockholder will be required, while a cross-purchase plan will involve many policies. If the stockholders vary widely in ages and percentage of ownership in the corporation, a stock retirement plan may not be equitable. With a stock retirement approach, the premiums are paid in proportion to the stockholders' ownership in the company. Those with the larger interests are paying larger portions of the premium, even though they do not have as much to gain as those with smaller interests. Proper insurance planning can reduce this problem.

Another factor to be considered is the existence of creditors' claims against the corporation. If a stock retirement plan is used, insurance proceeds may have to be used to pay creditors. With a cross-purchase plan, the proceeds are paid to stockholders so corporate creditors cannot attach them.

Other Aspects of Closely Held Corporation Insurance In general, the considerations involving the purchase of insurance to fund a business continuation plan for a closely held corporation are similar to those in the case of proprietorships and partnerships. The buy-sell agreement must cover essentially the same points. The ownership and beneficiary designations are similar, and the problem of uninsurable stockholders must be viewed in the same way.

ESTATE PLANNING

In this course the term "estate planning" refers to arrangements for the efficient transfer of property, at death, from one person to another person (or persons). The implications of this definition are important. First, virtually everyone has an estate. Therefore, estate planning should not be limited to those with large estates. In fact, estate planning may be more important for the owner of a small or medium estate than it is for a wealthy person because improper estate planning may have a proportionately greater effect on those with small or medium estates.

The accumulation of assets during a person's lifetime is largely outside the scope of the definition of estate planning employed here. The management of an investment program, for example, is part of the estate planning process when viewed broadly, but it is only indirectly related to the transfer of property at death. However, plans made during a person's lifetime may determine how property will be distributed. Thus, it is incorrect to assume that estate planning is important only at the time of death.

Every person has some form of estate plan since his or her assets will be distributed at death according to state law in the absence of a consciously prepared arrangement.

Many people have a plan that is so ill conceived that it hardly justifies the term "estate plan." An improper plan may distribute assets contrary to the wishes of the property owner or may result in an unnecessary diminution of values from taxes and estate administration costs. Therefore, efficient estate planning (1) distributes assets according to the desires of the property owner, (2) minimizes estate and inheritance taxes, (3) minimizes income taxes, and (4) minimizes probate costs. Conflicts often arise among these four basic objectives. For example, there may be a conflict between tax savings and the objective of distributing property to the desired persons, in appropriate amounts, at the desired time. If such a conflict exists, the property owner must decide which objective(s) are more important and how the conflicts should be balanced.

Parties Involved in Estate Planning

Designing and implementing an efficient estate plan can be simple or complex depending upon the circumstances of a given case. If a property owner has many types of property and a large estate, a substantial amount of expertise in several areas may be needed. Consequently, few financial advisors are competent to handle all aspects of a sophisticated case. What is needed, in complicated cases, is a *team* of advisors.

Normally an estate planning team consists of an attorney, an accountant, a trust officer, an investment counselor, and a life underwriter. An attorney is necessary to draft and review wills and other legal instruments. If taxes are a consideration, an accountant will be needed since that field is too technical to rely on unprofessional advice.

A life underwriter often provides two vital functions to the estate planning team. First, he or she normally is in the best position to initiate an estate plan (or a review of an existing plan). Secondly, he or she should be the most knowledgeable person available to select the proper insurance product to be used in an estate plan.

An Overview of the Estate Planning Process

Generally estate plans are developed in a series of five steps called the "estate planning process."

Gathering Facts The first step is to obtain facts about the property owner's present and anticipated estate and how he or she prefers to have the estate distributed. Normally this is accomplished by using a standardized questionnaire rather than relying upon an informal method of collecting the information.

Information regarding the names, ages, health, income, occupation, and residence of all close family members is essential, as is a complete description of the property owner's assets and liabilities. Each asset should be identified and valued, and the legal ownership of each should be determined. It should be clear, for example, if a savings account in a bank is owned individually or in some form of joint ownership. Included should be the property owner's status in any employee benefit plans and the OASDHI program. Anticipated changes in the subject's financial condition should be considered to the extent that they can be foreseen.

The current estate plan should be described completely. This involves questions about the property owner's will, any trusts in effect, and any gifts that have been made.

The property owner's desires for the transfer of the property at death should be ascertained. The subject must indicate to whom the property should be distributed, when the distribution should be made, and in what amounts. Perhaps a property owner will want a charity or educational institution to receive some of the property, in addition to family members. Maybe the children should not have complete access to the property until they reach a certain age. Very often these questions are complicated by business interests. For example, if a small business is to be transferred to a son, will the son have the necessary qualifications to manage the company? And if the son takes over the business, how will the other assets be divided? These questions illustrate the types of problems that may be involved.

Evaluating the Current Plan The second step is an analysis of the strong and weak points of the present plan. It can be tested by determining how the property would be distributed if the estate owner were to die immediately. Starting with this assumption, property must be classified (normally by an attorney) according to whether it would be included or excluded from the probate estate. Next, the amount of estate shrinkage that will occur when the subject dies must be estimated. Shrinkage is normal because of creditors' claims, estate administration costs, and taxes. If the property owner is married, these calculations should be made under several assumptions. One calculation would show the effect on the estate if the husband dies first; another computation would be based on the wife's prior death. In addition, the costs of successive estate transfers (assuming the second spouse dies shortly after the first) should be estimated.

The analysis of the present plan will determine the liquidity need at the property owner's death to pay debts, estate administration costs, and taxes, and to make cash transfers to beneficiaries. The plan should be designed so that the involuntary liquidation of any estate assets will not be necessary.

The legal instruments used in the present plan should be reviewed to see whether they distribute assets according to the property owner's wishes. They should also be checked to determine if they are up-to-date in view of prevailing legal and tax practices. Liberalizations in the tax law, for example, may not be incorporated into the current plan.

Formulating and Testing the New Plan The third step is to develop and test the revised plan to be certain that it overcomes the weaknesses of the old plan.

Execution of the New Plan After the new estate plan is developed, it must be implemented. Often this will require the purchase of additional life insurance and the execution of legal documents.

Periodic Review and Revision Estate planning is a continuing process. Laws, legal concepts, planning techniques, and the personal and financial circumstances of most individuals change over time. Therefore, estate plans should be reviewed and adjusted periodically (e.g., annually).

Fundamentals of Estate, Inheritance, and Gift Taxation

While tax planning should not dominate the estate planning process, careful consideration should be given to the tax consequences of an estate plan.

The estate tax is a federal tax imposed on the privilege of transferring property at death. It is levied on the estate itself, not on the beneficiaries or heirs who receive the property. In most cases the tax is the largest tax involved in an estate planning situation.

There are four basic steps in the computation of the estate tax liability. The first step is to determine the gross estate. Next, the taxable estate is determined by subtracting allowable deductions from the gross estate. The third step is to apply the federal estate tax rates to the taxable estate. The actual tax liability is then determined by subtracting credits that may be allowed against the tax.

The Gross Estate An individual's gross estate includes all interests (tangible and intangible) in real and personal property, wherever the property may be situated. The value to be attributed to each asset is its "fair market value," which is open to reasonable interpretations.

The executor must select as a valuation date either the date of death or the date exactly six months later. The same date applies to all property with the exception of property distributed, sold, or exchanged during the six-month period which is valued at the date of the transfer.

Property owned by a decedent is included in the gross estate. Examples include a home, business interests, real estate investments, bank accounts, stocks, bonds, mutual funds, household furnishings, jewelry, professional tools and equipment, and automobiles. The gross estate also includes accrued but unpaid income.

Property owned jointly with a spouse is valued either by means of the "fractional interest" rule or by means of the "consideration furnished" rule. The fractional interest rule treats property as belonging one-half to each owner. However, this rule applies only to property owned as joint tenants (or tenants by the entirety) by spouses and only when the joint ownership constituted a gift after December 31, 1976. If a married couple purchases a home after 1976 and elects to have the joint tenancy treated as a transfer for gift tax purposes, one-half of the value of the residence will be in the wife's estate if she dies first and one-half will be in the husband's estate if he dies first.

The consideration furnished rule applies to all jointly owned property that does not meet the above requirements. According to this rule, if the surviving joint owner can prove that he or she contributed to the original purchase price of the property, only the proportion contributed by the deceased owner will be included in the estate. Suppose, for example, that Mr. A has a joint bank account with his wife in the amount of $3,000. If Mr. A dies and if he originally contributed $1,000 and Mrs. A originally contributed $500 and no other deposits were made (but interest doubled the amount), two-thirds of the total $3,000 will be included in Mr. A's estate because he contributed two-thirds of the original value.

Surviving spouses often have difficulty proving that they contributed to the original purchase price. Without such proof the entire value is included in the deceased's estate.

Life insurance in which an individual has any incidents of ownership is also in that person's estate, regardless of beneficiary designation. The phrase "incidents of ownership" includes the power to (1) designate or change the beneficiary, (2) surrender the policy, and (3) assign or borrow on the policy.

The payment of premiums is not regarded as an incident of ownership; nor is the right to receive policy dividends.

If a person possesses any incidents of ownership, the full amount of the insurance proceeds will be included in his or her estate. In other words, either the full amount will be included or none at all. Furthermore, if the policy is jointly owned, the full proceeds will be included in the decedent's estate.

If an individual indirectly possesses an incident of ownership, the proceeds will be included in his or her gross estate. For example, a life insurance policy owned by a corporation that is owned by the insured will be included in the insured's estate.

The insurance proceeds can be kept out of an insured's estate by making certain that the insured possesses no incidents of ownership. This can be achieved easily at policy inception by having someone other than the insured purchase the policy. For example, the wife can apply for a policy on the life of her husband and possess all ownership rights. At the husband's death the proceeds will not be included in his gross estate. If the wife dies before the husband, only the cash value of the policy will be included in her estate.

It is possible to transfer all incidents of ownership of an existing policy to another person and thereby remove the policy from the donor's estate. However, the transfer may have income and gift tax consequences that should be examined carefully.

The tax laws and regulations do not detail how various types of insurance plans will be treated for estate tax purposes. Instead, specific insurance plans are treated according to tax rules that generally are not organized according to traditional types of insurance plans.

Group life insurance is included in an employee's estate if he or she possessed any incidents of ownership including the right to name the beneficiary. In recent years a number of states have specifically authorized employees to assign all incidents of ownersip in group life insurance policies if they choose to minimize their estate tax burden.

If a key employee life insurance policy is arranged properly, the company will possess all incidents of ownership and the proceeds will not be included in the employee's estate.

Normally when a party to an insured buy-sell agreement dies, the deceased has no incidents of ownership and therefore, the proceeds will not be a part of the estate. However, in a cross-purchase plan, the deceased's estate will include policies on the lives of the other parties to the agreement, and the value (roughly the cash value) is a part of the deceased's gross estate.

In the usual form of split dollar plans the insured possesses incidents of ownership. However, there is a general exception to the rule that either the full value or no part of the value will be included in the computation. If a decedent owned property that is subject to the payment of a debt (and the deceased or the estate is responsible for repayment), the value included in the estate is the full value minus the debt. In a split dollar plan the insured's beneficiary receives the face amount less the indebtedness to the employer for premium contributions. Therefore, only the amount payable to the employee's beneficiary is included in the deceased employee's estate.

In a split dollar plan, steps may be taken to remove all incidents of ownership from the employee. One method is to place all incidents of ownership with the employer and the employee's beneficiary. If the employee's beneficiary (usually the spouse) is given the ownership rights normally given to the employee, no part of the proceeds should be included in the beneficiary's estate if he or she should predecease the insured.

The gross estate of an individual includes any annuity values that exist at the point of death. If death occurs before benefit payments begin, the accumulated value of the contract is included in the estate. If death occurs after benefits have been started, the actuarial value of all future payments will be included in the estate.

Social security benefits are *not* valued in a person's estate, including the lump-sum death benefit and the value of monthly survivor benefits.

Any death benefits payable in installments under a qualified pension or profit-sharing plan funded by employer contributions are not included in an employee's gross estate if they are not paid to the employee's estate. This advantage of qualified retirement plans is not lost even if the employee has some incidents of ownership.

Death benefits incorporated in HR-10 plans and IRAs (both types of retirement plans are discussed in Chapter 12 of this text) are not included in a participant's estate if they are not paid out in a lump sum. If they are paid in a lump sum, they are included in the gross estate. The lump-sum payment is subject to a special income averaging rule and this income tax advantage may more than offset the additional estate tax liability.

For estate tax purposes nonqualified deferred compensation benefits are treated in the same fashion as individual annuities. The present value of any nonforfeited, post-death benefits is included in the employee's estate. This is despite the fact that there may be a substantial risk of forfeiting benefits in the plan.

The Taxable Estate   The next step in calculating the estate tax is to subtract allowable deductions such as incurred funeral and administrative expenses. Allowable expenses include mortician's charges, burial costs, cemetary plot costs, and monuments or headstones. Administrative costs include attorney's, executor's, and accountant's fees, appraisal costs, court costs, and necessary expenses to maintain (but not improve) estate property. Deductible administrative expenses are not limited to expenses associated with the probate estate but include expenses incurred to administer assets outside the probate estate.

Allowable deductions include claims against the estate such as personal obligations of the decedent that exist at the time of death. Obligations incurred after the decedent's death, such as an unpaid mortgage, are not deductible.

Casualty and theft losses during estate administration are deductible from the gross estate to the extent that they are not compensated for by insurance.

The next category is the marital deduction. If a person is married at the time of death, up to one-half of the decedent's adjusted gross estate or $250,000, whichever is greater, that passes (or has passed) to a spouse is deductible (subject to certain requirements). The adjusted gross estate is the gross estate minus funeral and administration expenses, debts, and losses during administration.

The amount of the marital deduction is limited to the value of the property that actually passes to the spouse. If, for example, all the requirements are met and a marital deduction of $100,000 is permitted but only $80,000 passes to the survivor, the deduction is limited to $80,000.

Most transfers from one spouse to another will qualify for the marital deduction, including property transferred by will, without a will, by joint ownership, by a trust, or by insurance. The method of transfer is unimportant with one exception. The survivor's interest in the property must not terminate or fail because of the passage of time or the occurrence (or nonoccurrence) of a certain event. This is known as the "terminable interest" rule. For example, property left to a wife "for ten years, with the remainder of the property going to the children" represents a terminable interest since the wife's interest ends after ten years. This type of disposition, therefore, does not qualify for the marital deduction.

The terminable interest rule assures that property will not escape estate taxation. Without it property could be left to a surviving spouse and then transferred to others without being taxed in the surviving spouse's estate.

Finally, contributions to charitable and religious organizations are deducted after the marital deduction, regardless if the transfer took place before or at the decedent's death.

After all deductions, a "tentative tax" is determined by applying the following rates.

The "tentative tax" is reduced by a tax credit according to the schedule shown in Table 14-4.

Table 14-4
Tentative Tax Rates

Not over $10,000	18% of such amount.
Over $10,000 but not over $20,000	$1,800, plus 20% of the excess of such amount over $10,000.
Over $20,000 but not over $40,000	$3,800, plus 22% of the excess of such amount over $20,000.
Over $40,000 but not over $60,000	$8,200, plus 24% of the excess of such amount over $40,000.
Over $60,000 but not over $80,000	$13,000, plus $26% of the excess of such amount over $60,000.
Over $80,000 but not over $100,000	$18,200, plus 28% of the excess of such amount over $80,000.
Over $100,000 but not over $150,000	$23,800, plus 30% of the excess of such amount over $100,000.
Over $150,000 but not over $250,000	$38,800, plus 32% of the excess of such amount over $150,000.
Over $250,000 but not over $500,000	$70,800, plus 34% of the excess of such amount over $250,000.
Over $500,000 but not over $750,000	$155,800, plus 37% of the excess of such amount over $500,000.
Over $750,000 but not over $1,000,000	$248,300, plus 39% of the excess of such amount over $750,000.
Over $1,000,000 but not over $1,250,000	$345,800, plus 41% of the excess of such amount over $1,000,000.
Over $1,250,000 but not over $1,500,000	$448,300, plus 43% of the excess of such amount over $1,250,000.
Over $1,500,000 but not over $2,000,000	$555,800, plus 45% of the excess of such amount over $1,500,000.
Over $2,000,000 but not over $2,500,000	$780,800, plus 49% of the excess of such amount over $2,000,000.
Over $2,500,000 but not over $3,000,000	$1,025,800, plus 53% of the excess of such amount over $2,500,000.
Over $3,000,000 but not over $3,500,000	$1,290,800, plus 57% of the excess of such amount over $3,000,000.
Over $3,500,000 but not over $4,000,000	$1,575,800, plus 61% of the excess of such amount over $3,500,000.
Over $4,000,000 but not over $4,500,000	$1,880,800, plus 65% of the excess of such amount over $4,000,000.
Over $4,500,000 but not over $5,000,000	$2,205,800, plus 69% of the excess of such amount over $4,500,000.
Over $5,000,000	$2,550,800, plus 70% of the excess of such amount over $5,500,000.

Table 14-5

Schedule of Unified Credits

Year	Tax Credit
1978	$34,000
1979	38,000
1980	42,500
1981 and after	47,000

For individuals who die after 1980, estates of less than $175,625 will incur no federal estate liability as a result of this tax credit. If a person has a gross estate less deductions of $175,625, Table 14-4 shows a "tentative tax" of $47,000, and this is exactly the amount of the tax credit shown in Table 14-5.

Actually a person's estate can be larger without incurring an estate tax liability. This is because credits against the tax are also allowed for state death taxes actually paid, foreign death taxes, and federal gift and estate taxes paid on prior transfers to the decedent.

The following example recaps the major points in the estate tax computation process. Assume that in 1981, Mr. A is sixty-three years of age and is interested in estimating the federal estate tax that will be payable if he dies soon. Mr. A's will states that Mrs. A will receive 50 percent of his adjusted gross estate. The other one-half of his estate will be divided equally between his two sons. Mr. A has made no gifts during his lifetime. Table 14-6 shows the details of the estate tax computation process involved.

The importance of the marital deduction is illustrated clearly in the above example. Without the deduction Mr. A's taxable estate would be $488,000 and the tentative tax would be $151,720. Even with the tax credit, the tax payable is $104,720. The marital deduction, therefore, will save Mr. A $82,840 in estate taxes.

The maximum marital deduction in this case is achieved by leaving Mrs. A one-half of the adjusted gross estate. If the adjusted gross estate had been estimated and a flat amount left to Mrs. A, the maximum advantage of the deduction might not have been achieved. For example, suppose Mr. A used the above figures and estimated his adjusted gross estate at $488,000. Based on this figure he leaves $244,000 to Mrs. A. This will not take maximum advantage of the marital deduction if Mr. A's adjusted gross estate increases before he dies.

Table 14-6

Estate Tax Computation

Assets: The estimated fair market value of "Mr. A's" assets are:	
Residence	$105,000
Savings account	5,000
Automobiles	12,000
Household furnishings	30,000
Other personal property	8,000
Common stock	46,000
Bonds	12,000
Business interest	240,000
Life insurance:	
Individual straight life	100,000
Group term	50,000
Life insurance on "Mrs. A" (cash value)	16,000
	$624,000
Liabilities:	
Mortgage on residence	$ 35,000
Business loan	50,000
Other estimated deductions:	
Funeral expenses	$ 20,000
Administrative costs	31,000
Estate tax computation:	
Gross estate	$539,000[†]
Funeral and administrative costs	51,000
Adjusted gross estate	488,000
Marital deduction	244,000
Taxable estate	244,000
Tentative tax (from Table 1)	68,880
Credit (from Table 2)	47,000
Tax payable	$ 21,880

[†]Assets ($624,000) minus liabilities ($85,000).

State Death Taxes   Most state death taxes levied can be classified into two basic types. One type is an estate tax which is imposed on the right to transfer property at death. In general, the states that use this approach pattern their death taxes after the federal estate tax. The state tax rates vary among the states but all are lower than the federal rates. The personal (and other) exemptions vary greatly, and the tax rates range from a fraction of 1 percent to 16 percent.

Most states employ an inheritance tax which is imposed on the right of beneficiaries to receive property from a decedent. The distinction between the two is that this tax is imposed on each beneficiary's share—not on the estate as a whole.

In computing the federal estate tax a credit may be taken for state death taxes paid subject to federally imposed limits that vary according to the size of the estate.

Some states employ death tax rates that equal the maximum credit under the federal law. Few states have lower rates. In many states the total state death taxes are greater than the federal estate tax credit and therefore, impose an additional burden on estates.

Federal Gift Taxes The federal gift tax is imposed on donors, not donees. Furthermore, a donee does not incur an income tax liability by receiving a gift, and a donor does not receive an income tax deduction for the amount of a gift. One financial motivation for making gifts is the desire to reduce the size of the estate, thereby reducing federal estate and state death taxes.

The federal gift tax law applies to all transfers, whether the gift is direct or indirect, real or personal, in trust or otherwise, or tangible or intangible. However, it is not the intent of the law to tax ordinary gifts such as gifts for Christmas, birthdays, anniversaries, or graduation. The law, therefore, contains an annual gift tax exclusion in the amount of $3,000. This exclusion is allowed for each donee and it is available each year. A person may give $3,000 or less to any number of individuals (family members or others) and not incur a gift tax liability. The limit, however, applies to each donee individually. If, for example, a father gives $2,000 to his son and $4,000 to his daughter in the same year, he could exclude the gift to his son but only $3,000 of the $4,000 gift to the daughter would be excluded.

The "gift splitting" privilege allows a married person to double the annual exclusion for gifts to someone other than to his or her spouse by assuming that the gift is made equally by the husband and wife. Thus, a married person may give $6,000 each year to each donee with no gift tax consequence if the other spouse agrees to the gift.

To qualify for the annual exclusion a gift must be a "gift of a present interest" and cannot be a "gift of a future interest." Basically this means that the use, possession, or enjoyment of the property by the donee cannot be postponed until the future.

Gifts for certain public or charitable purposes are not subject to limitation. That is, the donor is not taxed on these gifts, regardless of size. However, gifts to individuals, irrespective of need, cannot qualify for the charitable deduction.

A marital deduction is available for gifts to spouses. This is a lifetime (not an annual) deduction. Under this provision a spouse is allowed a deduction of $100,000 plus 50 percent of gifts over $200,000. These limits apply on a cumulative, lifetime basis. Furthermore, the gifts from one spouse to the other must meet the "terminable interest" requirements. In general, this means the gifts must meet the same requirements that apply to the estate tax marital deduction.

The underlying philosophy of the estate and gift tax laws is that property transferred at or before death should be taxed in the same manner. The estate tax is merely a tax on a person's last gift. Conversely, a person who makes a gift is taxed as if he or she had died.

Assume Mr. B has made no previous gifts and in 1981, gives his wife $80,000. Assuming the gift qualifies for the annual exclusion and the marital deduction, $77,000 of the first $100,000 of the marital deduction will be exhausted. If Mr. B gives his wife another $80,000 in 1982, it will be treated as follows. After the annual exclusion, the $77,000 remainder will exhaust the remaining $23,000 in the first part of the marital deduction. The difference of $54,000 will be taxable to Mr. A. The tax on $54,000 (Table 14-4) is $11,560 ($8,200 plus 25 percent of the excess over $40,000). Mr. A, however, is not required to pay a gift tax because he can use up a portion of his $47,000 unified tax credit. Mr. A's remaining unified credit will be $35,440 ($47,000 minus $11,560). Using a portion of his unified tax credit while he is alive will reduce the credit when it is applied to his estate after his death.

Two aspects of the estate and gift tax law are particularly important. First, gifts may actually exhaust all of the unified tax credit and as a result, federal estate taxes payable later may be higher than they would have been without such gifts. Secondly, periodic gifts are taxed at increasingly higher rates because the gifts are cumulative over life. When the gift tax is calculated, all previous gifts are considered and the latest gift is taxed using the incremental tax bracket.

Despite these limitations it is possible to reduce federal estate taxes by making gifts. One method is by taking advantage of the annual exclusion. If a husband and wife have three children, for example, they may reduce their estates by $18,000 each year. Over time, a married couple can reduce their estates substantially by making annual gifts.

A second possibility is to make gifts of property that is likely to appreciate. Suppose a husband and wife own a small apartment building worth $250,000. If they give the building to their daughter, the gift will be valued at $250,000, its fair market value at the time of the gift. If instead they retain ownership of the building and die years later, the value of the building, included for estate tax purposes, may be much higher.

The gift tax marital deduction can make gift giving advantageous. The value of property that is given to a spouse within the restrictions of the marital deduction escapes, or at least postpones, federal estate taxation. However, the estate tax marital deduction is reduced to the extent that the minimum gift tax marital deduction is used.

In giving gifts to reduce estate taxes the value of all gifts given within three years of death may be included in the deceased property owner's estate since they are presumed to have been given in "contemplation of death."

Wills and Trusts   Two invaluable instruments frequently used to develop an estate plan are wills and trusts. Their usefulness in many instances is independent of the size of the estate in question. However, the larger the estate, the more sophisticated the provisions of these instruments tend to become.

Wills.   Many individuals have no will and many others have a will that is badly out-of-date despite the fact that an up-to-date will is the cornerstone of an effective estate plan.

A will is the primary method of distributing property at a person's death according to his or her desires. A person who dies with a will is said to die *testate*. The consequences of dying *intestate* (without a will) often are unfortunate. If a person dies intestate, the property is transferred according to state laws of descent and distribution. The pattern of distribution varies from state to state, and it would be sheer coincidence if the property is distributed according to the property owner's desires.

A portion of the District of Columbia Intestacy Statute provides an example of how property might be allocated if a person dies without a will. Under this law:

1. If there are children and grandchildren, the surviving spouse takes one-third and the children and a child of a deceased child takes two-thirds.
2. If there are no children or grandchildren, the surviving spouse takes one-half and the decedent's father and mother take one-half.
3. If there is no mother and father, the surviving spouse takes one-half, and the decedent's brothers and sisters or their descendants take one-half.
4. If there are no children, grandchildren, father, mother, brothers, sisters, or descendants of brothers and sisters, the surviving spouse takes all of the real and personal property.

There are numerous variations in the intestacy statutes of states. Many have homestead (principal residence) exemptions and family allowances which differ greatly in amounts. The portion provided to a surviving spouse varies among the states and special situations, such as adopted children, illegitimate children, posthumous children, and children of half blood are handled differently in the various states.

There are additional advantages to having a will. First is the ability to provide income to the family while the estate is going through the estate administration process which may take many months or even years. During this period the family may be unnecessarily strained financially unless it is stipulated in the will that income will begin immediately after the property owner's death and will continue until the estate has been distributed.

Second, it allows the property owner to select the person to serve as the executor of the estate. This selection is important since it is the executor's responsibility to collect the assets of the deceased, determine and pay legal claims against the estate, and distribute the remaining assets to the proper individuals. Use of an incompetent administrator may result in an unnecessary decrease in value of the estate and a delay in the distribution of assets. Without a valid will (or with a will that does not name an executor), the probate court will appoint an administrator. Generally, the person selected will be the person entitled to the largest portion of the decedent's property. Often this is the surviving spouse who may not be particularly effective.

Third, problems with distributions to minor children can be minimized. Without a will minor children may be entitled to property that they do not have the legal capacity to manage. A guardian must then be appointed by the court which may result in unnecessary expenses and delays. Furthermore, the appointed guardian may not be the person the decedent would have selected.

Fourth, if an individual chooses, knowledge of specific property and advice for its management can be incorporated in the will. By placing this type of information in the will, the estate owner is assured that it will be read and its importance will be emphasized.

Fifth, a will facilitates the minimization of estate shrinkage by speeding up the settlement process. Delays may cause estate values to decline. Furthermore, a properly drawn will minimizes taxes. If a person, for example, wants to take maximum advantage of the marital deduction, the will should specify the spouse's share and the terms of the bequest.

Sixth, a will may be used to make gifts to whomever or whatever the testator chooses. Similarly, a person can establish a testamentary trust at death by means of the will.

Use of a will encourages coordination in the estate planning process. Coordination problems often arise because a will controls the disposition of property that passes through probate only. Life insurance, for example, is not controlled by a will but rather by the beneficiary designation in the contract. Another example is jointly owned property.

When property is co-owned with right of survivorship, the property passes automatically to the surviving owner when the other owner dies. For example, if a wife is the life insurance beneficiary and also receives the family residence as a joint owner, this may affect the best allocation of the probate property. The amounts provided to the wife in the will should recognize the amounts provided to her by other means.

Contrary to common belief, a will is needed by many small estate owners as well as by those who have large estates. Furthermore, a will should be written by an attorney since an improperly drawn will often causes estate settlement problems. Many state statutes limit the effectiveness of oral wills and wills that are not properly witnessed. A will should be reviewed and updated periodically with the aid of an attorney.

Trusts. Trusts may serve a variety of purposes in estate planning. Because of legal and tax complications, trust instruments should be drawn up by an attorney. The following section should familiarize the reader with the basic nature of trusts and how each type of trust accomplishes certain objectives.

A trust is an arrangement by which one person or organization holds legal title to property for the benefit of another person or persons. There are five essential ingredients for a valid trust:

1. Settlor. (Also known as a "grantor" or "creator.") This is the property owner who establishes a trust.
2. Trustee. This is the individual or organization that holds legal title to property provided by the settlor.
3. Property. (Also known as the "corpus" or "res.") A trust must have property of some type (or be expected to have property), otherwise it is a "dry" trust and invalid.
4. Beneficiary. A trust must exist for the benefit of some person, persons, or organization. There may be secondary or contingent beneficiaries of a trust.
5. Terms. A trust must have a purpose, otherwise a trustee cannot know how to administer the trust.

Trustees, by statute, have a fiduciary responsibility to fulfill the following obligations:

1. administer the trust solely for the interest of the beneficiary (or beneficiaries);
2. not delegate the administration of the trust;
3. keep and provide accurate records;
4. furnish information to the beneficiary;
5. exercise reasonable care and skill in administering the trust;
6. take, keep control, and preserve trust property;

7. keep trust property separate from other property, although the terms of the trust may allow a trustee to commingle trust funds with other funds;
8. make trust property productive;
9. deal impartially with beneficiaries;
10. cooperate with co-trustees; and
11. submit to the control of others who have the legal authority to direct the trustee.

Furthermore, the terms of the trust agreement may confer upon the trustee a number of powers that are not listed above. As long as the trust agreement does not violate the law, a settlor may direct the trustee to engage in a wide variety of practices. For example, the trust agreement may allow a trustee discretionary powers to incur expenses that are reasonable and necessary to handle the trust property, and the trustee may be allowed to sell, pledge, mortgage, or lease trust property. In recent years, however, the liability of fiduciaries has increased and many trustees are reluctant to accept a broad range of powers which leaves their actions open to question.

The trustee selected by the settlor may be an individual or a corporate entity. Four factors should be considered in selecting a trustee. First is the amount of experience the potential trustee has had in managing the type of property that will comprise the trust corpus and in handling the other functions expected of the trustee. Second, the stability and life expectancy of the potential trustee should be evaluated. The trust may be effective for a long time, and the death or poor health of an individual trustee might cause problems. By way of contrast, a corporate life expectancy is infinite. Third, the extent of the property owner's desires that the trustee have personal knowledge and take a personal interest in the beneficiary's welfare should be considered. Corporate trust departments tend to be impersonal, while an individual trustee may be a close family friend who is knowledgeable about the beneficiary's needs. Finally, the size of the trust should be considered. Many corporate trustees will not handle a trust unless the value of the trust property is in excess of a certain figure such as $100,000. Corporate trust fees, however, are not necessarily higher than those charged by individuals. In fact, trust fees may be small, especially if the trust property is managed as a common trust fund.

Trusts may be divided into two basic types: testamentary trusts and living trusts. Testamentary trusts are created by the grantor's will and do not become operative until death. With this type of trust a person maintains full ownership and control of the trust property. The fact that a trust has been established in the will does not interfere with the management of the property at all. In fact, the trust can be terminated at any time prior to the grantor's death. A living or *inter vivos* trust is created and becomes operative during the lifetime of the grantor. It may be revocable or irrevocable. It also may be funded or unfunded.

IRREVOCABLE LIVING TRUST. A grantor who establishes an irrevocable living trust makes an absolute gift of the corpus and relinquishes all rights to terminate, revoke, or change the terms of the trust. One advantage of this type of trust is that it provides a method of transferring property without having it go through the public disclosure associated with probate. Since wills are public documents they may be read by anyone. Furthermore, the delay and costs of probate are avoided but this advantage is offset partially by the cost involved with establishing the trust.

Use of an irrevocable trust reduces income taxes if several rules are followed. These rules are designed to make sure that the grantor has given away the property without retaining any property rights. If these rules are followed, the income from the trust property will not be taxable to the grantor but rather to the beneficiary if distributed or to the trust itself if not.

The most common reason for establishing an irrevocable trust is to reduce federal estate taxes. If the grantor survives three years (thereby avoiding the "in contemplation of death rule"), the corpus will not be included in the grantor's estate. Furthermore, if arranged properly, the corpus will not be taxed in the trust beneficiary's estate either.

An irrevocable trust might be preferable to making a gift outright if the grantor (donor) wants the advantages of a gift but wishes to exercise some control over the beneficiary's use of the gift. For example, if a father wishes to make a gift to his son to save estate and income taxes but is concerned that the son does not have the necessary managerial ability to handle the property, it might be wise to establish an irrevocable trust. This accomplishes the tax objectives, but the trustee can be empowered to manage the property according to standards established in the trust agreement according to the trustee's discretion.

One disadvantage of an irrevocable trust is that it represents a gift of the corpus and therefore is subject to the gift tax laws. The $3,000 ($6,000) annual gift tax exclusion is available (if arranged properly) and the exclusion applies to each trust beneficiary as a separate donee. The trust itself is not regarded as the donee.

SHORT-TERM TRUST. Short-term trusts (also called Clifford trusts, ten-year terminable trusts, or short-term reversionary trusts) are irrevocable for a period and then become revocable. They primarily are used to save income taxes. For example, consider a person in a high income tax bracket who has been providing or who would like to provide an income to another person or persons. If income-producing property is placed into a trust for a minimum of ten years and one day, the income will be taxed to the trust beneficiaries or the trustee rather than to the grantor. The trust can be terminated at will by the grantor after the designated period has elapsed. Once the trust becomes revocable, the grantor is taxed on the income, regardless of to whom it is distributed. This type of trust is most useful when the beneficiary is in a lower income tax bracket than the grantor. Furthermore, in order to not be taxed on the income, the grantor must not have a legal obligation to provide support to the beneficiary or if there is a legal obligation, the income payments cannot constitute support.

The trust must be in existence a *minimum* of ten years or for the lifetime of the beneficiary. The life expectancy of the beneficiary is not considered in determining the tax consequences of the trust. Generally, all the trust property should be placed in trust at one time. If the grantor makes periodic transfers to the trust, the ten-year requirement applies to each transfer.

While any type of property may be placed in a short-term trust, to be effective the property should be income producing for obvious reasons.

There are no estate tax advantages to the grantor in establishing a short-term trust. The property is part of the grantor's estate if death ocurs after the trust has expired. And if the grantor dies during the existence of the trust, the value of the trust property less the actuarial value of the income to be paid to the trust beneficiary is included in the grantor's estate.

The value of the trust property is not regarded as a gift, but the estimated value of the income on that property is subject to gift taxation.

If the trust income is accumulated in the trust, the trust pays the income tax. The trust beneficiaries pay income tax on periodic distributions.

Short-term trusts are often the best choice for persons who are providing income to aged parents. In many of these cases, income would be provided in any event and there is a large difference in the income tax brackets of the grantor and the parents. These trusts are also useful for high-bracket taxpayers who want to shift income to their children who are in low tax brackets.

REVOCABLE LIVING TRUST.   A revocable living trust is a highly versatile estate planning tool. Some of its possible advantages are:

1. The grantor may transfer financial management obligations to a trustee.

2. Property in the trust bypasses the probate process which may cut costs, shorten delays, and avoid publicity.
3. The trust may provide income to the family during the critical period after the grantor's death.
4. The trust may allow a business to continue without interruption after the grantor's death.
5. Minors and others with legal disabilities may be protected.
6. The trust will be less susceptible to attack by disgruntled heirs than a will because the trust will have been operative before the grantor's death.
7. The grantor may observe the operation of the trust while he or she is alive and make adjustments as needed.
8. It prevents the grantor's creditors from reaching the trust assets (at least in some states).
9. The trust can bring together property located in more than one state (eliminating the need for probate action in several states).

There are no tax advantages to a revocable trust. The grantor remains responsible for all federal income taxes, even if the trust income is paid to someone else.

There is no gift when a revocable trust is created because the grantor retains the power to revoke the trust. However, a gift occurs when income from the trust is actually paid to a beneficiary.

TESTAMENTARY TRUST. If a trust is not needed until the grantor's death, a testamentary trust may be appropriate. However, the advantages of a testamentary trust can also be achieved by means of a revocable living trust. This may be preferable in some instances since the grantor can observe the management of the trust and the establishment of the trust does not depend upon the will. If a testamentary trust is used, it will not become operative if the grantor dies intestate or if the will is denied probate. An unfunded revocable *inter vivos* trust is similar to a testamentary trust in that the trustee's fee and many administrative details are avoided until the grantor's death. The *inter vivos* unfunded trust may own life insurance policies and therefore automatically becomes funded upon the death of the insured.

In situations involving large estates the use of two testamentary trusts is useful as a way of minimizing estate taxes. In the typical situation, a person with a sizable estate is interested in taking maximum advantage of the federal estate tax marital deduction. This is easy to achieve; in fact, the maximum deduction will be available if the entire estate is left to the surviving spouse. However, if the entire estate is left outright to the surviving spouse, the estate tax may be large, not so much when the first spouse dies, but when the surviving spouse dies.

The usual method of minimizing estate taxes at the death of each spouse is to establish two trusts: a "marital deduction trust" and "nonmarital deduction" or "residuary" trust. Other common terminology referring to this two-trust concept is "marital and family trusts" or A-B trusts.

The marital deduction trust is structured to take maximum advantage of the marital deduction by placing one-half of the grantor's adjusted gross estate (or $250,000, whichever is greater) in it. The terms of this trust must meet the marital deduction requirements. At a minimum, the surviving spouse must have the right to all the trust income and the power to direct the trust property to anyone he or she wishes. Of course the trust will qualify for the marital deduction if the surviving spouse is given all the rights to the trust property.

There is no estate tax savings associated with establishing a marital trust since the marital deduction is available without a trust. Furthermore, the property in the marital trust will be subject to estate taxation when the surviving spouse dies.

A marital deduction trust is convenient if the surviving spouse is incapable of managing the property or if the property could be managed more effectively by a trustee.

If the amount of property placed in the marital deduction trust is sufficient, there may be no need to establish a residuary trust. The remaining portion of the grantor's estate may be left to children or to others. The basic objective of the residuary trust is to give the surviving spouse some rights in the property but not enough rights to make the property includable in the surviving spouse's estate. The spouse may be given the right to receive all the income from the trust and may receive the greater of $5,000 or 5 percent of the trust property each year (noncumulatively). Under certain conditions a spouse may be given additional amounts of principal.

It is best to place "wasting" assets (those that tend to lose value) in the marital trust and appreciating assets in the residuary trust. If the income from the marital trust is not sufficient for the spouse to live on, it may be best to exhaust the marital deduction trust corpus before entitling the spouse to touch the income from the residuary trust. The reason for this is that the property in the marital deduction trust is subject to taxation in the surviving spouse's estate, while the property in the residuary trust is not.

SPECIAL TRUSTS. Virtually all trusts may be classified into one of the basic types previously discussed. However, many trusts have a unique characteristic or an important provision, and these trusts are known by specific names. Three of the most important are (1) pour-over trusts, (2) life insurance trusts, and (3) sprinkle trusts.

Pour-Over Trust.   A pour-over trust receives assets from a will or another trust. While these trusts may be either revocable or irrevocable, or living or testamentary, most are living, revocable trusts. A pour-over trust is used to consolidate assets from a number of sources under professional management into a logical, integrated plan.

This type of trust is also useful in minimizing taxes. If a person has no incidents of ownership in a life insurance policy but the proceeds are payable to his or her estate, the proceeds will be included in the estate for tax purposes. This can be avoided by having the proceeds payable to a pour-over trust. The death benefits from a qualified pension or profit-sharing plan may also escape estate taxation in the same manner.

Life Insurance Trust.   The corpus of a life insurance trust is life insurance that is held by and payable to the trustee. These trusts may be revocable or irrevocable. The tax treatment of the trust, therefore, will follow its basic characteristics.

Life insurance trusts provide (1) greater flexibility than that obtainable with life insurance settlement options (discussed in Chapter 8), (2) restrictions and limitations on the use of funds, (3) an alternative to the appointment of a guardian for minor beneficiaries, (4) an avenue to avoid subsequent estate taxes when trust beneficiaries die, (5) investment management, (6) consolidation of assets, and (7) estate liquidity.

With regard to the last item, trust property will be included in the insured's estate if the trustee has a legal obligation to provide liquidity to the estate. As a practical matter, however, many life insurance trusts serve this purpose without imposing the legal obligation to do so on the trustee.

Sprinkle Trust.   Trusts that contain a "sprinkling" clause are known as "sprinkling" trusts. The financial needs of different trust beneficiaries may vary, especially over a long period. With a sprinkling clause the trustee can be given the right to use some discretion in determining the proper payments to the different beneficiaries. For example, the trustee may increase the income of a beneficiary when there is a special need, such as medical expenses or college education.

These trusts do have income tax implications. Income taxes will be less when low income tax bracket beneficiaries receive more income than others. Generally, the income will be taxed to the person who receives it. However, the income will be taxed to the grantor if he or she is able to direct the income spray or receives benefits from the income.

Chapter Notes

1. For our purposes, the most important exception to the transfer for value rule is that proceeds are not taxable if the transferee is a corporation in which the insured is a shareholder or officer.
2. Split dollar plans established before November 1964 do not involve any taxable income.
3. A company's rates for term riders cannot be used.
4. Terminology in the field of business insurance is confusing. This section is concerned with the financial losses to business interests when a sole proprietor dies or becomes disabled. Insurance that covers these losses is known as "business continuation insurance," "business purchase insurance," or simply "business insurance."
5. There are some important legal and practical differences among sole proprietorships, partnerships, and corporations. These distinctions are analyzed in detail in CPCU 6 and will not be emphasized here.
6. When there is a large deficiency in the insurance proceeds and the installment payment approach is not practical, it may be necessary to reorganize the company into a partnership or corporation. The surviving heirs would then become partners (possibly limited partners) or stockholders.
7. The number of policies required in a cross-purchase plan is always $n(n-1)$, where n is the number of partners.
8. For a discussion of individual state laws, see *Advanced Underwriting Service*, vol. 2 (Indianapolis: Research and Review Service), p. 14-21.

CHAPTER 15

Personal Loss Exposures and Their Treatment: A Case Analysis

INTRODUCTION

The previous chapters of this book have examined different potential loss exposures and ways in which such exposures might be handled within a risk management framework. In this context, techniques for meeting loss exposures such as loss prevention, retention and transfer techniques such as insurance were evaluated. In some situations, mini-cases were utilized. However, such cases involved only one personal loss exposure situation. This chapter will present one detailed, extensive case analysis that should enable the reader to utilize information gained in previous chapters of the text.

CASE FACTS

John Dover, age forty, is a successful advertising agency executive. He joined the agency, now called Mediamatics, Inc., fifteen years ago as a junior account executive when the entire agency staff consisted of eight people. The agency now has thirty employees, with 1977 billings of approximately $4 million.

With the agency's incorporation two years ago, John was elected treasurer and vice president. In this position, John personally maintains a limited number of client accounts and oversees the operations of all current and prospective clients. This job matches John's abilities well, and his expertise is a major reason for Mediamatics' continued growth and prosperity.

John's current salary is $55,000 a year. Since becoming an account executive within the agency (twelve years ago), his salary has increased at an average annual compounded rate of about 6 percent. For each of the past four years he also has received a sizable bonus based on the agency's overall performance as well as his individual objectives for new accounts and increased billings. The employee benefits John currently receives include a qualified profit-sharing plan, noncontributory group term life insurance coverage equal to one and one-half times his current salary, and a medical-expense plan which includes basic hospital and surgical coverage (Blue Cross-Blue Shield) and supplementary major medical coverage (commercial insurer). John's dependents also are protected under this medical-expense plan. The agency has just upgraded its benefits program by starting a short-term (twenty-six week) disability income program. The board of directors also is considering key employee insurance for certain employees including John. The amount of coverage recommended to the board is $100,000 per individual. When John was elected an officer of the agency, he purchased 1,000 shares of the corporation stock (par value $10). The other 7,000 outstanding shares are distributed 3,000 shares each to the chief executive officer, age sixty; the president, age fifty-eight; and 1,000 shares to the agency's other vice president, who is forty-three. There has been no formal discussion of what would occur within the agency upon the death or serious disability of one of these officers, although it has long been assumed that John would be the first promoted at the death or disability of either senior officer. He looks forward to such an executive position, but has no desire to change agencies or industries for such an opportunity.

John and his wife, Sue, thirty-five, have been happily married for twelve years and have three healthy sons, ages ten, eight, and five. Sue was a commercial artist before starting the family, and two years ago she began painting again, selling her art work locally on consignment. This past year she earned $5,000 from this, but she has no desire to return to full-time employment.

Personal financial matters are handled by John. They live comfortably but remain quite practical and economical in their preferences. All their property is owned in joint tenancy except for Sue's art works and supplies ($1,000), the savings bonds ($100 owned by each child), and the common stock and profit-sharing assets, which John owns. Their primary financial ambitions are to assure that their children receive a quality college education and that they maintain adequate financial protection for any unfortunate contingencies.

John has occasionally speculated for short-term profits in the stock market (with moderate success) and generally is willing to accept a moderate investment risk. Overall, John considers himself a cautious and analytical investor and essentially desires investments of long-term growth and stable cash flow. With his total 1977 tax liabilities being nearly 70 percent of his salary, he has been discussing with his broker feasible tax-shelter investments but otherwise has not considered changing his investment and property portfolio.

Besides his employee benefits from the company, John owns property-liability insurance on his home, on a farm he and Sue own, and on rental properties, and family and basic automobile coverages. Ten years ago he purchased an individual $50,000, five-year term life insurance policy which had a renewability feature which he exercised for an additional five-year period. Sue is named beneficiary of this policy as she also is on the group life insurance.

John and Sue recently signed their will, whereby at the death of either person all remaining property is left to the surviving spouse. They also settled on their major retirement goals—they have agreed that they want to comfortably maintain a home and a similar standard of living as just prior to retirement. They also would like to travel internationally but realize it might be difficult to do until John retires and/or the college expenses for the children have ended. Besides these priorities, they would like to provide their children and potential grandchildren some gifts during their lifetime and the balance of their estate when both are deceased.

Five years ago, they moved into their current residence which cost $52,500 ($42,000 mortgage, twenty years at 8 percent). With the betterments they have made and the rapid property appreciation in their neighborhood, John estimates the home's current market value to be $72,000. They have no desire to sell their home in the foreseeable future, however.

John also has interest in two other real estate properties. Three years ago (1974), he and a college classmate pooled their resources to invest equally in rental properties, which easily provide annual income to fund the mortgage and maintenance expenses. The value of his share of these properties is $52,000 (20 percent down, twenty-year mortgage at 8¾ percent). The properties are located in a growing suburban community and although they are twelve years old remain structurally sound and well kept. John plans this to be a steady source of income for at least ten more years.

The second property interest involves two adjoining family farms in the Midwest. Two years ago John inherited, through his aunt's will, a one-half interest of approximately eighty-nine acres with an appraised value of $2,000 per acre. John's sister also inherited eighty-nine acres. Since his sister has no desire for this property, John has been buying his sister's interest as it is transferred to her. To buy part of her interest,

Table 15-1
Loss Exposure Identification

Objectives	Loss Exposures
Short-Term	
1. Maintain adequate financial protection for unfortunate contingencies	1. Economic loss from death, accident, sickness, property and liability loss, and unemployment (pure)
2. Income tax planning	2. Excess income tax (speculative)
3. Complete purchase of sister's interest in the farm property	3. Insufficient earnings from accumulated assets (speculative)
4. Assist parents with retirement income	4. Insufficient earnings from accumulated assets (speculative)
Long-Term	
5. Assure their children a quality college education	5. Insufficient earnings from accumulated assets (speculative)
6. Maintain a similar home and standard of living at retirement	6. Loss of earned income at retirement (pure)
7. International travel in the future	7. Insufficient earnings from accumulated assets (speculative)
8. Contribute to their heir's welfare	8. Estate and probate settlement conflicts (speculative)

John obtained a second mortgage on his family home for $30,000, which he is financing over fifteen years at 9 percent interest.

The annual income from both farms has been consistently yielding an average return of 8 percent, and with rapid appreciation of land values John foresees these as stable and highly profitable assets. The property and income loss history of these farms has been minimal, and the current tenants who farm these properties seem quite competent and trustworthy.

Although John thinks the farms he has acquired will have a very positive effect on his family's financial future, he is concerned about future retirement income for his parents who are both over sixty-five. They have very little in savings, and John is determined to help his parents financially but is unsure of the best method. His goal is to give them $5,000 annually. Table 15-1 lists John's long- and short-term objectives and his major loss exposures.

LOSS EXPOSURE ANALYSIS

The first step in loss exposure analysis is compiling the family's

Table 15-2
Balance Sheet

Assets		Liabilities/Net Worth	
Current Assets		**Current Liabilities**	
Cash and Checking Account	$ 1,000	Credit Accounts Due	$ 400
Savings Account	5,000	Bills Payable	900
U.S. Savings Bonds	300	House Improvement Loan	1,500
Common Stocks (marketable)	5,000	Other	1,000
Other (art-works inventory)	1,000		
Total	$ 12,300	Total	$ 3,800
Long-Term Assets		**Long-Term Liabilities**	
Vested Profit Sharing	$ 12,500	Mortgage—Personal Home	$ 37,800
Farm Property	250,000	Mortgage—Rental Property	40,370
Rental Property	52,500	Mortgage—Farm Property	29,050
Common Stock (Close Corp.)	10,000		
Personal Residence	52,500		
Total	$377,500	Total	$107,220
Other		Total Liabilities	$111,020
Automobiles	$ 8,250		
Household Furnishings	7,250	Net Worth	$314,780
Personal Property			
(jewelry, clothes,			
sailboat, etc.)	20,500		
Total	36,000		
Total Assets	$425,800	Total	$425,800

financial data in a functional manner which permits appropriate analysis. The details of this family's financial situation are shown in Tables 15-2 through 15-6.

Not only must the current financial status be known, but also a prospective appraisal of the family's future financial status must be provided to plan effectively for forthcoming events. This forces the family and their advisors to anticipate future changes in their finances and security needs. The case implies that John is a successful and integral part of Mediamatics, Inc. and that he is in line for a top management position. Thus, it seems certain that his earned income will continue to increase at least equal to the 6 percent average. John is quite confident of his rental and farm properties and does not plan to change his investment portfolio, so it is also reasonable to presume that the yield on these income sources will remain fairly constant. No major

Table 15-3
Income Statement

Income		Expenses		
Earned Income		Ordinary Living Costs		$27,500
Salary—John	$55,000	Debt—Interest Expense		
Bonus	8,000	Bank Loans	200	
Income—Sue	5,000	Mortgages	6,200	6,400
Total	$68,000			
		Debt—Amortization		6,200
Investment Income		Insurance Premiums		
Farm (net)†	18,600			
Rentals (net)†	5,200	Auto	525	
Interest (taxable)	250	Life and Health	385	
Dividends	150	Property and Liability		
Capital Gain (long-term)	1,000	Personal	215	
		Investments and		
Total	$25,200	Properties	780	1,905
		Expenses Before Taxes		$42,005
		Taxes		
		Federal Income		$26,798
		State and Local Income		3,700
		Property—Residence		2,250
		Property—Investment		5,250
		Total		$37,998
Total Income	$93,200	Total Expenses		$80,003

† Net refers to the gross earnings less direct operating costs.

purchases or investments are foreseen, so the family's balance sheet and expenses also should remain fairly constant.

Thus, the current financial statements appear to be a reasonable distribution of the family's assets and liabilities and income and expenditures. Recognizing the implications of inflation and other economic factors, these statements can then be used in developing the family's financial plan.

The second step is analyzing the financial impact to identify the possible perils occurring within each loss exposure area and determine its frequency and economic severity.

Table 15-4
Federal Income Tax Statement

Gross Income		$93,200
Less		
Business Expenses	$ 850	
Property Expenses		
Maintenance	300	
Depreciation	2,250	
Interest	4,005	
Taxes	5,250	12,655
Adjusted Gross Income		$80,545
Less		
Interest	2,195	
Medical Expense	0	
Taxes	5,950 8,145	
Personal Exemptions	3,750	11,895
Taxable Income		$68,650
Tax (at 55% marginal tax rate)		$26,978
Less		
Credit		180
Tax Liability		$26,798

Premature Death

The economic losses most likely to occur in the event of premature death are:

1. loss of current income and future income potential;
2. extra costs and obligations, such as funeral costs, estate and inheritance taxes, loss of household services, and so on;
3. loss of credit standing, i.e., inability to repay current debts, limited chance of obtaining future credit, and so on;
4. loss of tax advantages, such as joint returns and gift and estate tax marital deductions; and
5. loss of career opportunities and/or business value.

Economic loss is created when a person has excess income or services on which others depend. In this case, the untimely death of Sue or John could create specific economic hardship to the surviving family.

To measure the severity of loss, it is necessary to analyze the surviving family's income and cash needs assuming the death were to

Table 15-5
Current Insurance Protection

Personal	Coverage
Life Insurance	
1. Group—term with wife, Sue, as beneficiary	$ 82,500
2. Individual—term with wife as beneficiary	50,000
a. 5-year with guaranteed renewal for 15 more years—option exercised 5 years ago	
b. lump-sum settlement option	
Disability	
1. Group—short-term (26 weeks) with 5-day waiting period	300/week
Medical Expense (Group)	
1. Basic hospital — reasonable costs for up to 60 days	
surgical — partial-service benefits based on cost schedule	
medical — up to $50 per day for 60 days	
2. Major Medical — $250,000 maximum benefit limit $200 corridor deductible $80\times$ coinsurance (percentage participation) on first $5,000 benefits	
Property and Liability	
1. Homeowners—Form 2—$100 deductible	
Coverage A—dwelling	70,000
C—personal property	29,000
D—additional living expenses	14,000
E—comprehensive personal liability	25,000/occurrence
F—medical payments	500/person
property damage to others	250/occurrence
2. Family Automobile Plan (2 cars)	
Coverage A—bodily injury liability	50,000/100,000
B—property damage liability	25,000/occurrence
C—medical payments	5,000/person
D—comprehensive	actual cash value
E—collision ($100 deductible)	actual cash value
F—uninsured motorists	5,000/10,000
3. Directors' and officers' liability	1,000,000

Other	Coverage
Property and Liability—Farm	
1. Farmowners—$100 deductible	
Coverage A—dwelling	$20,000
B—household property	10,000
C—additional living expense	2,000
F—farm buildings	50,000
G—personal liability	50,000
H—medical payments	1,000/person
	50,000/accident
2. Basic Automobile Plan (3 vehicles)	
Coverage A—bodily injury liability	50,000/100,000
B—property damage liability	25,000/accident
C—medical payments	5,000/person
D—comprehensive	actual cash value
E—collision ($100 deductible)	actual cash value
F—towing and labor costs	500
G—uninsured motorists	50,000/accident
Property and Liability—Rental	
1. Businessowners policy	
Section I —	
Coverage A—buildings	45,000
B—personal property	5,000
C—loss of income	7,000
Section II —comprehensive liability	500,000

occur in the immediate future. In general, a family has the following financial requirements:

1. *Cash for immediate needs*—to pay for funeral costs, estate and inheritance taxes, and immediate living costs.
2. *Readjustment fund*—income necessary to comfortably allow the family to adjust to new living conditions. This fund should be approximately one year's current salary.
3. *Dependency period*—income required for surviving parent to support children until they are self-sufficient or age twenty-two (assuming each finishes college). This should be approximately one-half of current annual salary.
4. *Pre-retirement income*—income required for spouse after children are independent and prior to normal retirement age (sixty-five).
5. *Retirement fund*—spouse's income requirement after age sixty-five. It is suggested that the annual income provided for periods 4 and 5 be at least one-half of current annual salary.

Table 15-6
1976 Financial Data—Mediamatics, Inc.

Billings	$4,000,000
Net income	125,000
Tangible assets	100,000
Retained earnings	85,000
Current value of stock	93.75/share
Property Valuations	
Farm (actual cash value)	
Dwelling	$ 22,500
Buildings	40,900
Vehicles	18,000
Tools and machinery	9,000
Cattle	85,000
Land	2,000/acre
Rental (replacement value)	
Building	$ 100,000
Personal property	10,000
Land	10,000
Residence (replacement value)	
Dwelling	$ 67,000
Household furnishings	8,250
Personal property	20,500
Land	5,000

6. *Emergency fund*—this is a contingency fund for unexpected needs, which should be invested until needed. Between $1,000 and $3,000 is considered adequate.
7. *Special needs*—this might include repaying outstanding debts, saving for college education expenses, and so on.

If John were to die, the surviving family members would have the economic needs shown in Table 15-7.

Since Sue provides a nominal portion of the family's income, the economic hardships of her immediate death should be viewed more as a loss of potential income than actual income. Of course, an additional hardship is imposed in the event of Sue's death due to the loss of her household services. There are two types of income needs, then, which must be considered. The *immediate needs* will be similar since most of the family's assets are currently jointly owned. The other income need at her death is the *readjustment fund*. The household and maternal

Table 15-7

Family Economic Needs

1. Immediate needs (assumes no inheritance tax)		$ 42,255
†Funeral costs = $ 5,065		
₊Estate tax = 30,970		
†Living costs = 6,220		
2. Readjustment fund (1 year's current salary)		$ 55,000
3. Dependency period (one-half current salary per year, decreasing proportionally as each child becomes self-sufficient)		$ 403,200
Sue and 3 children (11 years) = $302,500		
2 children (2 years) = 45,800		
1 child (3 years) = 54,900		
4. Pre-retirement income (one-quarter current salary for 13 years)		$ 178,750
5. Retirement needs (one-quarter salary, life expectancy of 21 years)		$ 288,750
6. Emergency fund		$ 3,000
7. Special needs		$ 203,000
Repaying mortgage = $107,220		
College education expenses = 95,780		
	Total	$1,173,955

†Estimated.

services which a mother currently provides are now being recognized as a significant loss not only in qualitative terms but in replacement costs, e.g., it was recently reported that to replace a mother's services currently costs about $7,000 per child. It is important, then, for the surviving family to have adequate financial liquidity to meet the immediate expenses at Sue's death (about $26,000), and have adequate funds to at least temporarily replace her household services (a minimum of $21,000 per year).

The frequency of this loss exposure is readily available in mortality tables. However, since death creates such a definite and catastrophic loss, the probabilities of the loss exposure's occurrence are inconsequential, and only the impact of the severity factor should be considered.

Disability

Serious accident or sickness which forces temporary or permanent curtailment of the total or partial activities of the family's income-earners can cause the same significant perils as the risk of premature death, i.e., loss of current and future income, loss of credit standing, loss of career opportunities or business values, and extra costs and obligations. This last peril can be especially disastrous if the medical care required is extensive in time and/or complexity. In fact, the total and permanent disability of the family breadwinner (in this instance John) can be economically more catastrophic than premature death because of these additional expenses and the requirements of time and assistance now placed upon the other family members.

The severity of this exposure is essentially measured in the same fashion as premature death. The income needs of the family will be greater, however, since John's subsistence costs must now be included, and additional medical and rehabilitation expenses will be incurred. These needs also are more variable because of the uncertainty of duration and required medical care of the disability or injury.

Income requirements must be separated into:

1. *Medical expense needs*—the costs of hospitalization; professional services, e.g., surgery, drugs, medical equipment, etc. Planning for these expenses is needed for all family members.
2. *Disability income needs*—the loss of income which will occur if the breadwinner, John, is disabled and unable to continue working and receiving income.

An adequate amount of protection for medical expenses is difficult to determine because of the volatility and severity of the loss exposure. It has been suggested that at least $10,000 *per cause per person* be available, and a minimum of $100,000 be on hand for expenses over the lifetime of the husband and wife (which includes the children during the dependency period).[1] An important element to consider is the rapidly rising costs of medical care, which increased 70 percent between 1967 and 1975, compared to a 27 percent increase in the Consumer Price Index (CPI) during the same period.

Disability income needs are essentially the same as or greater than the family's current income requirements since few if any expenses have ceased while extra medical costs have been incurred. Analyzing the family's income statement, pre-tax expenses are just over 66 percent of John's earned income. Assuming additional medical care expenses and continued tax liability on the property and investment income, a monthly income of $3,525 is required to satisfy the family's needs.

The frequency of disability of ninety days or longer (about 1.2 percent) is approximately 4.5 times greater than the probability of death at age forty. On average, about fifteen days per year per person in this family's income class will be lost to restrictive disability of some sort. Such statistics, when related to the severity of the loss exposure, imply that the disability risk is very serious.

Retirement

Retirement can be extremely difficult unless adequate savings and planning are initiated early. The most important peril with this loss exposure, then, is the loss of earned income without sufficient accumulated savings to meet retirement expectations. An indirect peril which can severely depress the real value of long-term savings and fixed annuities is inflation.

The possible severity of inadequate retirement income depends on one's retirement goals. John and Sue have stated their main retirement goal is to maintain a similar standard of living and home as at retirement. Assuming John's retirement age is sixty-five, the family's mortgages will be paid-up, so their income needs will be to match their "pre-retirement" standard of living.

The impact of inflation can severely deter one's ability to adequately save for retirement needs, however. For example, if $100 were invested for one year at 5 percent, the total amount at the end of year one would be $105. But if inflation was 7 percent that year, the $105 would be worth only $98 in real value; in other words, the $100 saved for one year actually lost $2.

In projecting John and Sue's retirement income needs, the purchasing power of a dollar of savings must be considered. Presuming wages increase relative to merit (productivity increases) plus the rise in inflation, using an average of John's salary in his last five working years, gives a good estimate of their retirement income needs. This "final-average" salary calculation does not protect them from the impact of inflation during their retirement years, however, and this peril must therefore be considered in the sources of retirement income.

Thus, assuming John's salary will continue to increase at 6 percent per year, their annual retirement income requirement will be $58,850. Assuming a 6 percent interest rate, John's life expectancy at age sixty-five to be fifteen years and Sue's twenty years, and that the surviving spouse will need two-thirds of retirement income for her (his) remaining years, the accumulated savings necessary when John becomes sixty-five is $692,107.

Unemployment

The peril of unemployment can lead to the loss of income, possibly the loss of credit standing if repayment of debt becomes difficult, and the loss (or interruption) of career opportunities. Maybe even more important, unemployment can place terrible emotional burdens upon the family. It is not the type of loss exposure that can be statistically measured as to frequency, so personal awareness or "intuition" of one's job security is necessary.

The advertising industry is rather volatile in regard to job security. However, John's long service with one agency and widespread respect throughout the industry seem to make it fairly unlikely that he would now lose his current job or have much difficulty in gaining a similar position with another agency. Therefore, the economic impact and likelihood of John being relieved of his current duties does not warrant financial planning beyond maintaining a family emergency fund which could be used for this event or any other unforeseen contingencies.

A more probable and critical source of conflict would be the death or serious disability of one of the other three agency stockholders, causing his or her share of stock to be sold or passed on to heirs. In a close corporation in which personal talents are so important, the successful working relationships among top management and stockholders is very important. It is unlikely that a stockholder's heir would have the same talent and management skills, and the heir's efforts to replace the stockholder could easily disrupt the profitability and work environment of the agency. If a stockholder or his or her estate attempted to sell the stockholder's shares of such a closely held corporation, the interested buyers would probably be very few, if any. Thus the selling price and value of the stock would seriously decline. It is questionable whether any of the "working" stockholders could purchase the shares until they drastically declined in price. As with the heir joining the management team, the purchase of these shares by an unknown or unwanted person could seriously disrupt the agency. And finally, the turmoil caused by the loss of an important stockholder could result in the loss of clientele and/or credit standing with current or future lenders.

It is important, then, for the four stockholders to have a written buy-sell agreement which establishes the method and price for transferring stock interests at death or in the event of incapacitating disability. In this manner the future of the agency will remain in control of the current management team. To fund this agreement, the remaining stockholders or the corporation must have $93,750 (1,000 × $93.75) if John or the other vice president leaves the agency, or if the chief executive officer or president should leave, $281,250 (3,000 × $93.75), readily available to purchase the stock, assuming the recent stock valuation will persist.

Property and Liability Loss Exposures

The economic loss from real and personal property damage can occur from a great variety of perils. The most prevalent are fire and lightning, windstorm, hail, explosion, smoke or water damage, damage by or to an automobile, riot, vandalism, theft, and glass breakage. The most important properties subject to these perils are the family's residence, the rental and farm properties, automobiles, and the family's sailboat.

The resulting damage from these events is known as a *direct* loss. Such losses also can create consequential *indirect* losses which must also be identified. The most important of these are additional living expenses, e.g., temporary housing, laundry, food, and clothing costs; debris removal; business interruption; and demolition costs.

The severity of property damage is essentially based on the maximum loss that could be incurred for various parts of the property. Several values can be used to define this loss potential, the most important being *actual cash value* and *replacement value*. The latter is the expected current costs to fully replace similar property. This type of valuation should be used for the personal residence and the rental property since the same quality and type of asset would presumably be constructed. The actual cash value is the replacement cost less physical depreciation and obsolescence. This valuation is more difficult to ascertain, but is more relevant for business property which will be replaced with better or dissimilar assets. In this case, the farm property should be valued by its actual cash value. The pertinent valuations for these various properties are provided in the financial statements. Property damage to the automobiles also is valued on an actual cash value basis, which for our purpose is the stated value of the income statement ($8,250).

The indirect losses are essentially extra costs caused by these direct losses. Property damage to the residence will cause additional living expenses, which insurers project to be approximately 20 to 30 percent of the dwelling's property value. The primary indirect loss from the farm and rental properties will be loss of income, which in 1977 would have been a total of $23,800. Debris removal and demolition costs are not significant enough to be concerned with in this planning process.

The frequency of property damage risks can be fairly accurately projected, discriminating by important variables such as income class, geographic location, age and condition of the property, sex, age, and past loss experience. Although these factors do not imply a high frequency for the Dovers, the fact that real property is a major portion of the family's assets and that automobile damage is such a volatile risk imply the need for adequate protection.

Personal liability can result from an act of negligence, a breach of contract, or contractually assuming the liability of others. It is essential that possible loss exposures be identified. They include:

1. owning income-producing property,
2. employing others to maintain this property (e.g., farm tenants),
3. owning automobiles and a boat,
4. personal activities, and
5. duties as a corporate officer.

Liability actions are becoming an increasingly troublesome area of tort law and can result in severe economic problems even for unintended negligence. The damages are sometimes a completion of expected services, but most often monetary damages are decided up to the family's total asset value or net worth. The frequency of this exposure is by no means as great or as easily measurable as property losses, but the severity can be catastrophic. Therefore, adequate protection of this loss exposure also is a necessity.

Estate and Probate Settlement Conflicts

Probate settlement refers to the passing of the decedent's privately owned property by the executor/executrix of the family's will. In this case, the probate estate will not be significant since the vast majority of assets are owned in joint tenancy which allows the property to pass to the surviving joint-owner outside of the will. This is beneficial since probate settlement often causes delay in passing property to heirs, offers opportunity for problems among creditors, relatives, or the general public, and can be costly because of attorney's and executor's fees. John's probate estate will include his common stock holdings ($15,000) and mutual funds ($12,500). This nominal probate estate offers no relief for the family's potential estate tax liability, however, and may provide liquidity problems for the executor in meeting the estate settlement costs.

Estate settlement refers to the passing of the person's total property interests to his or her heirs. This could transpire during one's lifetime and/or at death. The method of transferring this property can have great financial impact on the tax liability and continued welfare of the decedent's heirs. It is essential, therefore, that the family initiate effective estate planning, which will include the following:

1. planning how and to whom the decedent's property will be distributed and the estate settled;
2. planning adequate financial support for the decedent's dependents;
3. keeping estate transfer costs, i.e., death taxes, settlement and administrative expenses, to a minimum;

Table 15-8

Potential Estate Tax Liability

	John	Sue
Gross Estate	$578,200	$419,500
Less: Debts	110,220	0
Adjusted Gross Estate	$467,980	$419,500
Less: Marital deductions	250,000	250,000
Taxable Estate	$217,980	$169,500
Tax	60,970	45,040
Credit	30,000	30,000
Tax Liability	$ 30,970	$ 15,040

4. providing adequate liquid assets for the estate to meet these estate transfer costs, including repayment of debt; and
5. planning for the disposition of the closely held business interest.

The economic need for this planning is significant in this case. First, the potential estate tax liability, as shown in Table 15-8, would be $30,970 at John's death and $15,040 at Sue's death.

Table 15-8 assumes current market values, but the appreciation of asset values, especially the family's real estate holdings, could increase this liability significantly over time. It also must be remembered that the estate will pay taxes on the income earned in the year prior to the estate-owner's death, and the heirs must pay tax on the capital gains relative to transferred asset appreciation. Adequate liquid assets must be available, therefore, to satisfy these liabilities. Liquid assets also will be needed at John's death to repay the outstanding debt ($107,220), if it is called. Secondly, this points out the need for estate planning to minimize the estate transfer costs.

A sort of "boomerang" effect that will occur with the current provisions of the will and joint-ownership is the excessive estate tax at the death of the surviving spouse. The will and joint-tenancy arrangement transfer essentially all property to the surviving spouse. The problem arises that no marital deduction can be taken at the estate settlement of this spouse (assuming he or she does not remarry), which creates an enormous tax liability, as shown in Table 15-9.

Another essential need for estate planning is in the distribution of estate assets. As the case states, Sue is not interested or knowledgeable in the family's financial matters. For her to inherit not only the family

Table 15-9

Estate Tax Liability Without Marital Deduction

	Surviving Spouse Was Sue	Surviving Spouse Was John
Gross Estate	$419,500	$578,200
Less: Debts	0	110,220
Taxable Estate	$419,500	$467,980
Tax	128,391	145,335
Credit (assumes highest tax credit)	47,000	47,000
Tax Liability	$ 81,391	$ 98,355

income responsibilities but the management of the rental and farm properties therefore appears imprudent. Thought also must be given to the transferring of these assets to the children (especially if they are not yet of majority age) at the death of the surviving spouse or to leaving this choice to the spouse's discretion. Another consideration is the consequences that might result at the simultaneous deaths of both parents. It is necessary, then, for Sue and John to decide the financial support they wish to leave their dependents and the most efficient and financially sound method of distributing the assets under the varying possible circumstances.

A corollary to this is the fact that at present Sue will become a 12.5 percent owner of Mediamatics, Inc., and an equal partner in the management of the rental property. The need for a buy-sell agreement of the closely held stock in Mediamatics, Inc., has been previously discussed in the section on Unemployment. A similar arrangement also must be prepared by John and his college classmate to smoothly transfer their business interest at the death or incapacitating disability of either partner.

Excess Income Tax

The impact of taxes, especially federal income taxes, is becoming an increasing burden. The progressive tax system increases the tax rate as taxable income increases, while inflation decreases the real value of additional income. The taxpayer is in a losing position both ways.

The Dovers' situation is a pertinent example. John's earned income for the past twelve years has been increasing at about 6 percent per year, but if we assume an inflation rate of 4 percent, this cuts the increase by two-thirds. During this same period, the increased earned income has caused the tax rate to climb (at current rates) from 32 percent to 53 percent, or approximately 1.75 percent annually. The increase in *available* earned income, then, has only been 0.25 percent annually.

With the additional income sources the family has enjoyed in the past three years, this tax burden is magnified. The 1977 federal income tax liability of this family was about 40 percent of earned income and 30 percent of total income.

The objective of income tax planning, then, is to decrease the family's income tax liability and subsequently increase its disposable income. The Internal Revenue Code allows various methods of reducing taxable income through exemptions, deductions, and credits. The essence of tax planning is to fully utilize these tax reducing methods within the guidelines of the family's financial means and objectives.

Capital Asset Investment and Management

Speculative risks are events which have the chance of gain as well as loss. This essentially refers to the investment and capital budgeting decisions of corporations and the risk of capital loss or insufficient return on investment. The goal of the corporate financial manager is to maximize the probability of gain or return on each capital investment through accurate financial analysis and planning within the firm's objectives and budgetary constraints.

These concepts can be similarly applied to a family's situation. A family has investment decisions and income-earning assets which have similar risks of capital loss or insufficient earnings from the investment. Insufficient earnings in this context refer not only to cash flow needs but to the impact of unnecessary taxation. The goal of the advisor, then, is two-fold: to maximize the probability of gain on each investment, and to minimize the income and estate tax liabilities through proper planning and management of the family's assets. It is necessary, therefore, to identify the areas which demand this financial management and to measure their economic needs. It also is important to recognize the potential advantages available from proper income and estate tax planning.

The risk of insufficient earnings and income to meet financial needs seems a persistent problem to many families. The most efficient method of minimizing this risk is planning for one's needs by intelligently investing and managing one's resources. Intelligence in this context implies designing a priority schedule of these needs, purchasing investment vehicles that will attain these goals and satisfy the investor's

Table 15-10

Projected Educational Costs and Required Savings

Current Age of Child	Total 4-Year Costs	Annual Savings Required (5% Return)	Accumulated Savings Required
10	$27,270	$2,300	$15,185
8	30,710	2,010	15,511
5	37,530	1,780	16,374
	$95,510	$6,090	$47,070

utility for risk, and studying these investments to be sure they continually achieve the desired results.

John and Sue have established a primary financial objective of assuring their children a quality education. The estimates of the financial requirements to meet this objective are staggering. One source, using an inflation rate of 6 percent a year and current college per-year costs of $4,000, projects the costs for each Dover child as shown in Table 15-10; also shown are the annual investment and current accumulated savings required to meet this cost (assuming 5 percent return).

The other long-term objective which will require accumulated savings is their desire to travel internationally after the college expenses are completed. This objective could be included in their retirement needs, or can be funded periodically in a special account from their common stock interests or other resources. It is difficult to project costs of international travel fifteen to twenty years in the future, but inflating today's prices (say $3,000 per person for a ten-day European trip) by 3 percent per year would mean $4,650 must be accumulated. Assuming a 6 percent interest rate, this requires an annual savings of $200 per year.

The third step in this section is calculating the relative value of the loss exposure and then categorizing each objective by its impact on the family's financial welfare.

The *relative value of loss exposure* is a quantitative measure of each exposure's economic impact on the family's wealth, i.e., total net worth, if no means of loss exposure protection were available. The maximum possible loss or need for each exposure is considered in Table 15-11 as the total amount currently required to meet the family's requirements, which were essentially developed in the previous section. Some of these factors, such as income needs at death or disability, are based over a

Table 15-11
Relative Value of Loss Exposures

Objective	Loss Exposure		Relative Value ($)
1. Financial protection from unfortunate contingencies	Death		$\dfrac{1{,}173{,}700}{314{,}780}$
	Injury	Per case	$\dfrac{50{,}000}{314{,}780}$
		Per lifetime	$\dfrac{100{,}000}{314{,}780}$
	Disability		$\dfrac{254{,}880[1]}{314{,}780}$
	Unemployment		$\dfrac{13{,}392}{314{,}780}$ or $\dfrac{56{,}250}{314{,}780}$
	Property		$\dfrac{72{,}000}{314{,}780}$
			$\dfrac{55{,}000}{314{,}780}$
			$\dfrac{250{,}000}{314{,}780}$
	Liability		Could vary up to family's net worth
2. Maintain a similar home and standard of living	Retirement		$\dfrac{332{,}917[2]}{314{,}780}$
3. Contribute to heir's future welfare	Estate and probate conflicts		
	John		$\dfrac{30{,}970}{314{,}780}$
	Sue		$\dfrac{70{,}305}{314{,}780}$
4. Income tax planning	Excess income tax		$\dfrac{26{,}798}{314{,}780}$
5. Assure children a quality college education	Insufficient earnings on assets		$\dfrac{47{,}070}{314{,}780}$
6. Travel internationally	Same as #5		$\dfrac{1{,}128}{314{,}780}$
7. Purchase sister's interest in farm property	Same as #5		$\dfrac{3{,}000}{314{,}780}$
8. Assist parents with retirement income	Same as #5		$\dfrac{5{,}000}{314{,}780}$

1. This is the annual needs times 25, which is the difference between John's current age and retirement age, discounted to its present value at 5 percent.
2. This is discounted to its present value at 5 percent.

long period of time. For simplicity, this time variable has not been considered in discounting the need or loss figure to its present value.

This relative value of loss exposure must be combined with the qualitative factors of each loss exposure which were broadly referred to earlier to evaluate its total economic impact. The limits of the three categories, i.e., catastrophic, major, and minor, are a function of the family's attitude toward uncertainty. The case states that the Dovers generally are conservative in their buying attitudes and rather practical and thrifty. John is a moderate risk-taker in investments but is careful to find long-term and stable assets. John and Sue have based their major financial goals around the total family's needs.

Overall, these factors imply a rather strong aversion to risk. Thus, the objectives should be categorized in the following manner:

1. Catastrophic
   - maintain adequate financial protection for unfortunate contingencies
   - maintain a similar home and standard of living at retirement
   - contribute to their heirs' welfare
2. Major
   - income tax planning
   - assure their children a quality college education
   - assist parents with retirement income
3. Minor
   - purchase sister's interest in farm property
   - travel internationally

LOSS EXPOSURE EVALUATION

Analysis of loss exposures provides the advisor with a quantitative and qualitative examination of the family's objectives. The final product is the categorizing of objectives relative to the family's risk-aversion and financial priorities. It is the purpose of the third part of the process, loss exposure evaluation, to examine the various financial "tools" available to satisfy these objectives.

The objectives categorized as catastrophic must be entirely fulfilled before considering the lower priority goals. This is essential since the economic impact of these objectives on the family's financial welfare is absolute. The major- and minor-category objectives are then considered in the order of their listing within these two categories. In this way, the family will achieve its most important objectives within the limits of its economic and planning abilities.

There are four methods to achieve these financial goals. Each method can be considered separately and/or together with the other methods to attain the best plan of controlling the loss exposure. *Avoidance* implies eliminating or avoiding all causes of the loss exposure. This is the most drastic but decisive means of protecting against economic loss; seldom is it applicable in the personal loss exposure area. *Prevention* refers to various ways of reducing the probability of the loss exposure's occurrence or reducing the severity of a loss once it has occurred. This method is applicable to almost every family exposure to loss through technical and "common-sense" techniques. *Retention* means personally assuming the economic perils of the loss exposure, whether consciously or by being unaware of its existence. Conscious retention of loss exposure should not be taken unless a thorough cost-benefit analysis has been completed and adequate financial reserves are available. *Transfer* is the passing of the risk from one party to another. Insurance is the most common loss exposure transfer device, but other methods, such as hold harmless agreements and financial hedging, can be quite effective.

Thus, loss exposure evaluation requires the advisor to consider several elements. First, the priority schedule of objectives must be followed. Secondly, the feasibility of each method's "protection" must be analyzed relative to its satisfaction of the family's objectives. Finally, the advisor must be aware of the cost-benefit trade-off of each method so that the family achieves the maximum number of objectives within its budgetary limits.

Adequate Financial Protection for Unfortunate Contingencies

Premature Death The relative value of loss exposure for John's premature death is over three and one-half times the family's net worth. Also, this loss exposure may occur at any time, which implies the need for immediate and dependable financial protection. Avoidance is obviously irrelevant in this situation, and the dollar amount of financial protection required makes retention inappropriate. Prevention is applicable in the sense of the family maintaining good health habits and medical treatment, practicing defensive driving, and so on. In essence, however, this loss exposure is inevitable, and the potential economic severity on an individual basis requires transferring the exposure to a party which can provide the necessary financial resources regardless of when the risk occurs. The financial "tool" best suited for this situation is life insurance.

The economic requirements of the family at John's death were itemized in the exposure analysis section of this chapter. These needs can be further identified as liquidity needs and income needs. Liquidity

Table 15-12

Sources of Funds to Meet Liquidity Needs

Need		Source of Funds	
1. Immediate needs	$ 42,255	1. Social security	$ 255
		Life insurance	42,000
2. Emergency fund	3,000	2. Savings account	5,000
3. Special needs:		3. Purchase decreasing	
Mortgage repayment	107,220	term life insurance	107,220
College education expenses		Planned for separately	

needs include (1) immediate needs, (2) emergency funds, and (3) special funds. Income needs include (1) readjustment funds, (2) dependency period funds, (3) pre-retirement income, and (4) retirement income.

The liquidity needs are an immediate demand, or outflow, of funds at John's death. Therefore, these needs must be the first considered. The sources available to meet these needs are current assets, social security, and life insurance proceeds, i.e., cash and checking account ($1,000), savings account ($5,000), marketable common stock ($5,000), life insurance proceeds ($50,000 and $82,000), and the lump-sum social security death benefit ($255). Thus, the best means of funding the family's liquidity needs are as shown in Table 15-12.

The first two cash requirements are satisfied with available family finances, but it is necessary to purchase decreasing term life insurance for repayment of the family's mortgage debt. The coverage should be decreasing since the principal due on this long-term debt progressively decreases with each mortgage payment. The insured will be John, and the beneficiary(ies) will be the creditors. Assuming all three mortgages are held by the same institution and the coverage can be purchased from a life insurer for $2 per thousand, level premium for seventeen years, the annual cost will be about $214. It also is prudent to purchase the waiver of premium rider (assuming it is available in this policy, say for $.25 per thousand) so that this protection will continue without further premium payment if John becomes permanently disabled. The total cost, then, will be about $241 per year.

The income needs of the family are a function of the time periods outlined earlier. These needs can be more easily understood by a time-series graph, as shown in Figure 15-1. This graph expresses the income requirement on a monthly basis, to show the periodic death benefits required and currently available. The graph also assumes an inflation factor of three percent per year. This variable was not considered earlier

Figure 15-1
Time-Series Graph

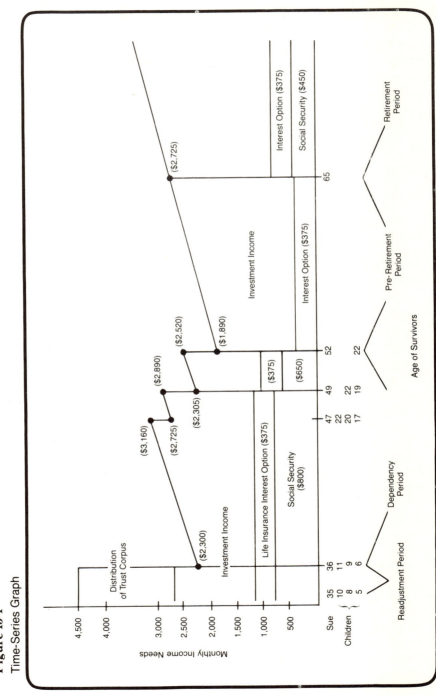

in this section but is extremely pertinent since inflation now appears to be a persistent factor in today's economy. Without considering this factor, the real value of the family's benefits received would be decreasing continually and thus inadequately provide for the family's financial needs.

The case states that Sue is neither interested in nor knowledgeable about financial matters. The family's income needs must therefore be managed by a competent third party, which implies life insurance settlement options and/or trusts. The significant advantages of settlement options are:

1. security of income and capital,
2. special income tax interest exclusion for the spouse,
3. payments guaranteed for life, and
4. flexibility feasible through withdrawal and commutation privileges.

The advantages of trusts are:

1. complete flexibility: trustee may be given broad discretionary powers, and
2. protection against inflation since trustee may have broad investment and asset management powers.

A trust arrangement would benefit the family by offering qualified management services to maintain their sizable investment income and protect against loss of purchasing power (inflation). There is a certain degree of downside risk to this investment income, however, so that the guaranteed periodic income of settlement options is therefore the best way to finance the family's income needs.

The trust corpus will include the real and personal property assets, or their settled value in the estate. Only $112,500 of the farm property will be transferred initially, with the remaining $137,500 transferring to the trust after the children have completed their college education (further explained in the financing of college expenses and retirement income for parents). The other assets included are annual income from the rental property ($5,000—explained further in the estate planning section), the marketable securities ($5,000), and the proceeds received for John's Mediamatics, Inc. stock ($93,750—further explained in the unemployment section).

The insurance proceeds available to meet the family's income needs will be $90,500, i.e., $82,500 from the group policy and the remaining $8,000 from the individual life insurance policy. Social security benefits of approximately $950 per month (the maximum family benefit) will be provided until the children have completed their college education. Between the ages of fifty-two and sixty-five, however, Sue will receive

Table 15-13

Program for Meeting Family's Income Needs

		Source	
Readjustment fund	$4,500	Life insurance interest option (at 5%)	$ 375
		Investment income (at 6.5%)	1,500
		Social security	800
		Distribution of trust corpus	1,825
Dependency period	2,300(+)	Life insurance interest option	375
		Investment income	1,500
		Social security	800
		(with 1 child)	650
Pre-retirement income	1,890(+)	Life insurance option	375
		Investment income	2,000
Retirement income	2,725(+)	Life insurance interest option	375
		Investment income	2,000
		Social Security	450

no social security benefits since she no longer has dependent children. After age sixty-five, she will receive approximately $450 per month.

The program shown in Table 15-13 will be established to provide the family's income needs. Various allocations could have been developed; there is no one right way of financing income needs. The most important consideration in any method, however, is the security of the income sources. Insurance contracts create a debtor-creditor relationship, such that the periodic payments are basically guaranteed. In the program above, the interest option with right of withdrawal is used throughout so that the spouse maintains financial flexibility to obtain additional funds from the insurance principal if investment income is insufficient. Any principal that remains at Sue's death can be passed on to her heirs to meet estate liquidity needs.

A fiduciary relationship arises with the creation of a trust; the trustee guarantees only that his or her actions will be ethical and in good faith, but by no means warrants continued earnings from the trust. It is therefore essential to choose a very competent trustee. In this specific case, the trustee must possess both investment and property management skills. It is probably most prudent to choose a corporate (bank) trustee who has access to the variety of necessary information and expertise. An annual fee of approximately $1,400 will be levied, but no fee is charged when the trust is created. Since John is "financially-oriented" to handle the family's assets during his productive lifetime, the trust should commence only at his death (testamentary trust) or incapacitating disability.

Consideration also must be given to the liquidity and income needs of the family at Sue's death. The family does not have adequate current/liquid assets to meet the immediate cash needs ($26,000). The readjustment period needs ($21,000 for at least two years) would increase total expenses to 107 percent of gross income. Thus, life insurance on Sue's life is required.

Through a transfer of ownership, the family's liquidity needs can be alleviated and the purchase of life insurance is therefore unnecessary for this purpose (see estate planning section). The readjustment fund is a temporary need while the children are at home and dependent. Term insurance seems appropriate, with a fifteen-year, $40,000 policy costing about $100 per year. A lump-sum or interest with right of withdrawal settlement option could be chosen. The beneficiary will be John with the contingent beneficiaries being the children.

Disability The occurrence of injury and disability from accident or sickness, as mentioned previously, is approximately 4.5 times greater than death for a male, age forty, and before age sixty-five, one out of every seven Americans will be disabled for five years or more. For as severe and frequent as this loss exposure is, however, it is probably the most "under-protected" personal economic exposure to loss.

Avoidance is possible by eliminating one's exposure to any hazardous situation, but this is improbable in today's active and mobile society. More realistic is the use of prevention practices to reduce one's exposure to accident or sickness. The types of prevention practices range from periodic medical examinations, good health habits, and sufficient first-aid skills to government regulations on carcinogenic agents and environmental pollutants. Retention is prevalent in the form of deductibles and coinsurance provisions. Deductibles are a cost-saving method for the buyer of health insurance, i.e., a larger initial deductible causes a decrease in the premium rate per benefit amount since the frequency of small insurance claims is greatly reduced. It is imprudent to retain all or a large portion of this exposure, however, because of the volatility of its frequency and severity.

The major means of protection from economic loss, then, is transfer through group and/or individual health insurance. There are two broad classes of health insurance: medical-expense insurance and disability-income insurance.

Medical-expense insurance covers the person's medical expense needs, which were previously described as the costs of hospitalization, surgical services, and general medical care. The Dovers currently have the following group medical-expense insurance coverage:

1. *Basic hospital and surgical*—coverage of reasonable hospital costs for up to sixty days per occurrence, surgical costs based on the policy's cost schedule, and regular medical or doctor's expenses, excluding surgical costs, of up to $50 per day for sixty days.
2. *Major-medical*—coverage of almost all medical expenses up to a $250,000 maximum, with a $100 corridor deductible and 80 percent coinsurance provision on the first $5,000 of benefits.

It was established in the loss-exposure analysis section that the family's minimum medical expense insurance needs should be $10,000 per person, per occurrence, and $100,000 maximum benefit per lifetime. The manner in which the basic plan benefits are provided and the high maximum limits on the major medical coverage make the family's current insurance protection adequate for its needs. They should be aware, however, of the types of benefits and possible personal expenses which this coverage produces.

This basic coverage provides hospitalization benefits on a service basis, i.e., pays for all reasonable costs within a specified duration (sixty days). Because of the rising costs of medical care, this type of coverage is more beneficial to the insured family. For the insurer, however, this type of contract is increasingly expensive and difficult to underwrite, so that the "reasonable" limits are becoming more stringent and initial deductibles are being required. The basic surgical benefits are paid on a scheduled basis, with the cost of each surgical procedure listed in the contract. The actual surgical charge can be substantially higher than those listed in the contract. The Dovers have to be aware of the possible personal costs of adding to the surgical benefit amount to meet the surgeon's fees and therefore should maintain an adequate emergency fund to meet such contingencies.

Besides the limitations already mentioned, a basic medical-expense policy often does not cover many types of significant medical expenses. This creates the need for an "umbrella" coverage of all these unprotected or excess costs not included in the basic plan. This family has a major medical plan that indemnifies almost all medical expenses up to a maximum benefit. The corridor deductible requires them to pay the first $100 of costs above the basic plan limits, and the coinsurance provision requires the family to pay 20 percent of the next $5,000 of costs. In other words, the family will receive only $4,000 of major medical plan benefits for the first $5,200 of costs above the basic plan limits, but beyond this point they will receive benefits equal to the reasonable costs incurred. The family must be aware of these possible expenses and maintain an adequate emergency fund to meet such contingencies.

Table 15-14

Disability Income Needs

Need	Source		Difference
$3,525/month	Short-term		
	Investment income	$2,000	$325
	Group insurance	1,200	
	Long-term		
	Investment income	2,000	725
	Social security	800	

The second class of health insurance is disability-income insurance. Its purpose is to replace a portion of the income lost because of the "breadwinner's" prolonged illness or rehabilitation. The benefit amount is a function of one's earned income with a maximum limit established in the contract. The benefit amount also may be limited by the person's unearned income, occupation, total net worth, and other personal factors.

It was established previously that the family's disability income needs are $3,525 per month. The family has three sources to currently obtain this income: investment income, social security benefits, and group disability-income insurance, as shown in Table 15-14.

The short- and long-term income needs unfulfilled by current sources can be satisfied by separate individual insurance contracts. However, it is better to obtain a long-term disability income policy with a 180-day waiting period for several reasons. The current short-term income sources are 90 percent of need already, so that it is questionable whether John could even obtain a short-term policy relative to an insurer's benefit "participation" limit and other underwriting standards. Secondly, the long-term disability exposure will have a much greater impact on the family's financial welfare. Investment income over a six-month duration usually will remain stable, but over a longer period and without John's management this income has a much greater risk factor. And, if the investment income source is not available or seriously decreases, the family's income needs will be neglected. Thirdly, social security benefits are provided on rather subjective and stringent conditions that limit the dependability of receiving these long-term benefits. Specifically, the disability must last five months and be expected to last at least twelve months or result in death before benefits will be provided. Also, the definition of disability is not being able to work at *any* occupation, which is much stricter than many commercial insurers' definition of total disability.

Thus, John should purchase an individual disability-income insurance contract that provides $725 per month to age sixty-five. The premium cost will average about $350 per year. This will assure John of a guaranteed minimum amount of periodic income to hedge against the downside risk of investment income.

Since the investment income is a major part of the family's disability income source, it is prudent to plan a trust arrangement which will commence when John is considered unable to manage the investment portfolio. The trust will be similar to that discussed previously for premature death. Besides providing a sizable portion of the family's periodic income, this trust can provide broad investment capabilities that allow protection against inflation.

Unemployment The unemployment peril is one usually considered to be a public responsibility and is dealt with through federal-state social insurance programs. These programs typically provide limited benefits for a short duration, generally fifty-two weeks or less. Unemployment can also result from other circumstances such as long-term disability or the death of a partner in a closely held business. This section will discuss these latter types of situations.

The loss exposure analysis section explained that the death or serious disability of one or more of the four stockholders of Mediamatics, Inc. could seriously disrupt its work environment and profitability. An orderly process for the purchase and reallocation of stock in this situation is necessary to maintain stability within the agency and to pay the stockholder or his or her estate the stock's fair market value.

The stock recently has been valued at $93.75 per share, which requires either $93,750 or $281,250, depending on which of the four current stockholders dies, to be readily available to purchase the stock. These funds can be accumulated in three different ways. Each stockholder can attempt to personally save adequate reserves to buy out the new stockholder. Assuming pro rata distribution of the purchased shares, this would require John to save $13,393 or $56,252 to purchase his number of shares. Not only would this amount of savings be difficult for John to afford, but it would take a long time for such a reserve to be accumulated. The death or disability of a stockholder could occur at any time, however, and thus the fund must be immediately created. Another problem with this method is that each stockholder is also dependent on the others to save adequately or else the buy-sell arrangement is dissolved.

The second method is for the agency to fund this buy-out arrangement through its current and accumulated earnings. Assuming the funds are available, the accumulation of this reserve can seriously hamper the financial flexibility and growth of the agency. Also, this buy-out may be required at any time, and the reserve must therefore be immediately available. Thirdly, such a large accumulation of earnings could be subject to accumulated earnings tax since the holding of earnings in indefinite anticipation of a stockholder's selling of stock is not considered a legitimate business need by the IRS. Lastly, this reserve is considered a corporate asset and thus subject to the claims of creditors.

The third and most appropriate method of financing this buy-sell agreement is by purchasing sufficient life insurance on the lives of the stockholders. Only a small, periodic premium is required to guarantee full payment of the necessary funds regardless of when the insured dies. Thus, the financial position of the purchaser of the insurance policy is not excessively disturbed, and the funds are guaranteed and immediately available. Also, it is an economical plan because the potential advantages of compound interest and the insurance principle are available.

Purchasing life insurance can be done personally by the stockholders (cross-purchase plan) or by the corporation (stock redemption plan). In this instance, the stock redemption plan is the most equitable method. This method is more practical since only one insurance policy on each life must be purchased, rather than three smaller policies being purchased by *each* stockholder. From a tax standpoint, it is more economical for the agency to purchase the policies, i.e., John (and presumably the other stockholders) is taxed at a higher rate than the corporation. This would become even more significant if the agency followed a common policy of increasing individual salaries commensurate with the premium costs incurred in a cross-purchase plan. Another factor is that the older stockholders also are the primary shareholders, which will cause John and the other vice president to incur a much greater premium expense in a cross-purchase agreement. In a stock redemption type of buy-sell agreement, the corporation pays the premium from its accumulated or current earnings, which implicitly means each stockholder is contributing relative to his proportion of stockholdings. The holding of corporate earnings to pay for these life insurance premiums is considered a legitimate business need, so any such accumulation will not be subject to the accumulated earnings tax. The cash values are considered corporate assets, however, so the agency must consider the possibility of creditors' demands.

Besides providing a smooth transition of management change, the formal buy-sell agreement serves several other valuable purposes. It establishes the value of the stock for estate tax purposes (presuming the valuation is reasonable) so that conflict with the IRS or probate and estate settlement delays to appraise the stock's value are avoided. Also, this established value will be used in calculating the transferred basis of the property and subsequent tax liability to the estate or heirs. Finally, the agreement assures the decedent's heirs of the value received for this stock, saving them and the estate the emotional and financial difficulty of attempting to sell close corporation stock.

So far, specific reference has been given only to the use of life insurance at a stockholder's death. As previously mentioned, the probabilities of serious disability actually are several times greater than the chance of dying before retirement. It is therefore necessary to plan for a buy-sell agreement in case of incapacitating disabilities in the same manner as for premature death.

The buy-sell agreement should be funded by the corporation for the same reasons given in the funding of life insurance. A disability-income insurance policy is not always a good funding mechanism, however, since the benefit limits are much less than the buy-out amount required and the benefit payments are often periodic over time (rather than paid in a single lump sum). Insurance companies are beginning to underwrite policies that meet these buy-sell needs, but alternative funding methods, either individually or jointly used, can include payment from (1) future corporate income or accumulated earnings, (2) a reserve or sinking fund, (3) borrowed funds, and (4) the cash value of the life insurance policy on the disabled shareholder.

One difficulty in a disability buy-sell agreement that does not exist in a death buy-sell plan is defining *what* is an incapacitating disability and *when* the buy-out should take place. To be objective to all parties, a specific definition and time period of disability should both be stated in the agreement. Obviously, these variables will significantly affect the family's financial planning and the possibility of money from stock redemption offsetting the necessary disability income.

Property and Liability Losses   As the loss-exposure analysis conveys, the Dovers have a wide variety of exposures to property damage and personal liability. In this area more than any other, then, it is important that John periodically review his potential loss exposures to assure identification of the many perils that could exist. Property and liability insurers often have checklists or guides that can be quite helpful for identification of both private and commercial property exposures.

Property and liability exposures also offer the best opportunity to apply the various methods of loss-exposure "protection." Avoidance should be seriously exercised to eliminate unnecessary exposures to perils. An example would be avoiding the unnecessary accumulation of flammable substances, such as gasoline and kerosene, in areas close to the residence and other combustible property. If these exposures are necessary, they should be minimized by various prevention techniques.

For example, the gasoline needed for household machinery should be kept in unbreakable, nonflammable containers and stored in a metal shed or similar structure away from the residence. Another prevention method against fire is the appropriate use of early-warning smoke detectors throughout the residence. A reputable insurer will have information to help a family recognize the need and implement the multitude of prevention techniques.

With the rising costs of property and liability insurance, retention is becoming a viable and practical alternative. A family should consider large deductibles except for excessive losses to decrease insurance premiums. Consideration must be given to the frequency and severity of the potential loss, but more importantly, the family should evaluate how much it can afford to lose. Several important points should be remembered in deciding on a family's retention limits, however. First, most property and liability insurance indemnifies the insured for the actual cash value of the property loss. The rapid depreciation of property in its early years, especially automobiles, causes its actual cash value after three to five years to be significantly lower. Secondly, casualty losses over $100 per year are tax deductible, which significantly tempers the ultimate financial loss particularly to a high-bracket taxpayer.

The high tax rate and available cash flow of the Dovers make retention an excellent cost-saving method for them. An excellent example is their automobile insurance. By raising the collision deductible from $100 to $250, they can reduce the collision premium about $60 per year; accepting a $50 deductible on comprehensive coverage can provide a $35 premium reduction. Assuming they incurred $250 collision damage, the net cash loss would actually be only $107.50, i.e., the $60 premium savings plus a tax deduction of $82.50 (55 percent tax rate) subtracted from the $250 loss amount. As the age of the cars increases, John should consider increasing his deductible to as much as $500. The increased premium reduction, tax deductions, and declining value of the property cause the family to accept little or no greater risk than at lower deductibles. John already is assuming a $100 deductible on his homeowners and farmowners insurance policies and therefore receiving a premium reduction on these coverages.

Although retention is becoming an increasingly viable alternative, there remain substantial financial loss exposures that must be transferred to another party, i.e., a property and liability insurer. Individual policies can be purchased to protect specific losses, but it is much more convenient and efficient to purchase a single policy which covers either specified or "all-risks," known as multi-peril coverages. John currently owns a homeowners-2 policy, family automobile plan, farmowners policy, basic automobile plan, and a small businessowners policy to protect the rental property. The amount of insurance needed should be based on the maximum possible loss the family could suffer. The current property values and related insurance coverages are listed in the family's financial statements.

Coverage A of the homeowners policy and small businessowners policy have an 80 percent coinsurance provision that forces the insured to maintain a proper amount of insurance to cover the dwelling's replacement value or pay the proportional difference at the time of loss. Eighty percent of $80,250 and $55,000 are $64,200 and $44,000, respectively, so John's current insurance amounts are sufficient. The differences are nominal, however, so John must be aware of the increasing replacement value of his residence and rental property in future years and discuss the need for additional coverage with his insurance advisor.

The broad form multi-peril coverages that John has on his properties cover the most prevalent perils, and his exposure to the excluded risks does not warrant the added premium expense of changing to an "all-risks" type of policy. However, the family's sailboat is not protected under the homeowners policy, so a personal property endorsement to include this item should be considered.

The indirect losses of property damage to the family residence and rental property are covered by these multi-peril policies. However, the income from the rental property is an essential source in satisfying the income needs of several other family risks, i.e., death, disability, education expenses, and so on. John should purchase business interruption insurance as a policy endorsement or separately to be sure these earnings will continue even though the business is shut down by an insured peril.

John also must consider his exposures to personal liability and his current comprehensive coverages. With the claims-consciousness and excessive damages being assessed today for negligent personal acts, it is recommended that a person of John's income level and net worth carry between $750,000 and $1 million liability coverage. John should therefore purchase an "excess" or "umbrella" liability policy of $1 million which will insure him for all liabilities and excess damages not covered under his current multi-peril or automobile coverages. The premium cost will be about $100 a year. John also should review his tenant contract to identify liability exposures and consider transferring them to the tenant through hold-harmless and waiver agreements.

Mediamatics, Inc., carries a director's and officer's liability policy of $1 million, which is sufficient to cover John's corporate liability exposures.

Maintain a Similar Home and
Standard of Living at Retirement

The goal of retirement planning is to accumulate savings sufficient to replace the annual earned income that the retiree will no longer receive. It was determined in the loss-exposure analysis section that the required accumulation when John retires at age sixty-five must be $692,107. This sum was calculated making several critical assumptions, the most important being John and Sue's life expectancy. Such actuarial statistics are based on the past data of large groups, and for the individual to match this expected time period is coincidental. Therefore, it is necessary to recognize the risk of outliving one's accumulated savings and plan for income sources which will continue throughout his or her actual lifetime.

The previous section also emphasized the effect of inflation on fixed retirement incomes. A final-average pay formula was used to reflect the productivity and inflation increases at retirement, but the problems of inflation during the retirement years still exist. The best means of coping with this problem may be to have variable rather than fixed income sources that reflect the rising cost of living.

John and Sue currently have three sources of retirement income: the company's profit-sharing plan, social security, and the family's investment income. If the profit-sharing plan were to continue contributing 10 percent of annual salary and John's salary annually increased at 6 percent, an accumulation of approximately $140,000 is feasible. With this sum, a joint and two-thirds survivorship annuity of $966 per month ($11,592 per year) can be purchased. Annual contributions of this percentage (or at all) are not assured, however, so to be conservative, a monthly annuity of $900 ($10,800 per year) will be considered. The projected maximum old-age social security benefit will be $879.60 per month ($10,555 per year). This benefit will increase by the automatic cost-of-living escalator if the CPI increases 3 percent or more within base periods. This income source is thus a hedge against inflation and also provides survivorship and lifetime benefits.

The investment income also is a hedge against inflation, and will presumably continue until both parents are deceased. The problem, however, is that the annual income amount is indefinite, with no guarantee that *any* profit will be earned. Assuming John sells the rental property by age sixty-five and continues to enjoy a profitable harvest from the farm during his retirement years, an annual income of $15,000 can be conservatively projected from this source. Thus, the Dovers' current retirement income sources will provide $35,138 annually.

The remaining annual retirement income ($23,712) could be

obtained through guaranteed-payment contracts because of the uncertainty of the profit-sharing and investment incomes. An agreement perhaps could be made that at John's retirement the cash value of the $100,000 life insurance policy will be used to purchase a joint and two-thirds annuity. Assuming a fifteen-year paid-up whole-life policy, the cash value when John is sixty-five is about $75,000, which will provide a $517.50 monthly annuity ($6,210 per year). Not only is this beneficial to John, but also to Mediamatics, Inc. as a fringe benefit to hold a key employee in a highly competitive labor market. It also serves its intended purpose of indemnification if John should die before retirement.

A second source of guaranteed retirement income is starting a Keogh (HR-10) retirement plan with Sue's self-employment income from her art. Assuming she continues to earn $5,000 per year, she may contribute $750 a year, tax deductible, to a qualified plan. Since emphasis is on guaranteed payments, the contributions could be invested in an annuity. Insurance companies currently are offering as much as 8 percent on straight-life annuities, so that about $54,830 would be accumulated when Sue reaches age sixty. This would provide a monthly annuity of $354.20 ($4,250 per year).

A $160,000 joint and two-thirds survivorship annuity could be purchased to meet the remaining retirement income need. The premiums could be paid with after-tax dollars by John, or through a deferred compensation arrangement with the employer. Since the family is currently in a very high tax bracket with a large proportion of unearned income, it is better for John to forego a portion of his future salary increases and enter into an agreement that the employer provide the annuity at age sixty-five with this yet-unearned compensation. The employer must retain approximately $3,300 per year to fund this agreement. Assuming a properly written agreement, John will be able to defer his tax liability on this amount until he receives the annuity payment at retirement, when it is presumed he will be in a lower tax bracket.

Contribute to Heirs' Welfare (Estate Planning)

The objectives of estate planning in this case were listed in the loss-exposure analysis section. The liquidity needs to meet estate transfer costs were planned for in the earlier section on premature death. The transfer of the close corporation stock was covered in the unemployment section. The remaining goals of this section, then, are to plan for the distribution of estate property and the financial support of the heirs, and to reduce the estate transfer costs to a minimum.

Table 15-15

Gross Estates

	Sue	John
Current assets	$ 6,200	$ 10,200
Long-term assets	377,000	483,250
Other assets	36,000	36,000
Life insurance proceeds	40,000	239,500
	$459,200	$768,950

At the death of either parent, the gross estates would be as shown in Table 15-15. John's gross estate has increased by the revaluation of his close corporation stock and the decreasing-term life insurance, and Sue's gross estate has increased by the life insurance purchased on her life. Using the maximum marital deductions and 1977 estate tax credit, the estate tax liability on John's estate is $67,784 and on Sue's estate is $37,344. John's estate must pay the income tax on $41,875 capital gains for the appreciation of the redeemed Mediamatics, Inc. stock, while Sue's estate or heirs (John) have no capital gains liability until they sell the appreciated assets.

The will currently transfers all property to the surviving spouse. If John is the first decedent, Sue thus owns all of the family's property. As stated previously, because of her lack of interest and financial expertise, the income-producing assets should be managed by a qualified third-party. The income from this property must go to Sue and her children to satisfy specific income needs at John's death (see premature death section). Therefore, the will should be changed to put all the income producing assets in trust(s) managed by a corporate trustee who has expertise in equity investment and real property management.

To satisfy the various family objectives and minimize the estate and income tax liabilities, multiple trusts and changes in property ownership should be initiated. The ownership of the rental property should be changed to joint-tenancy between John and his college classmate, so that at John's death his interest automatically will pass to the other owner. A buy-sell agreement with his classmate should specify an "income-continuation" plan which will pay the trustee $5,000 per annum until the fair market value for John's interest has been repaid (currently about 13 years assuming a time-value of money factor). The sale of this property will be considered an installment sale and capital gains can be prorated over the length of the installment periods. Also, this will avoid any management difficulties that may have arisen had this property been placed in the trust.

John should also take sole ownership of $150,000 of the farm property. By taking this from Sue's estate and using the full marital deduction and tax credit, her estate tax liability will be zero, and the total tax liability of both estates is $17,209 less than when there is joint ownership.

Finally, all incidents of ownership of the individual and group insurance contracts on John's life should be transferred to Sue so that the proceeds will not be in his estate. John will pay gift tax on the replacement value of the group and $50,000 term policy, but this cost will be more than offset by the estate tax savings of $22,815. If Sue is the first decedent, the replacement values of these policies will be in her estate.

Testamentary Marital Trusts A and B should be established in the will if John is the first decedent. Trust A should be formed on a percentage formula which allows the greater of one-half of John's adjusted gross estate or $250,000 to be transferred to Sue and similarly qualify for the full marital deduction. Trust B will transfer ownership of the remaining property to the three children. The available income from both trusts will be periodically distributed to Sue, but the property in Trust B will be outside of her estate. In case the parents should die simultaneously, a clause should be entered in the will stating that John will be considered the first decedent.

Finally, separate trusts from the marital trust will be established immediately so portions of the farm property income may be used to meet the children's educational expenses and parents' retirement income objectives (see appropriate sections). At termination of these short-term trusts, this property will revert to Trust B.

The result of these ownership transfers and trusts is the satisfaction of the estate planning objectives. Table 15-16 shows estate tax liabilities for both parties when either is the first decedent.

Income-Tax Planning

The goal of tax planning is to minimize the burden of taxes through legitimate tax allowances. These allowances eliminate or reduce the tax burden, i.e., deductions, exclusions, credits, and alternative tax methods; defer the tax liability; or transfer the tax liability to another taxpayer. Thus, an advisor should incorporate avoidance, prevention, and transfer methods to take full advantage of tax planning.

The Dovers' current income tax statement appears in the family's financial statements. The goal of this section is to minimize the tax

Table 15-16
Estate Tax Liabilities

First Decedent Is:	John	Sue
Gross Estate	$529,450	$364,200
Less—Debts	110,220	0
Adjusted Gross Estate	419,230	364,200
Marital Deduction	250,000	250,000
Taxable Estate	169,230	114,200
Tax	44,230	28,060
Credit	30,000	30,000
Tax Liability	$ 14,954	$ 0

At Death of Surviving Spouse:	John	Sue
Gross Estate	$250,000	$529,450
Less—Debts	0	110,220
Adjusted Gross Estate	250,000	419,230
Marital Deduction	0	0
Taxable Estate	250,000	419,230
Tax	70,800	128,338
Credit	47,000	47,000
Tax Liability	$ 23,800	$ 81,338

liability by assuring full use of the three "protection" methods mentioned previously.

Avoidance implies receiving tax-free income. The most common form of nontaxable income is interest on "municipal" bonds. The family income statement shows about $12,000 to $13,000 of excess income which could be invested in specific "municipals" or in municipal-bond mutual funds. Yields on these mutual funds currently are about 6 to 6.5 percent, which is the equivalent of 9.25 to 9.75 percent return on taxable investments (50 percent tax rate). The mutual funds also offer diversification to reduce the risks of default and individual price changes and professional, full-time portfolio management (for a slight fee). Often an investment of only $1,000 is required to join the fund, and entry and exit can be essentially at the investor's desire. Other tax-free income sources are the first $100 per year of common stock dividend income, and the proceeds of certain "employer-financed" employee benefits, such as group term life insurance and various group health insurance coverages.

Prevention (reduction) refers to the proper use of tax deductions, exclusions, credits, and deferrals. The Dovers could increase the tax deductions from adjusted gross income by making contributions to and accounting for travel and administrative expenses incurred in connection with donations to qualified charitable organizations. They also should be aware of medical expenses, which are deductible if greater than 3 percent of adjusted gross income, and cumulative casualty losses greater than $100, which could become more prevalent with the increase in property and liability insurance deductibles. A $750 deduction from gross income can be taken for Sue's Keogh (HR-10) retirement plan contribution. Another way to reduce taxable income is by using the long-term capital gains deduction and offsetting capital gains with short-term capital losses.

The family's tax liability also may be reduced by the use of alternate tax methods, such as maximum tax and alternate capital gains calculations. At this time, neither method will have much effect on the family's taxes, but the maximum tax will become increasingly important as John's earned income increases in future years.

Tax planning has its greatest impact on taxpayers with large net worth and income streams, i.e., the Dovers, since they have the resources to better achieve their objectives through tax shelters. This tax concept refers to commercial investments which offset other taxable income through deferral, debt-leverage, and conversion of ordinary income to capital gains. The Tax Reform Act of 1976 has greatly reduced the benefits of most tax shelters, however, with real estate being one of the only investments not radically affected by the new law.

John currently owns two income-producing properties (rental property and farm property) which provide several tax-shelter benefits. He can deduct from his gross income all expenses incurred in using these properties for business, such as maintenance, travel, repair, and other expenses. He also can defer some of the tax liability by using accelerated depreciation on the rental-property buildings and capital assets, and on various farm assets, such as the buildings, vehicles, and equipment, and certain farm animals. Current deductions also can be taken for soil and water conservation expenses and feed and other asset development expenses, although these deductions are limited by a new "at risk" provision. Investment tax credit is allowed when any of these depreciable farm assets is purchased, and their sale is a capital-asset transaction. John currently is depreciating (straight-line) only the rental property. Using accelerated depreciation on this and the farm assets, approximately $7,000 additional deductions from the gross income of these two investments can be attained.

The third method of minimizing the tax burden is to transfer taxable property to other taxpayers. Outright gifts can be initiated, although the increased gift tax rate and change in gift tax exclusions have reduced the effectiveness of this concept. A more practical method for John is to transfer income-producing property to his children and parents through short-term or "Clifford" trusts. The income from this property is then taxed at the lower rates of the trust beneficiaries and not included in John's taxable income. A gift tax on the discounted, reversionary value of the property will be levied at the time of transfer, but can be avoided by the annual gift tax exclusions. Also, the appropriate benefits of depreciation and business deductions discussed above are also transferred with these assets, or else John will receive beneficial enjoyment on this property and be taxed on the gross income.

A combination of these various tax-saving methods should be employed in the Dovers' financial planning. The result of this planning will be shown in the revised tax statement at the conclusion of the financial plan.

Investment Plans and Goals

The objectives of assuring the children's education, assisting parents with retirement income, purchasing John's sister's remaining interest in the family farm, and traveling internationally in future years are all dependent on the investment plans and goals of the family. The speculative risk with which these objectives are concerned is insufficient capital accumulation and earnings from the family's investment portfolio. To adequately control this exposure, a general understanding of the family's investment needs and constraints must be developed.

Any investment program must balance the characteristics of various investments, i.e., risk of capital and income, yield, liquidity, tax impact, future growth potential, and so forth, with the income and capital needs of the investor(s). In this specific case, John's investment portfolio is too heavily weighted with real property investments. Although these investments offer steady income, good potential for capital appreciation and yield, and certain tax advantages, the family needs a more diversified portfolio which offers liquidity for emergency needs, low investment risk, and reduced concentration of capital investment in one medium. In this way, changes in market price and interest rates, property damage to these properties, and other contingencies will not affect the family's welfare as severely. Also, investments should be considered which will relieve the Dovers of taxable income rather than increase it. This could mean investing in growth stocks that pay nominal dividends, municipal bonds or mutual funds that provide tax-free income, or tax-shelter vehicles that offset the family's other taxable income. Since this investment income is an integral long-term income source in this financial plan, another critical consideration is the security of principal and income of the investments. Thus, high-grade stocks and bonds in profitable and dependable industries should be evaluated to minimize the financial, market, and inflation risks yet provide a competitive yield.

Assure Children a Quality College Education The loss-exposure analysis section vividly showed the inflationary rise in four-year college expenses. Planning is becoming a necessity to assure children the education desired. It is impossible for John to contribute the required accumulated savings to meet these costs, so a plan must be developed to contribute annually the necessary funds. There are four ways this may be accomplished: (1) personal savings, (2) tax-exempt investments, (3) endowment insurance, and (4) short-term income trusts for the children.

Personal savings would demand a disciplined effort of approximately fifteen years to satisfy the savings requirements. Too many financial emergencies and/or temptations arise for this unstructured savings plan to be secure, and the investment earnings would be taxable income. Tax-exempt investments would avoid an increase in annual taxable income, but the market and default risks make this alternative questionable. Endowment insurance offers guaranteed income and tax-free investment income, but the yield on these contracts usually is low and the premium costs relatively high.

A short-term, or "Clifford" trust will accumulate the necessary funds and distribute them as needed, transfer taxable income from John's high tax bracket rate to the nominal tax bracket of the children, and not cause an immediate cash outlay to fund the trust (except for trustee's fees). The trust must exist for at least ten years, and John cannot retain administrative or other powers to control beneficial enjoyment. Thus, John should transfer $87,500 of the farm property to a trust which will exist until the college expenses have ended, specify the income earned from this property to be distributed to each child in the necessary amounts (assuming 8 percent return), and then have each child invest in an insured savings certificate. This will reduce John's taxable income by about $7,000 annually, yet return the property and income to him when he nears retirement and is more apt to need this income source. A gift tax will be levied on the initial transfer of property to the trust, but the gift tax annual exclusion for both spouses ($6,000 per child) will exempt them from any federal gift tax liability.

Assist Parents with Retirement Income John desires to provide his parents with $5,000 annual income to assist with their retirement needs. Essentially, he has three ways to fund this objective: (1) take the money directly from his annual income, (2) purchase a single- or joint-life immediate annuity, or (3) set up a short-term trust. The first method requires a disciplined savings program and could be interrupted at any time by a more urgent, immediate need for the funds. Also, the gift is made with after-tax dollars. The second method would create a single premium cost when the annuity is purchased that the family may not be able to afford.

A short-term ("Clifford") trust formed with income-producing farm property could provide for the parents' income needs and also reduce John's annual taxable income. John currently has no urgent need for the farm property and its earnings, and the savings in income taxes almost will offset the family's reduction in gross income. To qualify for this tax treatment, the trust must exist for the lesser of ten years or the lives of the beneficiaries, and John must gain no beneficial enjoyment from the trust or its property. This time requirement conforms to John and Sue's future goals and income needs to travel internationally and provide an adequate retirement income. A gift tax on the discounted reversionary value of the trust will be levied at time of transfer but can be avoided by the annual gift tax exclusions. Thus, this method requires no immediate or sizable cash outlay, effectively reduces the family's tax base for at least ten years, yet allows John to retain ownership of the assets to meet his future needs.

Purchase Sister's Remaining Interest in the Family Farm and Travel Internationally in Future Years The investment plan so far has emphasized the tax savings element by using short-term trusts to transfer the taxable income to other parties. These final two objectives should be provided with investment income which will diversify the family's investment portfolio yet not increase its tax liability.

The Dovers' net income before federal income taxes is $23,895 (assuming $12,000 annual income is transferred to the two short-term trusts and an additional $4,100 to cover the expenses for purchases of insurance and retirement annuity). The $23,895 could be invested in municipal bond mutual funds. These funds offer a diversified bond portfolio that is professionally managed and minimize the investment risks of individual municipal securities. They also offer easy withdrawal for emergency financial needs and provide annual interest income tax free. Assuming a 6 percent yield, approximately $1,400 will be accumulated annually, which is the equivalent of approximately $2,000 of taxable interest income.

The federal income tax liability will be paid from these mutual fund assets. The results of the tax-planning methods will reduce the tax liability to $15,830 as shown in Table 15-17.

Table 15-17
Reduction of Tax Liability

Gross Income (exclude $12,000 via Clifford trusts)			$81,200
Less: Business expense	$ 850		
Rental and farm maintenance	300		
Depreciation	9,250		
Interest	4,005		
Keogh (HR-10) contribution	750		
Taxes	5,250	20,405	
Adjusted Gross Income			$60,795
Less: Interest	2,195		
Charitable contributions	1,000 (estimate)		
Taxes	5,950	9,145	
Personal exemptions		3,750	
Taxable Income			$47,900
Tax: 14,060 + 0.50 (3,900)			16,010
Less: Credit			180
Tax Liability			$15,830

CONCLUDING NOTE

The case situation presented in this final CPCU 2 chapter has been designed to illustrate how the risk management approach can be applied to individual and family circumstances. Of course, there is no single set of absolutely correct answers to such complex and ever changing situations. Rather, the point is that certain principles can be applied in a logical manner to ensure that all future possibilities are recognized and dealt with in some reasonable manner. Factual information can be gathered about a family's financial situation and activities and summarized along with family goals and objectives. The results of such an effort can be used to identify the various loss exposures which confront the family. The potential loss exposures can in turn be analyzed in light of the family's resources and objectives. In this way, a family can reach informal decisions as to its needs, financial plans, priorities, and allocation of resources. This type of thorough, comprehensive risk management review and evaluation must be repeated every few years, because of the swiftly changing family circumstances.

Chapter Note

---

1. U.S. News and World Report, Money Management Series, *How to Buy Insurance and Save Money*, 1976, p. 112.

Bibliography

Advanced Underwriting Service. Vol. 2. Indianapolis, IN: Research and Review Service of America.

Advanced Underwriting Service. Vol. 3. Indianapolis, IN: Research and Review Service of America.

Allen, Everett T.; Melone, Joseph J.; and Rosenbloom, Jerry S. *Pension Planning.* Homewood, IL: Richard D. Irwin, 1976.

American Psychiatric Association. *APA Guidelines.* Washington: American Psychiatric Association, 1969, p. 12.

Automobile Insurance . . . For Whose Benefit? New York: New York Insurance Department, 1970.

Bellemore, Douglas H. and Ritchie, John C. *Investments.* 4th ed. Cincinnati, OH: South-Western Publishing Co., 1974.

Belth, Joseph. "The Rate of Return on the Savings Element in Cash Value Life Insurance." *Journal of Risk and Insurance,* Vol. 35, No. 4, December 1968, pp. 569-581.

Bernstein, George. "Critical Evaluation of the FAIR Plans." *Journal of Risk and Insurance,* Vol. 38, No. 2, June 1971, p. 275.

Bixby, Lenore. "Income of People Aged 65 and Older." *Social Security Bulletin,* Vol. 33, No. 4, April 1970.

Black, Henry Campbell. *Black's Law Dictionary.* St. Paul: West Publishing Co., 1968.

Blue Cross Association. "Questions and Answers About the Blue Cross Organization." Mimeograph, 1976.

Bushman, Donald M. "ESOPs: A Closer Look." *C.L.U. Journal,* April 1977, p. 33.

Calabresi, Guido. *The Costs of Accidents.* New Haven: Yale University Press, 1970.

Carlson, Robert S. "Aggregate Performance of Mutual Funds, 1948-67." *Journal of Financial and Quantitative Analysis,* March 1970, p. 1.

Cohen, Jerome B. "Common Stocks." *Financial Analysts Handbook.* Homewood, IL: Richard D. Irwin, 1975.

Evans, John L. and Archer, Stephen H. "Diversification and the Reduction of

Dispersion: An Empirical Analysis." *Journal of Finance*, December 1968, p. 761.

Fama, Eugene F. "The Behavior of Stock Prices." *Journal of Business*, January 1965, p. 93.

F.C.&S. Bulletins. Cincinnati: The National Underwriter Co.

Flood Insurance Manual. Arlington, VA: National Flood Insurers Association, 1975.

Ford, Gerald. *Economic Report of the President.* Washington: Superintendent of Documents, 1977.

Francis, Jack C. *Investments: Analysis and Management.* New York: McGraw-Hill, 1976.

Friend, Irwin; Blume, Marshall; and Crockett, Jean. *Mutual Funds and Other Institutional Investors.* New York: McGraw-Hill, 1970.

Gaines, Price, Jr. *1976 Time Saver for Health Insurance.* Cincinnati: National Underwriter Co., 1976.

Gregg, Davis W. and Lucas, Vane B. *Life and Health Insurance Handbook.* 3rd ed. Homewood, IL: Richard D. Irwin, 1973.

Havighurst, Clark C. and Tancredi, Lawrence R. "Medical Adversity Insurance." *Insurance Law Journal*, Vol. 613, February 1974, p. 506.

Head, George L.; Williams, C. Arthur; and Glendenning, G. William. *Principles of Risk Management and Insurance.* Malvern, PA: American Institute for Property and Liability Underwriters, 1978.

Holmes, John R. "Anticipated Growth is the Prime Measure of Potential Risk, Hence Potential Reward." *Financial Analysts Journal*, Vol. 32, No. 3, May-June 1976, p. 47.

"Homeowners Policy Program." Rev. New York: Insurance Services Office.

"How to Buy Insurance and Save Money." *U.S. News and World Report.* Money Management Series, 1976.

Investment Companies: Mutual Funds and Other Types. New York: Arthur Wiesenberger Financial Services.

Jonish, James E. and Lilly, Claude C. "The Federal Crime Insurance Program." Unpublished paper presented at the annual American Risk and Insurance Association meeting, 1974.

Karkowiecki, Marie. "Benefit Costs Climb 23% in 2 Years, Survey Finds." *Business Insurance*, Vol. 10, No. 21, 1976, p. 1.

Keeton, Robert E. and O'Connell, Jeffrey. *Basic Protection for the Traffic Victim.* Boston: Little, Brown & Co., 1965.

Kulp, C. A. *Casualty Insurance.* Rev. ed. New York: Ronald Press Co., 1942.

Levin, Jesse. "Growth Rates—The Bigger They Come the Harder They Fall." *Financial Analysts Journal*, Vol. 28, No. 6, November-December 1972, pp. 71-77.

Life Insurance Fact Book. Washington, D.C.: American Council of Life Insurance, 1977.

Life Insurance in Profit Sharing Plans. Information Bulletin No. 23C. Des Moines, IA: The Bankers Life.

Lilly, Claude C. "A History of Insurance Regulation in the United States." *CPCU Annals*, Vol. 30, No. 2, June 1976, pp. 110-111.

Long, John D. "Future Changes in American Insurance." *CPCU Annals*, Vol. 29, No. 2, June 1976, pp. 159-160.

Lund, Harry A.; Casey, Walter J.; and Chamberlain, Phillip K. "A Financial Analysis of the ESOT." *Financial Analysts Journal*, January-February 1976, p. 55.

Maisel, Sherman J. and Roulac, Stephen E. *Real Estate Investment and Finance*. New York: McGraw-Hill, 1976.

Mandel, Morris. *A Complete Treasury of Stories for Public Speakers*. Middle Village, NY: Jonathan David Publishers, 1974.

Mehr, Robert I. "The Concept of the Level-Premium Whole Life Insurance Policy—Reexamined." *The Journal of Risk and Insurance*, Vol. 42, No. 3, September 1975, p. 419.

Morse, R. R.; Hartwig, J. C.; Sager, F. W.; and Couzens, J. S. *Business Agreements for Use with Life Insurance*. Milwaukee: Northwestern Mutual Life Insurance Co., 1970.

The Nature of the Whole Life Contract. New York: Institute of Life Insurance, 1974.

New Group Health Insurance. New York: Health Insurance Institute, 1976.

New York Automobile Insurance Plan. New York: Automobile Insurance Plans Service Office, 1976.

O'Connell, Jeffrey. "Elective No-Fault Liability Insurance for All Kinds of Accidents: A Proposal." *Insurance Law Journal*, Vol. 608, September 1973, p. 506.

Pritchard, William G., Jr. "Social Responsibility in the Insurance Marketplace." *CPCU Annals*, Vol. 27, No. 1, March 1974, p. 46.

Private Passenger Automobile Manual. New York: Insurance Services Office, 1976.

2 Proceedings of the National Association of Health Commissioners, 1974.

Proceedings of the National Association of Insurance Commissioners, 1944.

2 Proceedings of the National Association of Insurance Commissioners, 421, 1974.

Proceedings of the National Convention of Insurance Commissioners, 1920.

Rabin, Robert L. *Perspectives on Tort Law*. Boston: Little, Brown & Co., 1976.

Recreational Vehicle Manual. New York: Insurance Services Office, 1976.

Rhodes, J. E. *Workmen's Compensation*. New York: Macmillan Co., 1917.

Rush, Richard H. *Antiques as an Investment*. Englewood Cliffs, NJ: Prentice-Hall, 1968.

_____. *Art as an Investment*. New York: Bonanza Books, 1958.

Ryder, Ambrose. *Automobile Insurance*. New York: Spectator Co., 1924.

Sharpe, W. F. and Cooper, C. "Risk-Return Classes of NYSE Common Stocks, 1931-67." *Financial Analysts Journal*, March-April, 1972.

Sherman, Sally R. "Assets on the Threshold of Retirement." *Social Security Bulletin*, Vol. 36, No. 8, August 1973, p. 9.

Source Book of Health Insurance Data, 1976-77. New York: Health Insurance Institute, 1977.

Stevenson, Richard and Jennings, Edward. *Fundamentals of Investments*. St. Paul, MN: West Publishing Co., 1976.

"Tax Facts on Life Insurance." Cincinnati, OH: National Underwriter Co.

Travelers Insurance Company. *The Travelers 100 Years.* Kansas City: R. M. Rigby Printing Co., 1964.

U. S. Bureau of the Census. "Money Income in 1973 of Families and Persons in the United States." *Current Population Reports,* Series P-60, No. 93, Washington, D.C.: GPO, July 1974, p. 9, Table 6.

U. S. Congress. House, Committee on Ways and Means, *Annual Report of the Social Security Administration for Fiscal Year 1975,* 94th Cong., 2d sess., 1976.

U. S. Congress. House, Subcommittee on Housing of the Committee on Banking and Currency, Housing and Urban Development Legislation. 91st Cong., 2d sess., 1970.

U. S. Department of Commerce. *Statistical Abstract of the United States 1976.* Washington: Superintendent of Documents, 1976.

U. S. Department of Health, Education, and Welfare. *Your Medicare Handbook.* Washington: Superintendent of Documents, 1976.

U. S. Department of Housing and Urban Development. *HUD News,* 10 March 1975, p. 3.

——————. *National Flood Insurance Program.* Washington: Superintendent of Documents, 1974.

——————. "Title 24—Revised as of April 1, 1975." Reprint. Washington: Superintendent of Documents, 1976.

Vogel, Ronald J., and Blair, Roger D. *Health Insurance Administrative Costs.* Washington: U. S. Department of Health, Education, and Welfare, 1976.

Why Disability Protection is Vital for You. Cincinnati: National Underwriter Co., 1976.

Index

D